INDIA IN RUSSIAN ORIENTALISM

India in Russian Orientalism

Travel Narratives and Beyond

AMARTYA MUKHOPADHYAY

MANOHAR
2013

First published 2013

ISBN 978-81-7304-997-2

Published by
Ajay Kumar Jain *for*
Manohar Publishers & Distributors
4753/23 Ansari Road, Daryaganj
New Delhi 110 002

Typeset by
Kohli Print
Delhi 110 051

Printed at
Salasar Imaging Systems
Delhi 110 035

To

Late Bankim Chandra Mukhopadhyay
(1905–81)—Father, Teacher
and
Late Madhuchhanda Mukhopadhyay
(Chhorhdi) (1944–84)—Sister, Friend

Note on Transliteration

The Library of Congress System has been used in the body text of the book for the transliteration of most Russian names and titles. But in the case of notes and citations the spellings of the names as they appeared in the sources have been retained, for many scholars use different spellings for these names and titles.

Contents

Notes on Transliteration 9

Preface 11

1. Introduction: Travel Narratives and Russian Orientalism 15

2. A 'White' Trader on his 'Sinful Voyage': Afanasii Nikitin and the Complexities of His Observations 56

3. An Ensign, an Envoy and a Violinist: India through the Lenses of Efremov, Daniebegov and Lebedev 89

4. Aleksei Dmitriyevich Saltykov: Prince, Painter, Traveller 163

5. Russian Orientalism *Par Excellence*: Vasily Vasilyevich Vereshchagin 213

6. Minaev, the Russian Exemplar: His Academic Indology and the Diaries 270

7. Afterword 335

Bibliography 341

Index 357

Preface

This is a book on Russian travelogues in India. While beginning with Afanasii Nikitin is an obvious choice, the end could go further to include figures like Theodore Scherbatskoy or Andrei Snesarev. But without claiming any authorial arbitrariness, I have chosen only these seven travellers including Afanasii Nikitin, Fillip S. Efremov, Rafail Daniebegov, Aleksei Dmitriyevich Saltykov, Vasily Vasilyevich Vereshchagin and Ivan Pavlovich Minaev, because in popular and even learned imagination about Russian travel narratives *in India*, not academic Indology (which is not the subject of this book), the names that have been chosen are the most influential, whether because of the interest of the lay Indian in them, or because of their place in troubled Indo-British colonial relations. The seven travellers who figure in this volume differ from one another far more than Russian 'Orientalism' does from the European meta-narratives. They differ in their social statuses, cultural upbringing, cognitive equipment, intellectual interests, purpose of visit, and in almost everything else. Nikitin, a trader, had come to India to make wealth in this fabled land of fortunes. Efremov, a Russian ensign, had also come in search of trading opportunities. Daniebegov, a wealthy Georgian had been sent by the king of Georgia to an Armenian merchant in India. Lebedev, the son of a priest and himself a musician and violinist, visited our land just because of his wanderlust and search of wealth, and only later became a self-taught Indologist. Prince Saltykov a Russian nobleman and painter, had set out for India via Persia in search of adventure. Vereshchagin, a member of the Russian gentry and a 'progressive' artist, came to India, after Caucasus and Central Asia, to search for his subjects of 'Orientalist' paintings and drawings. Minaev, an accomplished scholar of Pali, Buddhism and Sanskritic Indology, had come for mixed purposes of Indology and Russia's state interest.

Some of them left nothing but travelogues of varying comprehensiveness. For some others travel writing was not the main area of their creative activities, but was (as with Saltykov) only a pastime, or (as with Vereshchagin) a key to and a commentary on sketches and paintings, somewhat like Bernard Shaw's long prologues to his plays. Lebedev's travelling experiences were kept in various forms—letters to Russian authorities and East India Company officials, foreword to his books, reminiscences about his efforts at constructing Calcutta's first non-colonial proscenium, memoranda, etc. For Minaev, his diaries were a record of his daily Indological activities and programmes, plus brief notes on the socio-political stirrings of contemporary India and his assessments of them from the viewpoint of Russia's chances. Because the oeuvres of at least four of the travellers wandered beyond travelogues, and the author followed them in their wanderings, the preposition 'beyond' has been added in the title.

I posit with considerable hesitation and humility that though the book does not use Russian language sources, because I do not know the language, the book extends Russian Orientalism to India in a way not done before, except briefly in Alexander Morrison's article, 'Russian Rule in Turkestan and the Example of British India, *c.* 1860–1917'. *Bharat-Rus* by P.M. Kemp, *The Image of India* by G.M. Bongard-Levin and A.A. Vigasin, *Russia and India* by P.M. Shastitco, or *India in Russian Literature*, by R.H. Stacy, regardless of their considerable merits, offer what can be called a slapdash chronicle of Indo-Russian links. With a few exceptions erudite journal articles do not give priority to the Indian connection in their studies of Russians studying the east. Besides, due mainly to the enormous scope or limitedness of their coverage, close readings of texts is absent. Yet without such reading, it would be impossible to identify the different voices and their mix in Russian Orientalism, and to tease out their differences from British, French or German Orientalism. This is precisely what this book has on offer.

I became drawn to this arcane area primarily due to my obsession since childhood with Nikitin and Lebedev. But I should also record here my gratitude to people from whom I got help and drew courage. My teacher Professor Rakhahari Chatterji provided the first inspiration by urging me to look at Lebedev from new points of view. Professor Hayat Mamud, formerly of Rajshahi University, Bangladesh, the foremost expert on Lebedev in South Asia, gave me a copy of his enormous book on Lebedev, not available in any of the Kolkata libraries. Anindita Banerjee, a faculty of the Yale University, USA, who has broken new ground in research on Nikitin, sent me her article on Nikitin. Professor Hari S. Vasudevan, one of the foremost scholars of Russian history in India, never allowed a teacher of Social Science and a non-Russianist to feel like an interloper, and came forward with books, suggestions, occasional admonitions and what is most important, acceptance. Professor Himadri Banerjee of Jadavpur University also helped with books and encouragement. Without their help this book would not have been possible.

Sincerest thanks are due to the staff of the National Library, Kolkata and to the library of the University of Calcutta, for making available books of all kind, articles and other materials. I am truly beholden to the http://books.google.com/ for the books in the public domain and others that I have used in my research. The chapter on Saltykov would not have been complete without the digital books they made available. I have recorded my acknowledgements at appropriate places.

My wife, daughter and son helped with their healthy disinterest in such dated things. My friend Satybrata Ghosh gifted a valuable book.

All these words of thanks and acknowledgement do not, however, detract from my sole responsibility for the book's lapses.

AMARTYA MUKHOPADHYAY

CHAPTER 1

Introduction: Travel Narratives and Russian Orientalism

TRAVEL LITERATURE AS THE FOCUS OF STUDY

This is a book about seven Russian travel narratives in and about India, set in the general context of Russian Orientalism and Indology. One may wonder about the choice of Russian travel literature for the portrayal of Russian Orientalism. It is not, however, as open to question as it might first appear. Kate Teltscher points out that between AD 1600 and 1800, travel literature predominated among the various texts written and studied, and the vogue of travel literature was 'outrun in popularity among the reading public only by theology'.[1] Besides, while tracing Russia's own oriental past, Kalpana Sahni treats travelogues about Russia as the first respectable source.[2] Even more importantly, one of the latest books on Russian Orientalism has travelogues as the single most important resource.[3] And despite Vera Tolz's warning that travel guides do not usually claim to convey an 'objective depiction of the "Orient"',[4] they very often contain the most private and authentic expressions of a person's feelings that may reveal much about his country's Orientalist beliefs and practices. The study begins with Nikitin, an obvious choice, and ends with Minaev, in which case the choice is not so obvious. But the book is mostly about travellers who with only one exception predated institutionalization of Soviet Orientology and Indology, and are at the same time most remembered in India, whether by common or by learned Indians, not counting the Russianists.

'ORIENTALISM' AS THE ENTRY POINT AND ITS VOICES

There are two reasons why 'Orientalism' and postcolonial theory have been chosen as the anvil on which to test the travel literatures. The first is that ever since the publication of Edward W. Said's seminal work *Orientalism* (1978),[5] postcolonial analysis has become the dominant approach to interrogating the West's viewing of the East or 'the Orient'. And here we are considering how Russian travellers are viewing their East. Secondly, in the backdrop of the 'striking similarity' between the criticism of European Oriental Studies by V.V. Barthold and 'then more strongly and in an ideologically charged way' by Nikolai Marr and S.F. Oldenburg, on the one hand, and by Said on the other, Tolz claims that 'a clearly identifiable connection exists between Said and his Russian predecessors, thus arguing that one of the fashionable trends in the recent Western analysis of the history of European scholarship from the postcolonial perspective is, in fact, Russian in origin'.[6] Our query would be if such a connection can be seen even between the earliest travellers and Said.

Talking of Said, his aim was to unearth some coherence and continuity in the West's discourses about 'the Orient' or the East that legitimized a supposedly superior Western self in relation to an allegedly inferior non-Western 'Other', through the hidden, subterranean connection between colonial knowledge and colonial power. But in the more expansive senses 'Orientalism' was 'a style of thought based upon an ontological and epistemological distinction made between "the Orient" and (most of the time) "the Occident"', adopted by a huge number of poets, novelists, philosophers, political economists, and imperial administrators, which could accommodate disparate figures like Aeschylus, Victor Hugo, Dante and Karl Marx. It was moreover 'a corporate institution for dealing with the Orient . . . by making statements about it, authorizing views of it, describing it, by teaching it, settling it, ruling over it: in short for dominating, restructuring, and having authority over the Orient'.[7] In this sense 'Orientalism' becomes a Foucauldian discourse. And in its most encompassive sense 'Orientalism' was 'an imaginative cast of mind or style of thought' spread over roughly two millennia of Western consciousness about the East, a vast system or inter-textual network of rules or procedures that governs anything that is, or may be, thought, written or imagined about the Orient. In Said's conception the discourse is highly hegemonic; it silences opposition to such an unimaginable degree that no Oriental scholar or thinker could free himself or herself from its shackles. The stereotypes Orientalist discourse systematically produced about the Orientals and the Orient, such as the heat and the dust, the crowded marketplace, the terrorist, the courtesan, the Asian despot, the childlike native, the mystical East, etc., of the putative Orient, and the positional inferiority of the East that these pointed to, were bound to affect their thought processes.[8]

Such a pessimistic view is no more taken after Homi Bhabha's psychoanalytic approach to the claims of colonial power suggested that liberating questions can still be raised by the colonized. For, while colonial discourse pretends to be successful in its domination, below the surface of self-assured complacency the discourse conceals its radical anxiety about its declared achievements, and a lurking suspicion that the supposed difference between the West and the East cannot hide areas of sameness shown by the colonized population. Bhabha argues that this anxiety of colonial power creates large chinks in the assumed finality of colonial discourses. This could be used by the colonized to their advantage, as it leaves for them some considerable amount of agency, so that in spite of the vast structures of representational violence of the colonizers' discourses, it enabled the former to offer some resistance to them.[9] Said had unnecessarily minimized the spaces of such resistance. Ashis Nandy's remarkable book about the psychology of colonialism has shown such resistance by the colonized taking place in the spatial contexts of India and England.[10]

In the backdrop of this anxiety, the pretended superiority of Europe has deep psychological roots. As a modern commentator on 'Orientalism' points out in the context of a film portraying a French diplomat's infatuation with a leading 'lady' of the Beijing opera, and his downfall because of this obsession, 'Orientalism' is nothing but a pathology in the Western psyche. This pathology is, again, the result of 'two simultaneous desires: the personal quest of the Western male for Oriental mystery and sexuality and the collective goal to educate and control the Orient in political and economic terms. . . . Orientalism thus serves as both the individual and collective desire to possess the Orient, and the internal desire to appropriate the Orient'. This desire, however, becomes problematic for Ziauddin Sardar as neither the West nor the Orient are monolithic entities, but are rather complex, ambiguous and heterogeneous. If the Orient signified the ancient civilizations 'to the East of the West', then the West itself was not always 'the West' it now is, but was a product of a chequered history.[11] But after 'the West' developed, from a simple geographical designation into a cultural construct, it became the measure through which Oriental cultures were to be weighed and valued. However, the thing that was to be thus tested, the East, remained unspecified. This was because, as Sardar puts it so aptly, 'what is essential to the Orientalist vision is the desire not to know', stemming from the fact that any knowledge that may come from 'Orientalism' is judged not by its accuracy and utility, 'but by the degree to which it enhances the self-esteem of the Westerner. . . . The representations of cultures and civilizations to the East of the West that Orientalism came to signify were based on constructed ignorance'. That is why, according to Sardar, *The Travels of Marco Polo* remains one of the earliest authoritative and immensely popular historical sources of 'Orientalism, in spite of myriad problems of the integrity and historicity of the manuscripts. The reception of Marco Polo's travels and Karl Wittfogel's *Oriental Despotism* proves that 'Orientalism is a compendium, one that ranges over all its subject areas', where 'the history of the Western self, its ideas, doings, concerns and fashions' are present in all their forms, overtly or covertly.[12]

The 'compendium' is, however, not as monolithic as Sardar shows; and its politics is not as overpowering all through Europe, as he suggests. This conclusion is inescapable from Teltscher's recent work on India, where she argues that 'European writing of the seventeenth and eighteenth centuries' on India, and specifically 'British texts of the second half of the eighteenth century', do not constitute a single discourse, but several discourses. For, 'European and British texts create a network of intersecting and contending discourses about India', which, while sharing certain wide-ranging questions about authority in India, 'are diverse, shifting, historically contingent, complex and competitive', and conditioned by international and domestic concerns of Britain. As such they cannot be fitted into the straitjacket of 'a single narrative about colonial expansion of the British will to power'. Teltscher's deep probing of the diverse British and European texts of the seventeenth and eighteenth centuries compels her to say that they do not square with Said's presentation of 'Orientalist' discourse as 'monolithic and homogeneous', or with his contention about an 'unbroken, unchanging tradition of European representation of the East' right from Greek days to colonial times. Rather, it pays scant attention to the 'historical context . . . and neglects inconsistencies, contradictions and instabilities' of the discourses. In place of Said's certitude about 'an unshakeable assumption of European superiority' in Orientalist discourse, she notices 'the emergence of a much less stable sense of the European self; an identity that is shifting, various, and responsive to the demands of domestic policy and religious affiliation'. In consequence, the oppositions posited by Said—East/West, Other/Self—are significantly fragmented and eroded. Even if the narrative strategies were designed to put at a distance and 'subordinate India . . . at times they diminish Indian strangeness and challenge European assumptions of superiority.'[13]

C.A. Bayly has also problematized the Saidian equation of colonial knowledge and power,[14] as has Amartya Sen, who has additionally discovered some pattern in the diversities of European representations of India. Making light of Said's insistence on the 'uniformity and consistency' in discourses on the Orient, Sen focuses on 'several contrasting and conflictual Western approaches to understanding India', and finds that in place of the 'internal consistency' that Said claims to have found in 'Orientalism', there are 'several fundamentally contrary ideas and images of India'.[15] Sen identifies three voices in these representations: the 'curatorial', the 'magisterial', and the 'exoticist'. Arguing that in spite of Said's Foucauldian equation of knowledge with power, it is in the basic nature of human beings to pursue knowledge for its own sake, Sen describes such aspiration for knowledge as 'curatorial'. The second type of Orientalist knowledge, 'the magisterial', is definitely related with the power aspirations of colonial rule. But the third category of Orientalist knowledge, the 'exoticist' is typified by people who found India as a country full of fantastic things and ideas of an exotic kind. Sen found examples of 'curatorial' Orientalist knowledge in the writings of Italian Jesuit Roberto De Nobili, and of William Jones, English linguist and founder of the Asiatic Society of Bengal in 1874. The best exemplar of 'magisterial' knowledge was provided by James Mill. Typical of the 'exoticist' approach was the writings of the protagonists of the Romantic Movement in Germany, including Karl and Angust Wilhelm Schlegel, Johann Herder and Arthur Schopenhauer.[16]

APPLICABILITY OF 'ORIENTALISM' TO RUSSIA AND THE DISTINCTIVENESS OF RUSSIA'S 'ORIENT'

Before we enter into this question I would clarify that like Morrison I am using the term Orientalism 'without inverted commas to indicate a scholar who studies the East . . . and with inverted commas when referring to Said's largely pejorative use of it'.[17] While commenting on the applicability of the Saidian use of the word I would first point to Laura Chrisman's reminder that the essential principles and shapes of colonial regimes as also their effects were not the same for Dutch, French, Portuguese or British colonial rule.[18] It places in better perspective Nathaniel Knight's argument, cited by Morrison, that Russian Orientalism, whether in individual representations or considered as an entire corpus of knowledge, was 'idiosyncratic', distinct from its French, British, and German counterparts because of Russia's distinctive position between East and West.[19] But while critiquing Knight and Adeeb Khalid in applying Said uncritically to academic Russian experience in the context of a comparative estimate of 'applied Orientalism' in British India and tsarist Turkestan, the conclusions Morrison derives still strengthen our claim of applicability. The first conclusion is that 'in many respects there was nothing especially distinctive about Tsarist "Orientalism".' In Russia's relationship with its Asian borderlands, the overhyped 'Asianist' sub-strand of Slavophile thought, which envisioned Russia as a bridge between East and West, was hardly anything other than a 'way of legitimizing colonial rule, and a useful rhetorical device when confronted with Western European attempts to exclude Russia from the family of European nations'. It had little effect on the mentality or behaviour of the imperial ruling elite in Central Asia or Transcaucasia, or had hardly influenced colonial policy. Even if many 'Russian Orientalists were critical of European imperialism', or even if much if not all of their works were free of 'Orientalist' stereotypes, they did not set it off from British Orientalism in India. Talking of connections between the colonial state and Orientalist scholars, Russia's only distinctiveness was possibly that it allowed a much greater interpenetration of the worlds of scholarship and colonial rule than in the British Empire, as evidenced in the number of officers and administrators who became recognized authorities in the field of Oriental Studies, and the number of academic Orientalists who were attached to the administration in Turkestan. Secondly, irrespective of its effect on Russian rule in Turkestan, one can discern 'the existence of a pervasive and denigrating Russian "Orientalist" stereotype of all Muslims, and Sufi groups in particular, as "fanatical"', a legacy of the experience of war in the North Caucasus and the Andijan uprising. The only difference with British rule in India was that here there was a 'much more interventionist use of the knowledge created for them by Orientalists'.[20]

Referring to the problems of foisting Said's Orientalist conception on 'all other cultural and epistemic locales of modernity', here primarily the Russian, modern Caucasian scholar Madina Tlostanova points out that what one finds in Russia and her colonies in the nineteenth century is 'a secondary orientalism which is the direct result of secondary eurocentrism', where both of them 'reflect and distort the western originals in the Russian cultural and mental space'. In such a situation Orientalist constructs are compounded by the 'double mirror reflections', resulting from copying of Western 'Orientalism' with some changes and a hidden but nagging inferiority complex that 'Russia itself is a form of a mystic and mythic orient for the West', an 'intellectually colonized subaltern empire with the stressed imperial difference'. Here even the representation of the non-European Russian colonies of Caucasus and Central Asia as a part of the 'prototypal Orient—biologically inferior, culturally backwards [*sic*] and forever fixed and out of history' cannot rid the Russian elite observer from a deep colonial anxiety. It is that while he 'coded himself or herself as a European, albeit as second-rate one . . . the Orient that the Russian empire got through its colonial efforts was also second-rate, not like the one of Europe.' It was in this sense that Russian army officers referred to both wars and women in Caucasus and later in Central Asia as not interesting enough. In this situation there were two possible ways of encoding Russia's Orient. The first was of 'forgetting all about the second-rate Russian Asia' and focusing on the 'real and alien (for Russians) "Orient"'. The second was of 'editing Russia's own East making it fit the generally accepted orientalist stereotype'.[21]

But all these circuitous routes of establishing the legitimacy of Saidian 'Orientalism' for Russia's 'applied Orientalism' may be shown to be unnecessary. Khalid contends that Said himself kept Russia out of his analysis of Western Orientalism.[22] But to counter it, we do not need Tolz's finding that 'there is a direct link between Said and his Russian predecessors', and that while formulating his critique of European Orientalism, 'Said relied heavily on the works of several Arab authors who in the early 1960s initiated a major critique of Western Oriental Studies from a perspective that was at the same time Marxist and post-colonial nationalist'.[23] For, in *Orientalism* Said does include Russia among the colonial powers and leaves some scope for the possibility of treating Russia as an important Oriental player creating her 'Orient'. After recounting the achievements of British and French 'academic' Orientalism, he makes this important remark:

> By the end of the nineteenth century these achievements were materially abetted by the European occupation of the entire Near Orient (with the exception of parts of the Ottoman Empire, which was swallowed up after 1918). The principal colonial powers once again were Britain and France, although *Russia and Germany played some role* as well. [Italics added]

Of course, while talking about the 'flourishing knowledge industry' coupled with the 'accelerated attention paid by the . . .

European empires to the Orient' as the impetuses to the crystallization of 'Orientalist' structures and restructures, Said lays greater stress on the Russian imperial project in the East than on her academic Orientalism:

> Ever since the Treaty of Chanak . . . Britain's interests were more substantial in the East than France's, but we must not forget Russia's movement into the Orient (Samarkand and Bukhara were taken in 1868; the Transcaspian Railroad was being extended systematically), nor Germany's and Austria-Hungary's.[24]

But Said cites Lord Curzon's awareness and fear that though from 'the days of Sir William Jones the Orient had been what Britain ruled and what Britain knew about', still 'there were the other European powers, France and Russia among them, that made the British presence always a (perhaps marginally) threatened one'.[25] But if someone is still mentally hamstrung by Said's overemphasis on Western Europe as 'the West', we may take the view of David Schimmelpenninck van der Oye that 'Russian Orientalism is a particularly intriguing exception to Said's schema', where in the absence of separating seas, for Russians 'the boundary between "self" and "Other" is much less clear cut.'[26]

So, 'Orientalism', both as an imperial project and in its cognitive meaning of Oriental Studies as a discourse, is applicable for Russia too, and anyway if we accept Sen's identification of different voices in Orientalist representation by a country, it gives us a scope to ask if there is some correspondence between these voices and various national traditions of European 'Orientalism', or if there is any connection between imperial experience and the type of 'Orientalist' scholarship.

The trouble with differentiating these national traditions is that even many broad-minded Orientalists present 'Europe' or 'the West' as one unit and subsume it in Western Europe, taking Russia as no part of it. This was the point Sergei Serebriany raised against the writings of Wilhelm Halbfass who 'tries to tell us just one story, about how "Europe", or "the West", encountered India'. But since '"Europe" and even more so "the West" are not cultural monoliths', but are rather 'rich mosaics of various cultures and traditions', the 'narrative device of telling just one single story looks rather artificial and inadequate', hiding 'different substories and subplots . . . deserving . . . individual narration'. Serebriany concedes that 'it is largely a matter of scale and style whether the study of the encounter between India and the West should be told as one single story or as the sum of several different stories'. But he is not only sure that in the context of 'the present stage of our knowledge, it would be more fitting and more enlightening to try to tell separate stories, interconnected as they surely are, before weaving them into a general canvas'; but also that such a meta-narrative definitely ignores some subplots. So 'Eastern and Southern European strands ought also to be eventually woven into that general canvas'.[27]

But to be meaningful any discussion of Russian Orientalism has to be preceded by Russia's own sense of difference from the West, as well as from her East.

RUSSIA'S VIEW OF EUROPE AND THE DEVELOPMENT OF ACADEMIC AND APPLIED ORIENTALISM

Russian Orientalism is intimately connected with her identity *vis-à-vis* Europe, and her Asian east including India. Iver Neumann says that debate about Europe 'is a traditional staple of Russian intellectual life. Indeed the idea of Europe is the main "Other" in relation to which the idea of Russia is defined'. Moreover, this identity has its residence not in 'essential and readily identifiable cultural traits but in relations'. In consequence, 'the question of why and where and how borders towards "the Other" should be drawn' has assumed great salience.[28] Concentrating first on Russia's view of herself, one remembers that through many centuries Russians had nurtured, through interpretation or construction of geographical space, 'a variety of highly contrasting geographical or geopolitical self-images: visions in effect of Russia as a particular sort of geographical entity'. The only running theme was the sense of a 'discrete territorial massif between Europe and Asia', whether, as initially supposed, separated by the Azov-Tanais boundary, or as since the times of Peter the Great (1672–1725), by the Ural mountains.

Pre-Petrine Muscovy did not mind the superiority of Europe lying in the West of it. 'Isolated, self-obsessed and hyperxenophobic', she drew on the cultural roots of Byzantium, seldom seeing herself as a part of Europe. Ignoring a few exceptions, there was little mental openness toward Europe or endorsement of the idea of an overarching European pre-eminence. Rather in the self-belief of Moscow as the Third Rome, Russians flaunted 'a fully articulated ideology of their own national exclusivity as the chosen bearers of the true Christianity'. Insofar as Muscovites were aware of the categories of Europe and Asia, they belonged to 'formal physical-geographical designation'. For Mark Bassin this explains the indifference of the Muscovite literati to the fact that accepting the Tanais boundary placed a large part of the 'historical hearth of the Muscovite state in Asia'.

But this perception received a jolt after Peter the Great (1672–1725) undertook his reforms, which involved 'a fundamentally new understanding of the distinction between Europe and Asia and the significance of this distinction for Russia'. The new ideology unabashedly acknowledged the singular importance of the European continent and the unconditional pre-eminence of European civilization. Peter desired to give Russia a European aspect, reorganized thoroughly on European patterns. This went beyond renaming Muscovy from a *tsarstvie* or tsardom to an *imperiia* or a colonial empire, ruled by an *imperator* or emperor. The initiative to reorient Russia's political identity required recasting her geopolitical self-image in the direction of something more recognizably European in place of 'the expansive and rather formless agglomeration of lands and peoples sprawling out across the East European plain and northern Asia to the Pacific'. Here the fact that the Russian state straddled two continents acquired a new salience, pointing to a basic dichotomy in Russia's physical corpus shared by the Western empires, and produced further evidence of a natural affinity with them. For, like Spain or England, the Netherlands or Portugal, on a larger scale Russia too could be divided into two major components: a homeland or metropolis in the spatial location of the European civilization and a vast, but foreign, extra-European colonial periphery. Apart from providing the basis for the differentiation between Russia's European and Asiatic parts, this dichotomy imparted an entirely new immediacy to the old problem of the boundary across. In all subsequent redrawing of maps, in spite of efforts by conservative nationalists to revise this dichotomous geographical image, European and Asiatic Russia continued to demarcate 'a boundary . . . running directly south along the Ural (or alternatively the Emba) River to the Caspian', and embodied 'in a square column of granite, the word Asia carved on the east-facing side and Europe on the opposite', at Nizhnyi Tagil in the central Urals, to serve as a marker for this imaginary seam where the continents are supposed to meet.[29]

In pursuit of his emulation of Europe, Peter invited the French, English and the Germans, primarily the Germans, to set up the tsarist institutions of learning and administration, ignoring their 'derogatory references' to Russians, which were passed on to her Asiatic neighbours. Gone was Russia's former ease with her 'Oriental status', flowing from geographical contiguity with the Caucasus and Central Asia and resultant numerous contacts with many of the eastern civilizations, buttressed by the links forged with the Crimean Khanate since 1443, and with the subsequent Mongol rule from the thirteenth to the fifteenth century. Of course, the cultural distancing between Russia and the East did not immediately lead to full disengagement. Traces of earlier beliefs and influences, including polygamy, remained. Russian church architecture and icon paintings, as also a large part of written literature represented fusion with eastern cultures. But Peter I patronized German works, which enunciated alien codes of social conduct and discouraged Russian customs, and even sought to dissuade Russians from speaking in their tongue.

The changed winds led even gifted Russian authors like Pushkin, Alexander Griboedov, Nikolai Karadzic, V.G. Belinsky and others to write books decrying Russian culture and extolling virtues of Western ways of life. Russian aristocracy not only internalized foreigners' critiques of their demeanour and dresses, but made frantic efforts to gain recognition and acceptance from their detractors, even at the costs of rejection of their own culture and crippling self-abnegation. 'Russian culture and history were termed barbaric from the Russian pulpits of learning'. The claims by 'Normanist' historians that without intervention by the Normans the 'barbaric and backward Slavs' would have failed to usher in autonomous economic, political or cultural growth, was accepted without demur by the Russian court in the eighteenth century. As a result nineteenth century Russians sought to refute these charges by severing their own links with non-European cultures and trying to become more European. True to this secondary Eurocentrism Russians started regarding the Mongols and Turkic people, with whom they had centuries of close ties, as the ones who had incommoded Russia's development. From a sense of inadequacy, instilled by European scholars and writers, which they had internalized and now sought to pass on to their Asian neighbours, Russians distorted facts to turn the Mongol-Tartars as marauders and 'sworn enemies of Christianity'.[30]

The historiography of Russo-Tartar relations was a product of this new 'Orientalism'. Madhavan Palat explains Russia's 'deliberate silence' about the rule of Mongol conquerors for two centuries from the thirteenth to the fifteenth in this light.[31] His view finds echo in Nicholas Riasanovsky, who described the period of Mongol rule as 'the most traumatic historical experience of the Russian people',[32] though later scholarship established that the Mongol period rather represented 'a complex, multifaceted, and long term relationship between two peoples who were often but by no means always hostile'.[33]

Palat labels Russia's search for identity in her Asiatic parts as tsarist imperialism masquerading as 'Orientalism'. He deplores its soft-pedaling in specialized studies of the Russian empire, because of their penchant for 'incorporating expansionism into a posited *essence* of Russia', and their habit of 'presenting her in a state of endemic inflation since the sixteenth century, and thus inventing a part of the "Russian tradition"'. Three driving forces identified by Palat that justified Russian conquest of Central Asia and Turkestan were: 'the civilizing mission, the commercial and investment needs of Russian capitalism, and Anglo-Russian rivalry in Central Asia, otherwise known as the Great Game'. Palat shows, however, that since the early nineteenth century Russians systematically claimed that they were suffering from the unmitigated barbarism and violence, lawlessness and restlessness, ignorance, superstition, and fanaticism of the neighbouring 'Asiatics' and 'Orientals'. Charges of brigandage, raids and robberies in the steppe, rendering frontier settlements insecure, forced slavery of Russians, nomadic violence, feudal despotisms of Central Asian khanates, external fluidity of these systems and the internal amorphousness of their power structures, characteristics of the Oriental mind which needed tutoring and colonial pedagogy, and hence the colonial civilizing mission—all these served as ruses of Russia's expansion in her East. She succeeded in this because her charges, even if specious, 'derived from a collective European Orientalism to which Russia contributed and on which she drew'.[34]

But reducing Russian 'Orientalism' and its underpinning Orientology just to a defensive response to her inferiority complex regarding Europe (as Sahni argues) or to tsarist imperialism in the East (as Palat contends) would be both simplistic and inadequate, unless we distinguish between state policies and academic Orientalism. Tolz rightly points out that though it is customary to date the origins of Oriental Studies in Russia to the reign of Peter the Great, throughout the eighteenth century, however, Russian rulers did not go beyond attempts to train on an ad hoc basis a few people as translators and interpreters in the Oriental languages that were important for Russia's foreign policy. There were no academic Oriental Studies and no societies and centres in the field at the time. It was only in 1804 that the statutes of Moscow, Kazan, and Khar'kov universities introduced the teaching of Oriental languages there, and chairs in Arabic and Persian were created at the St. Petersburg University, established in 1819. Oriental Studies as an institutionalized academic discipline were, however, still far off. Instead, a few individual scholars worked in isolation in four existing centres of academic learning with a modest increase in the number of specialists in the 1830s. The situation changed only in the 1840s, when in the backdrop of the Westernizer–Slavophile debate over the essence of Russian national identity, a series of learned societies having Oriental Studies as an important academic concern came up. Amidst debates over their goals, the groups within these societies that pleaded for greater attention to Slavic Studies and to cultural and historic ties between Russians and other peoples living in the Russian state won the battle over research agendas. In the context of Oriental Studies this led to greater research focus on 'Russia's own Orient'—that is, the eastern borderlands of the Russian empire. So, like what their West European counterparts did under the impact of nationalism, Russian scholars decided to tailor their research agenda to the frontiers of the extant state. Still, till the early twentieth century no learned society solely catered to Oriental Studies. Rather, 'within the societies dedicated to studying Russia in its multi-ethnic and multicultural variety Russian/Slavic Studies co-existed with Oriental Studies'. Proliferation of learned societies with a clear specialization in Oriental Studies received a real boost only during the reign of Alexander II (1855–81), when liberalizing reforms and growing social activism were attended by another intensification of debate over Russian national identity, in which not only individual intellectuals but members of the ruling elite engaged. In the shock of Russia's defeat in the Crimean War and attendant increase in anti-Western sentiments, there was an attempt to define Russia's identity as separate from, and often in opposition to, Western Europe, and arguments about the impact of Eastern cultures and traditions on Russia acquired a new salience that did not recede or subside until the end of the imperial period. So, collation of knowledge about Russia's eastern borderlands gained new priority, culminating in a rapid growth of new societies and of branches of the existing ones in the borderlands themselves.[35]

Tolz locates this new priority for Oriental Studies in the second of the two 'Oriental Renaissances' experienced by Europe since the eighteenth century, the first associated with the Romantics, the second with modernism. It was when the second phase reached its peak between the 1880s and the 1920s that the Russians, whose 'national identity formation was particularly unsettled by modernization' made the most radical and far-reaching attempts to rethink the meaning of the Orient for Europe and herself. The push factors in this were the post-1880s industrialization and urbanization and attendant social changes, which placed existing norms, values and identities under challenge; and the novel policies of the tsarist government in administering the Russian empire, which combined the nationalization or Russification of the imperial space with the use of West European colonial methods of rule. Although the three revolutions in the first two decades of the twentieth century and the First World War put the cohesion of the Russian society under severe strain, finally leading to the fall of the tsarist regime and a passing disintegration of the imperial space, these also unleashed enormous creative potential, as well as intense intellectual and artistic ferment. This so-called Silver Age (1890s–1917) of Orientalism among Russian avant-garde artists searching for a unique Russian artistic style, and of engagement with 'Eastern' religions and cultures among broader circles of the Russian elite from members of the royal court to literati, was also enriched by academic Orientologists in St Petersburg. Prominent among them were Baron Viktor Rozen (1849–1908) and a group of his disciples, including Vasilii Barthold (1869–1930), Nikolai Marr (1864–1934), and Sergei Oldenburg (1863–1934).[36]

Tolz points out that two processes, closely connected but moving in opposite directions, shaped the contours of Orientalist research in this period. These are, nationalization, understood as 'the emergence of the nation as the structuring unit and the principal arena of scientific activity'; and internationalization, signifying heightened international cooperation as well as competition among scholars from different countries. The leading role taken by Rozen in guiding Oriental Studies through both the processes has been highlighted by Tolz and others.[37] But what about Saidian 'Orientalism', which quite a number of scholars studying Russia's ways with her Orient have engaged with, like Adeeb Khalid, Nathaniel Knight, Monica Greenleaf, Susan Layton, D. Brower and E. Lazzerini, M. Bassin, E.M. Thompson, Robert Geraci and others?[38] Tolz does not think that this perspective is competent enough to study this process. She gives her refutation with special reference to Khalid and Knight. Khalid concedes full relevance of Said's arguments to Russia, and provides an example of an Orientalist, who advised the government on a regular basis,[39] apart from maintaining that there were many other scholars keen to participate in the formation of government policies, which made them, in Khalid's view, 'automatic accomplices of Russian imperialism'. But Knight thinks that Russia's involvement with the Orient was profoundly different in nature from that of Britain and France, experiences of which formed the staple of Said's analysis. Moreover, Knight contends that academic Orientalists could not be easily seen as significantly responsible for Russian imperialism, because the tsarist government normally gave short shrift to their expertise. From this perspective, Tolz argues that though since the times of Alexander II Russian political and intellectual elites tended to believe that 'the government should copy the policies pursued by Britain and France in building national communities within the metropole and should take into account the example set by the creation of unified states in Germany and Italy', in the hope that 'Russia could be turned into a nation state with a particular type of social, political, and, maybe, even cultural cohesion, rooted in a common historical experience of living together', academic Orientalists, as distinct from Christian missionaries, particularly those involved in anti-Islamic polemics and government officials, did not support the policy of 'aggressive cultural Russification aimed at making the minorities Russian in language and culture'. On the basis of their published works as well as unpublished correspondence, diaries, public speeches, and reports addressed to the government by leading academic Orientalists, Tolz argues that the impact of nationalism on academics went beyond their desire to increase Russia's national prestige in Europe through their research, to lead to framing of research questions shaped by their view of themselves as nation-builders. So, the set of proposals put forward by the academics was unusual in the context of contemporary debate over the integration and assimilation of these minorities. The position of academics specializing in the Caucasus, Central Asia, and the native population of Siberia and the middle-Volga region was different not only from those who advocated voluntary assimilation in the western borderlands, where the strength of non-Russian national identities (for instance, among the Poles) was acknowledged, but was also different from that of xenophobic Russian nationalists of the early twentieth century, who opposed assimilation, because they regarded the minorities as threatening to the very existence of the ethnically defined Russian nation. The forte of the academic Orientalists was not only a kind of linguistic and cultural pluralism, unique in late imperial Russia, but their readiness to apply their arguments even to nationalities with weak or no sense of national identity and to propose pro-active measures aimed at forging such identities. Unafraid of possible growth of local nationalisms, but rather regarding it as beneficial for Russia's unity, they posited that the development of a 'European way of thinking', of which nationalism was one component, would make the worldview of the Russians and peoples of the eastern borderlands more similar.[40]

But though the above words may exonerate academic Orientalists between the 1870s and 1917, they do not allow us to forget that in spite of their insights Russia herself was changing, and not in just looking West. Tolz quotes Mark Beissinger's reminder that 'empires and states are inherently subjective constructs rather than simply objective entities', to make her point that 'it is often post factum, depending on whether a nation-building project succeeded or failed that the final judgement is reached over the imperial or nation-state nature of a polity'.[41] But as Jeff Sahadeo pointed out, Russian advances across the steppe lands generated sweeping changes not only for the conquerors, but for the conquered too. These defined both the character and status of Russia as an empire and forced the steppe and Central Asian peoples to alter not just political arrangements but ways of life. Imperial expansion offered a range of interactions and cross-fertilizations,[42] inevitably generating critiques about the real nature of Russia's eastward expansion.

RUSSIA'S IDENTITY: A STATE OR AN EMPIRE?

This question 'which is not only relevant for Russia's activities in the Caucasus and Central Asia but also touches at least three of our travel narratives, is far from settled academically. The answer that Sahni and Palat give to it echoes the tone of researches on Russia at the height of the Cold War, when both the tsarist and the Soviet State were considered as equally expansionist, as Russian-dominated 'empires' that skewed the natural nationalism of non-Russian nationalities.[43] The contentions of these researchers were premised on a simplistic view of nationalities as 'organic' communities, and of empires as entities 'obsessed with the suppression of national sentiments'. By the 1980s, however, under the influence of the constructivist models of E.J. Hobsbawm and Terence Ranger, Ernest Gellner, Benedict Anderson, Miroslav Hroch,[44] and others, which saw the modern nation as 'invented tradition' or 'imagined communities', and as products of post-industrial social and cultural processes, this differentiation between nationalistic aspirations coming from below and imperialistic impositions stifling them from above were similarly problematized. In tune with changing perceptions, post-colonial scholars started arguing that, let alone suppressing ethnic differences, modern empires encourage it and employ it as a governing tool.[45] Once the notions of 'nationality' and 'empire' were reopened in this manner, experts on imperial and Soviet Russia started questioning how germane or not to their field of study were contemporary theoretical exegeses of empires. Actually even the 'return of the repressed' perspective on the revival of nationalism in East Europe after the collapse of Soviet-type socialism in the USSR that some scholars found it opportune to adopt[46] has been frowned on by more objective scholars.[47] As Rogers Brubaker clarifies in an earlier work, 'The Soviet Union was a multinational state not only in ethnodemographic terms—not only in terms of the extraordinary ethnic heterogeneity of its population —but more fundamentally in institutional terms'.[48]

Brubaker's position has been reiterated by many Russian and more remarkably by non-Russian experts like Ronald Suny, Austin Jersild, Paul Werth, Leonid Strakhovsky, Igov Martynyuk and others. Suny points out how when in post-Soviet times Western writers resurrected the metaphor of 'empire' for Russia, what was once known and routinely referred to as the Russian state suddenly came to be universally decried as an empire, which either broke up because it was an empire, or was an empire because it broke up.[49] The critics forgot that in 'contiguous empires, where the distinction between the nation and the empire is more easily muddled than in overseas empires, ruling elites may attempt to construct hybrid notions of an empire-nation, as in tsarist Russia or the Ottoman empire in the nineteenth century'.[50] This is why, according to

Suny, consonant with her expansion into the Caucasus and Central Asia, Russia had embarked on a modern colonial project of identifying and categorizing its subjects. In their bid to address the empire's ambiguous position between Europe and Asia, and to describe the Asian 'other', scholars and writers did generate a Russian 'Orientalism'.[51]

The theme of contiguous empires was used by Jersild to contend that the emergence of an imperial imagination was primarily provided by political, ethnographic, and literary writing about 'famously exotic' North Caucasian mountaineers and their conquest and incorporation. However, the shaping of a new imperial purpose was a multinational creation by Georgian intellectuals, Ossetian, Abkhaz, and Dagestani teachers, missionaries, and officials co-operating with Russian bureaucrats. But still the Russian context of empire was quite different from the European, if only because 'Russia did not possess distant "colonies", but contiguous borderlands, and its enduring ancien régime social order and its "emperor of all the Russian (rosiiskoe) lands" pose a series of contrasts to the European experience'.[52]

In spite of geographical contiguity, lacking a coherent imperial ideology during the most of the nineteenth century, the Russian empire first resorted to religious conversion, and then to the codifications of the mountaineers' customary law.[53] Though late nineteenth century attempts by St. Petersburg to correct Russia's ambiguous identity as both nation and empire by encouraging assimilation and Russian colonization did not succeed, as far from being the epitome of Russianness many of the settlers were religious dissenters [as will be seen in the travelogue of Vereshchagin], still the conquest of the North Caucasus had a deep influence on the shaping of Russia's imperial ideology, upon which even the post-Revolutionary State drew heavily.[54]

Werth shows that even in the Volga–Kama region, which represented Russia's first imperial acquisition and whose indigenous inhabitants were Russia's first nationalities, dominated by a mix of Finnic and Turkic elements and Russian peasant settlers,[55] a 'pre-national' Russian empire was content for a long time with the population's loyalty to the dynasty, not caring about its (incipient) ethnic identity. The empire's confessional policy was a 'matter of negotiation and interaction',[56] which changed only after the Polish Rebellion of 1863 and the 'Great Apostasy' of 1866. The first made the loyalty of other ethnic and religious groups suspect. The second, in which over 10,000 Tartars petitioned the tsar for recognition as Muslims, made St. Petersburg more prone to represent 'fanaticism' as a general characteristic of Islam, and more determined to attempt 'containment' of Islamic influence in Russia's inner provinces.[57] Werth also points out that around 1860 Russia 'began to participate much more consciously in a larger European project of modern colonialism'. Dealing with its central point, namely, the Russian state's unfinished transition from religion-based to ethnic identity, Werth makes highly enlightening comparisons with 'hierarchies of religious confession' in Britain, France, the Ottoman Empire, Austria, Prussia and other German states, to show that the problem of determining where the 'empire begins' was not restricted to Russia.[58]

The purely post-colonialist take on the Russian empire building in 'Inner Asia' is questioned by I. Gerasimov et al. too for overlooking empire 'as a situation of undetermined boundaries and mutually open channels of influence that emanate not only from the culturally and technologically dominant centre, but also from the imperial periphery'. According to them the reluctance of post-colonial studies to pay attention to the problem of horizontal interactions between different elements and their obsession with the opposition between East and West make it necessary 'to search for new models to rethink the uneven space circumscribed by indefinite and porous boundaries'.[59] It is in this perspective that Gerasimov et al. pit the pioneering study of Russian imperial history by Strakhovsky, who analysed the situation of non-Russian peoples of empire from the point of view of their legal status; and showed Russia to be a national state, which, moreover, tolerantly handled its minorities.[60] There are other scholars who argue in geographical, cultural or political terms against the 'Orientalist' take on Russian expansion in Inner Asia, and contend that the words 'Asiatic' or 'European' or the word 'empire' are malapropisms in describing Russia's extension eastward. Martynyuk clubs their approaches under the rubric of 'Eurasianism', or 'Eurasianology',[61] and brings in P.N. Savitskii, a leading Russian geographer, who broached the concept of the Russian Empire 'as a unified geographical world unto itself, belonging neither to Europe, nor to Asia due to the cohesiveness of its biogeographical zones', in support of his position.[62]

Other scholars like G. Vernadsky shunned the word 'empire' in the Russian context, to seek conceptual refuge in the term 'mestorazvitie', meaning 'topogenesis', or place-development. For Vernadsky, the ethnographic unity of the landmasses was caused by the 'organic process of Russian peaceful colonization and eastward expansion, or in fact by the congruence between colonial settlement and "physiography"', complemented by 'biogeography'. Here the state, embedded in its environmental setting, espoused a single territorial massif of 'Russia-Eurasia' as a large-scale 'mestorazvitie', or a historical-cultural homeland of Slavic, Finno-Ugric, and Turkic ethnic elements, that acquired a so-called 'symphonic personality'. The history of the Eurasian space was primarily the history of a succession of empires. The Russian rule was better because it fitted better the structural organization of 'mestorazvitie' in all the aspects, obviating the need to employ explicitly the concept of 'empire', inasmuch as colonization itself is made to appear as quite a harmonious process.[63]

The terms of the debate, though inconclusive, have, however, established the relevance and salience of Russian Orientalism, both in the Saidian and traditional senses. But the Indian connection of Russian Orientalism has to be thrashed out yet to make the literature about Russian Orientalism and her identity relevant for us.

RUSSIAN ORIENTALISM, INDIA AND INDOLOGY

Schimmelpenninck shows that the Russian Empire's geography straddling two continents, its ambivalent relationship with the rest of Europe, and the complicated nature of its encounter with Asia have all given birth to a variegated and often surprisingly sympathetic understanding of the East among its people.[64] But Russia's interest in India has always moved beyond the purely academic, ever since the fiasco of the march of the Russian army towards India in 1801, ordered by Tsar Paul I at the height of winter through Central Asia as part of the joint Franco-Russian design of eliminating British presence in India.[65] And imperial calculations were never wholly absent even in the shaping of Russian Orientology about India. As Schimmelpenninck points out, even the academic curriculum was some-times 'designed to send a diplomatic message'. For example, when the Crimean War was at the boiling point, Bernhard Dorn, the Asian Museum's director, offered courses in Afghan languages to remind London about the vulnerability of British India. He informed the Minister of Education A.S. Norov that the English had started their unjust war in Russia in fear of her advance in Central Asia. Afghanistan being the only barrier between Russia and England's possessions in India, the English would 'tremble thinking that Russia might take a step here . . . England's Parliament will be stunned when it learns that Afghan is being publicly taught in Russia'. Of course, Schimmelpenninck reminds us that though the State viewed St. Petersburg's Faculty of Oriental Languages 'primarily in vocational terms', as 'a tool for its imperial ambitions', the professors led by Vasilii Grigoriev saw things differently. For them regardless of the importance of the 'the Faculty's practical goals', they were only 'part of its duties'. The 'academic study and dissemination of knowledge' was the main objective.[66] Again, Sergei Oldenburg, who according to Tolz was one of the architects of the so-called Silver Age of Russian Orientology, along with Rozen and others,[67] 'was not only a renowned specialist in the traditional culture of India, Central Asia and Far East, but also a liberal politician of the pre-Soviet epoch, a former member of the Central Committee of the Constitutional Democratic (Kadet) Party, and for a short time in 1917, even Minister of Education in the Provisional Government of the Russian Republic'.[68] It is impossible to contend that Oldenburg's Indological interests had no relationship with his politics.

Moreover, the presence of power relationship in Russian Indology is brought out by Morrison's point that the criticism of British rule in India in comparison with Russian rule in Turkestan on the part of the Russian military and civilian elite between 1860 and 1917 was a mere ploy. 'The subtext was not that Indians should be free to rule themselves, but that Russians would make much better imperial masters either because of their greater sympathy with Asian modes of thought or because they were more whole-hearted modernizers than the British. India was thus an obsession for metropolitan Vostochniki and military officers alike; they saw it as the key to Russia's imperial future as the world's greatest power, both temporal and spiritual'.[69]

From the words above Russia's academic and Romantic attachment to Sanskrit and to Sanskrit-based Indology, begun much before the second Oriental Renaissance of Tolz, would appear a little idealized, hiding practical concerns of Russia's expansion in the East, with India as a distant goal. It was not before the first half of the nineteenth century that Russia came out with a 'veritable explosion of books concerned with India', though since then, as evident in the entries of a standard bibliography like *Bibliographija Indii*, the publications have covered a wide range.[70]

While critiquing Halbfass' *India and Europe* for the marginal references to Russian Orientalists,[71] Serebriany does not mince words about the marginal position of India in Russian culture, both before the nineteenth-century, and after. In his opinion, 'in 19th century Russia there never existed a literary and/or intellectual movement . . . influenced by India', as that occasioned by German Romanticism. 'The comparatively low level of response to India on behalf of the classical Russian culture of the 19th century emphasizes the peculiar position of Russia in the 'concert' of modern European civilization'.[72] But G.M. Bongard-Levin and A.A. Vigasin's as well as R.H. Stacy's accounts of salience of India in Russian Orientalism, despite Serebriany's description of the former as pre-perestroika combination of 'solid scholarship and propagandist clichés', and the latter as too 'general' and 'rarely very satisfying',[73] might make Serebriany's views appear uncharitable. Though Bongard-Levin and Vigasin distinguish two basic trends in the development of European Sanskrit studies: 'the colonial and the romantic', comparable to Sen's categories of 'magisterial' and 'exoticist', and reserve the second to the German and the Russian tradition, they admit that Sanskrit studies in Russia and the establishment of new universities and departments teaching Oriental languages at the very beginning of the nineteenth century had 'practical require-ments of the Russian state', and the pressure of cultural relations with Europe in mind. But equally important as motivating factors were linguistic pride, occasioned by the perceived similarities of Russian with Sanskrit and their supposedly common origin, and Buddhism, professed by a number of Eastern nations existing on its borderlands. The theme of common origin of the two languages formed the subject of books by Konrad Gottlob Anton in 1809, and Friedrich Adelung in 1811. Ground was prepared for Count Sergei Uvarov's plea for an Asiatic Academy, which would undertake the publication of a Sanskrit dictionary and the translation of the Vedas and *Mahābhārata*. Stacy says this programme was never implemented.[74] But Bongard-Levin and Vigasin credit Uvarov's initiative for the foundation of the Asiatic Museum in Russia in 1818, earlier than similar institutions in France, Britain and Germany.

After this a continuous stream of research activities and publications started, even if the first ones were neither direct translations nor by scholars of Russian origin. These were Adelung's *Review of Literature in the Sanskrit Language* (1830) in German; Bernhard Dorn's *On the Kinship of the Slavonic and Sanskrit Languages* (1833); Robert Lenz's *Urvaśī* (*Vikramorvaśī*) (Kālidāsa's play, 1833), and catalogue of Sanskrit manuscripts in the Asiatic Museum in the Academy of Sciences. Systematic teaching of Sanskrit in the Oriental Studies programme of the Kazan University as a compulsory subject was started in 1842 by Pavel Yakovich Petrov, who translated the 'Abduction of Sita' from the *Rāmāyaṇa*, excerpts of *Gītagovinda* by Jayadeva, Sanskrit poem *Ghaṭakarparam*, a review of Hindu literature and a Sanskrit anthology containing excerpts from the *Mahābhārata*, *Rāmāyaṇa*, *Hitopadeśa*, *Kathāsaritsāgara*, *Brahmāṇḍapurāṇa*, and the *Rājatara giṇī*.

The next push came from Kaetan Kossovich's translations in 1844 of an excerpt from the *Mahābhārata* on 'Sunda and Upasunda' the *Story of Vidyādhara* by Jīmūtavāhana, an excerpt from the *Bhāgavatapurāṇa*, a translation of the first act from Śūdraka's

Mṛcchakaṭika, and the translation of Kṛṣṇa Miśra's *Prabodhacandrodaya*, in 1847. Kossovich also published several works as teaching aids for the Oriental Language Faculty, opened in St. Petersburg University in 1855. He praised Sanskrit as 'a model of a language with the most complete forms . . . most perfect structure' and 'perfect speech', and said that 'Russia needs Sanskrit scholars just as much as she needs mathematicians and historians'.

Another factor that kept up interest in Sanskrit studies was Slavophilism of the 1840s and 1850s, as evidenced in Alexei Khomyakov's book *A Comparison of Russian and Sanskrit Words* (1855), and Alexander Hilferding's book *On the Relation of Slavonic Language to Cognate Languages.* Together with Vassily Zhukovsky's lyrical transcreation of *Nala and Damayantī*, and A.D. Saltykov's romanticized *Letters about India* and accompanying pictures, Slavophile enthusiasm for Sanskrit sustained interest in Sanskrit-centred Indology. More serious researches appeared later, as St. Petersburg-based Otto Von Böhtlingk's huge oeuvre of Pāṇini's *Grammar* (1839–40), an erudite edition of Kālidāsa's *Śakuntalā*, a Sanskrit reader that included texts from the *Ṛgveda* (1845), Vyopadeva's *Grammar* (1846), Hemacandra's *Dictionary* (1847), a seven-volume Sanskrit lexicon: the *Great St. Petersburg Dictionary* (1852–75), a seven-volume *Concise St. Petersburg Dictionary* (1879–89), a three-volume book *Indian Sayings* (1863–5) compiling Sanskrit gnomic poetry, a German translation of Śūdraka's *Mṛcchakaṭika*, translations and editions of the *Bṛhadāranyaka* and the *Chāndogya* Upaniṣads, and a new edition and translation of Daṇḍin's poetry.

Buddhism was also a prolific source of Indological studies, based on Sanskrit, Mongol and Tibetan languages. Osip Kovalevsky, Polish scholar settled in Kazan, published in the 1830s *Buddhist Cosmology*, one of the earliest works on Buddhism in Europe. Anton Schiefner, a St. Petersburg University graduate, educated in Sanskrit at Berlin, wrote the *Sanskrit-Tibetan Dictionary of Buddhist Terminology* (1859) and a German translation of the *History of Buddhism in Tibet* by Tārānātha, a Tibetan historian (1869). Vasily Valilyev joined in with his three-part book *Buddhism: Its Doctrines, History and Literature* (1857–69), based on Chinese and Tibetan texts.[75]

The travel narratives I have selected are important because apart from being about India, all of them, with the lone exception of Minaev, predate the second Oriental Renaissance and the institutionalization of Orientology in Russia. I hope that they would give us an opportunity to measure the proportion of non-'magisterial' voices in Russian Orientalism, in the backdrop of the fact that though an overt power relationship was absent in Russian Orientalism and Indology, covert power aspirations always lurked in the background, as Morrison so aptly shows.[76] Still did absence of direct imperialism make Russian 'Orientalism' any different from the British and French versions of it? The question is important because long before books on 'Cold War Orientalism' started coming out,[77] 'Orientalism' turned into a subject of Cold War[78] discourse, where responses by Russian Orientalists were never direct as the books by Kemp, Shastitco,[79] and Bongard-Levin and Vigasin[80] would show.

But while going into what these travellers observed and attempting a close reading of the discourses, which sometimes would involve a 'deconstructive twist' and sometimes what Spivak says 'reading against the grain',[81] I want to clarify that what is at issue is not the 'mistakes' of their observation, or their failure to evolve a body of knowledge that stands up to the scrutiny of the present, but the evolution of a broad ranging perspective about different aspects of Indian society that were either heavily influenced or were relatively free of European archetypes of observing India. Below I give a short summary of these archetypes.

ARCHETYPES OF ORIENTALIST OBSERVATIONS OF INDIA

To early West European travellers India was a strange and confusing land, inhabited by people with utterly different outlooks on life. This was because, as Bernard Cohn points out, 'Europeans knew the world through its signs and correspondences to things known'.[82] Four themes dominated their literal or visual accounts of India: asceticism, *satī* (or suttee), Hindu divinity, and cartography.[83]

Asceticism

Asceticism, including performance of 'physical penance' by religious devotees to transcend their bodily and earthly desires, fascinated and perplexed early European travellers. To them ascetics appeared 'more like devils than men'.[84] To some others they were 'gymnosophists', followers of creators of the Pythagorean ideas of souls, essentially good and purveyors of salvation 'outside the established Church'. This perception later lost out to another reading, where the yogis became 'the perpetuators of superstitions'.[85]

Sexuality of Indian Women

The socio-psychology of Hindu women's general promiscuity and its binary opposite of self-immolation, termed '*satī*' (suttee), together with the seclusion of the 'invisible' Muslim women, which denied the travel writer his privilege as observer, engrossed the imagination of the European travellers. The fixation was natural in the backdrop of the pathology of 'Orientalism' as the personal quest of the Western male for Oriental mystery and sexuality.[86] With 'a body to be veiled, revealed or consumed in flames', an ambivalent compound of 'chastity, sexual appetite, and the death wish', the Indian woman was 'the fantasy woman in an imaginary land'.[87] This fantasizing is visible in the contradictory reactions to the 'inviolable privacy' of Muslim women, and the relative freedom and visibility of Hindu women. These inform the varying assessments of Hindu and Muslim women by John Fryer (surgeon to the East India Company between 1622 and 1681), Jean de Thévenot (a contemporary French traveller), or François de la Boullaye le Gouz, attracted to the sense of Indian female otherness, both Muslim and Hindu, 'heightened by their respective areas of sexual mythology'. Harem and voyeurism stand out in Gouz's illustration of a Mughal couple engaged in unlikely amorous mood before a voyeuristic female attendant; Sir Thomas Roe spotting parts of the bodies of two of the Jahangir's 'principall Wives' through the chinks in the window screen; Fryer, gaining entry as a physician, quoting Homer to 'confirm the myth of wicked dissipation' of women in the harem; and Niccolao Manucci, another doctor, describing the Mughal harem as a 'watery, sensual region', where combination of female sexuality and female power turned it into a place where customary political and gender hierarchies were inverted.

In the case of Hindu women the threatening side of female sexuality concerned occult religious practices, as in Tavernier's description of how 'at the marriage of a Virgin, the Bridegroome, to honour the Deullish Idoll, brings her afore the Pagode, or Idoll', to get her deflowered; or in others' accounts of 'the male dream, at least as old as Marco Polo, of the traveller having free access to another man's [frequently the host's] wife' [as is dwelt on at length by Nikitin in the next chapter]. Thus, John Ovington, chaplain to the East India Company, Luduvico di Varthema, Pyrard de Laval, Richard Head and others give a composite portrayal of Hindu women that is dangerously exciting: insatiable; offering themselves on the wedding night to strangers for deflowering them; sharing their beds to service the guests' carnal desires at their husband's behest or by their own volition; but also characterized by a lethal readiness to punish them with poisoning at the first sight of perfidy.[88]

Satī

If the sexuality of the Hindu woman was disturbing and yet enthralling, so was her willing self-immolation on the husband's funeral pyre. As an absolute negation of the widowed woman's physical self, and as a supreme example of conjugal subservience, *satī* flattered the European male ego beyond measure, and at the same time disturbed his religious self. As a reminder of spurned injunctions for 'the ideal life of chastity and fidelity to the memory of a deceased husband' for seventeenth-century English widows, *satī* became 'a potent image of conjugal fidelity'. The 'highly ambivalent masculine responses' to it reflected the European travel writers' perplexity.[89]

It was Niccolo Conti, Italian merchant, who in 1420 first drew attention to it. Oaten gives Conti's account of it in full, as he thinks it to be 'one of the best that we have from the pen of an early traveller':[90]

In Central India by which means most of India proper, the dead are burned, and the living wives, for the most part, are consumed in the same funeral pyre, with their husband, one or more, according to the agreement arrived at the time the marriage was contracted. . . . The first wife was compelled by law to be burnt. . . . But others . . . add to the splendour of the funeral ceremony by their death. . . . The deceased husband is laid on a couch, dressed in his best garments. A vast funeral is erected over him in the form of a pyramid. . . . The pile being ignited, the wife, habited in her richest garments, walks gaily round it, singing, accompanied by a great concourse of people, and amid the sounds of trumpets, flutes and songs. In the meantime, one of the priests . . . standing on some elevated spot, exhorts her to a contempt of life and death, promising her all kinds of enjoyment with her husband, much wealth, and abundance and ornaments. . . . When she has walked round the fire several times, she stands near the elevation on which is the priest . . . puts on a white linen garment, her body having first been washed according to custom. In obedience to the exhortation of the priest, she then springs into the fire. If some show more the timidity . . . they are thrown into the fire by the by-standers, whether consenting or not. [91]

If the iconic verbal description of 'suttee' was by Conti, then the exemplar of visual representation, as the widow leaping into the blazing pit, was by Dutch merchant Jan Huygen van Linschoten, provided in his 1595 *Itinerary.* [92] The artistic tradition of the leaping 'suttee', introduced through his drawings, accompanied by the observations in his book, and translated into Latin, French, German, and English, endured into the eighteenth century.[93] Examples of eighteenth century literary or visual representations that present 'suttee' as forced or drugged, sometimes with the viewer's claim of successful or unsuccessful intervention, are: an engraving by Pierre Sonnerat in the 1770s; experiences of another French traveller, L. De Grandpre, in Bengal in 1789 and 1790; Thomas Twining's description of 'suttee' near Calcutta in 1792; 'An Account of a Woman Burning Herself, By an Officer', in the *Calcutta Gazette* in 1785; and accounts by Reverend William Ward, a Baptist missionary at Serampore, near Calcutta, and by William Carey, the famed author of the *Dictionary of the Bengali Language*. Carey also undertook a census in 1803 of 'suttees' that returned 438 incidents that year within a 30 mile radius of Calcutta. And instances of 'sympathetic' and even admiring accounts of 'suttee' by foreign travellers include those by: Benjamin Crowninshield, an American merchant in India, in the ship's logbook in 1789; Maria Graham, in her *Letters on India*, published in 1814; and in paintings by Tilly Kettles (1735–86), Johann Zoffany (1733–1810), William Hodges (1744–97) and James Atkinson (1780–1852).[94]

Even in neutral accounts of *satī* feelings of observers were mixed, as in Pierre Le Moyne's *La Gallerie des Femmes Fortes* (1667); John Sym's *Life's Preservative against Self-killing* (1637); and Thomas Herbert's *A Relation of Some Yeares Travaile* (1634). The first saw it as a pagan, unchristian practice; the second as a necessary 'Law' aiming to preempt 'the frequent *poysoning* of masters and husbands, by their servants and wives'; the third viewed it as 'just reuenge, for their [Hindu women's] too much abused liberty, growne so audaciously impudent. . . .' Teltscher thinks rightly that this was a ploy to reduce the *satī* from 'the emblem of a faithful wife' to a bearer of endemic 'female licentiousness'. Efforts to explain *satī* either through social pressures and social conditioning, or through 'actual physical compulsion', ranging from drugging to coercive persuasion by wily Brahmins, are evidenced in the portrayals of Abraham Roger, Francis Bernier, Jean-Baptiste Tavernier, and Athanassius Kircher. While Kircher provides the example of denigration of *satī* through Christian lenses, attempts 'to reclaim her' or to view the act 'not from a Christian perspective, but treat her rather as a literary figure, a tragic heroine' are found in the observations of Italian traveller Pietro della Valle, William Hawkins, Catrou (Manucci's editor), and finally the poet John Dryden. The multi-farious reactions are traceable to the impossibility of reducing *satī* to a blind superstition, or demeaning it as a stage drama, just be-cause the *satī* did not return, increasing the perplexed 'incredul-ity' of European observers.

English attitude to *satī* changed only when 'the changeover from a mercantile and commercial to a territorial and administrative British presence' gave British colonial administrators a supervisory role over *satī*. They had to pass judgement over its voluntariness or otherwise, making the adoption of a classical literary framework an unavailable option. The colonial regime could not afford to elevate its female 'subjects to the status of classical heroines', thereby undermining its authority. The only problem was that *satī* being 'the only manifestation of Hindu female conduct that is substantiated by personal observation', differences of perception continued, and *satī* remained a 'powerful counter to stories of Hindu female promiscuity and occult sexual practices'.[95]

Hindu Divinity

The earliest European travellers' accounts from the sixteenth through the mid-seventeenth century represented the Hindu pantheon as little more than monsters or devils. Ralph Fitch's pejorative account of Hindu idols in his Eastern travels between 1583 and 1591, included in Richard Haklyut's *Voyages*, William Finch's derogatory remarks in *Purchas* about these 'stone images', together with wonderments about cow worship and deification of the excreta of cows are good examples of non-understanding of Hindu divinity.[96] All this changed under seventeenth-century winds of a growing scientific humanism, where differences in cosmology and religious practice could be accommodated. A new interest in information about Indian mythology created a demand for 'authentic' pictures of Indian gods. As Partha Mitter puts it, a 'new class of sources dating from the middle of the seventeenth century marks the beginnings of changing attitudes in the West towards alien societies and provides the essential key to the understanding of Indian iconography'.[97]

Cartography

Cartography too played a vital role in the acquisition of knowledge as power. A phenomenal increase in the population of British India coupled with the emergence of the colonial state and the growth of an overseas British society in India necessitated an ever-expanding documentation project, which would measure and map India into topography. An 'army of professional and amateur delineators, surveyors, topographers, natural historians, map makers, scholars, linguists, historians, antiquarians, archaeologists, engravers, artists, architects, and photographers' got involved. For, new descriptive and interpretive strategies were to be constructed and deployed 'if India was to be effectively domesticated. The devils of the 17th century travelers, with their satanic rites and satyrical priests, the wildness, the bizarre, and the weird had to be submerged if India was to be effectively and profitably ruled.'[98]

Broadly speaking, all these stereotypes are cast in rigid Saidian oppositions and binaries, like maturity/immaturity, civilization/barbarism, developed/developing, and progressive/primitive.[99] While searching for their depiction, sources and influence in the seven travel narratives, I remain conscious of the variations in the personal engagement of the 'Orientalist' with the world he encounters. But to the extent these archetypes are present with other observations in the narratives, they would show that if the attitude of despising the East as inferior and construction of the observer's self from this 'othering' can be called 'Orientalism', then it can be traced in the Russian psyche too well before the different birthdates of European or Russian Orientalism. Only these seven travelogues are chosen because apart from their availability in various English translations, my reading strategy of deep analysis of discourse precludes a large number of samples. Only two of the travelogues include perceptions of Caucasus, Central Asia, and India. I have maintained the connection in their cases, to show the disjuncture in Saltykov's representation and continuity in Vereshchagin's depiction.

Chapter 2 of the book deals with Afanasii Nikitin, a man who predated the controversies regarding 'Orientalism', and yet whose travelogue notices things having strong similarities with Saidian 'Orientalist' stereotypes. Chapter 3 clubs together three figures: Fillip S. Yefremov, Rafail Daniebeg, and Herasim Stepanovich Lebedev, mostly to show the difference of Lebedev from them and other contemporaries. Chapter 4 is devoted to Aleksei Dmitriyevich Saltykov and his 'exoticism'. Chapter 5 is on Vasily Vasilyevich Vereshchagin, the most typical Orientalist in the Saidian sense. Chapter 6 deals with Ivan Pavlovich Minaev, the most erudite among the travellers, and the most accomplished Indologist. The discussion of the travel writings and other artistic activities of these six travellers would always try to point out the specific mix of the 'magisterial', 'curatorial' and 'exoticist' voices in their observations.

NOTES

1. Kate Teltscher, *India Inscribed: European and British Writing on India 1600–1800* (Delhi: Oxford University Press, 1997), pp. 3–4.
2. Kalpana Sahni, *Crucifying the Orient: Russian Orientalism and the Colonization of Caucasus and Central Asia* (Bangkok: White Orchid Press, 1997), pp. 3, 14.
3. See, for example, Elena Andreeva, *Russia and Iran in the Great Game: Travelogues and Orientalism* (Abingdon, Oxon: Routledge, 2007), pp 1–12, and passim.
4. Vera Tolz, 'Orientalism, Nationalism and Ethnic Diversity in Late Imperial Russia', *The Historical Journal*, 48: 1 (2005), p. 130.
5. See Edward Said, *Orientalism: Western Conceptions of the Orient* (Harmondsworth: Penguin, 1978/1995).
6. Vera Tolz, 'European, National and (Anti-) Imperial: The Formation of Academic Oriental Studies in Late Tsarist and Early Soviet Russia', *Kritika: Explorations in Russian and Eurasian History*, 9: 1 (Winter 2008) (New Series): 56. She is referring to Vasilii Barthold (1869–1930), Nikolai Marr (1864–1934), and Sergei Oldenburg (1863–1934).
7. Said, *Orientalism*, pp. 2–4.
8. Leela Gandhi, *Postcolonial Theory: A Critical Introduction* (Delhi: Oxford University Press, 1999), pp. 75–7.
9. Homi K. Bhabha, *The Location of Culture* (1994), rpt. edn. (London and New York: Routledge, 1995), see specially chapters 3, 4 and 9.
10. Ashis Nandy's insightful description of the internal conflicts in Rudyard Kipling's mind between 'the Apollonian and the Dionysian *within* India and *within* the West', and Aurobindo's struggle and break with the West instilled in his mind by his father are registers of this resistance. See Nandy, *The Intimate Enemy: Loss and Recovery of Self under Colonialism*, 1st paperback edn. (Delhi: Oxford University Press, 1988), pp. 64–79, 87–96 and passim.
11. Ziauddin Sardar, *Orientalism*, published by arrangement with Open University Press (New Delhi: Viva Books Limited, 2002), pp.1–3.
12. Ibid., pp. 4–5, and 14–16.
13. Kate Teltscher, *India Inscribed*, pp. 2–8.
14. See C.A. Bayly, 'Knowing the Country: Empire and Information in India', *Modern Asian Studies* 27: 1(1993): 3–43.
15. Amartya Sen, 'Indian Traditions and Western Imagination', *Daedalus*, 126: 2 (Spring 1997): 4.
16. Ibid., pp. 18–19.

17. See Alexander Morrison, '"Applied Orientalism" in British India and Tsarist Turkestan', *Comparative Studies in Society and History*, 51: 3 (2009): 619–47, here 620.
18. Laura Chrisman, 'The Imperial Unconscious? Representations of Imperial Discourse', in P. Williams and L. Chrisman (eds.), *Colonial Discourse and Postcolonial Theory: A Reader* (New York: Columbia University Press, 1994), pp. 498–516, especially p. 500.
19. Nathaniel Knight, 'On Russian Orientalism: A Response to Adeeb Khalid', *Kritika* 1: 4 (2000): 705; and Knight, 'Grigor'ev in Orenburg, 1851–1862: Russian Orientalism in the Service of Empire?', *Slavic Review* 59, 1 (2000): 77, 99, quoted in Morrison, 'Applied Orientalism', p. 628.
20. Morrison, 'Applied Orientalism', pp. 644–7.
21. See Madina Tlostanova, 'The Janus-faced Empire Distorting Orientalist Discourses: Gender, Race and Region in the Russian/(post)Soviet Constructions of the Orient', obtained from *Worlds and Knowledge Otherwise*, www.jhfc.duke.edu/wko/dossiers1.3/contents.php-10k, last visited 9 May 2008, pp. 1–11, especially pp. 1–3.
22. Adeeb Khalid, 'Russian History and the Debate over Orientalism', *Kritika: Explorations in Russian and Eurasian History* 1: 4 (Fall 2000): 694–5.
23. Tolz, 'European, National and (Anti-) Imperial', p. 79. Tolz refers to Marxist sociologist from Egypt, Anwar Abdel-Malek, and his article 'Orientalism in Crisis', *Diogenes*, 44 (1963): 104–40, as an example.
24. Said, *Orientalism*, pp. 101, 191.
25. Ibid., p. 215.
26. David Schimmelpenninck van der Oye, 'Vasilij V. Vereshchagin's Canvases of Central Asian Conquest', *Cahiers d'Asie centrale* [En ligne], 17/18 | 2009, mis en ligne le 26 mai 2010. URL: http://asiecentrale.revues.org/index1196.html, retrieved on 6 August 2011, p. 185.
27. See Sergei D. Serebriany, 'Some Marginal Notes on India and Europe', in Eli Franco and Karin Preisendanz (eds.), *Beyond Orientalism: The Work of Wilhelm Halbfass and Its Impact on Indian and Cross Cultural Studies* (1997), 1st Indian edn. (Delhi: Motilal Banarsidass, 2007), pp. 79–80.
28. Iver B. Neumann, *Russia and the Idea of Europe: A Study in Identity and International Relations* (London and New York: Routledge, 1996), pp.1–2.
29. Mark Bassin, 'Russia between Europe and Asia: The Ideological Construction of Geographical Space', *Slavic Review*, 50: 1 (Spring, 1991): 1–17.
30. See Sahni, *Crucifying the Orient*, pp. xv, 8–18.
31. Madhavan K. Palat, 'Russian Imperialism', *Studies in Russia* 4:1 and 2 (1988): 188–90.

32. Nicholas Riasanovsky, 'Asia through Russian Eyes', in W. S. Vucinich (ed.), *Russia and Asia: Essays on the Influence of Russia on the Asian Peoples* (Stanford, CA.: Hoover Institution Press, 1972), p. 5.
33. Charles Halperin, *Russia and the Golden Horde: The Mongol Impact on Medieval Russian History* (Bloomington: Indiana University Press, 1985), p. 128.
34. Palat, 'Russian Imperialism', pp. 157–87.
35. Tolz, 'European, National and (Anti-) Imperial', pp. 55–8.
36. Vera Tolz, *Russia's Own Orient: The Politics of Identity and Oriental Studies in the Late Imperial and Early Soviet Periods* (Oxford: Oxford University Press, 2010), pp. 1–3.
37. Tolz, 'European, National and (Anti-) Imperial', pp. 53–81. Also see David Schimmelpenninck van der Oye, *Russian Orientalism: Asia in the Russian Mind from Peter the Great to the Emigration* (New Haven, CN: Yale University Press, 2010), pp. 186–9.
38. See Adeeb Khalid, 'Russian History and the Debate over Orientalism': 691–9; Nathaniel Knight, 'Grigor'ev in Orenburg': 74–100; discussion of Russian Orientalism in *Ab Imperio* : 'Theory and History of Nationalities and Nationalism in the Post-Soviet Realm', 1 (2002), http://abimperio.net; Monica Greenleaf, *Pushkin and Romantic Fashion : Fragment, Elegy, Orient, Irony* (Stanford, CA.: Stanford University Press, 1994); Susan Layton, *Russian Literature and Empire: Conquest of the Caucasus from Pushkin to Tolstoy* (Cambridge: Cambridge University Press, 1994), contributors to D. Brower and E. Lazzerini (eds.), *Russia's Orient : Imperial Borderlands and Peoples, 1700–1917* (Bloomington: Indiana University Press, 1997); M. Bassin, *Imperial Visions: Nationalist Imagination and Geographical Expansion in the Russian Far East, 1840–65* (Cambridge: Cambridge University Press, 1999); Ewa M. Thompson, *Imperial Knowledge: Russian Literature and Colonialism* (Westport, Conn.: Greenwood Press, 2000); and Robert P. Geraci, *Window on the East: National and Imperial Identities in Late Tsarist Russia* (Ithaca, New York: Cornell University Press, 2001).
39. Though Tolz does not name him, he was none other than Nikolai Petrovich Ostroumov, who arrived in Tashkent in 1877 as director of schools in the newly created province of Turkestan, retained his proximity to power in various capacities until 1917 all through the tsarist period, including editorship of the *Turkiston viloyatining gazeti*, the vernacular official gazette since 1883, to determine the contours of local cultural debates in the direction of Russian state interests. See Khalid, 'Russian History and the Debate', pp. 691–9.

40. Vera Tolz, 'Orientalism, Nationalism and Ethnic Diversity', pp. 127–50.
41. M. Beissinger, 'The Persisting Ambiguity of Empire', *Post-Soviet Affairs*, 11: 2 (1995): 149–84, quoted in ibid., p. 150.
42. See Jeff Sahadeo, 'Conquest, Colonialism, and Nomadism on the Eurasian Steppe', *Kritika* 4: 4 (Fall 2003): 942–54.
43. For the authorities who made these characterizations and the sources see, Palat, 'Russian Imperialism', pp. 184–7.
44. Eric J. Hobsbawm and Terence Ranger (eds.), *The Invention of Tradition* (Cambridge, UK: Cambridge University Press, 1983); Benedict Anderson, *Imagined Communities: Reflections on the Origin and Spread of Nationalism* (London: Verso, 1983); Ernest Gellner, *Nations and Nationalism* (Ithaca, NY: Cornell University Press, 1983); and Miroslav Hroch, *Social Preconditions of National Revival in Europe: A Comparative Analysis of the Social Composition of Patriotic Groups among the Smaller European Nations*, tr. Ben Fowkes (New York: Cambridge University Press, 1985).
45. Dipesh Chakrabarty, 'Postcoloniality and the Artifice of History: Who Speaks for "Indian" Pasts?' *Representations* 37(1992): 1–26; Ann Laura Stoler and Frederick Cooper, 'Between Metropole and Colony: Rethinking a Research Agenda', in Stoler and Cooper (eds.), *Tensions of Empire: Colonial Cultures in a Bourgeois World* (Berkeley: University of California Press, 1997), pp. 11–12, cited in Serhy Yekelchyk, 'Interpreting Russia's Imperial Dimension', *Canadian Slavonic Papers* (September–December 2004): 1–9. Retrieved from findarticles.com/p/articles/mi_qa3763/is.../ai_n 11849950/ on 23 May 2008.
46. See, for example, M. Ignatieff, *Blood and Belonging: Journeys into the New Nationalism* (London: Chatto and Windus, 1994), p. 2, cited in Michael Billig, *Banal Nationalism* (New Delhi: Sage, 1995), pp. 46–8.
47. R. Brubaker, 'Myths and Misconceptions in the Study of Nationalism', in J. Hall (ed.), *The State of the Nation: Ernest Gellner and the Theory of Nationalism* (Cambridge: Cambridge University Press, 1998), pp. 285–6.
48. See Rogers Brubaker, *Nationalism Reframed: Nationhood and the National Question in the New Europe* (Cambridge: Cambridge University Press, 1996), p. 23.
49. Ronald Grigor Suny, 'The Empire Strikes Out: Imperial Russia, "National Identity", and Theories of Empire', in Ronald Grigor Suny and Terry Dean Martin (eds.), *A State of Nations: Empire and Nation-Making in the Age of Lenin and Stalin* (New York: Oxford University Press, 2001), p. 23.
50. Ibid., p. 30. For a very insightful discussion on how Ottoman Orientalism might offer a close parallelism to Russian Orientalism in respect of Caucasus

and Central Asia, also see Ussama Makdisi, 'Ottoman Orientalism', *The American Historical Review*, 107: 3 (June 2002): 768–96.

51. Ibid., p. 46.
52. Austin Jersild, *Orientalism and Empire: North Caucasus Mountain Peoples and the Georgian Frontier, 1845–1917* (Montreal: McGill-Queen's University Press, 2002), pp. 4–7.
53. Ibid., pp. 89–109, especially 99–105.
54. Ibid., pp. 126–44, and 155–8.
55. Paul W. Werth, *At the Margins of Orthodoxy: Mission, Governance, and Confessional Politics in Russia's Volga-Kama Region, 1827–1905* (Ithaca, N.Y.: Cornell University Press, 2002), pp. 17–43.
56. Ibid., pp. 3–5.
57. Ibid., pp. 125–37, and 147–76.
58. Ibid., pp. 5, 42.
59. See I. Gerasimov, S. Glebov, A. Kaplunovsky, M. Mogilner, and A. Semyonov (eds.), 'In Search of a New Imperial History', Novaia imperskaia istoriia postsovetskogo prostranstva. Kazan, 2004, pp. 7–29, PDF article obtained from http:// www.zeitgeschichte-online.de/zol/portals/_zf/documents/pdf/ abimperio.pdf-,visited last on 26 April 2008, pp. 33–56.
60. Leonid Strakhovsky, 'Constitutional Aspects of the Imperial Russian Government's Policy toward National Minorities', in *The Journal of Modern History* (1941), 4(13): 467–92, cited by Gerasimov, p. 46.
61. See Igor S. Martynuk, 'Toward Understanding the Art of Modern Diasporic Ideology Making: The Eurasianist Mind-Mapping of the Imperial Homeland (1921–1934)', *Journal of the Interdisciplinary Crossroads, Thematic Issue: 'The Limits of Exile'*, ed. D. Kettler & Z. Ben-Dor, 3: 1 (April, 2006): 93–116, obtained from www.jic.in/contents31.htm - 15k - , last visited on 27 April 2008, here especially pp. 100–1.
62. P. N. Savitskii, 'Geograficheskii obzor Rossii-Evrazii [Geographical Overview of Russia-Eurasia]', in P. N. Savitskii, Rossiia – osobyi geograficheskii mir, pp. 1–69. (Praga: Evraziiskoe knigoizdatelsto, 1927), cited in ibid., p. 101.
63. G. Vernadsky, *Political and Diplomatic History of Russia* (London: Williams and Norgate, 1937); and Vernadskii, *Opyt istorii Evrazii: s poloviny VI veka do nastoiashchego vremeni. [Outline of Eurasian History: From the Second Half of the Sixth Century Till the Present*]. (Berlin: Izdanie Evraziitsev, 1934); both cited in ibid., pp. 106–7.
64. Schimmelpenninck, *Russian Orientalism: Asia in the Russian Mind.*
65. Palat, 'Russian Imperialism', pp. 188–90.
66. David Schimmelpenninck van der Oye, 'Imperial Roots of Russian Orientalism', in Michael Kemper and Stephan Conermann (eds.), *The*

Heritage of Soviet Oriental Studies (Abingdon, Oxon and New York: Routledge, 2011), p. 37.

67. See n. 36 above.
68. Mikhail Rodinov, 'Profiles under Pressure: Orientalists in Petrograd/ Leningrad, 1918–56', in Kemper and Conermann, *The Heritage*, p. 49.
69. Alexander Morrison, 'Russian Rule in Turkestan and the Example of British India, *c.* 1860–1917', *The Slavonic and East European Review* 84: 4 (October 2006): 666–707, especially p. 677.
70. R.H. Stacy, *India in Russian Literature* (Delhi: Motilal Banarsidass, 1985), pp. 41–2.
71. He said that in Halbfass's book 'references to things Russian are mostly cursory and brief'. For example, Afanasy Nikitin (the subject of our second chapter) is just mentioned in a note, by way of reference to a doctoral dissertation, and his contribution together with that of others is judged rather dismissively. His travelogue is included in a 'few, partly legendary, travel reports on India which reached Europe in the centuries before Vasco da Gama's expedition (1497–8)', which 'do not contain additional themes or additions to the available information in the field of religion or philosophy'. Besides, the name of another amateur artist and traveller to India, Prince Alexei Saltykov (1806–59), who visited India in 1841–3 and 1845–7, and who wrote and painted about India (subject of our fourth chapter), is mentioned in *India in Europe* only via a quote from Karl Marx. Only Helena Petrovna Blavatskaya (1831–91) found three mentions. See Serebriany, 'Some Marginal Notes', pp. 81–2.
72. Ibid., p. 84.
73. Ibid., n. 27, p. 98 n.
74. Stacy, *India in Russian Literature*, p. 43.
75. Grigori Maksimovich Bongard-Levin and Aleksei Alekseevich Vigasin, *The Image of India: The Study of Ancient Indian Civilization in the USSR* (Moscow: Progress Publishers, 1984), pp. 60–82.
76. See n. 69 above.
77. See for example, Christina Klein, *Cold War Orientalism: Asia in Middlebrow Imagination*, 1945–61 (Berkeley: University of California Press, 2003).
78. There are some scholars of International Relations who trace the beginning of the Cold War to 1917, the year of emergence of the Soviet Union. See F. S. Northedge and M. J. Grieve, *A Hundred Years of International Relations* (New York, Washington: Praeger, 1971), p. 249.
79. Petr Mikhailovich Shastitco, *Russia and India: Ancient Links between India and Central Asia* (Moscow: Vostok, 1992).
80. Bongard-Levin and Vigasin, *The Image of India*.

81. For this concept see Gayatri Chakravorty Spivak, 'Subaltern Studies: Deconstructing Historiography (1985)', in Donna Landry and Gerald Maclean (eds.), *The Spivak Reader: Selected Works of Gayatri Chakravorty Spivak* (New York and London: Routledge, 1996), p. 225.
82. Bernard S. Cohn, *Colonialism and its Forms of Knowledge: British in India* (Princeton, N.J.: Princeton University Press, 1996), p. 79.
83. See *South Asia at Chicago: Fifty Years of Scholarship*, IV, 'Recurrent Themes in the Representation of South Asia', http:// www.lib.uchicago.edu/e/su/southasia/50yrs4.html - 13k, last visited on 1 May 2008.
84. See John McClintock and James Strong, *Cyclopaedia of Biblical, Theological, and Ecclesiastical Literature* (New York: Harper, 1883), p. 468.
85. Cohn, *Colonialism and its Forms of Knowledge*, p. 79.
86. See nn. 11–12 above.
87. See Teltscher, *India Inscribed*, p. 68.
88. See for the observers and their observations, the sources, their publishing details and Teltscher's comments, Teltscher, *India Inscribed*, pp. 38–51, and 69–70.
89. Teltscher, *India Inscribed*, p. 51.
90. Edward Farley Oaten, *European Travellers in India: During The Fifteenth, Sixteenth and Seventeenth Centuries; The Evidence Afforded by them With Respect to Indian Social Institutions and the Nature and Influence of Indian Governments* (London: Kegan Paul Trench Trübner and Company Limited, 1909), p. 43.
91. Ibid., p. 45.
92. Linschoten visited Portuguese India in 1583, and lived here from 1583 to 1588. He was not considered to be a great traveller by Oaten, not having ventured out of the Portuguese settlements. For his itinerary, ibid., pp. 118–19. Oaten, however, does not refer to his drawings.
93. See Robert L. Hardgrave Jr., 'The Representation of Sati: Four Eighteenth Century Etchings by Balthazar Solvyns', in *Bengal Past and Present*, 117 (1998): 57–80, see *asnic.utexas.edu/hardgrave/Satiart.rft.html*. The engraving, Pl. 20, 'A Suttee', appears in the English translation, John Huygen van Linschoten, *His Discours of Voyages into ye Easte and West Indies*, tr. from the Dutch by William Phillip (London: John Wolfe, 1598), Hardgrave, 'Representation of Sati', note 16.
94. Ibid.
95. For the representations and their citations see Teltscher, *India Inscribed*, pp. 51–66.
96. Ibid., p. 23.

97. Partha Mitter, *Much Maligned Monsters: History of European Reactions to Indian Art*, 2nd edn. (Chicago: Chicago University Press, 1992), p. 48.
98. Cohn, 'The Past in the Present', in *South Asia at Chicago: Fifty Years of Scholarship*, IV, and n. 83 above.
99. See Leela Gandhi, *Postcolonial Theory*, p. 32.

CHAPTER 2

A 'White' Trader on his 'Sinful Voyage': Afanasii Nikitin and the Complexities of His Observations

The first of the marginalized Russian figures in Serebriany's list is Afanasii Nikitin [Afanasy, or Afanasij or Athanassius in Russian and other early sources]. His case partly questions the reasons two Soviet scholars cite for the marginalization of the Russian subplot: 'In spite of its considerable achievements . . . classical (academical) [*sic*] Indology did not for various reasons develop the necessary set of subjects for the study and comprehension of a country so complicated and original as India.'[1] For, many of Nikitin's observations in his journal, *Khozenie za tri morya* or *The Journey Beyond the Three Seas* [alternatively translated as *Voyage Beyond Three Seas*], bear out Said's contention that 'Orientalism' predates European colonialism,[2] apart from echoing many of the archetypes of 'Orientalist' observation mentioned in the previous chapter, as far back as in the fifteenth century.[3] More specifically, as we will see later in the chapter, he had already a set of preconceived notions about India derived from stereotypes of Khorasani travelogues, and was contributing to an 'Orientalist' discourse much before the Romantic or the modernist phases of Russian Orientalism took shape. In this also, as in his voyage to India, he was a pioneer.

BIOGRAPHY AND ITINERARY

Not much is known about Nikitin's life except that he was a merchant from Tver who visited India between 1469 and 1472.[4] Nikitin sailed to Iran via Astrakhan, the usual route of Russian merchants. His subsequent route was unusual for Russians. After his arrival by sea in the port of Cambay, he went to various places, spent a long time in Bidar in the Deccan, visited a place called Parvata, and then returned via Gulbarga, Koilkuoda, Kallur, Aland and Dabhol.[5]

The journey had a thin relation with the state, as Nikitin set forth 'down the Volga' taking his leave from Grand Duke and the Bishop and the Governor of Tver. The lower Volga, before Nikitin's voyage, was dominated by Tartar states, though Moscow, strategically located on the upper Volga, had already achieved some prominence, with power to collect tribute. The Grand Prince of Muscovy was trying to return the courtesy of an earlier embassy from the Shah of Shirvān, an independent Tartar state to the north-east of today's Azerbaijan, in 1466. Vasilii Papin, chosen for the task, was to go with a group of merchants, including Nikitin, desiring trade with Shirvān. Making the first part of his trip by river, Nikitin travelled south along the Volga-Caspian trade route. Proceeding downstream through areas marked by Tartar hostility, the Russian party tried to slip Astrakhan by night, but failed, and at the mouth of the Volga they were robbed by the Tartars. With boats destroyed, goods seized, men taken prisoners, and warned by the robbers fearing Russian reprisals against returning to Russia, the reduced party of twenty-two men continued on their original route to Shirvān. Next year Nikitin crossed the Caspian Sea, or 'Dorya Khvalitskaya', stopping at Derbent, where the merchants dispersed, as further journey without tradable goods was useless. But Nikitin persisted in proceeding towards India, though he had to earn his living in ways the *Journal* does not reveal. In 1472 he set on his journey back home, but died somewhere in Smolensk, never seeing home again.[6] 'Perhaps', says Hari Vasudevan,

> Russian myths carried some ideas of the strange puritanical *brahmanas* of this far-flung land. But, more significantly for a merchant, Mongols undoubtedly carried over some notions of the Sultans that had resisted them in the Sindh and the trade that existed across the Indian Ocean and the Arabian Sea.[7]

INDIA'S INTEREST IN NIKITIN

India's interest in Nikitin in India owed much to the developing Indo-USSR relations. It was as late as in 1955 that the local authorities at Tver erected a bronze monument to Nikitin on the bank of the Volga River. A story goes that his statue was raised because Nikita Khrushchev, visiting Premier of the USSR, wanted to set right his faux pas before Nehru that there *was* a statue of Nikitin in Russia. The episode seems apocryphal, as in Russia today Nikitin is something of a folk hero, with a Moscow-St. Petersburg train, a beer and a pop song named after him.[8] Anyway, the statue was featured on a Russian postage stamp in 2005, commemorating the 75th anniversary of the establishment of the Tver region (oblast).[9] In India, proving the close affinity between Nehruvian socialism and the Mumbai film industry,[10] Nikitin was the subject of a film where Nargis, Nehru's favourite actress, played the leading female role, and Oleg Stizhenov acted Nikitin's part.[11] The film, a joint Indo-Soviet production of 1957, was a much fictionalized account. Still, a senior Russian diplomat highlighted it in 2002 on the occasion of the inauguration of the laying of a monument of Nikitin at Alibag in Maharashtra.[12] The continuing interest in Nikitin is proved by the recent successful attempt by Indian historians and others to rediscover the Nikitin trail in an expedition, which started on 12 November 2006 and ended in 2007.[13] Indian historians' interest in Nikitin is not however new. Three eminent historians had in 1951 rated the *Journal* as a valuable source for studying pre-modern India.[14]

RUSSIAN FOREGROUNDING OF NIKITIN

There is a marked continuity in the adulatory Russian assessment of Nikitin from nineteenth century to the Soviet era. To Nikolay Mikhailovich Karamazin, the pioneer of Russian imperial history,[15] Nikitin was a forerunner of Tavernier, who longed for 'Russian Orthodoxy' even in a distant land and engaged in 'discussions with the natives about their religious dogmas'. Izmail Sreznevskij (1857) extols him for his intrepidity and inquisitiveness in distant foreign lands.[16] I.P. Minaev thinks this 'wonderfully clever and observant traveler . . . skips over many things . . . but everything important he treats intelligently'. He is placed on par with Vasco da Gama and others, who came to India later. For, nearly all the 'valuable facts for an insight into the life of ancient India and observed by his contemporaries . . . find place in his memoirs'. Moreover he 'excels many of them in impartiality, lucidity and keenness of observation; correctness of observation and sobriety . . .'. Minaev valued the work so highly that in his explanatory notes on passages from the *Voyage*, he 'cites parallels from the works of ancient travellers as well as from the works of contemporary geographers, travellers and historians', turning his commentary in essence into a companion piece for the *Voyage*.[17]

Twentieth century Russian Orientalists also praise the *Journal's* literary qualities, patriotism, humanistic love for native land, and capability of 'assessing foreign ways of life without compromising his own'. Even the 'foreign' elements in the text and its linguistic heterogeneity are branded as artistic devices to convey the religious alienation of an Orthodox Christian traveller eager to protect his cultural identity. They also regard Nikitin as a precursor of Vasco da Gama.[18] The integrity of his manuscripts has also earned praises.[19]

Both Bongard-Levin and Vigasin, and Kemp cite the incorporation of Nikitin's description in the *Sofiiskaya Chronicle* and other 'encyclopaedic collections' as proof of the 'keen interest in India that existed in Rus'. The former commentators regard the *Journal* to be a 'priceless source of information on Russian-Indian connections in the 15th century', when the image of India was 'formed, in the main, under the influence of Byzantine or West European literature'. The *Voyage* was 'a forerunner of a new stage in the history of contacts between Russia and India'. Apart from its authentic description of 'the distant country', a 'certain democratism' [*sic*], when describing 'with surprise (and possibly with some exaggeration) the luxury of the Indian grandees' and speaking with 'the same disapproval of the Russian grandees', makes the *Voyage* unique. Kemp also points to the integrity of its text, for which each of the seven copies of the manuscript was able to 'transmit the original quite correctly'. Additionally she finds in it perceptions of Indians 'from the lower classes of society when these were rare', and also insights into the social life of Russia itself'. It is claimed by Kemp to be 'one of the earliest secular books on travel in Russian', and one of the most realistic. For, atypically of early European travellers in Muslim India, Nikitin 'mixed with the common people and in particular with the Hindus'. Not being an accredited representative like later English travellers, but being rather forced even to hide his identity and survive under straitened circumstances, he could not help 'adopting local habits', and cultivating 'people in the lower condition of life', seeing public shows and royal processions, visiting temples and fairs as one of the crowd; entering into internal trade in the company of Hindu merchants, and visiting their homes. Consequently his book offers 'something like the point of view of the common man by those days'. Even Nikitin's lack of wealth, his lower status as a merchant in Russia, and his consequent inability to mix with the nobility are treated as advantages which bred in him some hostility towards the feudal aristocracy in Russia, visible in an obscure passage in the *Turkish*, like 'raste kam deret' [you have little truth (i.e. justice)]. These words supposedly paint Nikitin as 'something like the East European "democrat" or Man of the People to comment on Indian affairs'.[20]

After recounting the credit of Nikitin as a precursor of Vasco da Gama by twenty-five years, Alexander V. Riasanovsky argues that as a 'private traveller' Nikitin's experiences were bound to differ considerably from the royal Portuguese envoy. This explains the wealth of information we get from the book 'about the daily life, dress, customs and the social and economic circumstances of both Hindus and Muslims in India at that time'. There are also details about the goods available in various markets in India, their prices, the export taxes on them; distances between the places where these markets were located; the number of days required to travel these distances in those days; and animals found and sold in these markets, etc. Nikitin gives these pieces of information supposedly because he 'had undertaken the journey primarily for commercial purposes', and was possibly leaving notes for later traders. Also, 'despite its author's strong personal convictions', the *Journal* is 'remarkably free of bigotry', because some of the most interesting and valuable information to be found in it pertains to the religious customs and practices of the natives. However, Riasanovsky is not ready to view Nikitin as an 'East European democrat' of sorts or as a 'Man of the People'; nor as a 'social critic', despite the disapproving remarks in the *Journal* about Russian and Indian nobility. Rather the qualities and aptitudes he finds in him are his 'commercial practicality, on the one hand, and on the other, his deep religious faith . . . a faith, moreover, which was warm, sincere and personal; . . . his adaptability to strange surroundings, foods, and climates; his versatility in getting along with people of vastly different cultural backgrounds; his mental agility in overcoming communication barriers,' . . . his 'courageous and venturesome spirit' that accounts for the arduous journey he made; and his literary felicity, which, considering the time and circumstances, was no mean achievement in itself.[21]

A.S. Morris explains why not only Stalinist USSR, but pre-revolutionary Russia too projected Nikitin as Russia's own 'Marco Polo'. 'For the western world the age of discovery and exploration begins with the Portuguese and the end of the fifteenth century. For Russia, there was no age of discovery until the opening up of Siberia, but there were isolated journeys by literate travellers which indicate that from a very early period travel in Asia was accomplished with relatively little difficulty.' Nikitin was picked up, as the earliest of them, to stake the Russian claim to discoveries and explorations.[22]

NIKITIN IN WESTERN EYES AND COLD WAR COMPETITION

But just as Russia valorized Nikitin and his *Journal*, a part of Western scholarship doggedly sought to debunk him and his text. Two of their main planks of criticism were the timing of the projection of Nikitin and the expurgation of his text. Regarding the first, the contention of Lionel Tillettt,[23] that it was only in the Stalinist era of Soviet history that Nikitin's book caught on the imagination of Russians, appears highly unfair. Tillettt argues that for three and a half centuries the *Journal* lay buried in obscurity; and lack of popular interest in it and Nikitin continued even after the book was first 'published in Russian in 1853, and an English translation appeared in the same decade'. He alleges that pre-revolutionary Russian historians did not even think of placing Nikitin beside Marco Polo or Vasco da Gama; and the first generation of Soviet scholars viewing history strictly in class terms did not 'warm to this petty capitalist on a speculative mission'. But, since the mid-1930s three convergent Soviet policies rekindled academic interest in Nikitin. These were:

(i) the new interest in Russia's past greatness after the appearance of Stalin's decree on history in 1934, as a result of which Soviet historiographers started making exaggerated claims for Russia's past feats and exploits in scholarship, inventions, discoveries and explorations;
(ii) the emergence of India as the biggest non-aligned power in the world, which made it imperative for the USSR to win her friendship; and
(iii) the concept of the 'friendship of the peoples' that was evolved to make new friends with the help of the specious logic that irrespective of the activities of warlike rulers the peoples of the world had only cordial feelings for each other.

Because of these policy moves the *Journal* was 'brought out of obscurity', dusted, and though 'Nikitin's contact with India was brief and without cultural consequences', he was bracketed with world famous travellers and made to appear as the cultural ambassador of Russia. That is why all the important works on Nikitin are basically post-Stalinist.[24]

But this argument ignores the continuity of publications on Nikitin from 1821 to 1916, and from 1948 to 1960, pointed out by Kemp, including A. Lyubimov's detailed study in 1916 of the famous embassy of Vasilii Papin.[25] It is true that the importance of the book was not always known. It was only in course of his research in the Troitse–Sergieva (Trinity–St. Sergius) Monastery at Zagorsk near Moscow, early in the nineteenth century that Karamazin happened upon an early copy, named 'Troitskiī spisok', after the name of the monastery, in its library. The personal tone of the book depicting the author's numerous misfortunes and disappointments, loneliness, longing for home, nostalgic love for his own country, and sense of guilt for sins committed in his wandering life, appealed strongly to Karamazin's literary sense and nationalist sentiment. For, he was the exponent of a new approach to national history, the first historian to popularize and to romanticize the study of the past; and the founder of the school of 'sentimentalism' in Russian literature.[26] He extolled Nikitin for having 'traded along Malabar coast and discussed matters of faith and dogma with the inhabitants of the land', at a time when 'Vasco da Gama was only thinking of the possibility of finding a route to India via Africa.'[27] But all this was long before Stalin's rise.

So, the difficulty of achieving a balanced verdict is great, and Nikitin would have been astounded to know that his simple tale of a voyage over 'three seas'[28] would raise a gale that exceeded the fierce winds that buffeted his 'dabba'. For example, A.S. Morris, regarded as an objective critic, admits that the importance of Nikitin's manuscript has grown with improvements of translation and better identification of his route and deeper knowledge of his period, but advises against comparing Nikitin's journey to those of the Italians, Spaniards and Portuguese and others during or after 'the great Age of Discovery in Western Europe', simply because Nikitin 'belonged to feudal and illiterate Russia';[29] and his work, lying for long as obscure manuscripts, 'promoted no commercial or political expansion as did the works of Barbosa, Contarini or Martin Frobisher'. Morris brushes aside the 'Russian complaint' about neglect of Nikitin's tale by Western writers as 'inappropriate from the point of view of documentation of expansion of knowledge through geographical discovery'. Nikitin's account is important only 'as a contribution to the historical geography of India and the age-old caravan routes linking it with Europe'. He concedes that regarding Deccan India, only Nicolo de Conti's account predates Nikitin. Accounts by Arab writers who visited India before the Portuguese were 'unlinked to the European journeys', and anyway they visited only the coast and not the 'Moslem interior' like Nikitin. But all these concessions notwithstanding, Morris too finally regards 'Nikitin's work as something of an anomalous document, lying on the fringe of the general stream of geographical discovery, and too short and incomplete to stand on its own as a major contribution to geographical knowledge. . . .'[30]

Against Soviet Russia's glorification of Nikitin as its indigenous counterpart of 'outstanding navigators and travellers of the era of great discoveries', some Western scholars questioned Nikitin's alleged resistance to conversion to the Islamic faith, to put forth the controversial point that he might have actually converted to Islam, and was maintaining a kind of dual religion.[31] Others focused on the bowdlerization of his text by Soviet scholars.[32] So let us read him for ourselves.

'AFTER' NIKITIN: GOING IN SEARCH OF HIS OBSERVATIONS AND THEIR SOURCES

Cautious reading of the *Journal* is important because as a structuralist scholar has aptly commented, very often a 'writer's work can be received without being read: texts have effects without being read'.[33] Such caution is doubly important when a fifteenth-century book is 'translated' for transnational audiences six centuries later for contested purposes. The main concern for reading is of course how a description of fifteenth-century India 'after' Nikitin helps one understand the way in which 'Orientalism' has developed as a discourse. Here, there are three meanings of the word 'after' in a structuralist sense—(i) after Nikitin, i.e. 'later in time' than Nikitin; (ii) 'after' Nikitin as 'in the manner of', 'in agreement with', 'in honour of' and 'even in imitation of' Nikitin; and finally, (iii) 'after' Nikitin 'in the sense of "going in search of"' Nikitin.[34] The third meaning seems most appropriate for us, for it may reveal the relationship of Nikitin's book to the growth of a tradition of Orientalism in Russia since as early as the fifteenth century.

Of Nikitin's Archetypes of India and their Sources

While 'going in search' of Nikitin, charges of the inauthenticity of some observations, traded frequently between the defenders of West European and Russian Orientalism, are not granted supreme significance. The *Journal* has a good stock of such unrealistic observations. For example, the ornithological and zoological life in a place called 'Aland', a town 28 miles to the north-east of Gulbarga on the Deccan Plateau, where the 'biggest fair in Hindustan' is held in memory of 'Sheikh Ala-uddin', includes a 'Ghuggū', a bird which flies at night, crying 'ghuggû', causing a death in every house on whose roof it perches, and spitting fire whenever anyone tries to catch it; Mamons [or mythical ape-like creatures common in contemporary Arab-Muslim travel lore] prowling at night, catching fowl; or monkeys living in the woods, under 'a monkey prince who leads an army', and avenges any harm to his subjects by setting his army upon the offender, destroying houses and killing the offending householders. The monkeys have even a tongue of their own, and are possessive enough to leave on roads 'the young who are not like their mother and father'. The 'people of Hindustan' are said to pick up the orphans and 'teach them sundry handicrafts', though some of them they sell off at night lest they should flee back and some of them 'teach how to imitate players'. A full hundred of them are even included in the grand processions which the Sultan throws to amuse himself.[35] Other problematic utterances in the *Journal* are that 'All the Indian princes come of Khorassan, and so do all the boyars'; that Bidar was the political centre of India; and that at Bidar 'the full moon lasts for three days'.[36]

Riasanovsky, not a pro-Soviet scholar, regards the information about intelligent monkeys as one that 'was probably based on some folk version of the Rāmāyana epic heard by the Russian merchant during his travels'. He is even more dismissive in his comments on 'the gukuk bird'. Apart from guessing that it is possibly an owl, he ignores its 'fire-spitting' powers.[37] Vasudevan's explanation is, 'Typically, like many of the travellers of his day, Nikitin jotted down as fact most of the nonsense that was handed down to him concerning his environment—a curious combination of legend and fact'.[38] Bongard-Levin and Vigasin think it possible that 'he was acquainted with other "voyages" and under their influence, began to make notes in India which on his return he put together in the form of a special book', where in 'full agreement with the traditional medieval literature', many 'fantastic tales' he heard found place.[39]

Besides, if we look closely at Nikitin's observation of differences of the Indian way of life, like the ubiquity of the 'dhoti as dress; the nakedness of everyone, especially the women; the blackness of Indians; the sexuality of Indian women, the religious customs of the Hindus, Hindu divinity, etc., then we are faced with a paradox.

While some of them accord with the archetypes of 'Orientalist' observations, at least some are traceable to non-Russian Oriental influences. Nikitin's first reaction to Indians—both Hindus and ordinary Muslims—at a place called Chaul is their blackness, nakedness, and shamelessness, and his first presumption about them is their instinctive awe for and attraction towards the white man from the West:

> the land of *India . . . where everyone goes naked; the women go bareheaded and with breasts uncovered,* their hair plaited into one braid. The *men and women are all black.* Wherever I went I was followed by many *people,* who *wondered about me, a white man* [italics added].[40]

It is instructive to note that by nakedness Nikitin means that 'their prince wears a *dhoti* upon his head[41] and another about his loins'. The noblemen dress in almost the same way. The servants merely 'wear a *dhoti* wound about their loins'. All are barefooted. The women go 'bareheaded and with breasts uncovered', and children below seven 'go naked . . . and do not hide their shame'.

Nikitin is astounded that even in winter *dhoti* serves as the desired dress material, except 'for the princes and boyars' [noblemen], which in that season 'put on trousers, a shirt and a caftan', but even then 'wrap a *dhoti* about their shoulders, girdle themselves with another, and wind a third round their heads'.[42]

Apart from the archetype of nakedness of Indian women, their easy sexuality gets attention too. This is not apparent in the 1960 and prior expurgated editions. There the words are: 'In India strangers put up at inns and the food is cooked for them by women, who also make the guests' beds'. But these leave out the following words after 'guests' beds' in the unexpurgated version:

> *and sleep with them. If you would like to sleep with one or another of them, it will cost two shetel, otherwise only one shetel. These women are quite willing because they like white people* [italics added].[43]

In like manner two more of Nikitin's expurgated remarks harp on the loose morals of Indian men and easy sexuality of eastern women. The first, about the people at the temple at Parvat, says that 'there is no good in them, and they know not what shame is'.

The second reflects the Western fantasy about Oriental women related in the 'Introduction'[44]:

> And the wives sleep with their husbands during the day, but at night they go to the foreigners and sleep with them and pay them for it, besides supplying them with sweets and sweet wine, in exchange for their love. The wives like . . . white men, since their men are all black. And when a wife conceives a child by a stranger, her husband pays him a salary, and if the child is born white the stranger receives eighteen pieces of money, but if the child is born black, he gets nothing, but is welcome to the food and drink.[45]

Tillettt shows that in an excised passage in the account in mixed Turkish and Persian Nikitin gives 'the range of prices for Indian women as well as for slave girls, with their price graduated according to color'. This passage of three sentences was left out by the Haklyut society edition, as it was thought 'undesirable to supply in English', because of linguistic and social reasons.[46] It was kept in all the critical Russian editions including the one of 1960, but not in the translations. But in one instance, where the critical editions too have been bowdlerized, the 1948 and subsequent Russian editions of the text say about the inhabitants in one part of India that 'the people are all black and all wicked, and the women are all shameless (besstydnye); everywhere there is witchcraft, robbery, lying, and potions with which they kill their masters.' These words are retained in the modern 1960 multilingual edition, but in the Zagorsk version, which is kept in all these volumes the term is not 'besstdnye' but 'blyadi' (whores).[47]

How to explain the appearance in Nikitin's account of this 'Orientalist' archetype of easy Indian women sharing guests' beds to service their needs, with a lethal readiness to punish them with poisoning at the first sight of perfidy?[48] J. Lur'e considers Nikitin's 'narrative behaviour' as typical of a 'white man' and an 'alien'. He contends that 'black men and women (regardless of faith)', but 'especially Muslims, whom he perceived as rulers of the country' shocked the traveller's spiritual outlook as a Christian.[49] Morris insinuates that after leaving Junnar, Nikitin had to use 'various traveller's hospices or shelters many times on the roads' and was writing from experience.[50]

But still Nikitin's horror at not only prostitution of married women but their conscious choice of white men for lovemaking and reprodution of white children, and their husbands' approval of it, reminds one too strongly of the dangerous sexuality of Indian women as represented by Tavernier, Ovington, Varthema, Laval, Head and others.[51] Besides, such hatred for blackness among Indian people cannot come except through fixedly embedded binaries of black and white in the mind of the observer. Long back Oaten had aptly compared this 'disparagement of the people's "blackness" by Nikitin with a passage in the narrative of Abd-er-Razzak, famous Arab traveller in Vijayanagar in 1442. To the latter they appeared as 'neither men nor devils, at the sight of whom the mind takes alarm'.[52] One needs to know its sources.

Banerjee traces Nikitin's shocked reactions back to the influence of 'Chorasani' (Khorasani) travel narratives. Pointing to the 'creolized non-Russian elements in Nikitin's account' [remember Tillettt's reference to 'gibberish' and Morris's reference to 'a polyglot Turkic tongue'] and searching for 'the author's motivations for using them' as also 'the context in which they were generated', Banerjee posits that 'Muslim' merchants may have been the source of these non-Russian commercial and religious terms of Middle or West Asian origins. From this it is just a step that 'Muslim informants may have encouraged the Russian merchant to record his impressions and provided him the model to do so'.[53] Considering the dominance of foreign or outside Muslims, 'known as *Chorasani*' in the social hierarchy in fifteenth century Deccan, which was continuing in India since the time of Ibn Battuta (1304–77), and their knowledge of markets farther east, Nikitin's conscious choice to identify himself with these privileged outsiders from Central Asia, may have been dictated by the need for their guidance, which must have been indispensable in those pre-Gama days. To test this hypothesis Banerjee points to the parallels and similarities between *Chorasani* travelogues of sixteenth–seventeenth centuries, as of Badauni, Jamali and Hamadani about the Indian subcontinent, and Nikitin's *Journal*. First, like *Khozenie* most of these accounts had but sparse comments about the Indian markets, and were far more expansive about 'subjective impressions and commentaries about the land, people and customs'. Secondly, the *Chorasani* narrators were acutely conscious of their anomalous position of privileged outsiders and flaunted their identities of foreigner and Muslim. Nikitin too 'echoes their gesture' by recording his adopted name and title of 'Khoja Yusuf Khorassani' (*Chorasani*) in the *Journal*. Thirdly, Nikitin follows the 'other textual devices' employed by the *Chorasani* travellers to underline the superiority of their community and their affinity with the aristocratic class. It is under this influence that he informs that the royalty and gentry are made up exclusively by the *Chorasani*, while 'Hindusthani, the local populace, are pedestrian plebeians'. Thirdly, a 'close look at *chorasani* travel accounts demonstrates that the Russian merchant's individual impressions of Hindus mirror the precise terms that foreign Muslims used conventionally'. The people from Persia and/or Central Asia visiting India invariably highlighted the sparseness of clothing on the bodies of the Hindus. Nikitin's 'very first statement about the Indian subcontinent closely follows the *chorasani* tone: . . . Like the foreign Muslims, he connects paucity of clothing not with climatic or economic conditions but with deliberate immodesty and moral depravity, making women the chief target of his disgust . . .' Banerjee traces the striking similarity of words to this effect to 'their exposure to the same travel lore'. Fourthly, Nikitin's references to availability of comfort women at the inns also follows 'oral narratives circulating among *chorasani* travelers'. Banerjee cites, in support of her claim, an anonymous fourteenth century Arab travel account by Al-din al-Umari, where the narrator admits that his accounts of insatiable Hindu women simply borrow from the Central Asian tropes on their availability, and also extensive commentaries by Badauni and Jamali in this regard. So, either Nikitin had come across 'guest prostitution', endemic in the southern region of India where he was travelling, or his observations, as with those on dress, were 'predetermined by *chorasani* prejudice'. Banerjee bases the last hypothesis on the wordings of Nikitin's generalizations about Hindu women, which 'sound like much-used idioms about [Indian] fecklessness . . .'. Since such generalizations are juxtaposed with instances of sexual availability of Chinese housewives that he provides liberally in the text, the suspicion gets stronger that he had taken *Chorasani* presumptions about Indian women at face value and was convinced about them even before setting foot in India.[54]

Did *Chorasani* narratives also influence Nikitin's description of the religious customs of the Hindus, and of the Hindu divinity? Here Nikitin's own words can give us the answer. For example, his Hindu friends avowedly told him regarding their faith that they 'believe in Adam, and the Buts [Persian word for idol] . . . are Adam and his whole kin'. They further informed him that there were 'eighty four faiths in India, and everyone believes a But'. Some of them suggested a visit to Parvat, which Nikitin in his innocence describes as 'their Jerusalem, or Mecca in the Moslem tongue, where stands their chief *butkhanah* [Persian word meaning idol house]'.[55] In the subsequent passage idolatry, cow worship, nakedness, all the familiar archetypes of European 'Orientalism', jostle for attention. All the worshippers arrive '*naked*; with a cloth round their buttocks', '*though they wear jewels*', and 'go to the *butkhanah*, astride on oxen' [italics added]. Each ox has 'its horns encased in brass and wears about 300 bells round its neck, and has its hoofs shod'. While 'all these oxen are called "fathers" . . . and the cows are called the "mother"; they use the dung as fuel to bake bread and cook their food, and smear their faces, foreheads and bodies with the ashes. That is their sign.'[56]

Just as Bidar was the political centre of India to Nikitin, so Parvat was its religious hub, on the same rank with Jerusalem or Mecca. The godheads that Nikitin describes there with ill-concealed irreverence reveals his Eurocentrism. In the market of the stone-built temple complex, half the size of Tver, Nikitin saw carvings of '*buts*', as incarnations of Viṣṇu together with Lord Gaṇeśa, and Hanumāna, devotee of Lord Rāma, one of the central characters of *Rāmāyaṇa*, and very popular north Indian god. The very big carving of Hanumān, 'an ape like man', with 'a tail . . . seven feet long, slung over his shoulder', impressed him for the posture of 'his right arm . . . raised high and stretched out like the Emperor Justinian's at Constantinople'. The culture of nakedness had also invaded divinity, where *buts* had uncovered buttocks, and '*Buts*' wives are carved naked, in all their shame'. What also struck him as novel was the sight of devotees kissing the hoofs of a huge ox 'carved in black stone and gilt all over'.[57]

Nikitin's description of the cultural life of the Hindus and of the Muslims is so unorganized that it is difficult to classify them. So let us look at the whole and then sort them out for our purposes. Sometimes the description is quite factual, as for example when Nikitin points out that near the *butkhanah* 'old wives and young maidens shave their hair; beards and heads are shaved too. Then they go up to the *butkhana*, each has to pay a fee of two sheshkanis for the benefit of *but*, and horses are charged four fanams each'. He might be exaggerating when he claims that the 'number of those who gather at the *butkhanah* is 20,000 and sometimes even 100,000'.[58] His description of the food habits of the Hindus is also 'Orientalist', and sometimes self-contradictory. We learn that Hindus 'eat no flesh at all—no beef, mutton, fowl, fish, or pork', and 'have two meals a day', eating nothing at night. They 'drink neither wine nor mead', and 'do not eat or drink with Moslems'. They eat privately, not with friends or even their wives. 'They eat rice and khichrī with ghee [clarified butter] and various herbs', with their right hand, 'never touching it with their left hand . . . they never use a knife and have no spoons'. They also hide their food from Moslems 'lest they should look into the pot or at the food', which would pollute it. 'When eating, some cover themselves with a kerchief, so that no one may see them'.[59] But only two paragraphs back, while observing that the people of different 'faiths' among the Hindus 'do not eat or drink together, nor do they intermarry', he is on record that '*some eat mutton, fowl, fish, and eggs, but of no faith do the people eat beef* [italics added]. The habit of the Hindus of not eating before others could not also be as absolute as Nikitin made it out to be. For, he himself has proudly stated a little before that the Hindus 'did not hide from me when eating, trading, praying, or doing something else; nor did they conceal their wives'.[60]

In describing some other aspects of the religious and social life of Hindus Nikitin is in the familiar 'Orientalist' mode of compare and contrast,[61] as for example when pointing out that 'they pray facing eastwards, in the Russian manner', and 'raise high both hands and put them on the ground and stretch out on it'. The structure of Indian temples was a study in contrast, as was the Hindus' custom of cremation: 'Their *butkhanahs* have no doors, and face eastwards; the Buts too. And when someone dies, they burn him and scatter the ashes over water'. It is not clear what he means when he says, '. . . when a woman gives birth to a child, it is her husband who receives it;' but it is difficult to believe that 'a son is named by the father; and a daughter by the mother'. Observation of the form of social greeting among the Hindus is, however, influenced by *Chorasani* habits of genuflection to nobility: 'In coming or going, they bow after the fashion of monks, touching the ground with both hands and saying nothing'.[62]

Pursuing her Orientalization of the *Journal*, Banerjee points out that even Nikitin's theological paradigms were heavily influenced by those of the immigrant Muslims, which took India's polytheistic practices as their first object of attack. In this context Banerjee quotes Jamali's and Hamadani's shock to see that Hindus not only worship many gods but also trees, stones and animals, and Jamali's understanding of an ecstatic assembly in a temple as a kind of black magic, in which the women were out to harm him. She shows that in a similar vein Nikitin branded Hindu women as 'witches capable of poisoning their husbands', and that he too was disgusted by the bestial and/or nude deities at Parvattum, who reminded them of their 'naked' worshippers.[63]

But it is difficult to accept that *Chorasani* influences on the Russian merchant's individual impressions of Hindus were absolute. There are places in the *Journal* where he finds Hindus more open and trusting than the proselytizing Muslims. At Bidar he had confided to some Hindu acquaintances 'that I was a Christian and not a Moslem, and that my name was Afanasy, or Khoja Yusuf Khorassani in the Moslem tongue'. They also returned the trust.[64] This contrasts substantially with his attitude to Muslims, 'And so my Christian brothers of Rus, those of you who want to go to the land of India, must leave their faith in Rus and invoke Mohammed before setting out for the land of Hindustan'.[65]

Besides, even after the explanations of Lur'e or Banerjee, the ethnocentrism of Nikitin or his efforts at encoding himself as a white man is unmistakable. The comments of one of India's greatest mediators between the East and West on the ubiquity of the *dhoti* as covering of the body not only in different provinces of India including Nikitin's Malabar, but in different countries of Europe and in America in the context of climate, cultural difference and different conceptions of shame, put the ethnocentrism of Nikitin's observation in the most glaring light. Swami Vivekananda shows how not only Aryans wore it, but so did Greeks and Romans under the name of 'toga'. He also shows how in ancient India except in Bengal loincloth was sufficient for maintaining decency, though headgears were a must for both men and women. He shows how in ancient Buddhist sculptures both the father and mother of Buddhadeva are shown as wearing loincloths, and even Emperor Aśoka is shown wearing a *dhoti*. A *dhoti* like sheet was the attire of even Alexander the Great before his conquest of Iran.[66] A small trader might have not known all this, but was sure to notice the heat of Malabar.

Of History and Bidar

But despite problems of authenticity, ethnocentrism and accuracy in his observations there is something of permanent, even if of limited historical, value in Nikitin's *Khozenie*. First, he notices the gaps between the rich and the poor in Bidar quite clearly, though it may not be sufficient to entitle him to the claim of being termed a 'social critic' in the manner of Kemp. He found that in this populous land the 'countrymen are very poor, but the boyars live in luxury', 'carried in silver litters', preceded by horses, and followed by a large number of horsemen, footmen, trumpeters, drummers and pipers. The Sultan, even in outings for amusement, was accompanied by '10,000 [men on] horse and 50,000 [men on] foot . . . 200 elephants in gilt armour . . . 100 trumpeters, 100 dancers, and 300 spare horses in golden harness . . . 100 monkeys and 100 gaurikās or handmaidens.'

His description of the beautiful palace of the Sultan at Bidar, the pomp and grandeur of its tables and attendance, and the huge security and other staff engaged in guarding and maintaining it are enlightening.[67] So are his factual accounts of Deccan India's politics. He describes Malik-at Tujjar's campaigns against the outlying areas under Vijayanagar rule and their successes, the grand reception to him at Bidar, the wealth of Nizam-ul Mulk, the campaigns of Melik Khan and Farhad Khan, the luxury of the Sultan and his brother, his campaign, and the grand meeting of the Sultan with Malik-at Tujjar 'on the fifteenth day after Ulu Bayram, at Gulbarga'. He also relates how after taking many towns and villages and winning initial battles, the Bahmanis finally failed in the final war, because of the impregnable position of the Vijayanagar fort on the hills. Nikitin concludes very tersely, 'As for the big city they failed to take it'.[68]

Riasanovsky's point that Nikitin mistakenly supposed Bidar to be the political centre of the whole Muslim India does not decrease the value of his account of the campaign undertaken by the Bahmani Sultan Muhammad III against the fortress of Vijayanagar—an event 'marking the decline of the Bahmani state'. 'Since there are almost no Hindu historical records relating to the fifteenth century', says Riasanovsky, 'Afanasii Nikitin's eye-witness comments on the arduous siege tend to balance accounts found in Muslim sources'.[69] Oaten grudges the *Journal* the status of a substitute for non-Mohammedan records as Bidar had, 'not many years before his arrival, been made the capital of the Bahmani sovereignty in place of Culbarga [Gulbarga], the former capital'.[70] Morris considers the importance Nikitin gave to Bidar as 'only a minor distortion of the truth', since it was in fact the capital of one of the most potent 'successor States to the powerful fourteenth century Tughluq empire'. But Morris says there 'is no evidence to show that he actually saw the attack at the city of Vijayanagar, despite Kemp's assertion that he did so'. He also echoes Oaten's point that though the 'narrative contains some useful second-hand evidence as to Vijayanagar', its value is lessened by the fact that he did not visit the city.[71] Oaten, on his part, praises Nikitin for giving 'a fine picture' of the impregnability of Vijayanagar, 'which makes it difficult to believe he never saw the town'.[72] But while he regards his description of Bidar as 'probably true', his account of the Bahmani campaign against Vijayanagar is viewed as not more than 'sidelights on the almost unceasing war'. Oaten, however, does not place Nikitin below Conti in their portrayal of political India in the fifteenth century. For, 'the evidence of these two men for the political condition of

India is of far less value than its social institutions. When the Mohammedan writers leave us in the lurch as to a dynasty, a battle, or a date, Conti and Nikitin do not help us to fill the gap in our knowledge'.[73]

So Oaten's verdict is: 'Nikitin was not a cultivated or philosophic observer; neither does he compensate for his lack of a comprehensive grasp of the political conditions surrounding him by an accuracy of or minuteness of detail'. But still 'we could ill afford to dispense with him. His evidence for the Mohammedan sovereignty at Bidar, though not at par with that of Conti for Vijayanagar . . . has a definite value, while his remarks on Culbarga, as well as his second-hand information on Vijayanagar are not to be despised.'[74]

Of Imputed Secularism and Nikitin's 'Great Wails'

Was the *Journal*, as Soviet scholars say, 'secular'? It would be very hard to give that adjective to the travels. I would even argue that the word does not apply for Nikitin. This is not just because of Nikitin's grouse against the Muslims in India, against his harassment at the hands of the Tartars before coming to India, and oppression by the local Muslim ruler in India, which led him to comment that no religious freedom was there in India. He was obviously disgusted with the way in which the stallion he brought to India was taken away from him by one Asad Khan, servant of Malik-at Tujjar, the Vazir of Muhammad Shah III, Bahmani Sultan at Bidar, without giving its price and making the proposition that he would return both the stallion and its price to Nikitin if he converted to Islam. This is why he considered keeping one's Christian faith in India difficult. It can be said in defense of Nikitin's outburst against Islam in India that he was complaining not only from the perspective of his personal trading opportunities, but also the possibilities of Indo-Russian trade. But even then it would be very difficult to give a secular construction to the obstacles to Indo-Russian trade he mentions in the passage below:

> I was deceived by *Moslems*; they had told me of an abundance of goods [in India], but I found that there was nothing for our land. All toll free goods are for the Moslem land only. . . . But *we* shall not be allowed to take our goods free of toll. And the toll is very high, and moreover there are pirates at sea [*sic*]. And

all the pirates are pagans, not Christians or Moslems; they worship stone idols and are ignorant of Christ [italics added].[75]

The slender possibilities of Indo-Russian trade in the context of the market at Bidar, where not only horses, brocade and silk were sold, but 'black people' too; though regarding food items nothing but vegetables were available, and there were 'no goods for the land of the Rus',[76] pale beside the hazards of the journey back home. These are possibilities of piracy by pagan and idol-worshipping men who are ignorant of Christ. Besides, as sympathetic a commentator as Kemp herself shows that Nikitin had referred to the Muslims sometimes as 'Moslem dogs'.[77] Together they would not cook a good brew of secularism, in spite of Nikitin's felicity of mixing with followers of other denominations, particularly the traders. Besides, any reading of secularism in the *Journal* becomes unsustainable beside the great wails of the man, supposedly for being in the company of Muslims for too long, not having his hymn books with him, and being forced to keep fast with the Muslims. While travelling from Parvat to Bidar during the time of 'Ulu Bayram, the great Moslem feast', Nikitin was lamenting like a wandering lamb:

And I know not when Easter Sunday . . . occurs. So I try to guess with signs. With the Christians, Easter comes nine or ten days before the Bayram. . . . I have nothing with me—no books . . . when I was robbed the books were seized too. And I have forgotten all that I knew of the Christian faith and Christian feasts. I know not when Easter occurs, or Christmas, or Wednesday and Friday. And surrounded by other faiths I pray to God that he may protect me.

The fear of being 'surrounded by other faiths', so that his Christian purity may have been lost, which did not leave him during his return, problematizes Nikitin's secularism beyond any possible interpretation:

And I am going back to Rus thinking that my faith is dead, for I have fasted with the Moslems. The month of March has passed, and for a month I have not been eating any meat, fasting with the Moslems and eating nothing fat, no Moslem food, and taking two meals a day—nothing but bread and water. And I have prayed to God almighty. . . .[78]

Coming from a man who just a few pages back was describing in a xenologist vein the practice of the Hindus of not eating with people of other sects or with Muslims, this fear makes curious reading. To complicate matters, one of the excised portions also shows that along with dropping meat from his menu he had also said, 'and I had no relations with women'.[79] Anyway, overtly he seems eager to regain his faith by observing the rites of Christianity as best as he could and by repentance: 'In the month of May, I kept Easter at *Moslem Bidar, in Hindustan*. . . . O faithful Christians, *those who voyage to many lands fall oft into sin*, and rob *themselves of Christian faith*. And I have been yearning for my faith with all my heart'. [italics added]

Together with renewed observance of rites, Nikitin also relates how he resisted the pressure from the local Muslim notables to convert to Islam. But then he is assailed by doubts if he could maintain his faith after all. As he puts it,

> Melik the Moslem pressed me to adopt the Moslem faith. I answered him: 'My lord, you perform your prayers, I perform mine; you say five prayers and I say three; I am a stranger, but you are not.' But he said to me 'Indeed, albeit thou professest not to be a Moslem, neither dost thou know the Christian faith'. And then I thought over a great deal, and said to myself: 'Woe to me miserable sinner, for I have strayed from the true path and knowing no other must go my ways.

So, no option remains but to surrender to God: 'I have of necessity done nothing virtuous for Thy sake in my distress, and have lived all my days in evil'. Among these lapses were 'wasting four Easter Sundays in the Moslem land'.

The entreaty is to God, 'to lead me not away from the path', as against all these odds he had not 'forsaken the Christian faith; and God knows what may yet happen'.[80]

Referring to Nikitin's expressions of emotional crisis Vasudevan correctly points to 'wild deviations—almost great wails of agony that have no place in the run of the narrative'.[81] But beyond being deviations, out of place, or exposing the misapplication of the category of secularism for Nikitin, they reveal the religious crises of Nikitin and the resultant problem of identity.

BEYOND SECULARISM TO ESSENTIAL IDENTITIES OF NIKITIN AND HIS ORIENTALISM

Much of the recent research on Nikitin shows why he 'cannot easily be typed'.[82] Tillettt suggested that to get rid of 'a stereotyped Nikitin' we should 'allow him to speak for himself'.[83] But allowing Nikitin to speak for himself does not mean that he will only speak the words modern non-Soviet researchers will put in his mouth. For example, scholars like Gail Lenhoff, Mary Jane Maxwell or Anindita Banerjee have, in their different ways, sought to Orientalize Nikitin to such an extent that it raises new problems. Maxwell stands the entire debate on Nikitin's secularism on its head. She builds on Lenhoff's thesis that 'Nikitin did not keep his faith but converted to Islam', just as Conti and Varthema might also have been converted.[84] Thus, she gives an entirely different 'reading' of the lamentations of Nikitin as mentioned above and locates the degree and meaning of his spiritual transformation in the wider discourse on conversion and Islamization on fifteenth century trade routes. Making a departure from studies of the politico-economic process of mass conversion to the personal and spiritual factors motivating individual conversion within the context of 'social conversion' in its own contemporary cultural framework, she first points out that it was out of question in the fifteenth century to expect a person of any religion not to carry some sort of spiritual identity. So, without taking into reckoning the operation of spiritual factors in the conversion process in these times, or their relationship to secular factors, such as trade, a significant portion of the conversion process is bound to be overlooked.[85]

Maxwell reconstructs the progress of Nikitin to individual social conversion in novel, interpretive ways. She thinks Nikitin's efforts to recoup his losses in various markets of Muslim Persia in the next two years must have brought him into contact with Muslim traders, engendering a certain familiarity and respect for their traditions even before arriving in India. For, contrary to Russian chronicle accounts, relations between Orthodox Muslims and Russians were not just hostilities. Rather, behind 'the highly publicized wars and massacres between the Rus and the Tatars' there were social processes that facilitated camaraderie, and 'a modus vivendi' of coexistence. But nothing in Nikitin's past prepared him for his first shocking encounter with Hindus. This explains the disapproving tone of describing their cultural, social and religious practices. On arrival in India Nikitin could continue his movements in familiar Muslim circles of the Bahmanid kingdom, because he was already fluent in Persian and conversant with Muslim trading practices. But still his Christian background hamstrung his trading prospects, forcing his first trade-off of non-conversion to Islam, in that as a non-Muslim he could not trade in horses. Nikitin was rescued from the tough choice of confiscation of the horse or conversion to Islam, to be made within four days, that the local Muslim governor presented him with, by a certain Khoja Muhammad of Khorassan, known through business relations either in Persia or in India. But he was sufficiently rattled.

Maxwell believes that under overt pressure from political authorities to convert, and the constraint of relying only on Muslim merchants in plying his trade, Nikitin at this point superficially converted to Islam, without fully realizing the consequences and crises that would result from conversion. What Nikitin was attempting individually was 'conversion by assimilation'. It explains the pronoun 'we' that he used while describing his journey from Junnar to Bidar across the Deccan plain (possibly with Khoja Muhammad); the favourable phrases he used to describe the political, military, and economic superiority of the Muslims in India contrasted with the poverty and cultural otherness of the Hindus; and his observation that all the rulers of the region as well as their wives and ministers came from Khorassan. During the only instance of commercial relations with Hindus, in connection with the 'annual trade fair at 'Parvattum', he revealed his real Christian identity. But even so his subsequent comments on Hindu religio-social life suggest that he was ill at ease in their polytheistic world. After a few months with them, he returned to Bidar 'a fortnight before *Ulu Bayram*', to be subject to further spiritual transformation.

Proof of this spiritual transformation was that although he had thus far been able to mark time after the Russian Orthodox calendar, he now forgot the dates of Christian feasts and failed to keep them; and increasingly used Muslim holy days to keep track of time. His emotional outburst during the second sojourn at Bidar at this amnesia was thus according to Maxwell mainly a 'subterfuge'. Having put on record that he kept Easter in Hormuz; that he departed from Chaul in the seventh week of Easter; that the winter in Junnar 'set in on Trinity Sunday'; that Khan Asad had given him a deadline of four days 'till Our Redeemer's Day during the Fast of the Holy Mother of God' (a moveable fast) to convert; and that he had sold his horse at Bidar on Christmas Day; he could ill afford to forget the difference between Wednesday and Friday. This is not only because of the importance of Friday as day of congregational service as part of the five pillars of Islam, but also of his remembrance of Hindu days of fast. According to Maxwell, what the passage beginning with 'And I know not when Easter Sunday . . . occurs', shows instead, is that Nikitin was no more keeping the Orthodox holy days, but was now worshiping alongside Muslims.

For Maxwell, Nikitin's admission that he fasted with the Muslims during the month of March, i.e. he kept Ramadan, gives away his spiritual transformation. This is why he claims that in the month of May in 1473, he had 'kept Easter' alongside the Muslims who 'kept *Bayram* on a Wednesday'; and that he 'had begun to fast on the first day of the month of April'. Nikitin's yearning for his faith though Lent and Easter had come and gone unobserved four times [in 1469, 1470, 1471, and 1472—it is now 1473], due to loss of sense of Christian time, proves many things. First, Nikitin had not become a full convert. Though he had apparently kept one of the five pillars of Islam by fasting during Ramadan, he still refrained from eating meat at this period, i.e. period of Orthodox abstinence from meat during the forty days from Lent to Ramadan. Maxwell construes this admission as the strongest evidence of the Christian-Muslim syncretism that Nikitin practised during his travels. Secondly, Nikitin had real feelings of guilt even for this partial conversion. But still he could not resist the opportunity to maintain his spiritual and personal identity through communal worship. Not living in a modern, 'secular' space for Christians and Muslims, but in one marked by allegiance to a particular faith, what began for him as a syncretic form of counting days and months, combining both Russian and Muslim holy dates, gradually culminated in exclusively celebrating the Muslim holy days in place of Orthodox feast or fast days. Under its influence even his vocabulary at this period changed. He had convinced himself that the only way of maintaining his monotheistic faith was to participate in corporate worships and fasts that recognize 'one God—whether Muslim or Orthodox'. So, his prayers started closely resembling the most famous pious phrases of Islam, including the *basmala*, a must for Muslims before engaging in any worthwhile socio-economic activity. The prayers started being addressed exclusively to Allah rather than to the Trinity as before. The long prayer to Allah in creolized Arabic at the very end of *Voyage* praised Jesus as 'God's spirit' and not as God's son as in the opening prayer of *Voyage*. Maxwell reminds that the Qur'an refers to Jesus as a spirit created by God, but not God's son, as they eschew trinity. She also draws attention to the fact that Nikitin's last prayer echoes the 'Ninety-nine Most Beautiful Names of God', a popular Muslim prayer that cannot be traceable merely to loss of Christian hymn books.

Lenhoff's argument that Nikitin's neglect to pray to the Trinity or to invoke the Russian saints, together with Nikitin's admission that by avoiding returning to Russia via Mecca he had fulfilled only four of the five pillars of Islam, are used by Maxwell to describe Nikitin's state of quasi-conversion. This is because keeping the five pillars of Islam does not make one a Muslim, only saying the *shahada*, 'There is no god but God. Muhammad is the messenger of God', with conviction does. His position is best captured by the words: 'I am between faiths'.

The confusion of quasi-conversion leads to Nikitin's final epiphany while making plans for his return: 'As for true faith God alone knows it. . . .' Really, Maxwell thinks, he was now searching for ways to reintegrate his new Muslim religious 'habits back into Orthodoxy', not purely from spiritual motives. In his days, in Russia, apostasy meant death penalty. But his genuine spiritual conviction that the 'one God' of the Muslims was the same as of the Orthodox Christians is evidenced in his later prayers that invoked God's name in Arabic (Allah), Persian (Khuda), Turkic (Tanri), and Russian (Bog) for the welfare of Russia. Not having come on any spiritual mission, and rather for commercial reasons, once in direct contact with Muslim and Hindu spiritual culture in the Indian subcontinent, Nikitin still underwent a syncretic transformation, which in Maxwell's guess would have advanced to full conversion had he not returned to Russia. But still the phased 'process of superficial conversion' led to 'an altered spiritual identity', where spiritual and secular motives were intertwined.[86]

But was the final wail of Nikitin just a ploy to hide his new identity?

> Whither do I go from Hindusthan? . . . there is no passage from Hormuz to Khorasan, Jagala, Baren or Yazda. There is strife everywhere. . . . And there is no other way. And to go by the way of Mecca would mean to take the Moslem faith. . . . And to live in Hindustan would mean to spend all that I have, because everything is expensive here. . . .'[87]

This loud lament has more to it than the tensions of superficial conversion, or fear of punishment in Russia. Vasudevan looks at these wails from another perspective. He guesses that putting Nikitin's notes together in the *Chronicles of Moscow*, 'the scribes of the time made no distinction between the travel account that Nikitin had assembled in Fedosia, and other rough notes that he had with him when he died'. But even if Nikitin actually incorporated them while finishing his draft and was suddenly reliving those days in India, 'the interpellations indicate the cost of the great journey—a sense of loss as much as of gain that must be the fate of great travellers who become part of the path they traverse'.[88] Vasudevan thinks that Nikitin might have been quite comfortable with his identity of a Caspian merchant in the Caspian region. The ease deepened so much after entering Hindusthan that he slipped into Muslim practices'. The resultant tensions were with 'essential identities'.[89]

But what were Nikitin's 'essential identities'? Vasudevan argues that 'Nikitin's account itself does not betray the "Orthodox" *or* the "Russian" eye. It betrays the eye of an inhabitant of the Western Mongol Empire—hence the lack of surprise or interest in the Caspian or the customs of Islam in India'.[90] But could the "Orthodox" or the "Russian" eye be conceptually separated in those days? As Michael Khodarkovsky puts it, 'Religion defined the aggregate identity of the Russians in premodern Russia. To be Russian was first and foremost to be a Russian Orthodox'.[91] In that case, the fact that Nikitin did not see much novelty in the Caspian or Islam in India because of his heritage of the Western Mongol Empire, but while seeing Hindu India echoed some of the most dominant stereotypes of Western 'Orientalism', leads to a dangerous conclusion. It is that his putative Mongol persona or acquired *Chorasani* persona helped him see the differences that European observers saw much later. In other words Orientalism as a lens is not limited to the West European cognitive or imperial project. It is rather a conceptual blinker for observing differences further east.

NOTES

1. See L.B. Alayev and V.K. Vapha, *Indology (History, Economy and Culture)* (Leningrad: Nauka, 1968) p. 4, cited in Nisha Sahai–Achuthan, 'Soviet Indologists and the Institute of Oriental Studies: Works on Contemporary India in the Soviet Union', *Journal of Asian Studies* 42: 2 (February 1983): 323–43.
2. See nn. 7–8 of 'Introduction'.
3. See nn. 82–98 of 'Introduction'.
4. Bongard-Levin and Vigasin, however, claim that recent research has established that he stayed in India from 1471 to 1474. See *The Image of India*, p. 25.
5. Ibid. For a fuller account of the route with contemporary place names see Afanasy Nikitin, *Voyage Beyond Three Seas, Afanasy Nikitin 1466–72, with Hindi and English Texts* [*Khozenie za tri moria Afanasiia Nikitina*], ed. S.N. Kumkes (Moscow: Geografgiz, 1960), pp. 107–11, 113–15; and Alexander V. Riasanovsky, 'A Fifteenth Century Russian Traveller in India: Comments in Connection with a New Edition of Afanasiī Nikitin's Journal', *Journal of the American Oriental Society* 81: 2 (April–June 1961): 126–7. But the best description—in English—of the routes taken by Nikitin to India and back is to be found in A.S. Morris, 'The Journey Beyond Three Seas', *The Geographical Journal*, 133: 4 (December 1967): 502–5.
6. Morris, 'The Journey', pp. 503–5; and Nikitin, *Voyage Beyond Three Seas*, pp. 107–15.

7. Hari Vasudevan, 'The Solitude of Afanasii Nikitin in his "Voyage over the Three Seas"', in Geeti Sen and Molly Kaushal (eds.), *Journeys: Heroes, Pilgrims, Explorers*, India International Centre (New Delhi: Penguin Viking, 2005), p. 79.
8. Shabnam Minwala, *Times News Network*, 28 January 2002, www.russian-centre-mumbai.com/en/admin/.../shabnam_minwalla.doc, visited on 22 February 2008.
9. See Afansy Nikitin in Wikipedia, en.wikipedia.org/wiki/Afanasy_Nikitin, visited on 22 February 2008.
10. For this see Sudipta Kaviraj, 'The Culture of Representative Democracy', in P. Chatterjee (ed.), *Wages of Freedom: Fifty Years of the Indian Nation-State* (Delhi: Oxford University Press, 1998), pp. 147–75.
11. Stacy, *India in Russian*, p. 91.
12. See Shabnam Minwalla, op. cit.; and Vasudevan, 'Solitude of Afanasii', pp. 76–7.
13. See Sudha Mahalingam, 'The Challenges of Travelling through Russia', in *The Hindu*, online edition, 28 November 2006; and 'In the Footsteps of Afanasy Nikitin', By a Staff Reporter, *The Hindu*, online edition, 27 March 2007, www.hindu.com/2007/03/27/stories/2007032701190500.htm, visited on 1 April 2008.
14. See Ramesh Chandra Majumdar, Hemchandra Raychaudhury and Kalikinkar Datta, *Advanced History of India* (London: Macmillan, 1951), p. 363.
15. See Allison Y. Katsev, 'In the Forge of Criticism: M.T. Kachenovskii and Professional Autonomy in Pre-Reform Russia', in John T. Sanders (ed.), *Historiography of Imperial Russia: The Profession and Writing* (Armonk, N.Y.: M.E. Sharpe, 1999), pp. 50–7.
16. See Anindita Banerjee, 'By Caravan and Campfire: Chorasani Narratives about Hindustan and Afanasij Nikitin's "The Journey Beyond Three Seas"', *Die Welt Slaven* XLVIII (2003): 69.
17. For the relevant sections from Minaev's *Ancient India: Notes on the Voyage Beyond Three Seas of Afanasi Nikitin* (St. Petersburg, 1881) and the comments, see A.P. Barannikoff, 'Biographical Sketch of I.P. Minayeff', in Ivan Pavlovich Minayeff, *Travels in and Diaries of India and Burma*, tr. Hirendralal Sanyal, compared with the Russian text by Sunil Bhattacharya, language ed. Satish Chandra Sengupta (Calcutta: Eastern Trading Company, 1956), pp. 33–4. For the direct source of Minaev's deep appreciation of Nikitin, expressed in similar terms, though in slightly different words caused by differences of translation, see Ivan Minayev, *Old India—Notes on Afanasy Nikin's "Voyage Beyond the Three Seas"*, tr. Arun

Mohanty, ed. Eugenia Vanina and Irina Chalysheva (New Delhi: Har-Anand, 2010), pp. 29–31.

18. For appreciations by N.S. Trubeckoj (1963), V.P. Adrianova-Peretc (1958), D.S. Lichacev (1975), and B.A. Uspenskij (1994) see Banerjee, 'By Caravan', pp. 69–70.
19. Of the early manuscripts one was published in 1821. A more complete version appeared for the first time in the fifth edition of Karamazin's *History of Russia* in 1842, nine years before an authoritative edition as part of other sixteenth- and seventeenth-century Russian texts was published by the Petersburg University in 1851. A new edition of the book in 1948 focused more on the historical political situation of Russia at the time of writing it, and on the geography of the voyage, rather than on an evaluation of the data about India. The English translation through which Nikitin became known in India is, the one made for the Haklyut Society in 1857, by a member of the Russian Embassy in London. See Count M. Wielhorsky, 'The Travels of Athanassius Nikitin', in R.H. Major (ed.), *India in the Fifteenth Century*, Haklyut Series I, vol. 22 (1857), cited in Kemp, *Bharat-Rus* , pp. 14–15.
20. Bongard-Levin and Vigasin, *The Image of India*, pp. 7, 21, 25, and 29, and Kemp, *Bharat-Rus*, pp. 1–5 and 15–20.
21. Riasanovsky, 'A Fifteenth Century Russian', pp. 127–8.
22. Morris, 'The Journey', p. 502.
23. Lionel R. Tillett, 'Afanasy Nikitin as a Cultural Ambassador to India: A Bowdlerized Soviet Translation of His Journal', *Russian Review* 25: 2 (April 1966), pp. 160–9.
24. The publications cited are: a popular account of his travels by L.S. Baranov in 1939; a publication by V.V. Bogdanov commemorating the 475th anniversary of his venture in 1940; a number of critical editions of the *Journal* by B.D. Grekov and V.P. Adrianova-Peretc in 1948, N. Vodovozov in 1950, and the 2nd edition of Grekov's edition in 1957; popular geographies of his travels by a number of authors in 1949, 1950 and 1957; two children's stories based on his life in 1947; two biographies in 1951 and 1955; a novel by V.S. Pribytkov in 1956; and translations of Nikitin's *Journal* and works on him in Czech, Polish, and Hindi languages from 1951 to 1960. Ibid., pp. 161–2.
25. Kemp, *Bharat-Rus* , pp. 14–15.
26. See Riasanovsky, 'A Fifteenth Century Russian', p. 127; Walther Kirchner, 'The Voyage of Athanassius Nikitin to India, 1466–72', *The American Slavic and East European Studies* V (1946): 46–54; and Kemp, *Bharat-Rus*, p. 14.

27. Karamazin cited in S. Lur'e and L.S. Semenov, *Khozhdenie za tri moria Afanasia Nikitina* (Leningrad: Nauka, 1986), pp. 62 and 78.
28. The first sea was the Sea of Derbent, or Sea of Khawalis, the second was the Indian Sea, or Sea of Hindustan, and the third was the Black Sea, or Sea of Istanbul. See Nikitin, *Voyage*, p. 123.
29. Here the tone of treating Russia as Europe's Orient, which we discussed in the 'Introduction', is unmistakable.
30. Morris, 'The Journey', pp. 507–8.
31. Gail Lenhoff, 'Beyond Three Seas: Afanasij Nikitin's Journey from Orthodoxy to Apostasy', *East European Quarterly*, 13: 4 (1979): 431–47, especially p. 434.
32. See Tillettt, 'Afanasy', pp. 165–9.
33. Nicholas Royle, *After Derrida* (Manchester: Manchester University Press, 1995), p. 160. This particularly happens when a book becomes an important object of culture.
34. Ibid., pp. 2–7.
35. Nikitin, *Voyage*, pp. 112–13.
36. Ibid., pp. 111, 118.
37. Riasanovsky, 'A Fifteenth Century Russian', p. 128.
38. Vasudevan, 'Solitude of Afanasii', pp. 83–4.
39. Bongard-Levin and Vigasin, *The Image of India*, pp. 28–9.
40. Nikitin, *Voyage*, p. 109.
41. *Dhoti*, or *dhuti* in Bengal is a piece of cloth, pleated in different styles, that men used to wear as a covering for the lower part of their body, and still do. But here Nikitin is obviously referring to a turban or some sort of headgear.
42. Nikitin, *Voyage*, pp. 110–11.
43. *Nikitin, Khozhdenie za tri morya Afanasya Nikitina*, 1466–72, 2nd edn., ed. B.D. Grekov et al. (Moscow: 1958), pp. 74–5, cited in Tillett, 'Afanasy', p. 165.
44. See nn. 67–9 in Introduction.
45. See *Khozhdenie*, 1958, pp. 79 and 81, and for pages in English translation where omitted passages are present, see pp. 114 and 116, cited in Tillet, 'Afanasy', p. 166. The places, where this happens, 'Cheen' and 'Machin', may refer to Chinese towns. However, as Tillett points out, Nikitin discusses them with Indian places without locating them. See nn. 23 and 24, p. 166, ibid., pp. 166–7.
46. Wielhorsky, 'Travels of Athanassius Nikitin', p. 18 n., in ibid., p. 166. Morris also thinks that 'a mixture of delicacy and inability to render . . . a polyglot Turkic tongue, with some Arabic and Persian words, in all probability the international language of merchants using the Central Asian caravan

trails' into English was the reason of omission. See Morris, 'The Journey', p. 505.

47. Tillett, 'Afanasy', p. 167.
48. See n. 88 in 'Introduction'.
49. Ja. S. Lur'e, 'Russkij èuežemec v Indii XV veka', in Ja. S. Lur'e and L.S. Semenov (eds.), *Choženie za tri morja Afanasija Nikitina* (Leningrad, 1986), pp. 76, 80, and 84, quoted in Banerjee, 'By Caravan and Campfire', p. 70.
50. Morris, 'The Journey', p. 505.
51. See n. 88 in 'Introduction'.
52. Oaten, *European Travellers*, p. 37, 41–2 n.
53. Banerjee, 'By Caravan and Campfire', p. 70.
54. Ibid., pp. 71–5.
55. Nikitin, *Voyage*, p. 113.
56. Ibid., 115.
57. Ibid., p.113.
58. Ibid.
59. Ibid., p. 114.
60. Ibid., p. 113.
61. See Teltscher, *India Inscribed*, pp. 12–34.
62. Nikitin, *Voyage*, p. 114.
63. Banerjee, 'By Caravan and Campfire', pp. 70–7.
64. Nikitin, *Voyage*, p. 113.
65. Ibid., p. 111.
66. Swami Vivekananda, *Prācya o Pāscātya* [*The East and the West*], 25th edn., 41st rpt. (Kolkata: Udbodhan Karyalaya, 1902/2009), pp. 47–51.
67. Nikitin, *Voyage*, pp. 112–13.
68. Ibid., pp. 119–20.
69. Riasanovsky, 'A Fifteenth Century Russian', p. 127.
70. Oaten, *European Travellers*, pp. 32–3.
71. Morris, 'The Journey', p. 505.
72. Oaten, *European Travellers*, pp. 39–40.
73. Ibid., p. 36.
74. Ibid., p. 33.
75. Nikitin, *Voyage*, p. 111.
76. Ibid.
77. Kemp, *Bharat-Rus*, p. 19.
78. Nikitin, *Voyage*, p. 115.
79. *Khozhdenie*, 1958, p. 80; *Khozhdenie*, 1960, p. 115, cited in Tillett, 'Afanasy', pp. 167–8.
80. Nikitin, *Voyage*, pp. 116–17.

81. Vasudevan, 'Solitude of Afanasii', p. 84.
82. Ibid., p. 77.
83. Tillettt, 'Afanasy', p. 169.
84. Mary Jane Maxwell, 'An Orthodox Russian's Spiritual Voyage in the Dar al-Islam, 1468–75', *Journal of World History*, 17: 3 (September 2006): 243–66, obtained from Proquest Research Library, Document View, pp.1–19, http:// proquest.umi.com/pqdweb?index=3&did=1126906851 &SrchMode=3&sid+1&F, last visited 23 January 2008, here pp. 2 and 15–16. For Conti's forced conversion, later seeking of absolution from Pope Eugene the Fourth, the Pope's pardon and assignment of his secretary for penning Conti's experiences in Latin, see Oaten, *European Travellers*, pp. 28–32, especially p. 31.
85. Maxwell, 'An Orthodox Russian', pp. 3–4.
86. Ibid., pp. 4–13.
87. Nikitin, *Voyage*, pp. 118–19.
88. Vasudevan, 'Solitude of Afanasii', p. 87.
89. Ibid.
90. Ibid.
91. Michael Khodarkovsky, '"Ignoble Savages and Unfaithful Subjects": Constructing Non-Christian identities in Early Modern Russia', in Brower and Lazzerini, *Russia's Orient*, p. 17.

CHAPTER 3

An Ensign, an Envoy and a Violinist: India through the Lenses of Efremov, Daniebegov and Lebedev

We have seen in the last chapter that Nikitin's *Journal*, even in the pre-modern fifteenth century, reflected many of the known binaries of 'Orientalist' writing, even when the 'Continent of the Circe'[1] diluted his Russian-Orthodox identity. Of the three travellers we are focusing on in this chapter, Fillipp S. Efremov (1750–died after 1811), Rafail Daniebegov (probably last quarter of seventeenth century to middle of eighteenth century), and Herasim Stepanovich Lebedev (1749–1817), the first two belonged to the eighteenth century, and the third to the late eighteenth and early nineteenth century. All three predated the beginning of Russian 'Orientalism'. One wonders from where, in the case of the first two, voices of superiority akin to the 'magisterial' emerged in their observations, unless one dates the beginning of Russian 'Orientalism' further back, on the lines of Harsha Ram, who claimed that Mikhailo Vasliyevich Lomonosov's 'Khotin Ode' was the first articulation in the realm of literature of Russia's feeling of superiority over Asia.[2] But then one wonders equally how Lebedev was so different, unless we agree that the 'Orientalist' observer can be free of stereotypes.

The importance of all three stems from the fact that they fill an important gap in Russian observation of India. All came to the eastern parts of India when these were not on the iconic travellers' itineraries. So, they could provide an answer to Oaten's complaint that Conti 'does not tell us more of what he saw in Bengal, of which place at this date (1420) we know but little'.[3] While accounts of the first two Russian travellers belie this hope both in substance and attitude, though Kemp places them above British travellers who visited at the time,[4] Lebedev more than compensates for their blinkers.

FILIPP EFREMOV: BIOGRAPHY AND ITINERARY

In the 1770s a Russian ensign named Filip Yefremov (Fillipp Sergeevich Efremov in modern spelling), born in Vyatka, who had been forced into slavery in Bukhara, was obliged to return to his native land via India.[5] The first edition of the accounts of his travels appeared in 1786 under the title *The Nine Years of the Travels of the Russian Non-Commissioned Officer, Yefremov in Bukhara, Khiva, etc.* Its second edition came out in 1794, under the title of *The Travels of Civil Councilor Yefremov in Bukhara, etc.*[6] Kemp honours him not only as an important figure in the 'old series of overland travellers', but as the 'first Russian to visit British India and certainly the first to travel across the country'. His accounts are said to fill a gap in times 'when the impressions of individuals nearer the common people and not either officials, educated adventurers or missionaries were seldom recorded'.

Efremov's journey was as turbulent as Nikitin's. Taken prisoner by tribesmen on the Russian frontier near Orenburg and eventually sold in Bukhara, he managed to procure some tradable goods and money and to make his escape. But misfortune struck again, and after losing much of his goods and money he entered India as a helpless wanderer. Kemp says in the same breath that his book has 'little of particular factual importance for India', but is still an 'interesting . . . social document', contrasted with 'English travel and missionary books at that date'. Even the sheer paucity of information in the book becomes a virtue. Thus, despite traversing vast distances and 'having obviously met with lots of local people', including merchants, 'he does not mention a single one of the classic Indian anecdotes, or say anything about superstitious beliefs, barbarous customs or the mysterious East which so many travellers related. . . . That inherent dishonesty and degradation in the "Indian character" which so often broke the hearts of British writers at that time, never struck him either.'[7]

EFREMOV'S INDIA: BARBARISM, SLAVERY, IDOLATRY AND FORCED 'ANTARJALI'

Actually, after entering India through Tibet and Kashmir, and passing Delhi and Lucknow before coming down to Calcutta, Efremov leaves uninteresting details of journeys through mispronounced place names, of the modes of travel, and distances of these places from Moscow, things which would interest none but historical geographers. When he starts talking about places 'lying on either side of the River Ganges' and the people living there, he should have embarrassed Kemp. He finds the 'inhabitants . . . rude in their habits, not very sensible and lazy', engaging 'slaves to do their work for them'.[8] The words are sanctimonious from a Russian in the eighteenth century, as slavery continued in Russia up to the 1720s, and serfdom peaked in 1861, to endure in milder forms till redemption payments were finally removed in 1907.[9] And though Indrani Chatterjee's research about the status of domestics in ruling households of eastern India in the eighteenth and nineteenth centuries, uses the word 'slavery', they were little more than serfs.[10]

Far from reticence about 'superstitious beliefs, barbarous customs or the mysterious East', which Kemp claims, Efremov's depiction of riverside life in Bengal is crowded by the familiar 'Orientalist' archetypes of idol worship, asceticism and physical penance:

> Many of the Indians are of the Mohammedan faith or the idolatrous . . . A very considerable number deify the sun, the moon, the stars, cows, idols and other beings and make offerings to them three times a month. Sun worshippers wade into the river up to their knees when the sun rises and recite a prayer gazing at it and splashing water towards it; sometimes they look at it, pray and throw up some earth three times. The cow worshippers do not kill that animal, nor eat beef at all.

Efremov notices that the cow-worshippers do not even sell cows, fearing that they will be killed after sale, but says the next moment without any compunction that when 'a cow dies they remove their skin and make shoes of it'. Like Nikitin, he is surprised that idol-worshippers keep idols at the crossroads under makeshift shelters, and daub and clean their houses built on riversides with liquefied cow dung.[11]

So, quality of representation of India has not improved at all, even more than three hundred years after Nikitin. Rather, if the 'blackness', 'nakedness', shamelessness, polytheism and idolatry of Hindu India had troubled Nikitin, then his successors added the death rituals of Hindus and 'suttee' to the Orientalist litany of barbarous practices. Here is a very graphic description of Hindu death rituals:

They burn the bodies of the dead beside a river and then sweep the bones and ashes into the water . . . sometimes they may bring a sick man who is scarcely able to move or speak . . . and place him on the ground beside the water. An old man or *it may be his wife*, son or other relative *takes hold of the sick man's head and repeatedly souses it until he gasps*, after which they push him right into the water. When the water rises with the sea tide the bodies float on its surface and with the ebb they are carried by the current down into the sea [italics added].[12]

Superficiality of observation and attendant miscomprehension are difficult to miss in the description. Else Efremov could not have shown Hindus taking off the hide of dead cows to make shoes of it, and wives being party to the 'sousing' of terminally ill husbands to bring upon themselves the curse of 'suttee'. Nor had he any inkling of the complex psychological processes involved in the ritual of *antarjali jātrā* he is describing here, where a man whose death has been prognosticated by the physician is kept by the side of the river Ganga till he breathes his last, which incidentally is the subject of an offbeat Bengali novel and a not very bad film made of it.[13]

True to form, Efremov gives a skewed view of Calcutta's demography, where the 'inhabitants are English, *Greeks* and *Indians of many different tribes* [italics added]'.[14] Calcutta even in its earliest, unstable colonial days did not have a sizeable Greek population. Actually an early twentieth-century demographer calculated that in 1752, of the total population of 1,17,744 in Calcutta, the number of Europeans (400), Eurasians (3,500) and Armenians (250) were a little above 4,000. There were no figures for Parsees, Jews, Chinese, or Greeks.[15] Another source, however, mentions the number of Greeks, mainly traders, between 1770 and 1800 at somewhat less than 200 in Calcutta.[16] This apparently irrelevant detail speaks of the quality of his observation.

RAFAIL DANIEBEGOV: BIOGRAPHY, RELEVANCE AND ITINERARY

Rafail Daniebegov [Daniebegashvili in Georgian transliteration] was a wealthy Georgian who visited India five times at the end of the eighteenth century, spending an interrupted period of eighteen years. The origins of his travels lie in the traditional connections his family had with India, where his father had often been on official missions. For his first journey Daniebegov carried a message from the Georgian king Irakli II to the wealthy Armenian merchant Yakov (Hakop) Shahamirian,[17] to present the charter of a Georgian village to him for having sent a large sum of money to the king.[18]

That we are including a Georgian among Russian travellers needs explanation. According to a Western reviewer of Daniebegov's book[19] Georgia was reportedly threatened by neighbouring Muslim states, and some sections in Georgia wanted an alliance with England, in the interest of a possible Georgian-Armenian state, and promoting contacts with the English in India. However, during Daniebegov's third journey Georgia was incorporated into the Russian state in 1801. So, after returning in 1813, Daniebegov met one General Glazenap at Omsk, before completing his journey at Moscow, where his book was published in 1815. His dedication of the book to Tsar Alexander I shows his anxiety to stress his loyalty to the newly-formed Russian state. More importantly, noted Central Asian scholar David Wileman quotes L.S. Maruashvili, editor of a new edition of the travles to show that he made two later journeys. The report of the fourth journey, occupying the years 1815-20, and signed by Daniebegov, is in the Omsk archives. The report of the fifth journey, done in the years 1822–7, 'was discovered in the notebook of G.F. Gens, chairman of the Orenburg Frontier Commission'. So, the complete travelogue is a Russian product. Actually, Wileman questions 'the motives of Daniebegashvili's travels after the incorporation of Georgia in the Russian state in

1801. . . .' And he cites Maruashvili to suggest that the travels may have been related to the Russians' desire to develop trade with India, particularly with Kashmir, which did not come under British control until later in 1848'.[20] The book was not only published under the Russian form of his name, but Soviet Russia co-opted and aggressively 'sold' Daniebegov as one of its travellers. Basing his arguments on the publication of Daniebegov's travels in India and other Asian countries in 1969, with parallel versions in Russian, English and Hindi [in much the fashion of the 1960 edition of *Khozenie*], Wileman significantly stresses that as par the preface to the book, it was issued 'in token of friendship from Soviet geographers to the Indian National Committee of Geographers' on the occasion of the 21st International Geographical Congress held in New Delhi in 1968.[21] The 1815 Moscow edition carried the words 'translated from the Georgian' on its title page, though the Georgian original could not be traced. Wileman points out that though at the start of the book he claims to have set out on his journey on 15 March 1795, he gives no further dates for the whole of his journey,[22] enabling him to falsely claim to have travelled for eighteen years.[23] The Soviet cooptation of Daniebegov as their own and Wileman's determination to expose it are sufficient reasons to include him among the Russian travellers. For example, Wileman makes the oblique reference that this report includes details of political events in India, including British military activities in India and of the travels of one William Moorcroft, a person Maruashvili wrongly identifies as a British intelligence agent.[24] Kemp also includes him as a Russian traveller.

Daniebegov's book tells about a journey from Georgia through Mesopotamia to India, Ceylon and Burma, and during return, through Kashmir, Sinkiang, Semipalatinsk, and Omsk to Moscow. Though Kemp found from Daniebegov's notes on the places he had visited that he was perfectly 'at home', and 'able to mix with the local businessmen' easily,[25] the uneasiness with a different, non-Western civilization, typical of 'Orientalist' representation, frequently lurks in his accounts. Bongard-Levin and Vigasin mention 'short digressions on Indian religious customs, funereal ceremonies in Bengal, and the sacred city of Benares and so on' in the book, conveniently without comments, though not forgetting Daniebegov's notes on local resistances to British expansionism in India.[26]

Idol-Worship, Demography, 'Antarjalī', Suttee, and Stinking Ganga

In actuality, Daniebegov too expresses shock at the religious and cultural beliefs and practices of Hindus, who 'worship cows and water' in place of the 'all wise creator of all creatures', and for this reason 'go without shoes or slippers, counting it in their ignorance as an unforgivable sin to wear the hide of beasts on their feet'. He was amused that they 'kill no animals for food, regarding them as similar to themselves'.[27] His description of Calcutta's demography, except for referring to Indians as '*the original inhabitants*, who are all idolatrous and Mohammedans', and not as 'tribes', like Efremov, is as skewed. We know that there were many Armenians in Calcutta, 'who live in a very luxurious style and do a lot of business with the foreigners'; and that apart from Indians and Armenians 'there are English, French, *and above all Portuguese there*' [italics added].[28] We do not know what 'above all' before Portuguese means. But the picture was not factual. Just two years before Daniebegov's first journey 'the non-official European community of Bengal in 1793' numbered merely 585. The racial composition was as follows: 'Italians 40, Portuguese 39, Germans 20, Netherlanders 6, Spaniards 7, Canadians 4, Americans 2, Danes 2, Swiss 1 and Turk 1'.[29]

Daniebegov's understanding of the economics of colonialism was as naïve and simplistic as his demography. He sympathizes that out of the East India Company's 'yearly income of up to 500 million rupees . . . little remains to them of this sum' as 'they have to pay the wages to the very large army which is maintained here'. One reason why 'their expenditure is also great' was that in the British Indian army, Indian sepoys, called 'blacks', got the same pay as their white counterparts. The reason the 'blacks' got the same treatment was that 'the Indian army know its drills so well that they are in no way inferior to the British army'.[30] While saying this Daniebegov had no way of knowing that the 'rate of pay offered by the Company to a sepoy was not particularly handsome', though it was enough to attract men to Company service, and that a recruit had no chance of attaining an officer's commission.[31] Much later, Captain V.F. Novitskii, who stayed four months in India in 1888 as a guest of the Indian army, criticized the British 'for not making the Indian army a school for the civilization of the Indian natives', and teaching them to read and write, as was done in the Russian army.[32]

Much influenced by Caucasian-Russian conception of food, Daniebegov wonders that the Indians 'live only on rice and fish, bread is not eaten at all'. He seems even more surprised that in Calcutta 'they speak the same language as in the state of Pankhal [Bengal]'. After visiting other misspelled places in Bengal like 'Serampur' [Serampore], 'Chichra' [Chinsura], etc., he had to go as far as 'Marshitabat' [Murshidabad], a place 150 versts from Calcutta, where an 'Indian Nawab has his residence', [33] to find the first people who '*speak the real Indian language*' [italics added], which means that for him Bengali was not the common language even in Bengal.[34]

Like Eefremov, Daniebegov too was haunted by the death rituals and pollution of Ganga water from these, and outdid him to show how the river water stank from it. After devoting quite a few lines to the diseases endemic in Calcutta, and the role of polluted water in the spread of the diseases, Daniebegov pens these startling lines:

> Perhaps the water here would be suitable for us too, but inasmuch as it is the Indians' custom to throw dead bodies into the water after burning them a little in the fire, the water has an unpleasant stench from the bodies rotting in it, and *therefore it is not used for any purpose at all* [italics added].[35]

The last italicized words would look amusing for people who know that as late as in late nineteenth century Ganga water was used for drinking purposes even in zamindar houses, including that of Rabindranath Tagore.[36] Anyway, even after he moved west from Bengal, this obsession with bodies in Ganga water did not leave Daniebegov. At 'Azimabat and Fatoma' [Patna and Fatua] he observes with relief, 'Well water is used here, but the river water is not good for anything because the dead bodies thrown into it make it stinking and noxious'. He describes one scene of *antarjali* and a village of the 'undead' here:

Here there is . . . one of the most cruel customs with regard to the sick and infirm of both the sexes and all the ages, that if priests say from their observations of them that such people are near death, they place them in a coffin and carry them to the Ganges, where having carried them up to their knees into the water, they repeatedly pour water into their mouths and force them to pronounce the words 'Kina-Narain' [Krishna-Narain, (explains Kemp)] i.e. 'Lord God' . . . When one of these wretched people dies, then after placing his body for a short time on a fire they throw it into the river. Should it happen that he regains his health and strength, the priests declare him to be a wicked man displeasing to God; and therefore he is deprived of the right to live in the village and is compelled to move to a village specially made for such wretches on the other side of the Ganges. This village is called Murdun Ki Kram (Murdon Ki Gram) i.e. the village of the dead. The English collect no taxes from the inhabitants of this village. For, in accordance with the custom of the Indians, they reckon them among dead.[37]

Anyone who has read Tagore's moving short story 'Jivita o Mṛta' (The Living and the Dead)[38] and seen the limitless cruelty experienced by those who returned from the jaws of death even in nineteenth-century Bengal, or has read a classic Bengali novel dealing with traditional physician's practice of declaring *nidān*, i.e. diagnosis of irrevocably approaching death,[39] would not find Daniebegov in the wrong. But for the Russian traveller, the kaleidoscopic unfolding of Hindu cultural life, without the help of any binding and underlying thread that made it intelligible, made any hermeneutic understanding of a completely different culture and civilization impossible. This is why Daniebegov could so easily deride the wish of devout Hindus to die in 'Benares' (Banaras or Varanasi) and the ease with they could renounce their worldly possessions and even their families to ensure this end, as mere 'superstition', which 'has reached such a pitch' that they believe that 'if anyone dies in this city he will even be freed from all the torments in the next world which he might be obliged to endure'. After pointing out that 'All the inhabitants [at 'Benares' for sure] are cow worshippers and idol worshippers . . . they even rub their faces with her urine and cleanse defiled vessels with it',[40] Daniebegov finds further proof of the peoples superstitiousness in the fact that that at a place called 'Sirinagar', near the Nanda Devi mountain, a great fair is organized every year, where Hindus, 'living even five thousand "versts" away come here to worship the water of the Ganges'.[41]

Daniebegov's description of *satī*, at a place called 'Norpor or Far' (Nurpur according to Kemp, actually Nūrpur) is quite insightful:

An idol worshipper had died . . . Having placed the dead body on a richly decorated bier, they carried it to the place assigned for burning . . . He had two wives, who dressed in magnificent and costly clothes followed their husband's bier. As soon as they came to the appointed place the people made a huge pyre of wood over which they laid some planks and placed the body of the dead man on top. As according to the cruel custom *the wives out of love for their husband have to sacrifice themselves voluntarily to the fire together with him* the two richly dressed women seated themselves on the pyre on either side of their husband. The priests having poured plenty of oil and other combustible materials all over all three, suddenly set light to the pile from all sides, and these two innocent victims together with their husband's corps [*sic*] were drowned by the flames. The people standing around the burning pyre began to play various instruments and they continued until all had turned to ashes. . . . *Nevertheless women may choose not to perform this inhuman rite, their relatives and friends even try to persuade them to remain alive either for the sake of their children or the inheritance left by the husbands. But if they once decide*, if they approach the flames . . . and then suddenly feeling fear want to turn back, the watchers around the pyre threaten them with a different death—by the sword, in which case *the wretched women would not escape*, being regarded unworthy to live [italics added].[42]

In this description of 'suttee', as rich as that of Conti,[43] Daniebegov was sufficiently objective in the portrayal of the event and its conditions. An initial consent was needed, and at least some people were there to advise against it. But the women were 'innocent victims' all the same, because the consent was manufactured, even if by their conditioning; and once the consent was given it could not be taken back.

Daniebegov speaks of the resistances of Indians to the expansionist efforts of England in India quite appreciatively, and becomes complicit in the Anglo-Russian competition over control of the Orient. He shows how the people at a place called 'Fadipur' (Fatehpur) resisted the advance of the British, and women as well as men defended their city heroically and repulsed a British attack, killing

40 officers and as many as 2,000 soldiers. And then he relates how the 'common people' there, 'not wishing to be subject to the English elected their ruler from amongst themselves'. The resistance of the people of Srinagar in Kashmir also found approbatory mention: 'The English are exceedingly desirous of occupying this city, but up till now their wish has not been realized'.[44]

As only travellers can afford it, Daniebegov swiftly shifts his attention from the tragic customs of *satī* and *antarjalī* among plainsmen to the 'poor but cheerful' people of Kashmir, who in their Oriental foolishness ensured that their descendants remained poor too: 'The rich bury their gold and silver in the earth and keep it a secret which they do not reveal even to their friends, and which after the death of the person who has buried it, remains unknown'.[45]

On his way back, at Tibet, Daniebegov made special note of polyandry prevalent there, 'a very evil custom here and one quite contrary to common sense. If there are four brothers in a house they have one woman as their wife. The child born from them takes the name of the eldest brother, and in this way only regards one of them as his father.'[46]

What Daniebegov was describing regarding Tibetan marital system is known to anthropologists as 'fraternal or adelphic polyandry', called 'levirate' in which one woman marries several brothers, or 'sororate', when several sisters are simultaneously, or potentially, the spouses of the same man. Complex socio-economic reasons gave birth to all these forms of polygamy.[47] But while looking at it through the lens of monogamy, Daniebegov did not know or was forgetting that polygamy continued in Russia as late as the seventeenth century.[48]

HERASIM STEPANOVICH LEBEDEV

Lebedev frees us from all this ethnocentrism and 'Orientalist' stereotypes with a hermeneutic ability and humility that matched or exceeded even the most equipped of the 'Orientalists', including William Jones.[49] The great Bengali linguist Suniti Kumar Chatterjee rightly considered him 'an important link in the early history of Indological studies in Europe', whose real contribution to 'a better understanding between' India and Russia as well as Europe lay smothered under his image of 'an "adventurer" from Russia who had something to do with the drama in Bengal . . .' Chatterjee reminds us that it was only in 1955 that for the first time in India Lebedev's legacy was remembered at a meeting by the Indian People's Theatre Association in Calcutta, a cultural front organization of the Communist Party of India (CPI), close to the Soviet Union, on the occasion of the 160th year of Lebedev's first dramatic performance. Emulating IPTA, another leftist theatre group in Calcutta, the Little Theatre, staged four years later a play at the Minerva Theatre on 27 November 1959.[50] The renewed CPI-inspired remembrance created new problems, like a new popular image, best manifest in apocryphal likenesses of him in books and sculptures in public places.[51] This incomplete, new image persists because of the lack of coordination of the data that were culled about the most creative parts of his life in Russia and in the Indian subcontinent, and also lack of dialogue between Bengali/Indian and Russian/European scholars on Lebedev, as a result of which primary researches in Russia and in India, particularly West Bengal and Bangladesh did not complement each other.[52] This task was most ably done by Mamud combining all the available sources in his book in Bengali.[53] But an interpretive dimension to force the data to reveal more is needed.

Biography and Itinerary

Born in 1749 in a poor but respectable family of priests in Jaroslavl, Lebedev had only a desultory education because of his father's neglect. Until his fifteenth year he could do nothing more than read and write Russian apart from some proficiency in music.[54] He got his first opportunity of 'gratifying his desire for travel' through an embassy which was sent to Naples in 1775, under Count Andrey Kyrillovich Razumovsky. The decision of the Count to take Lebedev with him as a violinist suggests his musical talents. For, Razumovsky was himself a gifted composer, violinist, and personal friend of the greatest composers of Western Europe, namely, Joseph (Franz) Haydn (1732–1809), Wolfgang Amadeus

Mozart (1756–91), and Ludwig van Beethoven (1770–1927). The Neapolitan court led by Count Razumovsky was, however, 'obliged to stay at Vienna, owing to the military operations between the Austrian and the Prussian Courts'. So Lebedev decided to continue his journeys on his own by taking letters of recommendation to all the European courts from Prince Golitsyn, the then Russian Ambassador at Vienna, Count Razumovsky, and from Alexander Borisovich Kurakin, royal official and diplomat, addressed to Semyon Romanovich Vorontsov, full minister in the Russian embassy in Venice. The recommendations helped him not only in his journey to Paris and Etupes nearby, but also to the 'distant east'. Mamud finds that prior to coming to India he had toured Vienna in 1777–8; Germany and England in 1778–81/2; France in 1782; Italy in 1783; and England in 1784.[55] The itinerary proves that he went to England at least twice before coming to India, which explains his relative proficiency in English.[56]

The words above explode the myth supported even by Sahni, who says that Lebedev had 'disappeared', 'en route to the Russian Embassy in Vienna', and after 'his *disappearance act* . . . travelled around Europe eking out a living playing his violin . . . then all of a sudden . . . joined an English military band that was being sent to India'.[57] Actually Lebedev boarded the East India Company ship *Rodney* towards India, armed with important endorsements. They helped him in India also. For, on his arrival at the city of Madras on 28 July 1785, Lebedev was escorted by Captain Sydenham, the 'Town Major' [Mayor], and was given accommodation with all due haste, along with facilities for the exercise of his musical talents for the next two years. Impressed by his musical talents the Mayor also engaged him for two years on handsome terms as a teacher of violin.[58] Lebedev's credentials from some responsible and exalted official in England must have done the trick. For, in those colonial days one could not embark at an East India Company ship and come to Madras-Bombay-Calcutta at will, to bag an offer of £200 per annum in a two-year contract, when different types of company officials were not making more than £60–80 annually.[59] P. Thankappan Nair, however, deduces from this that 'Lebedeff's fame as a musician had preceded his arrival in Madras'.[60]

The last leg of Lebedev's outward journey was to Calcutta, where, from his own accounts he supposedly set foot in the month of August in 1787, though the date could not be specified.[61] The reasons why Lebedev left Madras for Calcutta was that though not materially unhappy, he found his situation comfortable but not challenging enough. So, 'infatuated by the general report, that Bengal was a more extended theatre for the animated action of the bolder race of Exploraters than Madras; and incited also by the emulation of enlarging my scale of knowledge in respect of things as well as men, I at once determined on visiting that country'.[62]

What caused the decision? Lebedev says that after gaining 'adequate means of subsistence with the help of the European residents' of Madras, he acquired some 'knowledge of the Malabar vernacular [Tamil]'; but got no opportunity 'to learn the wisdom of the Brahmins, written in [a] spiritual language which no Indian was capable of explaining to me in English'.[63] Mamud, however, detects the presence in him of both the desires of material gain and craving for knowledge, typical of the characteristics of the eighteenth century in Europe, a period in which the socio-cultural conflict between the Westerners and Slavophiles embodied in the rifts between the followers of Dostoyevsky and Turgenev was a long way off yet, but still the joining between the West and Russia that Peter the Great had achieved, brought the spirit of Enlightenment to Russia's doors. Lebedev symbolized two of its main characteristics, namely faith in his own abilities and the drive for discovering the unknown. So, Mamud does not subscribe to the view of many Lebedev experts that only quest for knowledge was involved. He cites Lebedev's own plain admission in his 'Memorandum' that he came to Calcutta 'not without an honest view . . . of improving my finance', and that Calcutta was the 'Prolific Spot where it was said that innumerable Sojourners most of all nations [*sic*] had rapidly acquired Competent fortune'. Mamud thinks that in this sense the epithet of an 'adventurer' given by George Grierson was apposite. But the mundane limits of this materialistic cleverness were burst asunder the moment the dream of Lebedev's innermost subconscious was released to come to the forefront: 'not the lust for money, but a deeper and much more far-reaching goal—discovery of the psyche of a new world [translation mine]'.[64]

After coming to the city of Calcutta Lebedev found even more admirers, including, the Town Mayor of Calcutta, other Colonels, Justices, Company's Counsel, and several other gentries.[65] With the resultant economic security, he started acquiring the knowledge that his book *A Grammar of the Pure and Mixed Indian Dialects* (*GPMEID*) is concerned with.[66]

In Calcutta: Fiddler on the Loose

Regarding Lebedev's musical career in Calcutta, the first evidence of his concerts was in an advertisement in the *India Gazette* and *Calcutta Public Advertiser* of 24 December 1787, discovered by Mamud, which announced a vocal and instrumental concert billed on 28 December at 8 a.m. The price of the ticket was 'one Gold Mohur each'. Just three days after the concert, on 31 December 1787, the same weekly carried a eulogistic review of the performance 'on the Violoncello' before a 'very numerous and respectable company'. Lebedev was praised for his skill and was ranked with known contemporary masters. *The Calcutta Gazette*, another weekly published from Calcutta, also 'confirmed the rumoured excellence of the performer . . . and fully justified recommendation and zeal of those who so laudably exerted themselves on this occasion for his encouragement'.

Mamud argues that what with the time required for the 'rumoured excellence' of Lebedev reaching Calcutta, collecting recommendation and 'encouragement', and forming a concert-team, this concert, held 3/4 months after Lebedev's arrival in Calcutta, was his first musical venture. Prior notification of the second concert, in the *Calcutta Gazette* of 31 July 1788 was first noticed by Saha. It began with his 'great professional merit in the musical walk', to suggest that in the backdrop of 'the present dearth of publick amusements' in Calcutta the imminent 'Bill of Fare for one nights [*sic*] musical repast' would be extremely welcome to its audience. The programme was finally on offer on 18 August 1788, in the *India Gazette,* and *Calcutta Public Advertiser* of the same date, and was favourably reviewed in the *Calcutta Gazette* of 21 August. The next available news of Lebedev's musical performance was in March 1791. Though Saha informs that Lebedev gave another performance of vocal and instrumental music on 9 April 1790 at the Old Court House, he does not give the source of this information. And Mamud found no documentary evidence of any such performance between 19 August 1788 and 31 December 1789 in any of the extant gazettes and weeklies. By his count between January 1787 and January 1797 Lebedev gave at the least ten and at the most twelve concerts, and at least once took part in another person's concert as a player of 'Violoncello'. The accounts of them given by Lebedev indicate that these were only partial sources of his finances, as receipts from these cannot explain his income of 5,000 sikka rupees, which he claims in his letter to Emperor Alexander I in 1801, to have earned in the city. Nor could these explain his stated monthly income of Rs. 400. It is clear that that just like Alexander Kyd, the 'Town Major', to whose son he gave lessons in music, he was in the payroll of other well wishers, friends and admirers who are mentioned in his writings, for giving lessons in the violin.[67]

Linguistic and Literary Endeavours

In the musical career of Lebedev in Calcutta, Mamud finds a mysterious, unexplained period from September 1788 to December 1789 (March 1790, if we accept Mahadev Prasad Saha's word that he gave a final concert on 9 April 1790). For, there was no advertisement for this period in the *Calcutta Gazette*. Mamud guesses from this that Lebedev was ill or outside Calcutta. This is because a man who had given twenty advertisements in the *Calcutta Gazette* about his concerts and dramas between 1791 and 1797 (when his financial misfortune began), and had been mentioned at least three times in the news about Calcutta in its pages, would not have been ignored for about a whole year.[68] My hunch is that it was the period when he was preparing himself for language learning. As Lebedev puts it:

> In the year 1789, at Calcutta I made my first application in researches of Indian literature, but to my great mortification, for the space nearly of two years, I could not meet with such interpreter as would scientifically explain the Shamscrit [Sanskrit] alphabet, which is used for the Bengal language, and otherwise called Pracrit [Prākṛt], or Bhadsha [Bhāṣā?], nor could I derive any

material assistance from the corrupted grammars of Indian dialects, written by Europeans, and which are without distinction entitled Hindostan Language. I was therefore nearly at the point of dropping the design altogether; but at that critical time, my Sircar (Steward) introduced to me a Bengallie schoolmaster, named Shree Golocknath-dash, who was grammatically skilled both in the Bengal Language, and the mixed dialects, and understood well enough the Shamscrit language.[69]

But giving this disproportionate importance to Lebedev's one year of absence in the papers is as unncessary as is to rely on a Russian novel which invented one fictitions teacher of Lebedev to explain Lebedev's sudden proficicency in Sanskrit and Bengali.[70] The violinist was during this time simply transforming himself into a linguist. He was struggling 'to learn the Bengali and the General mixed languages of Hindusthan and as far as possible Sanskrit', because without them any progress in Indological studies was impossible in India. Together with the learning of language Lebedev had 'translated a short but useful dictionary, wrote several dialogues, and a part of the calendar (3 months) . . . including the four initial processes of arithmetic.' He also 'translated . . . extracts of heroic poetry written by Bharat Chandra Ray'. Further, the '*necessity of a review of actuality* also made' him 'translate two English comedies, one named "Disguise" and the other "Love is the Best Doctor" into Bengali in general an [*sic*] useful language, *so that truth will triumph over falsehood*'(italics added). He 'wrote down under Bengali words their sense and pronunciation in Russian. Without this . . . even by educated good-hearted citizens who read only pleasing descriptions by honest commoner, a sweet-tongued story may be regarded as foolish, as unkempt, fluffy, solid and dirty.'[71] Elsewhere Lebedev has confessed that he took the help of his teachers in translating the two plays from English into Bengali.[72]

These biographical details are necessary to put in perspective the imaginativeness of Lebedev's efforts. What was the situation in India when Lebedev was perfecting his knowledge of Bengali and Sanskrit? One scholar says not without reason, that 'Between 1795 and the last quarter of the nineteenth century Bengal witnessed what was termed, even in its own time, a "Renaissance"'.[73] But Lebedev predates it. So, for Kemp the special value of Lebedev's work (*Bezpristrastnoe*) lay in the fact that while for the period 'maturing in the eighteen-twenties . . . there is very rich material . . . social documentation for the end of the XVIII century is much more limited'. The East India Company barred 'the possibility of frequent observers'; press was controlled; and anyway 'concerned itself solely with commerce and gossip of the English settlement'. Independent 'Indian-owned newspapers' did not exist, and 'a great deal of news-paper material relating to those years is said to have perished'. In European affairs 'military affairs dominated', and anyway interest was focused 'on affairs outside Bengal'.

What Kemp insinuates is that Lebedev filled a much needed gap in social history. More so because in his writings there is no reference to 'an anglophile middle class with a distinct ideology, such as twenty or thirty years later is so clearly apparent'; nor is there any vestiges of 'those partially westernized, waveringly anti-British "radicals" who gathered round the first vernacular press'. Yet Lebedev could also diagnose the early signs of a tension in the 'distinct Bengali sentiment', between 'a deep rooted resistance to cultural domination' and the opposing desire 'to adapt to the new and accommodate interests'. He detected signs of 'local interest in western education' that was not generated by 'intentional propaganda from without'. He came across people who were neither in service of the Company nor in business with it 'but had studied English on their own account while inspiring Lebedev himself with a tremendous love for Bengali language and literature'.[74]

The picture above may be a little idealized. For we know that in Calcutta the first sections of people who learnt English were those who had a commercial axe to grind with the Company and its officials; and the Bengali culture and literature that were taking shape under contact with the Englishmen was of a very low standard. From the second half of the eighteenth century to the second half of the nineteenth century, from Krishnanagar in the north to the urban centres of the nascent city of Calcutta on the side of river Hooghly, a very light kind of *jātrā* of folk theatre and religious ballads called *pāncāli*, and a vulgar type of combative poetry called *kobigān* purveyed by poetasters patronized by the *noveau riche* were the dominant forms of literature.[75] The Anglophile middle class Kemp speaks of, who detested even the new Bengalee literature, had not come into existence. Actually it is these considerations which put Lebedev's efforts in perspective. One may consider the view of a historian of Bengali drama regarding Lebedev's choice of the plays:

> The reason why the Russian used English plays translated into Bengali for his performances instead of original plays in the vernacular, was probably that there were no good Bengali dramas to be found as early as 1795. . . . In a critical review . . . Rājendra Lāl Mitra wrote in his journal *Bibhidhārtha Samgraha* of 1860 that he had read thirty four older Bengali plays, but he did not mention the titles of any one of them. . . . It is said that the poet Īsvar Chandra Gupta had a profound contempt for all the dramas of his own day . . . the eighth issue of Rājā Rām Mohan Rāy's newspaper *Sambad Kaumudī* of 1821 contains a criticism of an old Bengali drama. . . .[76]

The want of good plays was matched by that of attitude. One may be curious about how, a number of decades after Lebedev's translations of Bengali plays, the new English educated middle class was looking at what Lebedev called 'Bengali in general an [*sic*] useful language'. It can be best found in a satirical piece by great novelist-cum-essayist Bankimchandra Chattopadhyay (1838–94), written at least eighty years later, as the last but one piece in a book called *Lokarahasya*, written between 1886 and 1887. There a highly educated and sophisticated Bengali *babu* is shown to rail at his wife for reading Bengali books, because they were 'immoral, obscene, filthy', and because after reading them one gets 'demoralized'.[77] If even after eight decades this was the attitude to creative writing or translation in Bengali, it is not difficult to imagine how path breaking Lebedev's venture was. To understand this we pose the following questions about the reasons Lebedev gave of his translation of the two comedies:

(i) What is the *necessity of a review of the actuality*, which Lebedev speaks of, Bengali language being otherwise '*in general an* [sic] *useful language*'?

(ii) What 'truth' did Lebedev want to triumph over which 'falsehood'? Should we judge the question in the backdrop of the description of Bengali as '*in general an* [sic] *useful language*'?

(iii) Without what 'even by educated good hearted citizens who read only pleasing descriptions by honest commoners, a sweet tongued story may be regarded as unkempt, fluffy, solid [*sic*] and dirty, instead of holy and sanctified measure?'

To answer these questions we have to go beyond Lebedev's oeuvre —including the dictionary, avowed translation of Bhārat Candra Ray's poem, 'Vidyāsundar',[78] and the plays—to locate these efforts in the context of Russian and British Indology; contemporary realities of linguistics, lexicography and translations. We begin with *GPMEID*.

The Lexicographical Turn and A Curious Grammar Book

Lebedev's *Grammar* needs also to be seen more in terms of its context and intentions than its achievements, though a modern lexicographical analysis of the work would reveal its unappreciated value. Mindful of the fact that Soviet appraisal of the book differs widely from that of British and Indian scholarship, and that appreciations of the book have been ridden with differences of competing 'Orientalist' and postcolonial responses, we begin with the title page of the *Grammar*, which tells much about its contents. We know that Lebedev wanted to write a grammar for Sanskrit as well as local dialects, their compound words (*samāsas*), circumlocutory phrases and 'dialogues of the mixed Indian dialects commonly called Moors or Morish on daily useful subjects' for the benefit of the Europeans.[79] The whole book is unfortunately written rather haphazardly, as may be seen from the sequence of the sections. Again, grammatical differences between languages, like in the cases of conjugation of verbs, are shown rather confusingly under three heads: 'common mixed dialect', 'civil mixed dialect', and English Tongue, while dialogues are exemplified in 'the mixed Indian dialect', 'the English Tongue', and 'the Civil Shamskrit Bengal Language'.[80]

In the context of the linguistic situation in Calcutta, the attempt was nothing short of remarkable, particularly from a professional

Russian violinist and music teacher. Yet contemporary European Orientalist scholars tore *GPMEID* into shreds. For example, an anonymous reviewer in the *Asiatic Annual Register* derided Lebedev not only for taking on the earlier grammarians, including Jones, but also for 'the *singular title* . . . to his still more singular work'. While forgetting to 'inform' the readers 'what and how many languages he proposes to treat of', and flaunting a stanza from Vidyāsundar on the title page, *GPMEID* contained many more lexicographical oddities. One was that the grammatical rules were made 'applicable solely to Moorish tongue'; and in the section on vocabulary, styling a column head as 'The Civil Shamskrit Bengal Language' was comparable to 'supposing an Italian vocabulary to be styled one of the civil Latin Italian Language'. The reviewer wondered what Lebedev meant by his claim that 'the languages he treats of, are spoken in all eastern countries'; still more 'what reference his perplexed arrangement bears to the profound and philosophical system of Hindu grammarians'; and even more, and most importantly 'what portion of his work is calculated to facilitate the acquisition of the Sanscrit language'. While conceding that 'Hindustanee grammars', excepting that by John Gilchrist were 'unquestionably very defective publications', the reviewer vouched that a beginner would have 'got more useful information from either [Richard] Hadley's or [John] Ferguson's, than from Lebedev's.' Defending Jones from the attacks of one 'whose observations originate in mistaking Bengal pronunciation for a fit standard of orthography, whilst Sir William has adopted the more classic elocution of Benares and Mathura', was unnecessary.[81] Christophe Adelung, the famous German linguist, also found no enlightenment about Indian languages from the book.[82] In a subsequent publication he opined that 'this volume contains scarcely anything which its long title promises'.[83] Grierson said about *GPMEID* that, 'Not only is its system of transliteration detestably incorrect, but so is the whole account of the grammatical structure of the language'.[84] Later he went much further to comment that from the evidence provided by *GPMEID*, 'his knowledge of Hindostani must have been picked up in the Calcutta Bazar'.[85]

A linguist of Chatterjee's stature,[86] too did not view the work in a kindly light. He discovered no worth in the *Grammar* save its 'historical value'; and had only this much to say about Lebedev's efforts 'that his intentions were high and great but his actual performance fell very short of what he wished to do'. He did not think him to be 'a good linguist of both Bengali and the *Bazaar* Hindusthani . . .'. Lebedev's low competence in this language, 'which he calls "the mixed dialect" of Indian speech', was traceable to 'the influence of his informant, Golock Nath Das'. Chatterjee wonders that 'he even *had the hardihood to criticize*' Jones, '*whom he did not understand and who was far above the competence of Lebedev* as a scientific scholar' (italices added), as also George Hadley and John Ferguson, though he had failed to 'go beyond the narrow atmosphere of a Bengali debutant' in learning Sanskrit; and 'thought that the Bengali pronunciation of Sanskrit was the correct thing. . . .'[87]

Lebedev's Hardihood: Ferguson, Gilchrist and Lebedev Compared

The anonymous reviewer was not fair to Lebedev about the 'singular title' of *GPMEID*, because of its length and production of four lines of 'Vidyasundar' on the title page. The bilingual grammars of Hindustani in those days invariably had very elaborate titles, suggestive of the contents and the author's achievements, with adornments by lines of poems, as had Ferguson's and Gilchrist's books. The reviewer in the *Asiatic Annual Register* seems to have been unaware of the trend.[88] While wondering at Lebedev's 'hardihood' in criticizing Hadley and Ferguson, Chatterjee remains oblivious of the grammarians' war in the late eighteenth and early nineteenth century in India, and of the fact that Hadley too was debunked by Gilchrist. In his bid to 'corner the vernacular market'[89] Gilchrist labelled Hadley as an 'unqualified poacher in the field of Hindoostanee philology', his *Grammar* as representing a 'double imposition of wheedling people out of their money to purchase a mere Tom Thumb, by its alluring size and apparent simplicity, but also of their precious time'.[90]

Chatterjee was fully within his rights in trashing Lebedev's worth as a grammarian and lexicographer, as also in rating the linguistic works of German-Dutch scholar J.J. Ketelaer and Portuguese scholar Frey Manoel da Assumpcam (both published in 1743), and British students of Hindustani like Hadley and Ferguson above Lebedev for being more 'scientific' in transcription. He was somewhat less legitimately denying Lebedev full authorship of the book, saying 'possibly considerable portions of it were written in the Roman script for his benefit by Golok Nath Das or some other person'. He attributed the poor linguistics and transliteration in the book to Lebedev's dependence on them. He also rightly faulted Lebedev for imagining that in contemporary Calcutta 'there was a "mixed dialect", which we now call the *Bazaar* Hindustani of Calcutta, and that the purer forms of this "mixed dialect" also existed . . .' Anyway, 'he had no idea of standard or correct Hindustani. It is a sort of mixed up Bengali with Sanskrit'. Chatterjee is convinced that the book does not merit any serious study 'from the scientific point of view', its only worth lying in providing to a 'discriminating research scholar . . . some valuable side-lights as to the situation for the *Bazaar* Hindustani as it was used by Bengalis and others in Calcutta, particularly in their dealings with Europeans'. Finally, Chatterjee thinks, 'his work can be looked as a linguistic curiosity; but it also shows the genuine desire of a restless spirit from Russia . . . thirsting for exact knowledge of the East'.[91]

Bongard-Levin and Vigasin too could not say anything more than *GPMEID* being 'one of the first European grammars of modern European languages', having historical importance for 'students of the Calcutta dialect of Hindusthani at the end of the eighteenth century. . . .'[92]

Later Indian lexicologists too have criticized *GPMEID* on grammatical grounds. Tej K. Bhatia complains that even though Lebedev 'developed an extraordinary sensitivity to Indian culture and languages this sensitivity failed to translate itself meaningfully into his work on Hindi grammar'. Even though he 'fiercely attacked his fellow European grammarians for their insensitivity toward Indian culture and for their inadequate data collection, his work cannot be judged as more than ordinary'. The problem with his grammar is 'a massive interference from Bengali and Sanskrit . . . caused by his language-learning experience in Calcutta'.[93]

A Relook at the Grammar

Perspective of Russian Indology

GPMEID and Lebedev's other linguistic creations can, however, be viewed from two other perspectives: (i) Russian Indological context; and (ii) the dialogues it contains. Regarding the former, Lebedev's was 'almost the first completely original and noteworthy attempt' by a Russian at studying India and Indian languages. Russian interest in Oriental languages, begun in the early eighteenth century for administrative and diplomatic purposes, looked more at its immediate surroundings, Near East and Far East than at India; and scarcely had any need for Sanskrit or modern Indian languages. Though Georg Jacob Kehr (1692–1740) had proposed an ambitious scheme for modern Indian languages, it was not implemented and till the 1730s the only instance of linguistic Indology was the specimens collected by D. Messerschmidt at Astrakhan, which included specimens of the Devanāgarī and Tamilian alphabets, and specimens of Telugu among other things. Of course, there were some secondary translation works that have been mentioned by Stacy. But prior to Lebedev, the only direct link of Russian Orientalism with Sanskrit was provided by German Orientalist T.S. Bayer, who settled in Russia and published his papers on Tibetan, Mongolian, Chinese and Sanskrit systems of writing in 1728 and history of the Greeks in Bactria in 1738. As Kemp points out:

> No further original work of any kind appeared in Russia before Lebedev's return. . . . Shortly after Lebedev's return F. Adelung settled in Russia and gained an international reputation . . . as an orientalist and even as an authority on Sanskrit. But there is no doubt that Lebedev was the first person then in Russia with any real knowledge of living languages, and with much more real knowledge of India and Indian literature probably than Adelung. In the proper perspective of his times, Lebedev's apparently slight publications contained a number of original ideas.[94]

Perspective of Dialogues vis-à-vis Gilchrist and Ferguson

One of these original ideas was packing the dialogues with social content and civility. Looking at phrases related to travel in a number of English works on India from 1773 to around 1882, in books including Ferguson's *A Dictionary of the Hindostan Language* of

1773, and Gilchrist's *Dialogues English and Hindoostanee* of 1828, etc., an Australian post-colonial theorist finds Lebedev's dialogues far more polite. He compares the dialogues quoted from Gilchrist, symptomatic of his 'imperious approach to speaking to Hindi speakers', with the far more polite dialogues from Lebedev. Peter Friedlander first picks up a set of Gilchrist's dialogues 'in the context of how to speak to a boatman in the Calcutta area', to show how curt and imperious they are.[95] The talk with the bearers of a palanquin for a local journey has the same aggressive tone. It does not come out fully from Friedlander's partial quotation. So I go back to the original:

> I want a palanquin (or a chair) and bearers. What is their fare per day? Go straight forwards. Turn to the right. Turn to the left (hand). Go fast. Go a little slower. Go there, -go on, -stop. Stop here till I return. I will be back immediately. Run on before, and enquire if Mr.—be at home or not. Stop, stop put the chair down. Is your master at home? Take up the chair and go home. Carry this bundle home. Hand these things out of the chair. I dine at Mr.—'s, you *must* go there in the afternoon [italics added].[96]

The dialogues have been imagined in a way that they will teach other sahibs how to be ruthless in giving orders in Hindustani to menials and attendants. All this, however, shuts out any space for social communication from it. Let us look at the nearly unilateral conversation at dinner:

> Come take off my boots. Bring some wine and water. Cool the water well. Bring dinner if ready. . . . Bring some bread. Give me a clean knife and fork. Give me salt, mustard, pepper, pickles, vinegar, wine, meat, a clean plate. Take away the things. Open the Venetians. Bring pen, ink and paper. Carry this letter to Mr. —'s and wait for an answer. Take this one to Mrs. —'s and if she be out deliver it to the porter.[97]

Gilchrist's only example of social communication is self-referential —'Do you know my name?' Even this short-lived sociation is cut short when the lackey mispronounces his outlandish name. The servant says: 'Yes sir, it is Pin'. He gets the flak immediately, 'No, Block-head, my name is Fin and is written on this paper. . . '.[98] Sahibs are taught how to let off the servant after the final spate of orders about making bed, brushing curtains, cleaning shoes, etc.[99]

The tone of these dialogues is predictably peremptory. Nicholas Dirks points out that the connection between language and power comes out clearest in the efforts of Gilchrist 'to order and teach the vernacular languages of Bengali and Hindustani'. Gilchrist was concerned with 'teaching of imperative forms and lexicons relevant to the daily intercourse with servants and other inferiors'.[100] Bernard Cohn says after looking at Gilchrist's dialogues in various editions of his *Oriental Linguist* that he advised the young Englishman to be as curt as possible with his communicants, who were mostly his servants. Accosting the servant as *sunno* (hear) to put him 'on his guard', the officer was not even permitted to say 'give me a plate', but was just to mouth the word 'plate'.[101] It suited the purposes of the British officers, who learnt Hindustani, 'to exercise power and, because of that, were not careful of mastering the polite usages of the language or its grammar'. For them Hindustani was learnt 'as a tool of imperialism; quite literally as a language of command'.[102] The same point is made by Lahcen Ezzaher, who says in the context of rhetorical relationship between the East and the West, that 'grammar writing which British orientalists carried out during this period constituted one of the ideological apparatuses of empire'.[103]

Friedlander notices this master-servant discourse of the conversations of Gilchrist, and compares them with Lebedev's, to drive home the point that 'not everybody's experience of Calcutta was like Gilchrist's idea of how people should talk in Hindi with the locals', as it 'can be seen from the dialogues in Herasim Lebedeff's work which was published in 1801'. He admits that Lebedev's grammar was 'so confused that it is not very useful'. Still what Friedlander gives *GPMEID* credit for is 'a series of dialogues which seem to be transcriptions of conversations, the tone of which is strikingly different from Gilchrist's dialogues. Lebedeff is clearly talking to people with deference and as his equals in status and intellect'.[104] Friedlander gives the following dialogue as an example:

To enquire about the road on a journey. Friend (brother)? Sir. Pray, does this road lead to Calcutta. No, sir you have come out of the road. How far? About a mile. Which way then must I go? Go straight forward until you come to the bushes, then turn to your left. Is there any danger hereabouts? None at all, sir, excepting the darkness of the night. Friend, will you do me the favour to shew me the way? And I will give something for your trouble. Very well, sir, then let us go. Now, if you will keep this path you cannot miss the way. Very well, friend, there is what I promised you for your trouble. I thank you, sir, and wish your safety to your journey's end. I wish you the same. Good bye. Farewell, sir.[105]

Friedlander's efforts remind one of the current researches on the relations between colonialism and grammatical representation. As Tejaswini Niranjana says in the context of locating translation in postcolonial pedagogy, 'The desire of colonial discourse to translate in order to contain (and to contain and control in order to translate, since symbolic domination is as crucial as physical domination) is evidenced in colonial-missionary efforts to compile grammars of "unknown" languages'.[106] This is why 'European missionaries were the first to prepare western style dictionaries for most of the Indian languages, participating thereby in the enormous project of collection and codification on which colonial power was based.'[107] This motivation is, as Richard Steadman-Jones shows, particularly reflected in Gilchrist's lexicography.[108] It is no coincidence that John Gilchrist, and his partners, were vital informants for government in their search for direct knowledge.[109]

Friedlander's pointer to 'many more *European* views on how to communicate in Hindi with people than that of the British as typified by Ferguson, Hadley and Gilchrist' [italics added],[110] is best explained by different objectives of the three Indologists. Steadman-Jones shows how in Gilchrist's books on grammar and pronunciation and other aspects of linguistics, personal goals, political objectives of British rule in India, and the career prospects of the young officers of the East India Company were enmeshed. Regarding the first, Gilchrist thought that should he succeed in persuading the British community to learn Urdu, 'he would be able to supply the demand for pedagogical materials'. But Gilchrist's linguistic efforts had also 'an important political dimension. Texts and images of the late eighteenth century did place a great deal of emphasis on the role of knowledge in the construction and maintenance of the colonial regime'. But while established 'Orientalists' like Charles Wilkins saw the way to this to lie in the increased knowledge of Indians, lessening 'the weight of the chain by which the natives are held in subjection', Gilchrist was more partial to the interests of the British Empire.[111] This is why in one of his earlier texts he expressed 'concern that the ignorance of native language is com-promising the administration of justice', as native officers were allowed to take court transcripts outside the law courts for translation.[112] Playing upon the anxieties of the British community was the best strategy in this context. The acquisition of Indian languages was shown as the best tool for the colonial authorities to apprehend the reality of the political space they inhabit'.[113] But at the same time, as Steadman-Jones aptly points out, 'Gilchrist's belief that the British should study Urdu was a product of anxiety. While it is necessary to use Indian languages in order to ensure that administration is effective, to speak them badly could be potentially humiliating'.[114] So, as Steadman-Jones points out elsewhere, in all his published work Gilchrist emphasized 'the practical benefits that would accrue to the Company if more of its servants spoke Urdu', while always seeing 'his linguistic work as a means of advancing his own personal fortunes'.[115]

True to these mixed motives, Gilchrist showed how apart from furthering career prospects of new recruits to the colonial bureaucracy this linguistic knowledge could nip anti-colonial resistances in the bud, and claimed 'if the hindoostanee had been sufficiently understood at Vellore by European officers, the dreadful mutiny would have been prevented from taking place'. For, the 'sipahee' (Indian soldier), who first intimated the existence of the conspiracy, would have been taken more seriously.[116] He warned that English officers' lack of proficiency in Hindoostanee would cost Britain dear, but assured that after his books only the truly idiotic will remain weak in Hindoostanee, as he had 'strained every nerve . . . to teach every youth there [in India] to think and act for himself, by providing a true hindoostanee key to all the learning which exists in that region.'[117]

Ferguson's dictionary-cum-grammar of the 'Hindostan' language was also designed to cater to the needs of the Company rule in India, both political and commercial. The dedication page sought to ingratiate himself with the monarch for removing one of the causes, namely 'difference of language', of the 'difficulty in governing . . . distant and extensive territories'.[118] Apart from helping governance, the dictionary also hoped to increase colonial trade and commerce. 'The advantages', said Ferguson, 'which Great Britain derives from its commerce with Hindostan are great and important. . . . To render the language of Hindostan familiar to the inhabitants of this country is the most natural and effectual means of obtaining this end'.[119]

Unlike Gilchrist, Ferguson has treated dialogues separately, as simply examples of the meanings of words in part two of his dictionary. Though apparently innocuous, racist overtones may be teased out from some of the phrases, from unlikely places. The words for amorous favours from a beautiful woman are: 'A beautiful woman gives me great delight. I desire a beautiful woman. Madam, I am your slave. The Bengal women are amorous. Concupiscence increases from bathing'.

Regarding tips about how to bargain for less sophisticated and coarser women, one finds in the entries under letter 'B' the meaning of 'Bandee' (f. Bondmaid). The illustrative Hindustani phrase, with English translation is: '*Bandeeka kittna mool dega?* (What price shall I give for the bondmaid?)' Another entry under 'B', 'Bander' (f. Ape, Monkey), does not refer to climbing primates, but to the looks of natives: '*Kissa admee! Bander moffeek nuzzer auta.* (What a man. He looks like a monkey).' The illustrative phrase for the word 'Akhteehaar', (f. [1]Power, [2]Command, [3]Possession) is, '*Sahebka akhteehaar me hey*, it is in the (British) master's power'.[120]

By real contrast, while Lebedev's *Grammar* was also 'calculated for the use of Europeans', it wanted to provide a master key to the hidden treasures of the classical Indian tradition. As he put it:

> Every language has a peculiar idiom; and without obtaining a fundamental knowledge of the alphabet and grammar, and being able to peruse the Shamscrit or Bengal books and writings, little can be learned from conversation with the natives of the country, or even from the Brahmens themselves. . . . If, however, the incomparable construction of their alphabet and arithmetic, and their distribution in all the scientifical [*sic*] branches of the original arrangements were fully understood, it would be found that they have higher pretensions to literary reputation, and a more fertile and inventive genius than is generally attributed to them.[121]

With such a different objective, it was natural that Lebedev's dialogues would also be different. Gilchrist's dialogues, couched in such rough tones, covered orders for daily need, like eating and preparation of food (31 pages); personal service including dressing and preparing for bed (18 pages); travelling nearby as well as long distance (43 pages); sports and other leisure activities (27 pages); 'the memsahib's' tackling of servants (miserly 7 pages); studying (14 pages); commercial transactions (13 pages); finding fault with and abusing servants and eliciting information (13 pages); time and weather (5 pages); polite inquiries (predictably, 2 pages); routine military activities (5 pages); and health, medicine including consulting doctors (40 pages, clearly biased by Gilchrist's original profession of surgeon). As Cohn rightly says, the 'sahib, following Gilchrist's instruction, would quickly learn a considerable range of admonitions'. So, quite appropriately, in almost all the dialogues the mishap, mistake, or stupidity of the Indian servant is the theme'.[122]

But Lebedev's dialogues, called sometimes simply 'Bath-chiet', or sometimes as 'Hokie-cot, or Bath-chiet', are concerned with diverse matters of social intercourse. In my count they contain: discussions between two parents about their children's behaviour (2 pages and 20 sentences); features of the four parts of the world and of London (1 page and 8 sentences); salutation (1 page and 14 sentences); matters related to buying and selling (2 pages and 24 sentences); heterosexual conversation during a walk leaning to the romantic and very civil (2 pages and 22 sentences); the benefits of early rising; 'Fancy dialogue' about weather and human moods (1 page and 12 sentences); the enquiries about the road on a journey (2 pages and 18 sentences); way of enquiring from a merchant about a bill (1 page and 12 sentences); and, finally, 'Military Dialogue', 'To exercise the battalion', and 'To address the officers, and the soldiers' (2 pages and 21 sentences).[123] The dialogues exude civility and politeness, with what Dirks calls 'imperative forms and lexicons' being in the minimum. Words of polite address like, 'Give me leave', Sir', 'And what pray, Sir?', 'if you please', 'your humble servant', 'pray', 'friend', 'please', 'madam', 'excuse me', 'brother', etc., occurred fifty-two times in a total of one hundred and eighty one dialogues. The word 'sir' alone occurs thirty four-times in the dialogues. One reason behind the difference of Lebedev's dialogues from the other grammarians is the social content of them.

Dialogues: From Civility to Social Consciousness

The pervasive politeness of Lebedev's dialogues stems from the fact that he chose items of discourse that were almost never between the master or the servants or the superior or the inferior, and very frequently portrayed diverse social settings. For example, in one dialogue two parents are guardedly criticizing each other's wards. The first parent has not taken care to give education to his son. The second has even got his daughter educated (an unimaginably progressive step in those times). The choice of education in general and female education in particular for conversational lesson at a time when it was not even on the reformers' agenda,[124] makes the dialogue path-breaking and shows the difference of Lebedev:

First parent: Give me leave to tell you, the education of children requires the greatest attention.
Second parent: Without a doubt, but to what purpose do you say so?
First parent: To this purpose that the bad behaviour of children frequently proceeds from the bad education they have received.
Second parent: This happens sometimes, but what do you mean by this?

* * *

First parent: That if you, like a good father, had well tutor'd your son, he would never have play'd such a trick as he has done.
First parent: Very well, so therefore, you have your daughter tutor'd well;
Second parent: Without dispute, and I should be very sorry had she done anything that approaches to this.
First parent: How? What do you mean by this?
Second parent: How? This means, sir, that we should not be too hasty in condemning the conduct of others; and that those who caressing [criticizing? A.M.] others, should look well at home, whether there is not something lame there. [125]

The very next dialogue was a bit of information about the four corners of the world. In late eighteenth century the wide world outside was impinging on the consciousness of Indians. It must have been a favourite subject of conversation in a pre-modern society coming into direct contact with the West for the first time; and Lebedev introduced the subject with almost poetic sweetness:

In the East, there is plenty of riches; / and also in the west. / In the north, there is plenty of snow / and of wisdom too. / In the south, / most vines grow;/ however, the inhabitants / do not drink so much / as the inhabitants of the north. / How do you like / England? / Why, Sir, / it appears to me plainly / that in England / there is a great deal of wealth; / and I do think the city of London / is one of the largest in Europe. / its building, / how do you like? / really, they surprised me, Sir. / let us go, and see then? / if you please.[126]

There is nothing surprising in it that dialogues that come under the heading 'Salam-korte', or 'To salute', would be extremely polite.[127] But Lebedev's ingrained good manners or civility spills over even in a dialogue between a customer and a shopkeeper, funnily transliterated as 'Coried-korna, are bechnega' (Of buying and selling). Here even hard bargaining is carried on in a big clothes-shop in a tone overcautious not to offend. The dialogue runs like this:

How do you sell it? How is it a yard? / It's really worth eight rupees. / What! eight rupees? Impossible, *sir*, do you think I am so ignorant? [N]o, *sir*, excuse me. / We sell equally cheap to strangers as to our countrymen. / Well, you speak very well *friend*. [B]ut I will give you no more for it than seven rupees. / It (price) cost me more, *sir*. / Will you take seven and a half? / . . . I ought not to take less than eight rupees; but as you are my customer I will give it to you. / *Carrier, do you hear, good man*? / go with this gentleman to his house [italics added].[128]

In this slice of trade talks not only are the shopkeeper and customer strenuously polite, but the shop-porter is addressed politely too, transforming Gilchrist's commandingly accosting word *sunno* by adding the epithet 'good man' to it (*Mooteia shoono (soono) bhela adme*). Now, when commercial talks are so polite, it is no wonder that talks between a man and a woman going out on a walk would be especially tender, as in the following example.[129]

The extent to which Lebedev is trying to spruce up his dialogues is evident from his translation of the word, 'Randee', a normally derogatory word for women, equivalent to slut, into 'woman'. Actually, he may have been infusing a kind of civility in them that was not existent in normal Hindustani forms of speech. It is in keeping with the serious nature of the dialogues, some of which are quite didactic, as in one about the benefits of getting up early from bed,[130] while in another about weather, where both of the supposed speakers joke about the bright side of even bad weather.[131]

Other Ideas in Linguistics and Indology

Kemp refers to many original ideas of Lebedev in the field of linguistics. Though all of them do not stand scrutiny, some definitely do. One is 'his enthusiastic attitude towards living "vernaculars" as the vehicle for the expression of ideas and emotions and for new literary forms'. It is in this sense that Kemp treats him as a pioneer of 'modern literary movements at the time when even Bengali scarcely possessed a prose literature', and as, together with Golok Nath Das, 'joint authors of the first artistic prose in India'.[132] If we remember that really at this time Bengali prose was not only undeveloped, but was not applied to artistic creations,[133] then not only does Kemp's claim appear justified, but we can also find a key to the meaning of the '*necessity of a review of actuality*', which made Lebedev 'translate two English comedies . . . so that truth will triumph over falsehood'. The last words may have hinted at the alleged inappropriateness of Bengali for such creative purposes.

Kemp also quotes from Lebedev's *Impartial Observations* to give him credit for being the first to call attention to the 'striking parallels between Sanskrit and Slavonic which were such an exciting discovery in the first decades of the XIX century'. In her view both of these pioneering ideas went unnoticed because of Adelung's intellectual dishonesty. He mentioned Lebedev twice in his book *Historical Sketch of Sanskrit Literature* (1832); and in his 'Review of Lebedev's Hindustani Grammar' (in *Asiatic Annual Register*, vol. 4, 1802) appended a patronizing footnote for him. But while penning his book *On the Similarity of Sanskrit to Russian*, published in Germany, in 1811 in Russian and French, he did not acknowledge Lebedev's earlier work in this area.[134]

Kemp claims, less legitimately, that Lebedev may have anticipated not only Friendrich Schlegel but even William Jones in locating the origins of Aryans in India. For, Jones had already in 1792 deduced from his discovery of a common Indo-European linguistic family the notion of a common original race whose branches had migrated towards Europe and India,[135] though he did not regard India as their original home. Further, contrary to Kemp's claim, Lebedev may not have been the first to discover 'that a language like Hindustani, which served so many millions in India and even beyond India, was worthy of serious study and development',[136] as Hadley, Ferguson and Gilchrist clearly predate him in this realization. But he surely was the first in Russian to suggest these.

Some of Kemp's encomiums about Lebedev's linguistic wisdom and insights have done him more harm than good. For example, from Lebedev's observations about the 'sameness of the sounds (of Sanskrit words) with the Russian alphabet', and his perceptions of similarities in the phonetic systems of the two languages, rules of combining letters or sounds, and rules of changes of words, she gives him the credit of being the forerunner of 'the analysis of sound changes and phonetic equivalents worked out by comparative philologists a generation later'. She also appreciates him for arriving, through such observations, at a solution of the problem of transliteration that had eluded other non-Russian Orientalists, though it was one of Lebedev's weakest points.[137]

Besides, Kemp turns Lebedev's confusions about the identities and origins of north Indian and eastern Indian languages into insights. For example, any cursory reading of the *GPMEID* would show that declensions of personal pronouns in different 'cases' (transliterated as 'karok'), persons, numbers and genders have been done for four languages. These are 'Jargon mixed dialect', 'Regular mixed dialect', 'Civil mixed dialect' and 'English tongue'. Active and the 'active conjugation of the analysis of the three persons' in different tenses, numbers, moods, etc., have been done for three languages, the first two of the foursome being meshed to create a 'Common mixed dialect'.[138] Again, when suddenly inserting a long list of words pertaining to words 'which may be of great use to Anatomists, Doctors, Surgeons and to Searchers', he does it for three languages, 'The Mixed Indian Dialects', 'The English Tongue', and the 'The Civil Shamscrit Bengal Language'.[139] Further, contrary to Lebedev's claim about the dialogues being given in a way that the reader will gain after learning them 'the advantage of speaking the Mixed Dialects', and the felicity of 'expressing the sentences by them, according to the idioms of the Indians', the dialogues are given in only one 'dialect' and their English rendering.[140]

This is sheer mess. But still Kemp parrots Lebedev's rendering of his teachers' view that since 'the main modern languages were descended from an older Sanskrit or Prākṛt, it was logical to look for further subdivisions in Hindustani languages or dialects in their local forms'. Kemp praises him for trying, even if 'not very successfully . . . to fix and record the norms of dialects of Hindustani', including the 'popular speech of Calcutta itself and a more polished or "classical" form of educated intercourse'. She guesses that for Lebedev the 'mixed dialects' of Hindustani may actually have meant 'a wider system of closely related languages and vernaculars, which was nevertheless to be treated as a whole, and to be regarded as a common national heritage without its grammar'. She thinks that Lebedev was particularly receptive to this insight into the 'unity in diversity' of separate Indian languages as the linguistic situation in India was somewhat similar to the existence of a number of 'closely related and sometimes partly mutually intelligible Slavonic languages', supposed by contemporary theories to have evolved from Church Slavonic, the hieratic language of most of the Slavonic world.[141]

Now, while Lebedev definitely had better understanding of the relationship of vernaculars in north and east India with Sanskrit than Gilchrist, who thought Sanskrit to be a linguistic hoax perpetrated by the Indian priestly class,[142] he was grievously mistaken, even after his initial learning of Tamil, to think 'Morish' or 'Murs' to be the *lingua franca* of the whole of India. Kemp glosses over this misjudgement by saying that 'he did not go into that question', while taking Hindustani as a 'common national dialect', and Sanskrit as the national classical language.[143]

Anyway all these insights did not save Lebedev's grammar, even though Nair sought to defend it from the perspective of the demographic-linguistic situation of colonial Calcutta. In his view when

Lebedev was active in the city, Punjabis and Hindustanis, not Marwaris, were preponderant among the upcountry population in the Burrabazar and the surrounding localities. 'Lebedeff's grammar is concerned with the spoken language of these upcountrymen, strongly influenced by Bengali. . . . We should be cautious in criticising Lebedeff' as we do not have much literary texts to depend on the period of which the grammarian treats of.'[144]

Anyway, if we remember that as late as in 1815 Daniebegov was wondering that in Calcutta people 'speak the same language as in the state of Pankhal [Bengal]', then one gets a true measure of the distance Lebedev had covered even in the sphere of linguistics as Indology, in searching for an underlying unity in north Indian languages. Now, before delving into his theatrical innovations, we need to know about the two English comedies that he translated, the first of which was staged.

Dramatist, Director and Producer: Two Comedies and Their Authorship

The sources of the two comedies, *The Disguise*, and *Love is the Best Doctor*, are as with nearly everything concerned with Lebedev, highly contested issues. About *The Disguise* Kemp thinks it was an adaptation from William Popple's comedy *Double Deceit or the Cure for Jealousy*, first staged in London in 1776. Its Spanish setting came from *Two Strings to a Bow*, a farce adapted in turn by Robert Jepherson, from an older play by Thomas Vaughan.[145] But Mamud claims that after inspecting the manuscript of *Double Deceit* (1736) in the British Museum he has found no correspondence either in the names of the characters of *Double Deceit* and *The Disguise*, or in the number of characters, and their gender distribution.[146] Though silent in the autobiographical passages in *GPMEID* or in the *Impartial Observations* about the original author of *The Disguise*, in the handouts about the play distributed on 21 March 1796, Lebedev himself introduced it as a three-act comedy written by M. Joddrell, and translated by him.[147] But the identity of the man with the surname Joddrell became contested. Vladimir S. Vorobyev-Desiatovsky and R.K. Dasgupta[148] after their archival researches quoted different persons, W.P. Jodrell and Richard Paul Jodrell as the author. Sisir Kumar Das identified three persons, 'Dr. Jodrell', Paul Jodrell (1746–1831), and Richard Paul Jodrell, and said the first and the third was the same person and author of the play.[149] Mamud found in the British Museum two books written by Richard Paul Jodrell: *The Poetical Works of Richard Paul Jodrell, Esq* (London, 1814), and *Select Dramatic Pieces*, etc. (London: Printed for W. Lowndes, 1787). *The Disguise* was part of the second book. But finding the name of the author only in handwriting in black ink on the title page and nowhere in print, and also shaken by Lebedev's mention of the author's name as 'M. Joddrell, Esq' (with an added 'd'), he also cannot decide.[150]

Regarding the authorship of the second play, *Love is the Best Doctor*, Kemp and Nair regard it as 'one of the many almost unrecognizable adaptations of *Médecin malgré lui*, without any further enlightenment.[151] Das regards this much staged piece as a play written by Molière named 'L'Amour le Medicine', first translated and staged in 1669 under the name of 'Dumb Lady'. The translation named 'Love is the Best Doctor', was also played out on the Lincoln Inn Field stage long before on 4 April 1734. Das thinks that it was this later English translation that Lebedev retranslated in Bengali.[152]

Apart from the sources of the two plays, the identity of their translator too has been contested. Those who have hesitated to give credit to Lebedev include such famous names as Suniti Kumar Chatterjee, Hemendranath Dasgupta, Sisir Kumar Das, Kājī Dīn Muhammad, Kannada playwright and producer Adya Rangācārya, etc. While Dasgupta and Muhammad say the translator was Golock Nath Dash, without assigning any reason, Chatterjee gives Lebedev credit for the choice of the play, but not for the translation. Das and Rangācārya say with similar lack of ground again that he and Golock Nath Dash had jointly translated the play. This anyway seems to be the most widely accepted position.[153] Kemp also hints that he may not have translated the play, while writing that '[t]he Bengali dramatists completely rewrote the script, laid the scene in Calcutta, changed the characters into Indian roles with suitable Indian names and attributes, fitted in pantomime, and new humorous dialogues'.[154]

Credit for choice of the play does not say much about Lebedev, because he does not show much novelty or refinement of ideas here. As Kemp judges rightly, it was one of the 'Stock dramas of the English stage . . . constantly being revived and readapted . . . fairly typical of the theatre of that age . . . used over and over again by acting companies who adapted them *ad. lib.*'[155] But the controversy about translator's identity is unwarranted because Lebedev has in many places claimed both the credit for choice and translation in explicit terms. And besides taking considerable pride in the quality of his translation, he remembers his language teacher and other pundits for equipping him to do that, a sure enough sign that he did it himself. All this would be evident from the following words:

After these researches, *I translated* two English dramatic pieces . . . into Bengal language and having observed that the Indians preferred mimicry and drollery to plain grave solid sense . . . *I . . . fixed on those plays* . . . filled up with a groupe [*sic*] of watchmen, chokeydars; savo-yards, canera; thieves, ghoonia; lawyers, gumosta; and among the rest a crops [*sic*] of petty plunderers. *When my translation was finished, I invited several learned Pundits, who perused the work very attentively*; and then *I had the opportunity of observing those sentences which appeared to them most pleasing, and which most excited emotion*; and I presume . . . that by this translation the spirit of both the comic and serious scenes were much heightened, and which *would in vain be imitated by any European who did not possess the advantage of such an instructor* as I had the extraordinary good fortune to procure. [italics added].[156]

Apart from the impression given in the passage that Lebedev was closely following the impact of his translations on the pundits, one has also to remember his words that he wrote 'down under the Bengali words their sense and pronunciation in Russian', so that the thing would not appear 'as foolish [*sic*] as unkempt and fluffy, solid and dirty'.[157] In his 'Memorandum' too he not only stated that he translated the plays, but also that *The Disguise* was 'much contracted' in the process, because of the 'impossibility of filling up all the characters for the first time'. He also informed how the translation of *Love is the Best Doctor* was done in 'Superior Bengallie Language', and how to pander to the taste of Indians for 'mimicry and drollery', he inserted, in *The Disguise*, the subsidiary funny characters mentioned above'.[158]

But while questioning Lebedev's credit for translation of the plays, very few scholars have paid attention to the text of *The Disguise* in the only available translation. Madan Mohan Goswami, who browsed, micro-filmed and presented the manuscripts to the learned readers, informs that this play has two versions, one shorter and the other longer, both of which are kept in the Central State Archive of the (erstwhile) USSR in Moscow; and that while the one-act version comprises 58 pages and was translated between 1794 and 1795, the complete play, comprising 107 pages was done in English not after 1796. Goswami also notices that Lebedev took considerable pains to translate the original English play by providing Russian and Bengali equivalents of each English word, and giving their phonetic renderings in Russian. Each page of the manuscript has three parts, the original English on the left side, Russian in the middle, and Bengali translation on the right. His verdict is it is not impossible that Lebedev himself might have penned the unsigned, calligraphic manuscript, and also that 'Language-tutor Golock Nath Das and other pundits may have helped Lebedev in his work, but no native was the translator'.[159]

A balanced verdict on the case has been made a little difficult by the fact that the two Moscow manuscripts are not available in their original form, and unfortunately Goswami brought them out after unnecessary editorial interventions, which included separation of the English and Bengali texts; addition of punctuation marks in the Bengali translation that were not there, ignoring those in the English text, to facilitate easier reading of the Bengali translation; and addition of minimal Bengali translations in places where without them the play is not complete (as for example stage direction).[160] Mamud failed to gain access to the manuscript at the Moscow archive and to Goswami's microfilm, but found another manuscript of the full version of the play preserved in the Saltykov-Schedrin Open Library in Leningrad,[161] which after detailed textual analysis seemed to him to be in conformity with the fuller manuscript published by Goswami, and a reconstruction of the first draft. Since both the English and Bengali texts of the Leningrad manuscripts differ from the three Moscow manuscripts, he guesses that after the staging of 21 March Lebedev made the improvisations for future staging.[162]

Mamud argues that Lebedev was the translator of *The Disguise* from the syntactical arrangements of the prose, 'which is not of Bengali'. In the other 'samples of eighteenth century Bengali prose', 'whatever be the extent of arbitrariness in spelling, the paucity and irregularity of application of punctuation marks, and . . . malapropisms of Arabic and Persian words, the ordering of parts of speech and phrases conforms to Bengali idiom and speech pattern.' Accordingly Mamud cites some sentences from the Leningrad manuscript discovered by him that just cannot be written by any Bengali pundit. Neither is there any evidence of any emendation or refinement by any Bengali pundit in the text. From all this Mamud concludes that the debt that Lebedev acknowledged to Das or other pundits was more due to his respect for them, than to any real help he got from them in translation.[163]

But I think that even without any special pleading any casual reader could understand that the Bengali translation of *The Disguise* could not have been the work of any Bengali. A short passage would prove the point.

রামসন্তোষ : এত আমি সর্জ্জ করিয়া করে . . . (Ramsantos : After suffering so much for so long) . . . সুখময়: এক নির্ব্বুধ্যতা প্রেমেতে সমস্ত বিসয় দুর করিয়াছে, উহার দুরন্ত বাপের দ্বারায় (Sukhomoy: She has been rendered propertyless for her love by her wicked father) . . . সুখময়: এই এখন আমি হইলাম জেমন আমার উচিত ছিল করিতে (Sukhomoy: Now, I have become what I should have been). . . .

রামসন্তোষ : এই দেখ, তুমি চমৎকার হবে আমার মাথা আর পা অবধি নজর করিয়া এই বেলা অপকাসক্রমে (Ramsantos: See, you would be surprised if you take time to look closely at me from head to foot) . . . সুখময় : আর জখন একজন মনে হবে করিতে এক সুজোগ (Sukhomoy: And when some one would think of creating a chance) . . . ভোলানাথবাবু : প্রাণবন্দু! আমী পরম আরহ্বাদীত হইয়াছে তোমারে দেখে . . . (Bholanathbabu: I have been much pleased by looking at you) . . . ভোলানাথবাবু : সত্তি তাহার সুন্দর্জী আছে এবং সে অতি তুষ্ট আছে আমাকে . . . কেমন ঐ গরিব বেক্তী হবে চমৎকার জখন এই পত্র পাবেন । ও, ইহাতে বেস্ত করিবে উঁহাকে অতিবাদরুপ (Bholanathbabu: Truly she has beauty and she is much pleased with me.... How that poor man would be surprised when he would get this letter. It will disturb him uncommonly.)[164]

Apart from the wrong syntax, wrong subjects and objects of verbs, and wrong verb forms are certainly not expected from a Bengali pundit, whether as translator or as editorial help.

Lebedev as Theatre Producer and Director

This aspect of Lebedev's creative activities forms the subject of most of the conventional researches on him. After *The Disguise* was staged first as a one-act play on 27 November 1795 and as a three-act play on 21 March 1796,[165] there was no further staging of the play as Lebedev had to leave Calcutta as a victim of conspiracies of a number of people. How did Calcutta's first proscenium come into being and how did Lebedev first conceive and execute it? Fortunately for us Lebedev gives us many accounts of it. In the 'Introduction' to *GPMEID* Lebedev says:

> After the approbation of the Pundits [to the translation of *The Disguise*]—Golucknath-dash, my Linguist, made me a proposal, that if I chose to present this play publicly, he would engage to supply me with actors of both sexes from amongst the natives . . . —I therefore, to bring to view my undertaking, for the benefit of the European public, without delay, solicited the Governor-General, Sir John Shore . . . for a regular licence; who granted it. . . . Thus fortified by patronage, and anxious to exhibit, I set about building a commodious Theatre, on a plan of my own, in Dom-Tollah, (Dom-Lane) in the centre of Calcutta; and while in the meanwhile I employed my Linguist to procure native actors of both sexes,—in three months both Theatre and Actors were ready for representation of the Disguise. . . .[166]

After gaining Shore's permission, Lebedev first approached the manager of the Calcutta Play-House, the only theatre in existence at that time, for some of the staff of the theatre, 'but he refused, and with his friends laughed at the foolish venture'. Rebuffed, Lebedev 'returned . . . with a burning resolve', to build his own theatre 'in a hired house at 25 Doomtala which accommodated three hundred persons'. He also decided to become his own 'architect, the commander and manager over carpenters, cabinet-makers, bricklayers and other workers'. After the construction work was completed '*just like my fellow countryman Volkov of Yaroslav*', he 'tried in Calcutta, *as if in Moscow*, to decorate the floor reserved for staging scenes with painting according to Bengali taste' [italics added].

Even with his 'numerous cares and anxieties', he found time 'to teach the comedy business to. . . . Bengalees—three women and ten men.' After completing all preparations for production, he invited his friends to the rehearsal, who after witnessing this unforeseen spectacle spread the news 'in the city and to the suburbs'; and the public pressure was such that Lebedev had to 'fix the date [of the first show] without any postponement'. In the first show *The Disguise* was staged as a one act play, keeping in view the poor knowledge of Bengali among the Europeans. But audience reaction showed that a second show of the complete play was in demand. First, after 'every scene was presented without any confusion', there was, among the audience 'some murmur for the shortness of the matter which did not give full satisfaction'. Secondly, the gathering was such that even if the theatre had three times the capacity it would not have sufficed. Thirdly, Justice John Hyde sent him a personal letter inquiring if he 'had translated the whole comedy'. As a result of these encouraging signs Lebedev took the initiative of staging the whole three-act play on 21 March 1796 in his theatre, and emboldened by its success requested the Governor-General for permission to present both the Bengali and English versions of the play.[167]

The key to Lebedev's motivation in introducing the proscenium in Calcutta lies in the words 'just like my fellow countryman Volkov of Yaroslav' and 'as if in Moscow'. A brief look at the theatrical tradition in Russia up to his times is essential to get the full import of these statements, and to understand why Lebedev was emulating Volkov; why 'as if in Moscow'; and why he chose comedies.

Emulating Volkov

Like many other aspects of European modernity, theatre was not 'a cultural institution indigenous to Russia'. It remained exotic to the working class as late as up to the nineteenth century and to the aristocrats until the second half of the seventeenth century. Before that what Catriona Kelly calls 'revels and rituals' ruled the day.[168]

Deriving from either folk arts or both pagan and liturgical ceremonies, these were performed by 'peripatetic entertainers' called 'skomorokh', and though immensely popular with ordinary Russians, they were distrusted by the Monarchy and the Church, being finally driven to the outer regions of the country.[169] Royal patronage came only when after becoming tsar of Russia in 1645, Aleksei Mikhalovich Romanov (1629–76), partly to please his new wife and partly to mark the birth of their first child, mandated the court performance of a play based on a story from the Bible, and also ordered a clergyman to organize a small court theatre in Preobrazhenskoe, his summer residence.

Ecclesiastical dramas staged by church schools, borrowing freely from abroad in terms of contents, and characterized by amateurish and novice-like performances, also sustained interest in theatres till Peter the Great, early in the eighteenth century, correctly diagnosed the propaganda potential of drama, and tried to institute a popular theatre playing secular pieces. However, his coercive methods, while securing some hundreds of spectators, stifled genuine enthusiasm, till attention reverted to the court when imported ballets and operas became fashionable in Moscow and even in the newly-built St. Petersburg. The limitations of the attempt were that the actors were always non-Russian and the tone of the plays was 'strictly moral when prescribed by the Church and flippant within the royal precincts', both discouraging innovation.

School theatres also sustained the interest, till in the middle of the eighteenth century theatre at the royal court too assumed a new character, with plays that began 'to hymn the power and splendour of the Russian empire'. The companies invited to sing the paeans were predominantly foreign, and put on performances of different types, like opera, comic opera, ballet, commedia dell'arte and drama. But, finally, all these strands did not coalesce or cross-fertilize one another to create a tradition of Russian theatre staging indigenous Russian plays with Russian actors.

The real breakthrough is credited to Fyodor Volkov (1729–63), stepson of a Yaroslavl merchant and manufacturer. To organize a theatre he converted an old tannery, with his brothers, a student seminarist, and a barber, which in 1750 developed into a professional town theatre that sold tickets for admittance. But its cramped premises proving inadequate, a fundraising campaign was launched, and a new building, seating one thousand spectators, was eventually built. During its construction Volkov acted as an architect, painter and stage engineer; and thereafter became its director and its leading actor. Rumours of the success of the Yaroslavl theatre reached the ears of Tsarina Elizaveta Petrovna, who had the whole team and their support staff brought to St. Petersburg. Volkov's team performed Alexander Sumarokov's (1717–77) tragedy *Khorev*, and later his comedies and more substantial tragedies, and Volkov became the leading actor in Russia. The company was disbanded in the summer of 1752. But eleven leading actors including Volkov were retained in St. Petersburg, and some of them were enrolled in the Land Forces Cadet School, to be taught by Sumarokov. After they completed their course of instruction on 30 August 1756, the tsarina issued an edict which informed that a Russian theatre was already envisioned for which a particular house was earmarked, and actors would be 'put under contract'. The maintenance costs of this theatre were to be borne by the state; and Sumarokov was to be entrusted with the management of this theatre. The significance of this edict was that it declared the theatre a state institution, 'the public purse being charged with its upkeep'. Initially there were no women in the company, the female roles being performed by men. But in 1757 a notice was given for the recruitment of actresses for the state company, and the first actresses made their appearance. In 1759, the theatre was placed under the jurisdiction of the court department, which increased its autonomy. In 1761, after Sumarokov's retirement, Volkov became the director of the Russian Theatre, till his death in 1763.

The company's repertoire included tragedies by Sumarokov and plays and operas of Moliére; numerous works contributed by the Empress Catherine; and enduring satires written by Denis Fonvizin (1745–92), posing serious questions about the responsibilities of the landowning class and over-Frenchified manners of polite Russian society. The theatre itself, with encouragement from the top, had grown rapidly in popularity in all levels of society, with Tsarina

Catherine building a Grand Theatre, later called the Bolshoi, and the Imperial Theatre School. Major provincial towns now vied with each other to establish theatres to celebrate this new medium.[170] It is true that the origins of theatre in Russia owed to what Louis McReynolds terms 'legitimate stage'.[171] So that, even when theatres came up through private initiative the state controlled them. But still the theatre fever had caught on. Privately-owned theatres including those of serf companies proliferated both in the mansions of Moscow and on the landowners' county estates. Professional theatre companies also started appearing in the provinces in early eighteenth century. After their proliferation was countered by a 1775 decree on 'On Establishments for Provincial Administration', many theatres were erected at the initiative of the local administration. But, anyway, despite the statism in the envisioning of theatre in Russia, it was coming of age. It was evident in the exulting utterance in the introduction to the *Dictionary of Dramatic Arts* (1797): 'Everywhere one hears of theatres in the course of construction or already in existence, and actors of good standing are appearing in them.' In this universal enthusiasm for theatres, even in the towns without special theatres, public theatres arose on the foundation of serf theatres.[172] Of course, even after this spread, conservative tastes, characterized the stage for some time. These included eulogizing the tsar, monarchy or the Romanov dynasty as saviours of Russia, or Russification of historical characters.[173] But the stage for the stage had been irretrievably set.

Starting out on his journey in 1775, Lebedev must have seen much of it. Anyway he had taken Volkov as his role model, to become architect of the theatre and its director. The words 'as if in Moscow' shows he was replicating the Russian scene in Calcutta. Choice of a comedy for staging might have been influenced by the Russian tradition. As A.D.P. Briggs points out, not only in the eighteenth century, but later too, comedy was the forte of Russian theatre. 'Russia has no great tradition of classical, tragic or historical drama able to claim unalloyed quality and international renown. It was in the flourishing field of Russian comedy that artistic advances were soon made and then multiplied.'[174]

Lebedev's Bengally Theatre in Perspective

Whatever may have been the reason of Lebedev's experimentation with the Bengali stage, to get a measure of its immense significance, we have to look at the beginnings of theatre in colonial Calcutta. Modern Indian theatre was born in the eighteenth century out of the initiative of Englishmen in Calcutta, comprising East India Company officials, soldiers, merchants, and missionaries. They built Calcutta's first public theatre, 'The Play House', in 1753, which in a strange premonition of the 'volatile mix of performance, power, and culture that would mark the modern Indian theatre', Nawab Siraj-ud-dowla chose as an offensive post in his siege of Calcutta.[175] After this came the 'Theatre at Calcutta', inaugurated on 21 December 1773, with the expert guidance of David Garrick, legendary actor, manager, producer and playwright (1717–79).[176] Continuing enthusiasm about dramatic performances led to the building of another theatre, the 'New Play House', better known as the 'Calcutta Theatre', in 1775, financed through public subscription. Patronized by Warren Hastings, and others, the new theatre emulated the ones at Drury Lane and Covent Garden, back home in London, in its architecture, settings, machinery, staging conventions, and dramatic repertory; and survived up to 1801. New stages, both big and small, were built and started doing thriving business thereafter, though apart from the one known as Mrs. Bristow's Theatre (1789–90), all the others—like Wheeler Place (1797), Chandernagore Theatre (1808), Athenaeum (1812), Chowringhee Theatre or Public Subscription Theatre (1813–39), Dum Dum Theatre (1817–24), and the Sans Souci (1839–41)—appeared after Lebedev's Bengally Theatre.

There were, however, some important differences between these playhouses and Lebedev's theatre, sometimes missed by the historians of the stage in Calcutta, who like Rakesh H. Solomon locate Lebedev's theatre in the 'intercultural beginnings in Bengal', and link the production of a Bengali play simply to the spread of the culture of theatre among Bengali elites.[177] The first point of difference was that these 'Sahib' theatres were wholly British in stagecraft, with 'pit, gallery and boxes' and other paraphernalia.

Their alien ambience was strengthened by the fact that the plays presented were English, in which English performers entertained English audiences, and the running of the theatre down to the ushers and doorkeepers was done by Englishmen.[178] Of course, in a concession to European theatre architecture, Lebedev too equipped his play house with boxes, pit, and gallery, charged different fees for them, and announced the performance in an English newspaper.[179] But still he tried 'to decorate the floor reserved for staging scenes with painting according to Bengali taste', and the advertisement in the *Calcutta Gazette* too harped on the innovation of a 'New Theatre in the Doomtullah Decorated in the Bengalee Style'.[180]

Ramesh Chandra Majumdar justly wonders what the words 'Bengali taste' or 'Bengalee Style' signify.[181] Balwant Gargi thinks that it meant that 'the stage was decorated with red-and-yellow religious motifs'.[182] Ahindra Chaudhuri, a legendary early twentieth century Bengali actor, thinks that Lebedev may have decorated the stage floor with traditional auspicious Bengali symbols. Mamud adds that the word 'floor' may have meant for Lebedev background scenes of local motifs in the proscenium stage, simply because the locales in the adapted play were Lucknow and Calcutta, two Indian cities. He infers this from the fact that Lebedev employed a stage scene painter like Joseph Battle before the third staging of the play.[183]

But whatever these words may have meant, this was no mean achievement in an age in which at all the big or small colonial theatres 'maintenance of distinct European standards remained a matter of deep concern'.[184] Besides, Lebedev attempted many other innovations in the production. Not only was the cast revolutionarily mixed in a Bengali adaptation of an English play, but the show was 'to commence with Vocal and Instrumental Music', rendering an 'Indian Serenade', where to the musical instruments 'held in esteem by the Bengalees, will be added European'. More daringly, the musical ensemble was 'to set to music' the 'words of the much admired poet Shree Bharat Chondro Ray'. The added incentive was that between the acts 'Some amusing curiosities will be introduced'.[185] So the 'earliest known attempt to start a truly Bengali theatre for the production of plays in the vernaculars' was an intercultural package.[186]

Then why was not this effort adequately taken notice of? As Rustam Bharucha complains,

> What has happened to the Indian theatre since . . . Herasim Lebedeff . . . initiated 'the modern Indian theatre' with two Bengali adaptations of European farces . . . seems to be of no interest to interculturalists. Nor are they concerned with the assimilation of colonial models like the proscenium theatre, which have been totally transformed in the company- theatre tradition that flourished in all parts of India. . . . It is our 'tradition,' our much glorified 'past', to which they have turned. . . .'[187]

In a similar vein Solomon too decries discrete historiographic approaches in Indian theatre histories, dictated by particular historical and cultural moments, which hinder a proper appreciation of particular contributions in the totality.[188]

An objective appraisal of how important Lebedev's efforts were in the Calcutta dramatic world can rid us of such conceptual blinkers. We are not going into the details of how the machinations and manipulations of the officials of the East India Company and of theatrical entrepreneurs close to them aborted Lebedev's enterprise after only two performances. He himself has given a heartrending account of how a 'musician friend at that time not known as my enemy' recommended to him 'the scene painter Joseph Battle, who painted the company's scenes' and a few actresses 'tutored to make acquaintance with him'. Battle had become his partner by giving him false information and assurances, and with his accomplices, whom he had enrolled into the staff, ruined his theatre through innumerable means—physically destroying the decorations and before putting the building on fire, engaging him in false lawsuits, pressing false debt charges against him and even getting him arrested in one, to force him to leave Calcutta in a penniless condition and as a physical wreck. Lebedev himself attributed all this enmity and conspiracy to the competitive anxieties of the entrepreneurs of the Calcutta Theatre and their friends in the East India Company, as he had heard from many quarters that he 'won't get such help as will be accorded to the theatre run by the officers of the Company and members of the English nation'.[189]

But Mamud does not subscribe to this simple conspiracy theory.

In his view in contemporary Calcutta with its concentration of wealth and rapidly increasing non-Indian as well as Indian population,[190] it is unconvincing that the 'Bengally Theatre', with only two shows of a Bengali play in four months, would have been weaning away so many non-Indian theatre-lovers from the 'Calcutta Theatre' as to turn the English theatre entrepreneurs jittery. The 'Wheeler Place Theatre', which appeared in 1797, just two years after 'Bengally Theatre' was gutted, was not subjected to similar hostility. Considering the barbarian, mean, cruel and unified opposition that was meted out by contemporary English society towards Lebedev, Mamud thinks that it must have thought of him as a Russian spy. The decline in Anglo-Russian relations in the wake of Catherine the Great's policy of southward expansion and the resultant Russophobia of Britain which was heightened after Tsar Paul and Napoleon Bonaparte made a joint plan of invasion of India,[191] had increased the suspicion of the British about other Europeans in the port city.[192] Mamud shows from Russian sources how the Russian embassy in London got excessively curious at this time about British activities and politics in India, and how after Lebedev came here, they became hopeful of more direct and correct information. No Russian or other scholar has got any clue yet about Lebedev's connection with espionage. But Mamud thinks this was the main reason why he was so harassed, from his finding that Thomas Roworth, the boss of 'Calcutta Theatre' who was at the root of all the adversarial activities against Lebedev, was, at least in 1790, an 'Assistant' in the British Secret Department. The mean behaviour to Lebedev could be traced to the dilemma of the British rulers and mercantile groups, who were convinced that Lebedev was a spy, but lacked any positive proof. So they resorted to threatening and harassing him to force him to leave Calcutta. To buttress his point Mamud quotes a handwritten document of the British Secret Department, registered and sent on 10 June 1794, and received in London on 1 July 1795, where apart from Lebedev at least two other Russians are mentioned as possible spies. For Mamud all this suggests that Lebedev *was* on the list of suspects.[193]

But Lebedev's unfortunate exit from Calcutta harmed theatre in Bengal beyond measure. The next initiative was possible only after

1831, when Prasanna Coomar Tagore established the 'Hindoo theatre', which staged only English plays and plays translated into English. 'The first Bengali play to be performed at the Bengali amateur theatre was *Vidyasundar*, adapted from Bharatchandra's poem . . . at Nabinchandra Basu's theatre at Shyambazar'.[194] But it was of a completely different genre, called 'garden theatre'. There Basu 'organized various spaces available in his mansion' for 'a mixed audience of more than a thousand drawn from Hindu and Muslim as well as European communities'. The 'play ran from 12 midnight till 6.30 in the morning' on '6 October 1835 (some historians claim it to be 1833 or even 1831)'. It was a misnomer for a stage, as 'the audience was required to follow the actors to the various places, where scenes from the play were enacted'.[195]

This dramatic performance was in no way comparable to Lebedev's proscenium, though Calcutta had to wait for about three decades even for this. As Sudipto Chatterjee rightly points out:

> Lebedeff had . . . activated an apocalyptic clock that started ticking a patient countdown . . . to . . . almost eighty years later with the foundation of the National theatre in 1872. The endeavours of Lebedeff and Basu represent the two disparate factors—the foreign and the native, the Anglicist and the Orientalist—that would eventually determine and define the hybrid character of Bengali theatre.[196]

But Chatterjee's labeling of Lebedev's efforts as 'Anglicist' is problematic in the backdrop of Lebedev's approach to the Indian civilization, which is so distinct from what is termed as 'Orientalism in Reverse'.[197]

LEBEDEV'S ORIENTALISM

One good entry point into the nature of Lebedev's Orientalism is to compare his attitude to the Brahmin pundits with that of West European Indologists like William Jones. Teltscher, starting from Said's debunking of the myth about Jones of a scholar-saint as inadequate though correct, follows Ranajit Guha's insight, to show how the primary motivation of Jones in learning Sanskrit was his distrust of court pundits and his resolve to stop the helpless dependence of the Company on their perjuries for interpretation of ancient legal texts during trials. His denigration of pundits ended only after he conquered them, when his scholarship needed 'the ultimate stamp of authentication: pandit status'. In the 'narcissistic colonialist demand for narrative', the deceitful pundits were 'transformed into respected fellow scholars', as celebratory proof that 'the Other loves the self'.[198] In this self-serving strategy of recognition of the pundits, Jones was following the example of his predecessor N.B. Halhed, in codification of Hindu laws. Halhed in *A Code of Gentoo Laws: The Ordination of the Pundits* (1776), wanted to establish that his eleven Brahmin pundit collaborators commanded 'a degree of personal respect little short of idolatry in return for the advantages supposed to be derived from their studies'.[199] Jones also chose a committee for the compilation of his *Digest of Indian Laws*, the members of which were 'men of integrity and learning', got them entered on the government payroll, and particularly stressed the prodigious 'learning, virtue, memory and health' of Jagannatha Tarkapanchanana. Lord Cornwallis also lionized this man and the benefits expected 'from the Annexation of his Name as a Compiler and from his Assistance'.[200]

But though Tarkapanchanana was placed on such a high pedestal, the committee clearly had Jones as boss. And Lord Teignmouth took it as a measure of Jones's charisma that the exclusivist 'professors of the Brahminical faith' should choose 'to submit to the direction of a native of Europe, for compiling a digest of their own laws'. Teltscher shows the strategy to be overcoming the obstacles of '[E]xclusivity and secrecy', to create a situation where 'British expertise surpasses indigenous knowledge', and 'the pandits have been out-pandited'.[201]

But Lebedev has no such ambivalence regarding Indian pundits, simply because his conception of India was different.

Indians and their Culture

The premise of this different conception was that Indians were at par with Westerners in civilizational terms, if not higher. In the chapter devoted to contemporary Indian society in *Bezpristrastnoe*, Lebedev claims that 'Indians are far from being savages and have more right to ascribe that reproach to those who treat them more cruelly than the most bloodthirsty ferocious wild beasts'. Indians bore '*no resemblance to idolators*' (italics added), and recognized as savages those 'self-imposed newcomers who, to our misfortune, sacrificing the human race to their insatiable greed for enrichment devour up whole kingdoms.[202]

The italicized words above probably overstate the monotheistic aspect of Hinduism. But perhaps Lebedev could make such a sweeping statement mainly because, unlike his predecessors, he was not looking at Indians only in terms of their degenerate present, but also, and even more, in the light of their classical past. He strongly believed that Indian Vedas were not only older than the Hebrew scriptures, but were directly revealed 'from the creator of the world through the first man', and that the festivals of the Hindus are nothing but commemoration of that first communion. It is from this perspective that he gives in *Bezpristrastnoe*, a sketchy account of Hindu theology, Hindu rites and customs, science and social system through the lens of Indian categories. It does not mean that he was essentializing an India from her ancient texts. Rather, he emphasized that to present an authentic view of Hindu society these texts had to be read with current interpretations and the oral tradition. But, still, for Lebedev Indian culture was a living one, traceable back to its ancient sources. In words that we would find Tagore echoing many years later, he insists that even after continuous wars and invasions there had been no fall from that cultural pinnacle, and Indians had retained their pristine, if Oriental qualities. All the aberrations of Indian society, all the 'heathen' customs that had sneaked into it, were exogenously induced, 'by reason of the un-interrupted enemy attacks on their country, so that they are perforce almost obliged to forget their own humanity. Yet with all these oppressions and tyrannies committed against them, with all the deceptions born of them, they persevere in an undeviating virtue worthy of emulation'.[203]

In tune with his opinion that the defects of the extant Hindu social system cannot be explained in isolation from the effects of foreign influence and oppression, Lebedev accounts for the contemporary degeneration of the character of Indians in terms of the logic of necessary caution in their dealings with the colonizers:

> Although Indians . . . have a very tender conscience and are more inclined to uprightness and loyalty, nevertheless having been taught to do so by the treacherous foreigners trading with them, they are not ashamed to pay out the ignorant stranger with deceit. . . . They are not disposed to get the better of others . . . and have no need to envy any other nation, but by the example of foreigners dealing with them . . . they also know how to use the proper key to unlock the heart and water the pious souls of dissimulating politicians. . . .[204]

Lebedev and the Pundits

In the context of such empathy for Indians it is no wonder that Lebedev's experiences with, and attitude towards, the pundits would be different from that of Jones. It is best seen in the new light in which the 'exclusivity' and 'secrecy' of Brahmins is presented:

> In India itself it is not possible to get information on these matters (language, customs, rites etc.) except from the Brahmans, who look upon the Europeans who now live among them as . . . either inhuman persecutors or as . . . despised pariahs who are employed among them for fetching and carrying all manner of filth out of their courts and houses.

Lebedev informs that neither with Goluck Nath Das, nor with other pundits, did he have to pay for his lessons, as Brahmins do not put knowledge on sale, and that he recompensed them through lessons in music. According to Saha the reason why he did not meet with obstruction or intransigence from the Brahmins 'may be that unlike the then European scholars he regarded the pundits as teachers and not simply as clerks'.[205] Kemp thinks they accepted Lebedev for his zeal in bringing out 'an object hitherto unknown to Europeans', namely, 'the claims to recognition of their traditional culture' and 'a juster and more rational view of their beliefs and social organization'. Kemp pitted Lebedev's approach to acquiring Indological knowledge against that of Anquetil Du Perron, a pioneering European scholar of Oriental literature and ancient Sanskrit texts, whose studies were carried out '"en militaire", a pistol at his hand, a sword at his side'. He built up his famous collection of manuscripts through fraud, forgery, and Company help. But rather than fetishizing dead manuscripts, Lebedev, who respected pundits, laid considerable stress on 'contemporary interpretations and oral tradition'. For, 'Comments and interpolations were necessary for understanding'. Kemp thinks that his original ideas about the continuity of tradition, the interdependence of the study of ancient and modern languages, and the relationship between present quotidian customs and past tradition were not only rare in the eighteenth century, but anticipated later proponents of the value of the continuous tradition in India like H. Oldenburg.

Along with his respect for the pundits as crucial bearers of a continuous tradition, Lebedev was bitterly critical in his private correspondences of East India Company officials who posed as scholars and 'laid sacrilegious hands on India's cultural treasures'.[206]

The Wonder That Was India

Against the complexity of India's culture and civilization, Lebedev's Indological efforts appear largely amateurish. Apart from his *Grammar*, his main Indological researches are contained in *Bezpristrastnoe . . . or The Impartial Observations on the Brahmanian Systems in Eastern India* (1805); three manuscripts about Indian mathematics; and his translation of parts of the episode of 'Vidyāsundar', part of the famous book of verses by Bhārat Candra Rāy, *Annadāmangal. The Impartial Observations*, in its nineteen chapters, set in three parts, tries to capture the society and culture in eastern India. Part one of the book, about the eras 'Som, Ṛta Anya', seeks to enlighten the readers about the Brahmanical educational system established on the basis of true knowledge in the first lunar era. In its seven chapters it touches on: (i) the creation of the world; (ii) sacred monotheism and the indivisible trinity; (iii) the gods manifested to Indians in many forms; (iv) the stars and other celestial bodies at the start of the first lunar era; (v) the creation of all the worldly creatures; (vi) the start of the measurement of time in India; and (vii) the four Indians eras. The second part is about the basis of Indian knowledge derived from observation of nature during the primeval solar era running according to solar systemic laws and the second lunar era running according to lunar systemic laws named Dvāpar. The five chapters of this part are concerned with: (i) the divisions of the natural world; (ii) the division of the world into planets and degrees; (iii) the stars and other celestial bodies at the start of the solar era; (iv) the months and their symbols and the six seasons; and (v) the origins and ordering of tables in the Indian almanac. The third part is about sacred Brahmanical rites and cultural usages. The seven chapters of this part deal with: (i) sacred Brahmanical rites and consecration of children five times with charmed waters; (ii) temples and their decorations; (iii) main festivals of India and their spiritual celebration; (iv) the hierarchies in the naming of the Indian people; (v) the riches of East India; (vi) customs and usages of India; and (vii) Indian trade and commerce.[207]

Let alone being translated into English the book has been very recently rendered in modern Russian. But even from portions translated into English the affinity of Lebedev with Indian culture looks striking. The treatment of the Bengali-Hindu calendar is not only lyrical but brings out the responses of Indians to seasons with classic accuracy. The first month Boiśākh (April–May), is marked by 'pleasant weather—the South Malay wind . . . [and] fragrance of many flowers'. Jyaiṣṭha, the second, is known for 'the best apples in the world . . . called . . . Am (m) or Mango, and . . . many other fruits and flowers'. Śrāvaṇa, the fourth, 'is the equinox, the season in which night is known from the day by the night flower Kumud which grows with blue and white blossoms that open [up] in the night and close up in the day; while day is known from the night by the day flower Padva (Padma) with red and white blossoms that spread out at the day and close at night'. It is the month when 'rivers are so swollen with rain that in many places the land roads are impassable'. In Bhādra, the fifth month, 'peace falls upon the overflowing rivers from the rain, and a pleasant season begins', which lasts for several months, and is congenial for trade and commerce. Aśvin, the sixth month is known for 'the Great feast', which 'in honour of the almighty Wisdom called Durga is celebrated'. Phālguna, the eleventh month, is not only hot, but 'the insupportable monsoon wind . . . enflames the blood of all creatures and the life-giving sap in trees and sets fire to the thoughts in men themselves', with the song of the 'Indian thrush called Kokil', and the humming of 'bees and beetles'. In Caitra, 'the twelfth month, great abundance of honey and various other sweet things are gathered'.[208]

The seasonal cycle is followed by the description of the public festivals and ceremonies, and their essence. Lebedev enlightens that the Indians' 'reverence for the highest being has already been demonstrated in all above mentioned rites and festivals set up in commemoration of god's great mercies and in witness of their gratitude'.[209]

Apart from these, three manuscripts of mathematics, two of which Mamud says he has seen personally, betray Lebedev's extreme curiousness about Indian counting methods and mathematics, and a letter of his wife shows that up till the last days of his life he was engaged in preparing these for publication from his own press.[210] No Russian or Soviet researcher has commented on them. Mamud has seen, besides, two handwritten, self-contained slim books, presented to the tsar. The first manuscript, containing 72 written foolscap pages, has six chapters devoted to India's counting and measurement units; currency units and units of weights and measures, and various other data about Indian mathematics. The last chapter contains counting procedures in Sanskrit, Bengali and Russian. There is also a multiplication table together with the ways of reading it in Bengali, Russian transliteration and Russian. The second manuscript, contains without chapters 35 written pages, and by Lebedev's admission is mostly about *namata* (*nāmtā*—multiplication table) and *gunana* (*gaṇanā*—counting), prevalent in Bengal. It also contains one *ārjā*, or formula simplifying complex calculations in those days. Mamud has not seen the third manuscript, preserved in the Moscow Archives, among the collections relating to foreign affairs, but informs that it is no separate project, only the introduction to the first manuscript.[211]

The third item in Lebedev's Indological writings is the translation of *Vidyāsundar*. There is no doubt that he made the translation in Calcutta, because there is mention of it in his letter to Vorontsov[212] on 15 July 1797. But little light has been thrown on the manuscript by Russian or Soviet experts, except the information from Vorobyev-Desiatovsky that Lebedev copied the first part of the verse, and along with its transliteration in Russian, translated every line and feat in the manuscript. He also has informed that in the 85-page work Lebedev *had* also included notes on names of things and people and meanings of unknown words.[213] Suniti Chatterji insinuates that Lebedev did not translate it himself, as in the manuscript written by another hand Lebedev gave 'under each Bengali word its pronunciation given in Russian letters', with 'the Russian equivalent of the Bengali word', making it 'a very close line to line translation—really . . . a Bengali-Russian crib'.[214]

Evidently, this work remained incomplete, and anyway the totality of Lebedev's Orientalist oeuvre is not impressive. But Lebedev's 'curatorial' brand of Orientalism consisted less in its achievements than in its outlook and attitude. Confronted with 'the wonder that was India', Lebedev stressed more its civilizational affinity to Europe than its strangeness. As Kemp points out, 'Lebedev repeatedly introduces a subject with an expression like 'just as in Europe', or 'in the same way as we do'. This makes him 'an obscure forerunner of those comparativists who at least postulated a common historical background for Europe and Asia'. While the attitude 'is typical of certain Enlightenment trends in the XVIII century', Lebedev's lack of 'concrete knowledge of ancient history', made him adopt 'a mystical explanation of the similarities to be observed in myth and ritual'. But still his portrayal took away from 'Hindu custom the exaggerated orgy, sadism and senseless superstition', which 'missionary hypocrisy invested it with'.

Lebedev, Hinduism and Jones

To substantiate her argument Kemp shows how the Hindu Goddess Durga, the butt of missionary attacks for paganism, is sought to be likened by Lebedev to 'the mother of Christ called Usha Chasha, that is the Giver of Light, in whose honour the Christian Greco-Russian Church celebrates a feast on the very same day'; and how its image 'scarcely differs from the image of the Mother of God depicted by Christians. . . .'

Kemp also shows how public exhibitions of self-tormentation and mutilation, present in Hindu rituals, denigrated by European observers, were sought to be 'rationalized by Lebedev as voluntary sacrifice of saints, symbolically teaching the people the trials of those who desire to reach moral perfection and salvation in this life'. Kemp goes further to demonstrate how drawing these parallelisms further, Lebedev gives Russian equivalents for 'the rites of anointing of the East Indian Church', and also for the orders of Brahmins ('patriarch', 'archbishop', 'archimandrite', etc.) and Kṣatriyas ('despot', 'prince', 'president', 'chief of police', etc.). Kemp cites Lebedev's occasional references to instances of folk customs like libations to the dead, associations of rituals with seasonal happenings, harvests and cropping, to 'church feasts', or holidays to commemorate benevolent rulers and national heroes, which are nothing but 'reasonable' and largely educative dramatization of religio-historical traditions and moral ideas. She finally quotes Lebedev's denigration of the Europeans' double standards when testing them on the anvil of reason:

> The allegorical representations which the newcomers cannot penetrate because of their ignorance of the original Sanskrit language, seem strange to them; but the Indians have greater reason to be surprised at the strangers when they boast of their orthodoxy while forgetting that the Saviour himself set forth his teaching in parables.[215]

Of course, objectivity demands pointing it out that Lebedev was no pioneer while underscoring these similarities and drawing these parallelisms, and William Jones did it on a much larger and sophisticated scale. But, by the same token, if a lack of 'concrete knowledge' of ancient Indian and Western history is adduced as the reason behind Lebedev's naiveté, then the charge would apply with equal force to Jones. In his discourse 'On the Gods of Greece, Italy and India', Jones claimed that Hindu deities do not essentially differ from those of the Greek and Roman pantheons. Though Jones began by saying that he does not seek to demonstrate dogmatically any strict correspondence between the gods, later he threw caution to the winds, while drawing parallels between the three pantheons, identifying 'Rama' with 'Dionysos of the Greeks, 'Phoebus' with 'Su'rya', and 'Diana' with 'Ca'li'. Similarly in 'A Hymn to Camdeo', Jones thinks of Kāmadeva as 'evidently the same with the Grecian EROS, and the Roman CUPIDO'. With 'new and peculiar beauties' in 'his person and arms, his family, attendants, and attributes', the god, according to Teltscher, is not much more than a regional variant of Eros or Cupid. In a similar vein, in 'A Hymn to Indra', the king of gods in the Hindu pantheon is shown as feasting on nectar at his abode in Mount Suméru, just as the Grecian gods do on Mount Olympus. Likewise in 'A Hymn to Surya' the god is likened to Phoebus with his horse-drawn chariot, though his horses, unlike Apollo's, are green; and in a hymn dedicated to Lakṣmī, her birth from the waves is compared with the nativity of Venus.[216]

But there are a few crucial differences between the motives of Jones and Lebedev all of which place the 'curatorial' streak in Lebedev's Orientalism on a higher plane. This streak can be teased out by asking why were Jones and Lebedev trying to find these cultural similarities. Teltscher does not think that Jones's *Hymns* merely offered 'Indianized versions of classical stories'. She rather thinks that Jones 'tries to fix these myths in a familiar landscape', and chooses them because of their 'poetic possibilities' and the ease with which they could be 'absorbed into the English tradition'. Thus while tracing the English literary influences on the hymns,[217] Teltscher trashes the claim made by John Drew, in *India and the Romantic Imagination*, that Jones was not as much interested in Hindu myths as an alternative to classical mythology, as in finding out 'the common spirit which had inspired in these diverse cultures a not dissimilar pantheon'. This is because in making this point, Drew depended solely on 'A Hymn to Narayena', an atypical hymn, though even there the influence of Milton on the words is strong.[218] Besides, she shows that this practice of literary annexation of Indian myths and godheads becomes clearer if one looks at the set of prints, which illustrate Jones's essay, 'On the Gods'. While conforming to the iconic grammar and the tone of late eighteenth century East Indian paintings, the gods are framed 'with a fringe of exotic foliage'.[219]

Teltscher also shows how in the 'Hymn to Lacsmi', Jones makes the 'power/knowledge' frame of his researches amply clear. The first proof of this frame is evident in his advice that rather than 'misspending our time in learning the Pagan Theology of old Greece and Rome', Englishmen 'must consider that the allegories contained in the HYMN to LACSMI constitute at the moment the prevailing religion of a most extensive and celebrated empire', the industry of whose people '*adds to the revenue of Britain . . .*' [italics added].

The second proof is the shifting positions of Jones in the hymn. In the opening two stanzas he addresses Lakṣmī as a devotee in the second person, but towards the end of the third stanza, Jones takes on 'the extraordinary role of the goddess's adviser on colonial and religious matters', counselling her to facilitate the replacement of the 'wizard lore' of the Brahmins by the 'wand of empire' and by 'laws, by myriads long rever'd'.[220]

It is this power/knowledge frame that we do not find in Lebedev's Indology, even though its range and depth fall far short of those of Jones and other English Orientalists. According to Mamud the reason for this difference of Lebedev is that because of his Slav psyche he was free from the 'superiority complex' that the long memories of plunder of Indian wealth had created in the minds of Portuguese, Dutch, French and English people. The way Mamud compares Lebedev with Jones, and places him as an Indologist buttresses my point.

> It is incontrovertible that he did not have William Jones's weapons of expansive knowledge of languages and culture; it was only through this eternal Russian 'humility' with the help of which he came so close to India's culture and civilization. Among the foreign travellers to India he was possibly the only one who could be called 'the Fool', his value naturally being very small to English and German Orientalists. But to us he is venerable just for this helpless love . . . distinguished as a unique exception in the community of foreign Indologists for the pains he suffered for his love for India.[221]

But this singular traveller and Orientalist, after he left Calcutta in December 1797, heartbroken and penniless, was allowed to take only a small portion of his personal belongings, manuscripts and a few other manuscripts of classical Sanskrit treatises.[222] He was, however, taking with him his enduring love for India and his indomitable urge to present her to the Russian people. It was this compelling and possessing desire that made Lebedev suffer all the indignities during his journey to Africa, England and then back home,[223] and still preserve enough fire to establish the first printing press in Europe where Bengali type font was used.[224] Even in Russia he was not given due honours, being assigned an eighth grade job in tsarist administration as translator in the Asiatic Department of the Collegium for Foreign affairs,[225] making the pursuit of his life's work even more difficult. He is so much loved here probably because Bengalis love their tragic heroes.

NOTES

1. I am borrowing the term from Nirad C. Chaudhuri, *The Continent of Circe: Being an Essay on the People of India* (London: Chatto and Windus, 1966) (Bombay: Jaico Publishing House, 1974).
2. See Harsha Ram, *The Imperial Sublime: A Russian Poetics of Empire* (Madison, Wisconsin: University of Wisconsin Press, 2003), pp. 64, 77–8. From 'Oda navziatie Khotina' (Ode on the taking of Khotin) of 1739 to 'his penultimate ode to Catherine II, in which an Arctic maritime route is suggested' for Russia's conquest of China, India, and Japan, Lomonosov consistently pleads for Russia's eastward expansion.
3. Oaten, *European Travellers*, p. 41.
4. For travellers who came before and after them, see J. Courtney Locke (ed.), *The First Englishmen in India* (New Delhi: Munshiram Manoharlal, 1997).
5. Bongard-Levin and Vigasin, *Image of India*, p. 37 also see *Great Soviet Encyclopedia*, a translation of the 3rd edn., vol. 9 (London: Collier Macmilian Publishers, 1975), p. 75.
6. See Filip Yefremov, *The Travels of Filip Yefremov in the Kirghiz Steppes, Bukhara, Khiva, Persia, Tibet and India and His Return thence to Russia*, in *Russian Tavellers to India and Persia 1624–1798: Kotov, Yefremov, Daniebegov*, tr. and ed. P.M. Kemp (Delhi: Jiwan Prakashan, 1959), p. 45.
7. Kemp, *Bharat-Rus*, pp. 114–16.
8. Yefremov, *Travels*, pp. 87–9.
9. See nn. 30–1 of 'Introduction'.
10. See Indrani Chatterjee, 'Slavery and Household in Bengal, 1770–1880', Ph.D. Thesis, 1996, School of Oriental and African Studies, cited in Swapna Banerjee-Guha, *Men, Women and Domestics: Articulating Middle Class Identity in Colonial Bengal* (New York City: Oxford University Press, 2004), p. 19.
11. Yefremov, *Travels*, p. 89.
12. Ibid.
13. See Kamal Kumar Majumdar, *Antarjalī Jātrā* (Kalikata: Kathashilpa [1369] 1962); and a film based on it by the well known Bengali director Goutam Ghosh, *Antarjalī Jātrā* (*The Voyage Beyond*) in 1987.

14. Yefremov, *Travels*, p. 90.
15. See A.K. Ray, 'Appendix' in Ray, *A Short History of Calcutta: Towns and Suburbs*, Calcutta, Census of India, 1901 (Calcutta: Riddhi-India, 1982), p. 143.
16. 'Greeks, The', in *Banglapedia, National Encyclopedia of Bangladesh*, www.banglapedia.org/httpdocs/HT/G_0203.HTM, visited on 4 Decem- 2010.
17. Bongard-Levin and Vigasin, *Image of India*, p. 55.
18. Kemp, *Bharat-Rus*, pp. 112–13.
19. *A Journey to India by Rafail Daniebegov: A Georgian Nobleman*, translated from Georgian (into Russian), Moscow 1815, in Kemp, *Russian Travellers to India*. See also David Wileman, 'Review', of *The Travels of Rafail Daniebegashvili in India, Burma and Other Asian Countries, 1795–1827*, ed. L.I. Maruashvili, Academy of Sciences of the Georgian SSR, Vakusthi Institute of Geography (Moscow: Progress Publishers, 1969), pp. 103–4.
20. Wileman, 'Review', pp. 107–8.
21. Ibid., p. 107.
22. Ibid., pp. 103–4.
23. Ibid., p. 107.
24. Wileman, 'Review', pp. 107–8. This is anyway unfortunate and exposes the Cold War competition in the field of Orientalism. William Moorcroft was a selfless veterinary surgeon who along with George Trebeck crossed the Himalayas in 1811, without East India Company's help, to bring Turcoman horses to improve the studs and explore the possibilities of trade across the Himalayas. Both of them met with death on their return journey. See William Moorcroft and George Trebeck, *Travels in the Himalayan Provinces of Hindustan and the Panjab; in Ladakh and Kashmir; in Peshawar, Kabul, Kunduz and Bokhara, 1819–25*. Prepared for the press from *Original Journals and Correspondences by Horace Hayman Wilson*, First published, London: John Murray, 1841 (New Delhi: Munshiram Manoharlal, 2005).
25. Kemp, *Bharat-Rus*, pp. 112–13.
26. Bongard-Levin and Vigasin, *Image of India*, pp. 55–8.
27. Kemp, *Russian Travellers*, pp. 103–4.
28. Ibid., p.110.
29. Holden Furber, *John Company at Work: A Study of European Expansion in India in the late Eighteenth Century* (Cambridge, Mass.: Cambridge University Press, 1951), pp. 256–7.
30. Kemp, *Russian Travellers*, p. 110.
31. See John A. Lynn, 'The Heart of the Sepoy: The Adoption and Adaptation

of European Military Practice in South Asia, 1740–1805', in Emily O. Goldman and Leslie C. Eliason (eds.), *The Diffusion of Military Technologies and Ideas* (Stanford, California: Stanford University Press, 2003), pp. 54–5.

32. V.F. Novitskii, 'Voennye ocherki Indi', quoted in Morrison, 'Russian Rule in Turkestan', pp. 684–5.
33. Kemp, *Russian Travellers*, p. 110. The recovery of the actual place names, here and later, from Daniebegov's rendering of them is by Kemp. 150 versts are 99 plus miles, whether by modern or ancient British standards. But he was perhaps miscalculating the distance.
34. Ibid., pp. 110–11. Was he referring to the Urdu that he might have found the nobility speaking in Murshidabad?
35. Ibid., p. 110.
36. See R.N. Tagore, *Chhelebelā* (My Boyhood Days), Rabīndranāth Thākur, *Rabīndra Racanābalī* (*Collected Works of Tagore*), low-priced edition on the occasion of Tagore's 125th birth anniversary (Kolkata: Visvabhāratī, 1986–91), vol. 13, p. 712
37. Kemp, *Russian Travellers*, p. 112.
38. See Rabindranath Tagore, 'Jīvita o Mṛta', *Galpaguchchha*, *Rabīndra Racanābalī*, vol. 9, pp. 317–24.
39. See Tarashankar Bandyopadhyay, *rogya Niketan* (*Home for the Healing*), 8th rpt. edn. (Calcutta: Prakash Bhavan, 1969). Here the venerated traditional *kavirāj* has declared *nidān* even for his doctor son; and after a contention with his doctor grandson, which spans the whole novel, succeeds in making him realize that this was nothing but helping the patient at the terminal stage prepare for the life beyond. See pp. 7–9 and passim.
40. *Daniebegov,* in Kemp, *Russian Travellers*, p. 113.
41. Ibid., p. 115.
42. Ibid., pp. 117–18.
43. See Oaten, *European Travellers*, pp. 43–5.
44. Ibid., pp. 116, 119. Kemp deduces somewhat unwarrantedly from this account of resistance by the 'common people', supposedly tradesmen and artisans, that the way these were boastfully related before a visitor means that 'a tendency towards broad-based resistance must have been forming in the towns, foreshadowing the active part taken by artisans in the I857'. See Kemp, *Bharat-Rus*, p. 113.
45. Kemp, *Russian Travellers*, p. 120.
46. Ibid., p. 121.
47. See D.N. Majumdar and T.N. Madan, *An Introduction to Social Anthropology*, 4th edn. (New Delhi: National Publishing House, 1989), pp. 83–4.

48. See Sahni, *Crucifying the Orient*, p. 8.
49. For elements of the power/knowledge syndrome in Jones, see Teltscher, *India Inscribed*, pp. 192–228.
50. Suniti Kumar Chatterjee, 'Foreword', in Herasim Lebedeff, *A Grammar of the Pure and Mixed Indian Dialects*, 3rd enlarged edn., edited with notes, biographical sketch and bibliography on the writings of Lebedeff by Mahadev Prasad Saha (Calcutta: Firma K. L. Mukhopadhyay, 1801/1988), pp. xxiii, hereafter *GPMEID*.
51. See Hayat Mamud, 'Foreword', *Gerasim Lebedeff* (Calcutta: Paścimbanga Nāṭya Academy, 1995), n. p. for the books. It is a shorter Bengali version of the far larger book on Lebedev in Bengali written by him, titled *Gerasim Stepanovich Lebedeff* (Dhaka: Bangla Academy, 1985). I shall hereafter refer to the shorter and later book as *Gerasim*, and the original, larger version as *Lebedeff*. For independent and autonomous researches and scholars on Lebedev in India, Germany and Russia see Hayat Mamud, *Lebedeff*, pp. 13–60. A statue of Lebedev is in front of the Girish Park metro station in Kolkata.
52. Ibid., pp. 2 and 67.
53. Ibid. Much of the data in this chapter will be based on this work; though the interpretation will be my own.
54. 'Preface' to *The Impartial Observations on the Brahmanean System in Eastern India*, quoted in Saha, 'Gerasim Stepanovich Lebedev', (hereinafter Saha, 'Gerasim'); P. Thankappan Nair, 'Lebedev's Life in Calcutta' (hereinafter, Lebedeff), 'Introduction', in *GPMEID*, pp. i, xxxi-xxxii and 1–2.
55. See Mamud, *Gerasim*, pp. 9–11; Mamud, *Lebedeff*, pp. 69–72. Mamud quotes more modern Soviet sources to claim that Lebedev left Russia not in 1775 but in 1777, and not at the age of 25, but at the age of 28. See *Lebedeff*, pp. 24, 178.
56. Mamud, *Gerasim*, p. 11.
57. See Kalpana Sahni, 'Light Within: Foreign Exchange: Fiddler on the Loose', *Daily Times*, Saturday, 9 April 2007, http/ sajshirazi.blogspot.com/2007/04/foreign-exchange-fiddler-on-loose_08.html - 31k – visited last on 23 October 2008.
58. 'Preface' to *The Impartial Observations*, cited in Saha, 'Gerasim', p. xxxii; Nair, 'Lebedev's Life', pp. i-ii; Lebedev, 'Introduction' to *GPMEID*, p. 2; Mamud, *Lebedeff*, p. 74.
59. Mamud, *Lebedeff*, pp. 74–6; Mamud, *Gerasim*, pp. 12–14.
60. Nair, 'Lebedev's Life', p. ii.
61. Cited in Mamud, *Lebedeff*, p. 78, 'Appendix', pp. 395–6. This 'Introduction' slightly differs from the one reproduced in Saha, *GPMEID*.

62. Lebedev, 'Introduction', p. 2.
63. 'Impartial Observations', in Saha, 'Gerasim', p. xxxii.
64. Mamud, *Lebedeff*, pp. 214–15, and 386; Grierson's view in *Calcutta Review* (October–December, 1923) cited by Mamud, p. 263.
65. Mamud, *Gerasim*, p. 14; Lebedev, 'Introduction', p. 2; Mamud, *Lebedeff*, pp. 80–1.
66. 'Impartial Observations', in Saha, 'Gerasim', p. xxxii.
67. For advertisements of these concerts and musical performances see Mamud, *Lebedeff*, pp. 80–5; Mamud, *Gerasim*, pp. 17–18; and Saha, Gerasim', p. xxxiv. For Lebedev's computation of his income, its sources, and its purchasing power in contemporary Calcutta, see nn. 87–94 in Mamud, *Lebedeff*, pp. 181–91.
68. Mamud, *Lebedeff*, pp. 84–5.
69. Lebedev, 'Introduction', p. 3.
70. The novel *Gerasim Lebedev 1st. roman*, written by Vera Alekseevna Smirnova-Rakitina (Sov. pisatel, 1980), has Bhagat Das as the teacher of Sanskrit, and through Barranikoff this fiction has been accepted by some Russian Lebedev experts. See Mamud, *Lebedeff*, p. 91.
71. Lebedev's letter to A.A. Samborsky, the archpriest of St. Petersburg, in Saha, 'Gerasim', pp. xxxiv-xxxv.
72. See 'Preface' to *Bezpristrastnoe sozertsanie sistem vostochnoy Indii Bramgenov svyaschenuikh obryadov ikh I narodnuikh obichayev* (1805), cited with comments in Mamud, *Lebedeff*, pp. 91–2.
73. See Sudipto Chatterjee 'Mise-En-(Colonial)-Scéne: The Theatre of the Bengal Renaissance', in J. Ellen Gainor (ed.), *Imperialism and Theatre: Essays on World Theatre, Drama and Performance* (London: Routledge, 1995), p. 20.
74. Kemp, *Bharat-Rus*, pp. 121–3.
75. See Asit Kumar Bandyopadhyay, *Bāṅglā Sāhityer Sampurṇa Itibṛtta* (*A Complete Account of Bengali Literature*) (Calcutta: Modern Book Agency, 1998–9), pp. 265–75.
76. P. Guha-Thakurta, *The Bengali Drama: Its Origin and Development*, Trübner's Oriental Series, first published in 1930 by Kegan Paul, Trench, Trübner & Co. Ltd. (London: Routledge, 2001), p. 45.
77. Bankimchandra Chattopadhyay, 'Bāṅglā Sāhityer Adar' (Appreciation of Bengali Literature), *Bankim Racanabalī* (1954), vol. 2, 15th rpt., ed. Jogeshchandra Bagal (Calcutta: Sahitya Samsad, 2004), p. 4.
78. Bharat Chandra Ray (1712–60) was a leading poet of the eighteenth century, and Lebedev's favourite. *Vidyāsundar*, the first part of his trilogy, was and is famous for its lyrical eroticism.

79. *GPMEID*, title page, and p. 95.
80. Ibid., passim.
81. 'An Account of the Books for 1802', in *Asiatic Annual Register, or, A View of the History of Hindustan and of the History, Commerce and Literature of Asia, for the Year 1802*, London, printed for J. Debbett, Picadilly, and T. Cadell Jun. and W. Davies, Strand, 1803, http://books.google.com, retrieved on 11 October 2010, p. 41.
82. Johan Christophe Adelung, *Mithridates, oder allgemeine Sprachenkunde*, 3 vols: 1806–17 ('Mithridates or General Linguistics'), translated and cited by Mamud, *Lebedeff*, pp. 29–30. The source was first cited among Indian researchers by Mamud.
83. *An Historical Sketch of Sanskrit Literature*, from the German of Johan Christoph Adelung (Oxford: D. A. Talboys, 1832), p. 29, quoted in Saha, 'Gerasim', p. xlv. Grierson, *Indian Antiquary* (1903): 2, quoted in ibid.
84. Grierson, *Indian Antiquary* (1903): 2, quoted in ibid.
85. Grierson, *Calcutta Review* (October–December 1923): 84–6, quoted in ibid.
86. Suniti Kumar Chatterjee's *The Origin and Development of the Bengali Language* (Calcutta: Calcutta University Press, 1926), is regarded as the most authoritative account of the evolution of the language.
87. Chatterji, 'Foreword' in Saha, 'Gerasim', xxvi.
88. If *GPMEID* had a long title containing 183 words, including publishing details and four lines from Bharat Chandra Ray's famous verse *Vidyasundar*, then the title of John Gilchrist's famous book, *Oriental Linguist*, had 128 words, including 3 lines from poet Souda in Roman script with diacritical marks. Another book by Gilchrist, beginning with the curious but vaunting words, *The Hindee-Roman Orthoepigraphical Ultimatum* had 71 words in its title, while *A Grammar of the Hindoostanee Language*, had four lines of Souda in Urdu and Roman letters reproduced on the title. John Ferguson's work, *A Dictionary of The Hindostan Language*, has 81 words including publishing details. See John Bothwick Gilchrist, *Oriental Linguist: An Easy and Familiar Introduction to the Popular language of Hindoostan* . . . (Calcutta: Ferris and Greenway, 1798); Gilchrist, *The Hindee-Roman Orthoepigraphical Ultimatum* . . . (London: Black, Kingsbury, Parbury and Allen, 1820); and John Ferguson, *A Dictionary of The Hindostan Language* . . . (T. Cadel in The Strand, MDCCLXXIII).
89. See David Lelyveld, 'Colonial Knowledge and the Fate of Hindustani', *Comparative Studies in Society and History*, 35: 4 (October 1993): 670.
90. Gilchrist, *Oriental Linguist*, p. i. Actually pages i to iii are devoted to the busting of the myth of Hadley's scholarship.

91. Chatterjee, 'Foreword', pp. xxvi–xxviii.
92. Bongard-Levin, *Image of India*, p. 42.
93. Tej K. Bhatia, *A History of the Hindi Grammatical Tradition: Hindi-Hindustani Grammar, Grammarians, History and Problems* (Leiden, The Netherlands: E. J. Brill, 1987), pp. 90–1.
94. Kemp, *Bharat-Rus*, pp. 140–3; Stacy, *Russia in Indian Literature*, pp. 17 and 35; and Mamud, *Lebedeff*, p. 219.
95. John Gilchrist, *The Anti-Jargonist Or A Short Introduction To The Hindoostanee Language* (Calcutta, 1800), pp. 233–4, cited in Peter Friedlander, 'Travel Talk: Phrases for Travellers in India', coombs.anu.edu.au/SpecialProj/ASAA/biennial-conference/2004/Friedlander-P-ASAA2004.pdf, p. 7, retrieved on 1 October 2008. The same conversations are to be found in *Oriental Linguist*, p. 133.
96. Gilchrist, *Oriental Linguist*, pp. 134–5. The same dialogues have been reproduced in *Dialogues, English and Hindoostanee; for Illustrating the Grammatical Principles of the Strangers' East Indian Guide and to Promote the Colloquial* (London: Kingsbury Parbury, and Allen, 1826), p. 24 without capitals in the beginning of sentences and even for 'I'. Actually, sometime in his career Gilchrist shunned the use of capitals.
97. Gilchrist, *Oriental Linguist*, p. 135.
98. Ibid.
99. Ibid., p.136.
100. Nicholas B. Dirks, 'Foreword', in Bernard S. Cohn, *Colonialism and its Forms of Knowledge: The British in India* (Princeton, N.J.: Princeton University Press, 1996), p. xiv.
101. The first set of Gilchrist's conversations was published in the *Oriental Linguist* in 1798, which was reprinted and revised in 1809 and 1820. Bernard S. Cohn, 'The Command of Language and the Language of Command', in ibid., p. 39.
102. Tariq Rahman, 'The British Learning of Hindustani', *Pakistan Vision*, vol. 8, no. 2, pp. 19–20, www.pu.edu.pk/psc/journal/PDF-FILES/Tariq-2%20new.pdf -, visited on 13 November 2008.
103. Lahcen E. Ezzaher, *Writing and Cultural Influence: Studies in Rhetorical History, Orientalist Discourse, and Post-Colonial Criticism*, Comparative Cultures and Literatures series, vol. 18 (New York: Peter Lang, 2003), p. 66, cited in Kermit E. Campbell, *Rhetorical Review*, 2: (February 2004), http://www.nnrh.dk/RR/index.html, p. 12, visited on 13 November 2008.
104. Friedlander, 'Travel Talk', p. 10.
105. *GPMEID*, pp. 110–11, see also citation in ibid.

106. Tejaswini Niranjana, *Siting Translation: History, Post-Structuralism and the Colonial Context* (Hyderabad: Orient Longman, 1995), p. 34.
107. Ibid.
108. See Richard Steadman-Jones, *Colonialism and Grammatical Representation: John Gilchrist and the Analysis of the 'Hindustani' Language in the Late Eighteenth and Early Nineteenth Centuries* (Oxford: Blackwell Publishing, 2007).
109. C.A. Bayly, *Empire and Information: Intelligence Gathering and Social Communication in India, 1780–1870*, paperback edn. (Cambridge: Cambridge University Press, 1999), p. 167.
110. Friedlander, 'Travel Talk', p. 11. Friedlander does not distinguish between Russian and British as Europeans.
111. See Richard Steadman-Jones, 'Etymology and Language Learning at the Start of the Nineteenth-Century', in Piet Desmet (ed.), *The History of Linguistic Grammatical Praxis: Proceedings of the XIth International Colloquium of the Studienkreis 'Geschichte der Sprachwissenschaft'* (Leuven 2–4 July), pp. 189–207. Leuven: Peeters, 2000. http://books.google.com, retrieved on 11 April 2009.
112. John B. Gilchrist, *Preface* (*to A Dictionary of English and Hindoostanee, A Grammar of the Hindoostanee Language and The Oriental Linguist*) (Calcutta: The Mirror Press, 1798), p. xxvii, cited in ibid., p. 194.
113. Ibid., pp. 193–5.
114. Steadman-Jones, 'Etymology and Language Learning', p. 194.
115. Richard Steadman-Jones, 'Richardson's Barometer: Colonial Representation in Grammatical Texts', in Natasha Glaisyer and Sara Pennel (eds.), *Didactic Literature in England 1500–1800: Expertise Constructed* (Aldershot: Ashgate Publishing Limited, 2003), p. 156.
116. Gilchrist, *The Hindee-Roman Orthoepigraphical Ultimatum*, pp. vii–xviii.
117. Ibid., p. viii.
118. 'Dedication' in Ferguson's *Dictionary*, n.p.
119. 'Preface', in ibid., p. a.
120. Since the original work lacks pagination, page numbers cannot be given. The reader has to go by entries.
121. Lebedev, 'Preface' to *GPMEID*, p. 8.
122. Cohn, 'The Command of Language', pp. 39–40.
123. *GPMEID*, pp. 96–113.
124. At Lebedev's time there were few supporters of female education in India. Raja Rammohun Roy (1772–1833) was an exception in spite of the elitist nature of his educational reforms. See Henry Verner Hampton, *Biographical Studies in Modern Indian Education* (Freeport, New York:

Books for Libraries press, 1970), pp. 57–8. But his efforts started much later after Lebedev's departure. Jotiba Govindrao Phule opened the first school for girls of the low and untouchable castes with his wife Savitribai in Pune then in Bombay Presidency in 1848. It was also not before the 1860s that Manockjee Cursetjee, known enthusiast of female education wrote to Sir Stafford Northcote pleading for promotion of female education in India and establishment of 'The Alexandra Native Girls' English Institution', which was first opened in response to this letter in 1863. See Rosalind O'Hanlon, *Caste, Conflict and Ideology: Mahatma Jotirao Phule and Low Caste Protest in Nineteenth-century Western India* (Cambridge: Cambridge University Press, 1895), p.118; and *The Victoria Magazine* (London: Emily Faithfull) XI (May–October 1868): 185–6.

125. 'Bath-chiet dooay babes' or 'A Dialogue between two Parents', *GPMEID*, pp. 96–8.
126. Ibid., pp. 103–4.
127. Ibid., pp.104–5.
128. Ibid., p. 106.
129. For examples, see 'Bath-chiet. Firneka waste. Dialogue. About a walk', ibid., pp. 107–8.
130. 'Bath-chiet. Borgome bechonase ootna. In the morning from bed to getting up', ibid., pp. 108–9.
131. 'Bath-chiet. Mojlesie ak bath chiet. Fancy dialogue', p.109.
132. Kemp, *Bharat-Rus*, p. 144.
133. Examples of nascent Bengali prose before Lebedev are a letter written by Naranārayaṇ, the king of Cooch Behar in 1555; a letter written by Mahārājā Nandakumar to his son in the middle of the eighteenth century; Bengali books in Roman letters—*Vocabulario em idioma Bengalla e Portuguese* and *Crepar Xaxtrer Orth Bhed*—by Portuguese scholar Frey Manoel da Assumpcam and *Brahman-Roman-Catholic Sambad*, by Dom Antonio da Rozario, local Bengali Hindu Zamindar, kidnapped by the Portuguese, and converted to Roman Catholicism, all published in 1743; and *A Grammar of the Bengal Language*, or *Bodhaprakāśam Śabdaśāstram* for the benefits of the Englishmen (*firinginãmupkārārtham*), by Nathaniel Brassey Halhed, written in 1778. The last named book had only one example of prose from a property-related petition; all other examples were from *payār* metric system. But there was no attempt to use Bengali for literary translations. See Bandyopadhyay, *Bānglā Sāhityer Sāmpūrṇa Itibṛtta*, pp. 279–86.
134. Kemp, *Bharat-Rus*, pp. 144–5.
135. P. J. Marshall, 'Introduction', in Marshall (ed.), *The British Discovery of*

Hinduism in the Eighteenth Century (Cambridge, 1970), p. 15, cited in Christophe Jaffrelot, 'The Idea of the Hindu Race in the Writings of Hindu Nationalist Ideologues in the 1920s and 1930s: A Concept between Two Cultures', in Peter Robb (ed.), *The Concept of Race in South Asia* (New Delhi: Oxford University Press, 1995), p. 329.

136. Kemp, *Bharat-Rus*, p. 146.
137. Ibid., pp. 144–5.
138. *GPMEID*, pp. 32–8, 47–84.
139. Ibid., p. 95.
140. Ibid., pp. 98–102.
141. Kemp, *Bharat-Rus*, pp. 146–9.
142. Cohn, 'The Command of Language', pp. 37–8.
143. Kemp, *Bharat-Rus*, pp. 148.
144. Nair, 'Lebedeff's Life', p. xix.
145. Kemp, *Bharat-Rus*, p. 172; Nair, 'Lebedeff's Life', p. vii.
146. Mamud, *Lebedeff*, pp. 284–5.
147. Istoricheskii Archiv, no. 1, 1956, picture with p. 180, cited in Madanmohan Goswami (ed.), *Kālpanik Saṃbadal* (Calcutta: Jadavpur University, 1963), p. 6.
148. For Vorobyev-Desiatovsky, 'Gerasim Stepanovich Lebedev', ISCUS (Spring, 1957), and Dasgupta, 'G.S. Lebedev (1749–1817): The First Russian Indologist', *Oxford Slavonic Papers*, VII (1957), and other information see Mamud, *Lebedeff'*, pp. 280–1.
149. Sisir Kumar Das, 'Chadmabesī', *Gandharva* 4:4 (May–July 1962), cited in Mamud, 'Lebedeff', p. 282.
150. Mamud, *Lebedeff* 'Lebedeff', pp. 281–3, 285–8, 313.
151. Kemp, *Bharat-Rus*, p. 173; Nair, 'Lebedev's Life', p. x.
152. Das, 'Chadmabesī'; Mamud, *Lebedeff*, p. 282. Also see Stanley Hochman, *McGraw-Hill Encyclopedia of World Drama: An International Reference Work*, 5 vols., vol. 3, J-N, 2nd edn. (London: McGraw-Hill, inc, 1984), p. 36.
153. See Chatterjee, in Bireswar Bandyopadhyay, *Bāṃlādeśer Sam* (1972), p. 3; Dasgupta, 'Rangamance Pratham Bangālā Abhinay', in *Rūp o Ranga* (1924): 260-61, 'Theatre-er Kathā' in *Sonār Bāṃla*, Autumnal Issue (1945): 267, and *Sāhityer Kathā* (1946); Das, *Gandharva* 4: 4 (May–July 1962): 9; Dr. Kajī Dīn Muhammad, *Bāṃlā Sāhityer Itihās* (History of Bengali Literature) vol. 4 (1969), p. 2; Adya Rangācārya, *Indian Theatre*, translated by Arun Mitra as *Bhāratiya Theatre* (1975), p.145—all cited in Mamud, *Lebedeff*, pp. 276–8. Also see Sujit Mukherjee, *A Dictionary of Indian Literature*, vol. 1: *Beginnings—1850* (New Delhi: Orient Blackswan, 1999), p. 205.

154. Kemp, *Bharat-Rus*, p. 173.
155. Ibid, p. 172.
156. Lebedev, 'Introduction', p. 5.
157. Lebedev, 'To Samborsky', Saha, 'Gerasim', p. xxxv.
158. Lebedev, 'Memorandum', wholly excerpted in Mamud, *Lebedeff*, pp. 385–93. See especially pp. 388–9.
159. See Serial Fund No. 195, Archive Unit No.1, File No. 6075 (one act) and 6076 (complete), in Goswami, *Kālpanik Saṃbadal*, pp. 8–9.
160. Ibid., pp. 18–19.
161. Kept in the Indological records of F.P. Adelung as manuscript number 79.
162. Mamud, *Lebedeff*, pp. 288–92, and 298–9.
163. Ibid., pp. 279–80.
164. Goswami, *Kālpanik Saṃbadal*, pp. 74, 78, 80, 88, 90, 91, 92 and 93.
165. See advertisements in Calcutta Gazette of 26 November and 17 March 1796, in Nair, 'Lebedev's Life', pp. ix and xii; letter to Samborsky, where along with the date of staging he informs him that it was staged in one act and was also abridged 'because very few Europeans understood due to difficulty', Saha, 'Gerasim', p. xxxvi; Lebedeff, 'Introduction', in *GPMEID*, p. 6; and handout on the day of enactment on 21 March 1796, cited in Mamud, Lebedeff, Appendix, p. 407.
166. Lebedev, 'Introduction', pp. 5–6; also 'Memorandum', Mamud, *Lebedeff*, p. 399.
167. Lebedev, 'To Samborsky', Saha, 'Gerasim', pp. xxxv–xxxvii.
168. See Catriona Kelly, 'The Origins of the Russian Theatre', in Robert Leach and Victor Borovsky (eds.), *A History of the Russian Theatre* (Cambridge: Cambridge University Press, 1999), pp. 18–40.
169. A.D.P. Briggs, 'Pre-Revolutionary Russian Theatre', in Neil Cornwell (ed.), *The Routledge Companion to Russian Literature* (London and New York: Routledge, 2001), p. 64.
170. The foregoing account has been constructed from Victor Borovsky, 'The Organisation of the Russian Theatre 1645–1763' and 'The Emergence of the Russian Theatre', in Leach and Borovsky (eds.), *Russian Theatre*, pp. 41–55 and 60–8; and Briggs, 'Pre-Revolutionary Russian Theatre', pp. 64–7.
171. Louise McReynolds, *Russia at Play: Leisure Activities at the End of the Tsarist Era* (Ithaca, New York: Cornell University Press, 2003), p. 14.
172. See Borovsky, 'Emergence of the Russian Theatre', pp. 61–4.
173. Briggs, 'Pre-Revolutionary Russian Theatre', p. 66.
174. Ibid., p. 67.
175. See Rakesh H. Solomon, 'Culture, Imperialism, and Nationalist Resistance:

Performance in Colonial India', *Theatre Journal: Colonial/Postcolonial Theatre*, 46: 3 (1994): 337–40, courtesy http://www.jstor.org/stable/3208610, p. 338.
176. Kalman A. Burnim, *David Garrick, Director* (Carbondale: Southern Illinois University Press, 1973).
177. Solomon, 'Culture, Imperialism, and Nationalist Resistance', pp. 337–40; Nandi Bhatia, *Acts of Authority/Acts of Resistance: Theater and Politics in Colonial and Postcolonial India* (Ann Arbor: University of Michigan Press, 2004), pp. 35–8.
178. Ibid., p. 340.
179. See the photograph of the advertisement in Mamud, *Lebedeff*, p. 405.
180. Lebedev, 'To Samborsky', Saha, *Gerasim*, p. xxxix, and insertion in the *Calcutta Gazette* of 5 November 1795, Thursday, reproduced in Nair, 'Lebedev's Life', p. vii.
181. Ramesh Chandra Majumdar, *History of Modern Bengal* (Calcutta: G. Bharadwaj, 1978), p. 552.
182. Balwant Gargi, *Theatre in India* (New York: Theatre Arts Books, 1962), p. 108, cited in Solomon, 'Performance in Colonial India', p. 340.
183. For Chaudhuri's assessment and Mamud's own see Mamud, Lebedeff, p. 346.
184. Bhatia, *Acts of Authority*, p.12.
185. *Calcutta Gazette* of 5 November 1795.
186. Guha-Thakurta, *The Bengali Drama*, p. 43.
187. Rustam Bharucha, *Theatre and the World: Performance and Politics of Culture* (London and New York: Routledge 1993), p. 4.
188. Rakesh H. Solomon, 'From Orientalist to Postcolonial Representations: A Critique of Indian Theatre Historiography from 1827 to the Present', *Theatre Research International*, 29 (2004): 111–27.
189. Lebedev, 'To Samborsky', Saha, 'Gerasim', pp. xxxvii–xlii.
190. Mamud cites A.K. Ray, *A Short History of Calcutta: Town and Suburbs*, (Calcutta, 1982), p. 143, and David Kopf, *British Orientalism and the Bengal Renaissance: The Dynamics of Indian Modernization, 1773–1835* (Calcutta, 1969), p. 178 to show that in 1752 the estimated population of Calcutta was 117,744, including more than 4,000 non-Indians . And in the survey of Calcutta's population that Lord Wellesley ordered in 1801–2, 60,000 people lived in Calcutta proper and the population within a 25-mile radius of the city was 2,225,000. He assumed that in the last decade of the eighteenth century this number had increased at least fourfold. Mamud, *Lebedeff*, pp. 95–6, and 196.
191. See n. 21 of 'Introduction'.
192. See Chattar Singh Samra, *India and Anglo-Soviet Relations 1917–47*

(Bombay, 1959), pp. 3–4, Vinodini Terway, *East India Company and Russia 1800–57* (New Delhi, 1977), p. 9, Bernard Pares, *A History of Russia* (London, 1965), p. 328, and Captain Gervais Lyons, *Afghanistan: The Buffer State (Great Britain and Russia in Central Asia)* (Madras/London, 1910), pp. 100–3—all cited in Mamud, *Lebedeff*, pp. 97–102, and 196.

193. Ibid., pp. 102–3, and 199.
194. Ajit Kumar Ghosh, *Dinabandhu Mitra: Makers of Indian Literature* (New Delhi: Sahitya Akademi, 1998), p. 12.
195. Chatterjee, 'Theatre of the Bengal Renaissance', p. 19
196. Ibid., p. 20.
197. See Sadik Jalal al-'Azm, 'Orientalism and Orientalism in Reverse', Reading 8, in George Ritzer and Zeynep Atalay (eds.), *Readings in Globalization: Key Concepts and Major Debates* (Chichester, Malden: Wiley-Blackwell, 2010), pp. 54–7.
198. As Said characterizes Jones's academic purpose: 'To rule and to learn, then to compensate Orient with Occident: these were Jones's goals, which, with an irresistible impulse always to codify, to subdue the infinite variety of the Orient to "a complete digest" of laws, figures, customs and works, he is believed to have achieved.' See Edward Said, *Orientalism* (1985), p. 78. Ranajit Guha suggested that British historical research in India is traceable to its frustration with the 'collusive chicanery of native agents', who were hiding information from their colonial masters, and their resultant turn to the writing of their own history. See Guha, *An Indian Historiography of India: A Nineteenth Century Agenda and Its Implications* (Calcutta: Centre for Studies in Social Sciences, 1988), p. 5, both cited, in Teltscher, 'Sir William Jones and the Pandits', pp. 192–200, with the quoted comments.
199. See Thomas R. Metcalf, *Ideologies of the Raj* (New Delhi: Cambridge University Press, 1998/2005), p. 11.
200. Garland Cannon, *The Letters of Sir William Jones*, 2 vols. (Oxford: Oxford University Press, 1970), pp. 803 and 923, cited in Teltscher, 'Sir William Jones and the Pandits', p. 199.
201. Lord Teignmouth, *Memoirs of the Life, Writings, and Correspondences of Sir William Jones*, p. 314, and Teltscher's comments cited in ibid., pp. 199–200.
202. Lebedev, 'Preface' to *Bezpristrastnoe*, cited in Saha, 'Gerasim', pp. xlvi–xlvii; and Nair, 'Lebedev's Life', pp. xix–xx.
203. 'Preface' to *Bezpristrastnoe*, cited in Saha, 'Gerasim', p. xlvii.
204. Ibid., p. li.
205. Saha, 'Gerasim', p. xlvi.

206. Kemp, *Bharat-Rus*, pp. 127–30.
207. Mamud, *Lebedeff*, pp. 238–9.
208. Kemp, *Bharat-Rus*, pp. 155–7.
209. Ibid., p. 153.
210. Letter, written to the Emperor on 27 July, 1817, cited in Mamud, *Lebedeff*, p. 240.
211. Mamud, *Lebedeff*, pp. 240–3.
212. For Vorontsov see n. 56 above.
213. Vorobyev-Desiatovsky, 'Gerasim Stepanovich Lebedev', pp. 56–7, cited in Mamud, *Lebedeff*, p. 243.
214. Suniti Kumar Chatterjee, 'Foreword', p. xxiv.
215. For the quoted passages from *Bezpristrastnoe*, cited in Kemp, and her comments, see Kemp, *Bharat-Rus*, pp. 150–4.
216. See Jones, *Asiatick Researches* I: 256, 262, 265, and Jones, *The Works of Sir William Jones*, vol. VI (London, 1799), pp. 313, 315–16, 325, 340, 348, 350–1, 353, 358, all cited in Teltscher, *India Inscribed*, pp. 206–8.
217. Teltscher, *India Inscribed*, pp. 208–9.
218. John Drew, *India and the Romantic Imagination* (Delhi: Oxford University Press, 1987), pp. 45–82, cited in Teltscher, *India Inscribed*, p. 209.
219. Teltscher, *India Inscribed*, pp. 209–18.
220. Jones, *Works*, vol. VI, pp. 356–7, 365, cited in Teltscher, *India Inscribed*, pp. 218–19.
221. Mamud, *Lebedeff*, p. 225.
222. Saha 'Gerasim', p. xliii; Kemp, *Bharat-Rus*, p. 182. For details of the belongings and books see Mamud, *Lebedeff*, pp. 136–7, and 228–31; Saha, 'Gerasim', p. xliv; and Nair, 'Lebedev's Life', p. xxii.
223. See Mamud, *Lebedeff*, pp. 135–6, 137–45 and 155–9.
224. It is widely believed that the first Bengali typeface was used in Europe by its creator Charles Wilkins in 1808, in his book *Grammar of the Sanscrita Language*. But still there is no doubt that Lebedev's press became known all over Europe because of its type fonts of English languages. The proof of this is a letter to Lebedev from France as *Directeur de la nouvelle Imprimerie en letters indiennes á St. Pétersbourg*, inviting him to join a project to set up, with combined financing, a huge press for Sanskrit and Indian languages. See V.S. Vorobyev-Desiatovsky, 'Russian Indianist G.S. Lebedev (1749–1817)', in *Essays on the History of Russian Orientology*, Collection 2, p. 60, and Friedrich Adelung, *Mithridates*, p. 206, cited in Mamud, *Lebedeff*, p. 238.
225. For relevant documents see Mamud, *Lebedeff*, pp. 161–7.

CHAPTER 4

Aleksei Dmitriyevich Saltykov: Prince, Painter, Traveller

INTRODUCTION

A test case of the broadening of vision of nineteenth-century Russian Orientalism as a result of the Enlightenment and the first 'Oriental Renaissance' associated with the Romantics, is Prince Aleksei Dmitriyevich Saltykov's (1806–59)[1] representation of India, taking it to a high point unmatched before, excepting the earlier maverick efforts of Lebedev. A Russian nobleman born to Prince Dmitri Nikolaevich Saltykov and Anna Nikolaevna Leontieva in 1806, Saltykov enrolled into the diplomatic service with the Russian State Collegium for Foreign Affairs when he was eighteen. But after short stints in Europe and the Middle East, he tired of it and decided to spend his days travelling and painting. At thirty-four he took voluntary retirement and moved to Paris to pursue his new mission, and plan his travel to India, undertaken between 1841 and 1846. In 1848 he published a selection of his letters (*Pis'ma ob Indii*), sent to a family member during his India tour, in French. That the book, translated into Russian in 1851, caught the fancy of the reading public in Russia is no wonder. Already, in the backdrop of the Westernizer–Slavophile debate over the essence of Russian national identity, learned societies having Oriental Studies as an important academic concern were proliferating, and Sanskrit- based Indological works of scholars like Petrov, Kossovich, and Böhtlingk had made India a familiar name outside the confines of Orientology. Anyway, the book earned Saltykov the sobriquet of 'the Indian', and found several editions, as did his verbal and visual impressions of India both in his *Pis'ma ob Indii*, first serialized and later published in Moscow in 1851, and a series of sketches, published in Paris in

1853 (*Habitants de l'Inde dessines d'après nature par le prince A. Soltykoff*).[2]

A TRAVELOGUE IGNORED AND STEREOTYPED

All these factors, together with Marx's attention to Saltykov's representation of India in *Lettres Sur L'Inde Voyages* make the subsequent scholarly amnesia about this book and about *Dans L'Inde et En Perse*, truly surprising. Marx expected to see:

> At a more or less remote period, the regeneration of that great and interesting country, whose gentle natives are, to use the expression of Prince Saltykov, even in the most inferior classes, 'plus fins et plus adroits que les Italiens',[3] whose submission even is counterbalanced by a certain calm nobility, who, notwithstanding their natural languor, have astonished the British officers by their bravery, whose country has been the source of our languages, our religions, and who represent the type of the ancient German in the Jat and the type of the ancient Greek in the Brahmin.[4]

Actually, this quote gained for Saltykov a brief entry into Halbfass's *India in Europe*.[5] Otherwise he had been pushed to cold oblivion. Till date there has been just one translation of his travels and that too only of the portions relating to those in Punjab, the Himalayas, and Delhi during his second voyage,[6] though he travelled throughout India, described places and made extensive paintings of them.[7] Marginalized even in the discourses on Russian Orientalism, he is mentioned by Kemp only for leaving, some 'interesting observations', whose value 'decreased proportionally to other forms of documentation'. Kemp also remembers him for his caricature of 'the gloomy John Bull and the successful English 'shopkeeper', which were 'entertaining', and for the ridicule Saltykov allegedly heaped upon 'the triumph of the "shopocracy" over the broken feudal aristocracy', amidst 'the undercurrent of unrest in all but a minority of puppets and compradors'. She highlights the 'bored contempt' with which this aristocrat regarded the 'philistine narrowness, social snobbery and vulgar ostentation of the businessmen and officials who regarded India merely as market or a career' for otherwise unsuccessful young gentlemen. Kemp harps on the disgust with which Saltykov described British bureaucrats and speculators, all of whom were really 'shopkeepers'; 'pensioned rajas'; 'Parsi merchants' serving as factotums of the 'new masters', much 'like the Jews for us in White Russia'; and Dwarkanath Tagore's anglophile circle at Calcutta.

Kemp also shows him as one who saw in anguish ancient cities decaying; fine architecture crumbling into ruins; official indifference generating blindness about the aesthetic value of the old culture; narrow feelings of victorious superiority allowing the public display of the descendants of Hyder Ali and Tipu Sultan to viewers like captive animals; and the all-pervading officialdom stifling all differences. Desiring to present Saltykov only as a critic, Kemp misinforms that in spite of the artist's admiration for the natural beauty and exotic attractions of the country the changes brought about by British colonialism wearied him sufficiently to leave it without much sorrow.[8]

But Saltykov did not leave the country in hurry, but rather visited it twice to stay for a total time of five years; wrote a long travelogue of two voyages; and drew a good number of pictures, only some of which he produced in the album. And it would be difficult to classify the representations in the travelogue or in the pictures in the album,[9] drawn between 1841 and 1842, as either 'magisterial', 'exoticist', or 'curatorial'. Actually they are a free combination of all the stances, but with a redeeming aesthetic detachment that is difficult to miss.

Many contemporaries in the Anglo-Saxon world and even in India missed this 'exoticist' and 'curatorial' tone of Saltykov's oeuvres. In the *Westminster Review* of 1854, an anonymous reviewer rated *Voyage dans l'Inde et en Perse* even lower than a 'posthumous work on Western India' and another on 'Forest Life in Ceylon', the latter 'full of social sketches and sporting adventures'.[10] The reviewer blamed the limitations of observation in Saltykov's book on his exalted social stature:

> He traverses India throughout its entire extent, from Bombay to Calcutta, and from Ceylon to the Himalayas—always en grand seigneur . . . receiving the hospitalities of governors and governors-general, and having the splendours of barbaric courts displayed for his express gratification.[11]

Another softer review of Saltykov's travelogue on India also sees him as an aristocratic socialite. Calling him loosely the 'first Russian traveller' to have come to India, it mentions how he was well received at different places by the Governor of Bombay, the Political Agent, the Governor-General of India, Secretary to the Government of India, etc. Contentwise it treats only Saltykov's observations in Simla and its surroundings, like how at Simla he mixed with the limited English society, comprising only 50 English gentlemen and 100 English ladies with their children, without any club, etc. It shows how tiring of this place as also of its society and its droves of monkeys, Saltykov retired into the interior of the hills to observe the people and the nature of these places.

But, all the same the reviewer exonerates Saltykov from any anti-British parochialism, if only because 'he sympathized with English social and political life more than almost any foreigners'. He mentions how Saltykov shows Englishmen and Englishwomen as heroic. But, 'being very much preoccupied with material interests', they (the English) do not much enjoy what is distinctive of India, despising 'all that which differs from the ideas received in their country'.[12]

Of course, Saltykov has also been indirectly charged with Eurocentrism. While praising the travelogue for its directness of observation and authenticity, an American reviewer extols the revealing contrasts it demonstrates between the oriental and the occidental ways of life. But the examples of truthful observation of the Persian culture that the review gleans could squarely place the book among 'Orientalist' tropes pursuing the 'othering' strategy so characteristic of them. These are the duplicity of a Persian aristocrat, to claim an exorbitant price for a shield which he first presented to the Prince as a gift; the present by the 'Persian Schah' after much fanfare of 'a tall, lame bay horse', which his groom refused to admit into his stables; and the 'disenchanting' sketch of 'Mohammad-Schah' that Saltykov drew, and which made the king look like a common tradesman.[13]

Another conscious attempt to fit Saltykov into an 'Orientalist'-Eurocentric framework, through a selective reading of the travelogue, points to the supposed acceptance by him of the European 'stereotype of the strangler' or Thug in India. Martine van Wœrkens shows how Saltykov falls prey to this stereotype, spread and popularized in France by writers like Eugéne Suë, René de Pont-Jest, and Henri Vernes. Allegedly, Saltykov not only accepted it without any demur but also helped in the process of development of this stereotype into a 'media image', through his verbal and visual representations. This is because 'Soltykoff in his *Voyages dans l'Inde* . . . told how these sorts of statuettes [of thugs in action] were made', and visited the Lucknow prison where 'the director showed him 'very well made statuettes of colored plasters, representing all sorts of massacre scenes perpetrated by Thugs.'

Saltykov has been accused of subscribing to this stereotype because he 'bought the portrait of an eighty-nine year old man who boasted of having strangled 999 persons', being moved by the realistic nature of the work.[14]

DIFFERENCES FROM TWO CONTEMPORARY BRITISH AND FRENCH TRAVELOGUES

One good way of measuring to what extent Saltykov was/was not shackled by these archetypes is to compare him with other travellers who came to India roughly at his time. For this we may compare his reactions to the scene of sacrifices at a temple at Amber in Rajasthan, the Shila Devi ka Mandir, with those of Anglican Bishop and missionary Reginald Heber, who visited the cities in 1825; and Frenchman naturalist Victor Jacquemont, who visited here in 1832. Heber's account is typically suggestive of the British 'magisterial' perception of the inferiority of barbarous India. He tells of being guided to the temple through 'a dark low arch into a small court', where, to his surprise, he was suddenly faced with 'a *pool of blood* on the pavement, by which a *naked man* stood with a *bloody sword* in his hand', and 'the *headless body* of the poor animal' [italics added]. Though the priest continued to tinkle the bell, Heber could guess from the 'embarrassment' of the guide that 'they had intruded at an unlucky moment'. Strangely, the priest did not in his embarrassment withhold from Heber the privileged information that 'in ancient times, a man was sacrificed here every day'. After its discontinuance displeased the goddess, who told Jai Singh in a nightmare that thereby her image was being 'suffered to be dry', the king, too afraid to disobey and unwilling to meet the demand 'to its *ancient extent of horror*', 'substituted a goat for the human victim'.[15]

Elena Karatchkova compares Heber's account in the 'classical first person narrative', allowing an effortless switch between 'events and encounters', 'village descriptions' and 'personal encounters', 'ethnographic data' and 'local gossip', with the descriptions of the same incident by Jacquemont and Saltykov. She shows how while describing the palace temple complex at Amber, Jacquemont informs the readers of the presence of devout 'Brahmans and fakirs' in the temple, who offer a goat to the goddess every day, and of the fact that it substituted for the practice of human sacrifice at Amber, a custom that was till recently practised in the Himalayas and was even then in vogue among the indigenous tribes of central India.[16] Then Karatchkova gives the account of Saltykov, which is different from both of them:

> I entered a heathen temple, where preparations for the sacrifice of a victim were under way: it was a goat. Sixty years ago, the victim would have been human. They brought the victim and positioned it in front of the idol; the Brahmin poured some water on his head, and muttering prayers, scattered around yellow flowers. Then a child and another adult dragged the goat to a place covered with sand, where they instantly severed its head off with a razor like knife . . . the head and the first blood went into a copper bowl, which they placed in front of the idol and closed the curtain. . . . When the curtain was drawn, the animal's neck was lowered into a pit to drain the rest of the blood. *We left and ate our breakfast in a pleasant garden* adorned with a red marble kiosk. [italics added].[17]

Comparing these three descriptions Karatchkova rightly points out that this last description 'adopts a stance of an objective observer with a strong stomach. . . . The passage above is characteristic not only of a typical bravado of a young Russian aristocrat, but also of Soltykoff's personal style'. Explaining the non-existence of the British induced 'magisterial' version of 'Orientalism' in his book, Karatchkova comments that together with Heber and Jacquemont, Saltykov too 'stood outside the British society there'.[18]

But in my view Karatchkova somewhat wrongly brackets Heber, Jacquemont and Saltykov together. The case of Heber is most contestable. As an Anglican priest he was the most closely trapped by the dominant British perceptions of India, if only from a religious angle. For example, Heber was both let down and revolted by the scene of sacrifice, which was not only gory but also sinister, and turned 'magisterial'. In his own words, 'I felt, I confess, for an instant my hand instinctively clench more firmly a heavy Hindoostani whip I had with me, the butt-end of which would, as a last resource, have been no despicable weapon'. Besides, at the end of the description Heber penned a poem about Kālī, which stereotypes her as a blood-thirsty goddess whose 'robes are wet with infant tears', and 'whom the blood,/Of man delights three thousand years'.[19]

True to this spirit of 'magisterial' superiority, while describing the town of Calcutta, Heber describes its Hindu residents as afraid of straight fights with 'an equal, however severely he may be provoked', and capable only of clandestine murders of women out of jealousy and of children for their 'silver ornaments'.[20]

Heber's mode of easy switch between 'village descriptions'/ 'gossip' and 'personal encounters' in his travelogue, is seen again in a description of a suttee which he did not experience at the time of its happening, but reconstructed from the description of his 'native servants', to claim that the 'unhappy widow' had been 'stretched out' under the husband's funeral pyre, with a bamboo laid across her. Unfazed that 'these particulars . . . differ from the account of a similar and recent ceremony, given by Baptist Missionaries', Heber complained about how hard it is to gain, in this country, accurate information as to '*facts which seem obvious to the senses*' [italics added].[21] He resorts to the familiar accusation of colonial secretiveness and withholding of information from Pax Britannica's need for more information; without realizing the full import of his words: 'Perhaps these particulars vary in different instances'.

Heber's account was also replete with 'Orientalist' archetypes of the 'austerities and idolatries' of the Hindus; servile adulation to a 'a tall, large, elderly man, nearly naked', by his followers 'who suddenly knelt down one after the other, and catching hold of his feet, kissed it repeatedly'; a gymnosophist[22] 'who held his hands always above his head, and had thus lost the power of bringing them down to his sides';[23] and a Muslim *fakir*, who was 'very nearly naked', with 'insanity strongly marked in his eye and forehead'. He could not be typed because he refused financial help. While running off, 'singing, 'La Ilaha ul Allah!' his otherworldliness 'answered to the idea of the Arab Mejnoun, when he ran wild for Leila'.[24]

The role of pre-determined notions and gossip in Heber's account comes out not only from his admission: '*In general, however, I must own that these spectacles are not common, at least as far as I can yet judge, as before I came to India, I expected to find them*' [italics added].[25] It is also apparent in his decision not to visit an important centre of Hindu pilgrimage, Bṛndāban, for prior information about 'ancient' but 'mean' buildings, and 'its amazing swarms of monkeys, and the no less amazing crowd of filthy and profligate devotees, who crowd round every stranger, not so much asking as demanding alms'. His unpleasant surprise at the sway of Hinduism in Bṛndāban, an important centre of Hindu pilgrimage, because of 'its vicinity to the capital of Islam in the East [Delhi]'[26] also reveals the 'Orientalist desire not to know'.[27]

While nearly all the main archetypes of European inscription of India are present in Heber's analysis, hardly leaving any scope for a different sensibility Karatchkova attributes to the Bishop, neither does she convince me that Jacquemont was completely free from ethnocentric biases. For, in many places in his main travelogue, he is clearly 'magisterial', and openly supportive of British policies. Even culturally he is too 'French' to be fully objective in depicting Indian reality. His magisterialism is manifest in his request to his father in a letter to go through 'the five octave volumes of [James] Mill's *History of India*'. For it is 'beyond all comparison the best work on that country'.[28] He despised the Asiatic Society of Calcutta, and explained to the Chief Justice of India, why he 'sent no paper' to it. He disapproved of Oriental Studies because 'Sanskrit leads to nothing but Sanskrit'. This 'wonderfully complicated' language is 'like one of those machines which never leave museums'. Its only contribution was to the 'manufacture of theology, metaphysics, history intermingled with theology, and other stuff of the same kind; triple nonsense for the makers and the consumers—for foreign consumers especially—nonsense = 1/0. . .'.[29]

Of course, the 'magisterial' note of Jacquemont's account regarding the essentialized Orient in India is tempered by an empathetic approach toward contemporary India. He was mastering 'Hindostanee vocabulary' fast and was talking with commoners because, he sought to 'penetrate into their existence, their feelings, their notions'. He said 'I am impregnating myself with India, instead of dipping the tip of my finger in it, as many English do, who pretend to study this country.'[30]

But the Eurocentrism in Jacquemont's observation comes out clearly in his reactions to the famous Ellora caves. There, the temple structure reminded him of 'a Gothic Church in miniature', with nothing 'wanting: the nave, the choir, and that kind of gallery which contains the organ in our churches'. Beside the majesty of the cave temples the pyramids of Egypt were 'but a trifle compared to the labour which must have been required for excavating these palaces and temples out of this solid rock'. But the idols always put him 'a little out of temper'; for, 'they give the idea of bad reasoning, and the caves of Ellora are peopled with them'.[31] Jacquemont's paradox was that he wanted the temple without its divinities.

SALTYKOV'S DIFFERENT PICTURESQUE INDIA

The tone of representation in Saltykov's travelogue is also not free from this mixture of voices. But he still cannot be bracketed with Heber and Jacquemont. For, despite the coexistence of the 'magisterial' with the 'exoticist' and the 'curatorial' in Saltykov's approach, an aesthetic detachment keeps the first subdominant. This would become apparent if we look at his travelogue and the pictures in the album,[32] drawn between 1841 and 1842. But to find out the difference of Saltykov, we have to remember his own admission that the discourse on travel in India is different from that in Persia. For, in spite of his 'predilection for Persia', India 'is infinitely more interesting'. That is why after recovering from a period of homesickness, he resolved to make as many sketches of the wonders of nature in India as possible, so as not to 'make me completely contemptible in my own eyes and yours', however, unequal were his talents to the task.[33] The upshot was an extravaganza of verbal and visual representations about: Indian cities and their inhabitants; courts of big and small native kings; temples, shrines and religious places; natural settings in rural and urban areas; outlandish birds and beasts; Hindu idols and festivals; the decadence of the historical places; nascent civil society of the new cities; good or bad social practices and even vices of the traditional society and culture; and changes brought in by British rule. The tone is mainly 'exoticist'. An occasional dose of European superiority lurks in depiction of dependent kings and their courts. A liberal transculturalism that seldom looked down upon the difference of India pervades.

Cities Old and New

Saltykov's portrayal of some towns and cities in India, celebrates both similarities and differences, despite the initial shock of a cosmopolitan Russian nobleman seeing Oriental cities for the first time. So while the general trend of depiction may resemble main-stream 'Orientalism', one should watch out for odd sentences, occas-ional turns of phrases or expressions, and see how through them he was shaking off post-Enlightenment European blinkers to develop the hermeneutic ability to understand them.

The need for this perspective would be borne out by Saltykov's first impression of Bombay, immediately after reaching India. Definitely he was startled by the difference of the place and its multiculturalism. Native men are 'almost bare or dressed in white', with 'skin the colour of bronze, the face and sometimes the shoulders and arms painted as if on pastel, often wearing turbans of pink, white, yellow or green'. The women were also half bare, or strangely draped by gauzes of different hues, burdened with ornaments of silver and gold all over their bodies, and wearing odoriferous flowers in their hair. He also noticed small quite grotesque Indian temples, filled with 'monstrous idols', surrounded by groups of emaciated fakirs, with long fingernails and claws sharp as those of eagles; old women frightening to see, dishevelled and with wild eyes; large crowded ponds lined with stone steps where they wash the dead; silent chapels of Parsees; noisy Indian 'pagodas'; a wide-spread smell of musk coming from musk rats, which abound in the city, and live down the ground there; and 'sounds of a barbaric music which almost never stops'. He felt that 'in this city nothing is what seems at first'.[34]

But then what struck Saltykov most about Bombay was the stark contrast between the lifestyles of the natives and the Englishmen. Passing through the streets of Bombay he often saw, 'Hindu wedding ceremonies taking place, with an air of practical joke or farce'. For both the bride and the groom were small children; a boy of ten or twelve being married to a girl of five or six. Both were stark naked, 'but laden with rings and bracelets, smeared with yellow'. They were 'presented a number of times the water that they take into the mouth to throw at each other', amidst 'a din of drums and violins'. But shifting gaze to the excellent pavements he saw 'English horsemen in rich equipages, women decked with the latest research (in fashion) in London and Paris (des femmes mises avec la recherche de Londres et de Paris), *side by side with this poetry of the primitive times, refinements of modern civilization*' (italics added). While beautiful English country houses, built in the Italian style in the midst of trees and magnificent flowers, made one imagine being in Palermo, when one's 'eyes meet those naked men with long hair, in the background of light green banana trees, dark coconut or slender and tall areca', then his imagination transported him 'into the regions of South America'.[35]

Here, transcending the bareness of the adults or the nudity of the child bride and groom, and the absurdity of the customs of child marriage, Saltykov's message of the coexistence of the 'poetry of the primitive times', and 'refinements of modern civilization' at the same place shows him to be an 'exoticist'.

Calcutta affected Saltykov differently, and quite appropriately the emphasis was more on its culture than on its architecture and cityscape. Of course, he noticed on both sides of the river 'attractive country houses of the rich English people, of Italian and simple architecture', and the palace of the Governor-General, 'like a large fragment of the winter palace of Saint-Petersburg'. The walk every evening by the river reminded him of St. Petersburg on the 1st of May, with the difference that one did not see 'many pedestrians there'. But when 'one leaves the palaces where live the fashionable from here and . . . goes into the city (because the beautiful quarters are at the end, as in London)', one goes bang into the Orient, with 'narrower, but also clean streets, extremely animated, where are the bazaars of the natives, almost naked population, less black than that of Madras, and with long hair'. He visited the house of 'one of the first dignitaries of the East Indian Company', whose house passed for one of the most elegant in Calcutta, and saw that there was a sparseness of furniture to prevent the interception of the air, which, in Calcutta 'one makes circulate artificially with such hard care'. He would have liked 'to say something good' about this capital of India; but found it difficult, as even in the middle of October 'the heat is dreadful; the country is low and wet; there is no air to breathe . . .'.

At Calcutta too the thing that struck him was the juxtaposition of the Western and the Indian in the social and cultural life of the city. In the theatre, playing an English comedy, the 'actors are very good and the room is pretty, well-lit, filled with huge fans that go all the time at the ceiling'. A great Hindu festival was imminent that would 'last two weeks', and 'at the end of the festivities idols would be thrown into the river amidst great tumult'. One of the 'civilized natives' in Calcutta had invited him to witness 'notchs or Indian dances . . . that he will give in five or six days and which will last three evenings in continuation', as part of it. He also met another 'Hindu, *also civilized*' [italics added], who was connected with commerce and who passed for 'one of the richest private individuals of India in the estimation of natives', and was planning to visit Europe, namely 'Dwarkanot-Tagor'.[36] Saltykov also spent an evening with this 'Europeanized Indian', who 'had willingly taken on the task' of acting as his agent, in his country house outside the city, where, after a satisfying elephant ride and dinner they listened to Meyerbeer and Donizetti played on the organ. But 'the jackals made such a din around the house that one could hear almost nothing'. The host 'appeared embarrassed about this hitch, *not having any idea of the strange poetry of the thing for me*, a European' [italics added].[37] With this ear for the strange poetry of jackals and the hermeneutic ability to appreciate Indian culture in spite of its alienness, Saltykov describes the 'notch' to which he was invited, at French-occupied Chandernagore, 'a small town', inhabited by forty thousand French Indians'. The festivities gathered momentum slowly, with 'dances of bayadères', to which Europeans were invited. At Chandernagore, Saltykov was at two of these dances, and what struck him was that while in the well lit halls, a balustrade separated the dancers, musicians and distinguished European guests, still everyone was '*allowed*, however he is dressed', which struck him as 'very noble'. Saltykov describes the native audience as 'almost naked people, bronze color, with quiet and sweet faces and features which have almost never anything vulgar'. The comments on the dancers have also no racist overtones:

> The garment of bayadères, in gauze of various colors, is very curious. One of the dancers seemed to give herself more importance, and during rest she smoked a silver houka in a rather proud attitude, on the floor. Her pants of pink gauze, sticking at the top, and widening a lot downward until forming like a skirt, had seams furnished with slender braids from behind, three on every leg. . . . Her musician was a beautiful young man, dressed in extremely fine gauze, quite sticky, with a small bonnet also transparent, and an immense and splendid hair, much like that of our deacons. As for the women, they were all small, delicate and had black teeth although they were still very young. [38]

Apart from lack of ethnocentrism in the depiction of the looks of the Bengalis, eulogies for the social inclusiveness of festivities, factual reference to the blackness of the dancers' teeth at young age, possibly from use of *miśi*, and their general ugliness,[39] objectivity marked Saltykov's description of the *neveau riche* city nobility, and their organization of 'nautch' during Durga Pūjā celebrations, visited by Englishmen and other Europeans.[40] Saltykov finds them imitative of the *sahibs*. He met 'several rajas, Indian Lords', who 'try hard to know English manners, and . . . adopt a very ugly whimsical dress, and go for outing driving their cabriolets.'[41]

'Civilized natives', or 'Europeanized Indians', representing the parvenu nobility of Calcutta in the backdrop of a contrast between the modern and the traditional in Calcutta forms the subject of a picture. In a round carriage drawn by two strong horses, a Bengali family of five men and one veiled woman are travelling, in a festive mood. Sitting on one of the horses is one attendant, and another is running behind the carriage in tunics and shorts. The carriage races past a thatch under a huge banyan tree where people are smoking their *hookah* in a relaxed manner and looking on.[42]

Saltykov's impressions about traditional Indian cities and towns differed according to the nature and quality of the city life, as he was mainly after local colour. He was disappointed with the temple city of Benares, as 'this city is . . . neither as large nor as antique and dark' as he had painted in his imagination. It was 'a compact cluster of three storey houses', and 'small conical temples'; full of Brahmins, *fakirs* and crowned bulls, elephants bathing in ponds, and parrots flying everywhere.[43] Delhi was always more interesting, because of its capacity to accommodate both tradition and modernity, whether in its pre-colonial history embodied in its rich architectural heritage;[44] its cultural diversity; or its potential as a source of antiques for the collector. It was in this sense that in its soul the city was more a Mughal achievement where the English were just chance occupants. The architecture of 'this metropolis of India, or more correctly . . . of Hindustan', as seen from the top of a minaret of the first mosque which he climbed captivated him. He agrees with the muezzin that the mosque was the 'largest and most beautiful perhaps in the world'. He praises the palace of Mughals, surrounded by the Red Fort, behind which lay the 'vast cluster of houses with Italian terraces like those of Naples', and beyond which yet were 'the ruins of tombs and scattered fortresses in arid deserts'.[45] Four years later too, when contemplating from the top of one of the slim minarets of the biggest mosque the Mughal capital, 'still wrapped in the mysterious grey twilight of the morning', he imagined that the 'Grand Mughal slept in its marble palace, surrounded by gardens, courses, diverse kiosks, elegant mosques, and a heap of huts forming alleys, powdery and rustic, the whole enclosed in a magnificent battlement of ancient stone of red colour, whose high walls and the Moorish towers form a vast square on a flat ground at the edge of the Yamuna river'.[46]

But for Saltykov Delhi was not just its nostalgic past or home of 'the curiosities which are still in Delhi after all the plunders which it had to bear, until finally the English people restored peace and safety there'.[47] Nor was it simply 'an inexhaustible mine' for the 'sipehrs' (shields), armours, and straight sabres that he chose to call Indo-Germanic because of their strange shape. He bought many of these antiques at a cheap price.[48] Interestingly he puts his own experience of inspection of arms in a picture captioned purchase of arms at Delhi.[49] Even in the unlikely month of November, cholera was unfortunately creating havoc in Delhi, taking a daily toll of twenty in a population like that of Rome.[50]

Jaipur in Rajasthan was 'a beautiful city, built in an elegant Moorish style, in the middle of a desert, and populated with two hundred and fifty thousand souls'. Amber, an ancient city which Saltykov miscalculates to be eight versts (or 5.30 miles) from Jaipur, had 'a fort in the rocks, which reminds one of Granada and the Alhambra, except its large ponds, and gardens, mysterious and dark'.[51] Lahore was, however, an 'Orientalist's' paradise, what with its 'high walls, towers and ramparts . . . compact cluster of tall buildings in a terrible state of disrepair, which together form a dark and stinking cesspool', or its 'winding lanes, so confined', that when negotiating them on the back of elephants Saltykov was always touching the walls and fearing that they will be crushed by one of the slender buildings whose 'four or five floors seem to yield under the weight of their inhabitants', Equally alarming was the 'triumphal gates under which one passes from a quarter of the city to another', and the 'alleyway . . . full of horrible sewers where one slips, and of dangerous holes where the elephant is obliged to make steps of ridiculous square dance'. In the streets below one saw

> shops of disgusting food, and miserable or wild beings, draped as the witches of Macbeth, or nudes, with long beards; hideous eunuchs, fakirs smeared with ash and faces grotesquely painted, some covered with skins of tiger or leopard, and with fantastic turbans, plumed and crested, but very soiled, the others absolutely bare, howling or sounding a copper horn of the length of a man; fanatics in exaggerated costumes, entirely black, pretending to aim at you weapon of arrows, long guns with matchlocks, interminable spades or swords.

But when one looked above at the windows and balconies, one found they were 'loaded with courtesans and brilliant dancing girls in bright gold and jewels, making graceful salutes'. Some of them 'held hens and cocks in large numbers, filling the air with their cackling'. The 'mixture of parried girls and fowls', the latter 'roaring with laughter at my European appearance', made Saltykov sometimes 'forget the dangers of such a journey'.[52]

To any careful reader the above passage would appear romanticized and over-exaggerated, with too much happening too soon on a street. The hyperbole gets a repeat in a picture where a spear-wielding young prince/nobleman on a huge caparisoned elephant driven by a 'mahout'; soldiers brandishing spears on another smaller pachyderm and two horses; a woman in burqa on a third elephant; a standing spearman; and a half naked flutist and an idler on the street, and young women looking down from roadside balconies, render the narrow city street suffocating with images.[53] This is precisely why N.S. Kapany and K. Brown compare Saltykov with other contemporary European artists, like Emily Eden, and an anonymous 'a lady', who also admired the Sikh court of Ranjit Singh. In their view while Eden's lithographs, and those 'by a lady' depicting 'Entrance to the Holy Temple at Umritsar', are tinged with a calm and delicate appreciation of the characters, architecture and natural environs of Lahore, the lithographs of the Russian prince, including 'Une Rue de Lahore', are 'wildly and wonderfully Romantic—it is hard to believe they were in the same place'.[54]

If the houses and archways in the city of Lahore were ramshackle and precarious, then the cityscape of Amritsar was even more dangerous. After mentioning the death of a young prince from the collapse of a door, Saltykov writes, 'I tremble all the time whenever I cross on the back of an elephant under a door of Amritsar'. For, if an elephant touched a single brick of the low arches in disrepair, the entire structure would fall. But then, in his characteristic style, rather than using this opportunity to criticize Oriental sloth, Saltykov again looks away from the roads to the balconies, where women 'perched'. They had 'heavy jewels even in their ears and noses, with chains that stretch from the nose to the ears, so that', he could 'hardly see their charming faces'. Saltykov was lost in these graceful girls, greeting those below respectfully from their precarious balconies or terraces, clad 'in tight pants as with men, in cavalier postures, draped in a veil with borders of gold or silver'. Entering the bazaars in the narrowest and wildest areas of the city, on an elephant, followed by soldiers of the Sikh cavalry, Saltykov drew some satisfaction from the fact that the pachyderms knocked over with indifference everyone who came their way.[55]

Shifting to Lahore proper, Saltykov speaks admiringly of the Moorish-Indian architecture and the splendid gardens of Shalimar, or Shalimar-Bagh, also known as the hanging gardens of Lahore, 'perhaps because of the way in which it is laid out in several terraces one rising above the other'. This 'Versailles of the kings of Lahore', was distinguished by a big area of 'ornamental lakes animated by a quantity of ducks and gray geese; innumerable fountains and symmetrical cascades', all so artistically organized that 'they fill all the air of this paradise with a fine and imperceptible rain. . . .'[56]

If the hill town of Simla was a sort of Baden Baden and a 'boring Carlsbad in the Himalayas',[57] then Agra was like Lahore another exemplar of the archetypal Oriental city, and in terms of 'the ratio of Moorish architecture, perhaps most admirable'. It left Delhi and Cairo far behind. Its marble monuments, 'each one single in its kind, of a taste pure, majestic, and with complicated details, but harmonious', did not disturb 'the pure simplicity of the architectural lines'. By contrast the countryside was 'flat and ugly', as also dusty. One could see 'arid plains strewn with tents, camels and elephants; people preparing food in the open air; women carrying water, all of which was covered with dust; long bazaars, narrow and full of people, bordered with Moorish houses provided with balconies'. Various Indian edibles were sold in an exposed condition; as were toys, hookahs, tobacco and bright clothing, though of a coarse workmanship, in this 'Orientalist's' dream.[58]

Temples, Shrines, Divinities and Festivals

Searching for the spectacular and the picturesque in India, Saltykov gave detailed descriptions of temple complexes and of courts in India, with a singular openness of mind and detachment regarding their positive and negative aspects. The temple complex at 'Cond-jévéram' (Kancheepuram) got its character not only from the four elephants attached to it, but also from the men and women who filled Saltykov's apartment, to get some pictures of themselves.

Saltykov had to pay them liberally, but did not mind, partly because of the supreme beauty and diversity of the place and partly from a sense of guilt of indirectly participating in British colonial exploitation: 'We become a sponger in this country'. But he could not help it, 'because if Lord Elphinstone had not by generous attention sent to me French products of his magnificent kitchen, and his cellar, admirable and unique maybe in India, to what would I have been reduced?' Talking of the temples, sculpturally, they were 'all magnificent, incomparable', with the 'most imposing architecture, the most extravagant details'. Architecturally they were majestic, 'with enormous palm trees and banian trees, and galleries, colonnades, courses, plazas'. The place was culturally enthralling, with 'a crowd of old Brahmins, youth and children, almost naked, striped with yellow and white on the forehead and chest, the ones striped horizontally, serving Schiva (Śiva), the destructor, the others perpendicularly, serving Vischnou (Viṣṇu), the conservator'. To see the jewels of the temple, Saltykov had to pay 'tens of rupees', but reasoned that 'I do not have any other expenditure than this here, because I am accommodated and fed for nothing by the government or rather by Lord Elphinstone'. The only thing that disagreed with him was the local food which he describes with utter disapproval.

Saltykov describes with the same catholicity the large number of monkeys in the temple complex 'more or less venerated'; religious-communal marks on the face of the elephants 'horizontal or perpendicular . . . according to whether they are devoted to Vischnou or Schiva'; a shaven Brahmin seated on an elephant, acting as an 'admirer of the devil', and holding 'in front of him a copper vase filled with green leaves'; some musicians walking in front of the actor on foot or mounted on a cow, with a timpani which he played with frenzy; and two bells suspended on the elephant, and a species of horn or trunk. This seemed to him to be a 'serious practical joke'.[59]

But here there was nothing of Heber's bitter critique of the alms-demanding natives, swarms of monkeys, meaninglessness of rituals, or self-righteous contempt for greedy locals. Rather what stands out is his critique of the imperviousness of Englishmen to the majesty of the temples. As he says in the context of the jewels of the idols:

> Some Englishmen had recommended to me to see them, as the only thing worth seeing, . . . in Condjévéram, all the remainder being only native dirt and beastliness; one of many proofs of the low confidence to be given to what we hear, because these objects were very little compared with the infinite interest of the rest.[60]

Saltykov also gives a visual representation of two ornate temple precincts. In one, alive with caparisoned elephants, camels, priests, temple-dancers and devotees, elites and commoners come to pay honour to two deities, 'preserving and destructive', at a place 40 miles from Madras. The second picture shows a holy place of pilgrimage of Hindus in Karnataka, with female devotees with earthen pitchers on their heads, and male devotees with sparse clothes. To the right better dressed men and women are standing in a kind of physical proximity that betokens an amorous atmosphere far removed from religious piety. Another picture shows a religious procession at Rameswaram in south India before the balcony of a Hindu temple. Here three caparisoned elephants with their drivers, male drummers beating on drums and other percussion instruments, flutists, well-dressed dancing women, and a Brahmin with a flower garland in his hand conjure up a festive and carnivalesque atmosphere. To the right, a European, dressed in suit, leaning upon an unopened umbrella, serves as a symbol of 'Orientalist' observation.[61]

With the same catholicity Saltykov describes the city Madurai (in Tamil Nadu) and its Hindu temple as a 'magnificent, quite white pagoda, all white, raised high in the middle of a vast pond, surrounded by greenery, where peacocks walk and fly'. The old palace of the former kings of the country also gets accolades. A picture of one such temple in his album adds to the verbal depiction.[62] The palace, one part of which was purely Indian, while the other was 'a little bit Moorish', designed by 'an Italian architect, two hundred years ago', was constructed by the King of Madurai, named 'Trimalnaïak',[63] a man 'with a snub nose though elongated at the same time, big moustache, protruding buttocks and well bent loins'. What struck him in the principal temple were innumerable parrots of various colours, brought as offering from various regions of India, and suspended in cages; and troops of monkeys belonging to nobody, living on the roofs and in the courtyards of people, making war 'when they meet, being species of races, or, as one would say rather here, different castes, and each one defending his district'.[64]

The enchantment with the Hindu temple of Madurai did not pass on to that of 'Djagarnate, or more correctly Djaganate', as he helpfully informs the readers, located in the 'dirty Indian city' of Puri in Orissa, whose stink was 'atrocious'. Though Saltykov felt like the 'Paria of Bernadin Saint-Pierre',[65] coming to know that in 'this sacred temple no unclean person is ever admitted', though he could 'walk all around as long as he wanted', it was quite enough for him. He drew the temple from outside, but did not include it in the album, as it seemed to him 'extremely ugly', despite being eight hundred years old. But this Pariah-like status did not engender any rancour in his description of the head-priest, 'Tchatissàni-Djôg-Naik', 'a large and grand Brahmin, suffering from an attack of elephantiasis, which however does not seem to inconvenience him much', and adding that he was an amateur mimic of the tones of parrots and hummingbirds.[66]

Saltykov shows apparent similarity with European 'Orientalists', when he refers to monstrous idols in grotesque temples in Bombay,[67] and speaks of Goddess Kālī, in stereotyped terms. In a passage describing the Thugs in India he shows the tutelary goddess of the stranglers to be 'the goddess of the evil, of death, adored by the Hindus, and represented with all the funeral horrors'.[68] Again when telling about a fair held in her honour at a place called Kheri, in Saltykov's calculation about 30 versts (or about 20 miles) from Simla, he refers to her as 'the goddess of the evil and blood', one who evoked passions, as evident in the dances of two thousand mountain dwellers, 'the women whirling slowly and stirring up their bodies voluptuously', and 'the men making strange movements, holding up their sabres, almost delirious about it, and drawing from the arc and darting at the others blunt arrows, which however hurt. . . .'[69]

But the stock epithets about the dark goddess are almost routine utterances, because in his Enlightenment-induced openness and readiness for comparison and classification Saltykov does not have real problems with Hindu divinities. This is why he can describe the idol of Goddess Durga worshipped at the residence of a rich man of Chandernagore, in late autumn, together with the immersion ceremony in a detached way. The idols were 'colossuses of painted wood, made especially for the occasion'. There were:

> the goddess Durga, the pink woman with ten arms; another white goddess on her left which answers, in what was said to me by the *civilized Indians*, to *Minerva*, another goddess still, [with the colour of the blue of sky]; and a dark green man with a moustache and favourites (the favourites are of ancient use in India), with his horns and with a malicious air, brought down, devoured by a fabulous lion, and skewered over the market in addition, by a silver plated lance that the goddess Durga plunges securely in his breast stained with blood, while the lion eats into his stomach. All this was surrounded with an immense semicircle, consisting of all the small gods of the Indian Olympus [pantheon].[70]

The faithful description of the image and its iconic grammar, together with the acceptance of the suggestion of 'civilized Indians' of the affinity of Goddess Sarasvatī with Minerva, the goddess of learning, is proof of Saltykov's catholicity. That is why during the immersion on the fourth night he 'went there by a car to enjoy the show'. A painting by him of an immersion procession of the goddess Kālī shows us this openness even more clearly. There the Goddess is borne on a litter with drummers (*dhakīs*), torchbearers, flutists, and other people with only their loins covered with white cloths, to a place that looks like a 'burning *ghat*'. The welcoming man at the farthest point on the left, also carrying a torch, with his uncovered buttocks and only partially covered loins in front, seems to be the priest.[71] The festive-religious atmosphere of the procession hardly squares with the image of the 'the hideous heathen god'.

A similar detached openness informs the description of the triangular green flags with Indian divinities with thousand feet and thousand arms, painted on silk that some of horse riders and elephant drivers were carrying during the reception of Saltykov and others at Amritsar.[72] It comes out in his observation about the food habits of Indians which fly in the face of his predecessors' comments about the ingrained vegetarianism of Indians. He found that it is 'allowed among certain Hindu castes to kill game'. The sanction supposedly came from 'god Rāma having lived in the woods and being nourished by pheasants, peacocks, etc.'[73] Glossing over the faulted mythology, this openness of mind is evident also in the following description of a Hindu religious procession in Benares, in which were participating 'an infinite number of people of all sex and age, equipped or rather painted as gods, goddesses and other powers celestial and infernal', including 'Crichna (Lord Kṛṣṇa)' painted in blue sapphire, 'Rāma 'very pink, armed with a shield and a straight sabre', and 'people painted and dressed up as monkeys with long tails and pointed muzzles'.

This objectivity leads Saltykov to take the stories of Indian children acting as divinities, mounted on chariots in these processions being sacrificed later with a grain of salt. His revealing comment is: 'I hope that it is only one of these tales which one so often makes up for the travellers'.

In the same vein, the 'Orientalist' image of the blood-thirsty goddess is punctured in the description of another procession, where he refers to 'a woman coloured in almost black blue, dis-hevelled, upright, placed on a stage, pressing with her feet a man painted in white and pink, whose head was hidden in a hole between stained linens of red'. As if the last three words are not enough, she is described to have held with one hand 'a head made of paperboard by the hair', while with the other she 'held up a sabre, and lowered it with a furious air on the dead man'.

In this lighthearted depiction of the deadly goddess in a procession, Saltykov relates how he inadvertently entered seated on his elephant in this procession featuring 'gleaming torches, wars of giants in the open air, monsters made of paperboard', held in front of the house of the Raja of Benares with his 'wide white hat', and how only after 'hearing the bursts of laughter from all the spectators of Benares', he 'finally realized' his 'position, *because I seemed to want to play a part in this scene*' (italics added).[74]

The breaking of the dyad between the seer and the seen, through conveying the carnivalesque air of the religious procession faithfully, comes logically after Saltykov's suggestion that the story of later killing the children dressed as gods might just be gossip meant for the gullible tourists, a thing which Heber would never have imagined.[75]

Saltykov describes the religion of the hill men in the last village approaching the Borendo pass, showing 'the frankest idolatry', with a sort of amused wonderment:

> The other day I saw a Hindu god with long hair and a fringe like a skirt, attached to a sort of litter. This was violently shaken for an hour, God knows why, by two men dripping with perspiration, for the burden was too heavy for them; while others blew immense drums and copper cymbals. . . . I left them shaking their god to climb back to my tents. . . .[76]

This objectivity and catholicity is evident in Saltykov's description of most of the kings, courts and their regal styles in India, excepting that of the last Mughal Emperor in Delhi.

Of Kings, Courts and Royal Pageants

Probably because Saltykov toured India as a 'grand seigneur', and was privileged to see 'splendours of barbaric courts', these occupy significant space in his journal. But it is not just their grandeur that he depicts, and in this depiction his voice is not free of mixture. The travels throws light on the existential moments of choice for diverse monarchies in India under Company's rule and their results: precocious child kings and puny kings of small kingdoms with their hollow and mirthless pageant and their anachronisms; kings retaining many if not most of the cultural markers of Indianness amidst surface adoption of European culture; the helplessness and surrender of small princes in India to the Company and its pathos; and the uneasy surrender of large kingdoms and its tragedy. It is not that in the description of the courts of Tanjore, Pudukkottai, Thiruvanthapuram, Gwalior or Amritsar he is not affected by some of the normal stereotypes of the 'Orientalist' view. But he glosses over them and very often draws attention to more positive aspects of the courts with an ease that is truly rare.

For example, after being initially refused permission of a visit by the King of Tanjore in Madras, Saltykov went into the reasons of the king's bad temper. He informs that after his father was dethroned by his uncle, he was put into a dungeon where he was being slow-poisoned, till a widely respected German missionary rescued him.

He escaped, and solicited 'the support of the English'. The Company installed the young prince on the throne. But it exacted the heavy price of letting 'all the State of Tanjore' to be 'governed by the English people', 'the king being a boss only in his fortress and in the surroundings', and allowed to control and defend, with one gun-carriage only, a space containing about ten thousand inhabitants. The prince got the fifth part of the net incomes of the province, apart from retaining his fields. This was the deal even though the father of the present king was 'a devoted friend of the Europeans'. After the German missionary died he was 'inconsolable', and had 'a beautiful marble mausoleum' built to his memory'.

Apart from showing this human touch, Saltykov refers to the king's harem in oblique and uncritical terms, oddly in course of describing the disposition of the king's forty elephants. After talking about seven tigers and five leopards held by the king and adding that one of these tigers 'was a curiosity, because its hair was gray, and the stripes were barely visible', he mentions that some of the elephants belonged to the king's wives, and then throws in casually, within brackets, that he had three hundred of them in his castle. This information too is sought to be justified as 'an inevitable feature in a warlike nation of Marathi origin which had conquered this country less than one century and a half ago'. Before the reader can even pause and wonder, he is fed with the information that the other elephants were intended to serve the temple, which had immense granite towers which rise until naked among the clouds and 'a monstrously huge bull made of a single block of black stone', which was 'three times as big as the rock of the statue of Pierre le Grants in Isaac's square'.[77]

An attitude or European superiority peeps out from Saltykov's description of the king and his court, when he shows the king sitting on his throne of ivory, under a canopy of brocade, in a dress of golden gauze, with an air of self-importance:

On his breast and his plumed turban, of a strange form . . . shone large stones, and among others a disproportionate emerald shining like a third eye suspended above his nose; the turban was Marathi. . . . Several servants shook gilded fans and packages of peacock feathers behind the throne. . . . The incense burned on the steps of the throne, and a herald proclaimed aloud the greatness, power, the rare qualities of his master, his beauty, his courage, strength, etc. Nothing was missing from the effect of *this bizarre scene which had at the same time a theatrical, antique and childish character* (italics added).

But with this condescension goes tolerance, as for example, while showing how the king descended from his throne to engage him in a friendly chat in English about their 'respective health, the mutual pleasure which we felt to see each other and the warm temperature'. Labeling it with sophisticated banter as 'one of those conversations of a lively and deep interest', Saltykov tells how at the time of departure the king covered him with flowers from head to foot, splashed him with rose water, and anointed him with quintessence of sandalwood, a herald proclaiming all the time the titles and qualities of the prince.[78]

Mixed feelings of pity and admiration mark his account of a small court at Poudoucota (Pudukkottai in modern Tamil Nadu) whose child king of eleven wore a suit like 'that which on the theatres of Europe the Turkish characters and especially caliphs of Baghdad carry.' Saltykov expresses surprise 'to see that the majority of these out of date costumes of theatre and masquerade, that one calls Turkish in Europe', and that he 'had always supposed to be of imagination, come in the fact from this remote country'. But in the same breath he praises the young king and his still younger brother for their proficiency in English, as for the 'small gold sabre', which 'had superb ornaments of emeralds and fine pearls'.[79]

Again the way in which Saltykov received the king of Tanjore, coming to him in full regalia and pageantry, at Saltykov's home in the king's return visit, shows how receptive he was to Indian standards of hospitality. Saltykov seems quite apologetic about his mistakes in greeting the king ceremonially. He completed all the steps, but was genuinely sorry for not having the 'black oil' the king had anointed him with. His next comment brings out the goodness of the king: 'The king, who likes much these ceremonies, enjoyed helping himself all the time because of my inexperience, and smiled at my clumsiness with an air of pleasant protection'.[80]

Read with the mixed appreciation of the court of the child king at Pudukkottai, this episode reveals Saltykov's attitude. Not stopping at describing the young king's mastery of the English language beyond his age, he extols the impressive character of the royal reception he granted, with gold or silver caparisoned elephants, and well-bred and well-harnessed horses, with plumes on the heads, and the extremely graceful turban of the little prince, crowned by a tuft. He affectionately relates the elaborate parting ceremony, in which the prince forgot to anoint him with rose oil in his haste, as also the joy of the 'little guy' in presenting to Saltykov and his companions a rose-sprinkler, which when opened, threw up a thin jet of water, rising to the ceiling for a few seconds, and inviting them to dip their hands in it. 'Then it was real fun for him', to present heavy necklaces and bracelets of flowers to them, and to distribute golden betel leaves among them. Saltykov describes even the alien atmosphere of the farewell honours, with the same sympathy: 'The palace courtyard and the streets of the city or village were lined on our passage with a stark naked black militia, some with sword in hand, but the largest number had spades or muskets. The leaders were on horseback, dressed in soft colours of the other world.'[81]

There is no shock here about Oriental nakedness, though almost in the next paragraph he talks about the 'immense trumpets . . . in which one blew with a meritorious zeal, and which made a terrible noise'; and 'an immense parrot out of gilded wood, on a long stick', both of which were carried close to the royal palanquin, with the oblique comment that it 'appears definitely that these Indians invent very little that they can make effect with'.[82]

More revealingly of his difference, Saltykov focuses on the civility of the courts, and their efforts at maintaining authentic tradition under the veneer of Westernization. That is why he was tolerant of the king of Travancore and his anglicized brother, in spite of their funny sartorial imitations and European manners, and of being, together with the prime minister 'completely European in their conversation'. The Raja with his 'white chiffon gown with gold spangles, a feather in his turban decorated with small stones', looked every inch 'a Russian trader', and unbecomingly timid and nervous, so as to 'tremble in front of me'. His brother was more fearless with his 'half-Hungarian costume', in which he looked extremely funny. He was fascinated with European manners and very annoyed with his Nair caste, 'which put in almost every possible obstacle in his relationship with us'. Though the ministers were 'highly educated and completely decent', and wore 'all the true Indian costume and open sandals in the chamber', 'their spirit is European, at least seemingly'. The brother of the Raja came to attend European dinners 'with his entourage of naked people', though not touching anything and 'chewing his betel constantly'. The eagerness of the prince and his brother to acquire Western ways was manifest in the portraits they had got made by a passing Austrian painter for all the royal family. But Saltykov was not only 'overwhelmed with the courtesies of this court', but also by their zeal in keeping their tradition alive. The anglicized brother also sent him 'a quantity of dishes of his table; *the menu was composed only of vegetables, but excellent*', and he came himself to explain to him the recipes, served on leaves of banana tree by way of dishes'. Besides, he presented to him 'two Indian drawings, one representing the blue god with his white nursemaid, the other one depicting the taking of Ceylon by the monkeys of Rama', and just at the time they were departing for Quilon, invited him, to his 'inexhaustible . . . regret', to a dance that was to take place, depicting Lord Rāma's victorious return after conquering Lankā; in Saltykov's words, 'history of Adam, who, at the head of an army of monkeys, arrives from Ceylon at Travancore'. Saltykov's comment after seeing the costumes for this was '*I had never seen anything as baroque as this fantastic wardrobe*' (italics added).[83]

At other places, Saltykov seems to be looking at these anaemic representatives of political India in a pensive mood. In hardly concealed sympathy, he relates how Mysore was re-conquered by the British from Tippo-Saïb (Tipu Sultan), where they had 'reinstalled the old descendant princes, under the supervision of the English government. Having administered his state very badly and having been riddled by debts, the king was obliged to let police chiefs, appointed by the supreme government of India manage the affairs of his country'.[84] A nostalgia for their lost glory lurks from behind the seemingly neutral observation of the country of Kourgs. At Marcara, the capital, Saltykov finds a Hindu palace with stone elephants at the entry, lying abandoned, as the jungle gets thicker and thicker, because the king of this 'good and warlike people was dethroned and is today relegated to Benares'.[85]

Once Saltykov's description of the civility of the court took a slightly romantic turn; as for example, at Gwalior (in present-day Madhya Pradesh). Here the charming fourteen year old cousin of the king, lived 'as a recluse in keeping with the ways of the Indian people of high ranking', and sat on a 'chair encrusted with mirrors and hidden by a green curtain in which a hole closed by a small net was ingen-iously created'. From here the young princess could approach, without being seen, and train her fine ear and her pretty mouth'. Saltykov sat on the ground close to this small hole, and heard a sweet voice ask '*a saab atcha haï*?' (How are you sahib?] Replying '*kharab neï*' (doing not too badly) he also asked about her health to her; whereupon, the 'charming princess, with the natural sagacity and promptness still left with the primitive tribes of India, replied, without hesitating, that she was perfectly well'.[86] One feels tempted to compare this scene with Thomas Roe's voyeurism about Jahangir's 'principall Wives'.[87]

The sympathetic but condescending attitude toward the Indian kings gives place to pure, unalloyed admiration in the description of the splendour of the capital and court of Sher Singh, son of Ranjit Singh, in Lahore. Saltykov's effusive description of the welcoming party is captured even in the somewhat bland translation of H. Garrett.[88] Seeing from a distance the line of elephants and the mass of cavalry, he felt himself 'back in ancient days'. The Sikh horsemen mounted on 'magnificently equipped . . . fiery horses', reminded him of the 'invasion of the Huns', as depicted by Raphael 'in a fresco in the Vatican'. And the 'regular cavalry of the King of Lahore', in their cuirasses and helmets, coats and gauntlets of mail, plumes in their helmets, and tight trousers of gold, velvet, and silk 'looked very much like Circassians'.[89] Though Garrett omits them, his words, 'Avoir sous ses yeux un spectacle pareil, tandis que l'Europe est plongée dans une civilisation aussi prosaïque que celle de la Chine, et voir des hommes dans toute leur poésie primitive, tels qu'on était chez nous au moyen âge, n'est ce pas bien intéressant?', quite clearly shows that he was comparing Europe to her disadvantage.[90]

The colourfulness of the reception did not of course blind Saltykov to the social inequalities in contemporary Punjab, or to the sorry sight of Sikh power giving in before British strategy. It is with these insights that one has to read Saltykov's description of how while the greater lords, decorated with precious stones, were on elephants with seats of solid gold or silver, and in howdahs of golden sheet, behind them, clinging to the pachyderms were stable boys, stark naked or scarcely covered with dirty linens. Likewise, behind the radiant riders in gold, silk and velvet, on splendid saddles—and superb messengers on elephants too—one could see grooms nearly nude or with sparse clothes, some of them clinging to the tail of the horses of their masters.

This social inequality, coupled with recent political subjection, makes ironical the raw display of Sikh power, in the seemingly innocent sight of 'young Sikh dandies, strutting about in clothes of gold; enveloped in pink or white gauze; armed with daggers, swords and pistols; with upturned moustaches, and beards separated in the middle of the chin and combed up towards ears in a wild coquetry.' Even more tragic was the sight of the Akalis, still not reconciled with British primacy in Punjab, hurling abuses at the British envoy and his Russian companion. They were

> people of a curious and strange costume, with high turbans, everyone in black, daggers and feathers fixed in the turban, the moustaches and the beards trained up towards eyes, swamping us with insults, roaring with all their strength and brandishing their sabres against us, someone with even two sabres, one in every hand . . . privileged, too strong, and too numerous a sect to be controlled by the government of the King of Lahore.

The government hardly dared to touch them, unless they committed some atrocity, and 'all the mass of Sikh troops, and all these thousand elegant riders avoided them and let them offend us'.[91] Amidst this display of power and defiance more sorrowful was the sight of their prime minister offering propitiatory money and the seeming reluctance of the envoy to accept it, on the lines of what Max Weber would call the 'rational accounting methods and a legal separation of company wealth from personal wealth'.[92] But this has to be read in Saltykov's words, even if in my weak translation.

For, while he offered to the British political agent, seated on a running elephant 'an enormous bag full of rupees', he 'put it between his feet', this being a 'a gift . . . which the English people can never appropriate, since by an order of the government all this is counted and taken over by the East India Company, which restores it to Indians in another form'.[93]

As if in expiation for this description of subservience, Saltykov extols the spectacle of the King's wealth in the 'state audience' granted by him:

> What a sight! I could hardly believe my eyes. Everything glittered with precious stones and the brightest colours arranged in harmonious combinations. The green garden was decorated by a huge crowd of Sikhs in yellow, red, rose, white, gold, silver, green, lilac and azure, all armed and strikingly arrayed, some of them in coats of mail. . . . In the midst of this bevy was the king . . . a big stoutish man of forty, covered with the most beautiful jewels in the world. On his right arm was the Koh-i-Nur, the finest diamond that exists. He greeted Mr. Clerk cordially and invited us to seat ourselves on silver chairs, while he and his favourites placed themselves opposite to us in chairs which, as well as the footstools under their feet were made of Dutch Ducats melted down . . . all the passages and platforms were covered with superb shawls as far as one could see. Further back horses with costly trappings pawed the ground impatiently.

Further, Saltykov later dilutes any suggestion of superiority of the Company's rational accounting methods over Oriental Despotism while describing the demeanour of the king before the political agent and the gift-bringing subjects. This comes after reference to a 'lively conversation', between the king and the political agent, which was 'like any other official interview and interspersed with long pauses, during which each party cudgelled his brains to produce some elegant phrase about the good relations subsisting between the Sikhs and the English—relations about as cordial as those between the wolf and the hunter'. Then Saltykov shows the king's lofty disinterest in gifts. 'The presents of the English government were then brought in. . . . The King threw a careless glance', though these 'signified that the English government recognized him as King and were, therefore, of great importance to him'. For, 'Sikh etiquette required this seeming indifference'. He accepted monetary presents from his subjects with similar indifference, though this was 'one of the ways of raising revenue'.[94] As for presents of the dancing girls, 'Sometimes he took the rupees mechanically, sometimes he pushed away slowly the hand which offered them, sometimes he put some in the very hand offering money', while conversing with the political agent, in an 'absent-minded and friendly' way.[95]

Saltykov's love for the Lahore court was also due to the egalitarian attitude of the king, whose 'simple and unaffected air . . . distinguishes him'.[96] Thus, while showing him and the English guests of honour three of his best horses, their bridles and saddles adorned with the most precious jewels, and making them parade in the water of a tank with all these luxurious trappings and then bringing them up to the terrace for better viewing, 'the king appeared agitated like an ordinary person, on an equal footing with his courtiers and us'.[97] Similarly, when the king was leading them around the gilded chambers of the inner apartments of his palace, the dancing girls who had followed them from below were allowed a rare proximity. The king 'did not pay any more attention to them than if they were domestic cats, or rather children of the house. He let them pass close to him and in front of him, and avoided pushing them, though his walk was sometimes incommoded by it'. Again, when travelling with the king from one room to another and being offered Champagne with cold joint of chicken and game, on small plates, without forks or spoons, Saltykov realized that here 'everything is patriarchal and warlike. The king, in the middle of his courtiers, is on an equal footing with everybody, a warrior as the others. He is simply approached without ceremony'.[98] The simplicity of the king was also borne out from the fact that he sent two mountebanks or mimes, dressed as a fakir and a tall woman, and then again as an Akali in fury, to Saltykov's tent to entertain him.[99] Saltykov concludes that there 'is so much good nature, kindness and even of innocence in this king, that, although with a rather ugly figure, he is charming, and one would say that with this timid and simple air he possesses an indomitable courage in danger'.[100]

Saltykov finds the riches of the king incongruous with his subservient position. With harnesses of horses engraved with big emeralds and enormous pearls; saddles made of gold; hunting on a grand scale joined by 'fifty elephants, richly harnessed, with saddles of brocade and the howdahs of gold'; and 'thirty splendid horses from the stable, all covered with precious stones';[101] and the magnificent garden of Shalimar, the king was heir to the past glory of the court. Speaking of the 'garden with all its paths papered with Kashmir shawls, and all these horses stamping on these shawls; the intoxicating smell of dancing girls', he tells his correspondent, 'say to me if it were or not the case to exclaim with poor Tom of King Lear, 'God keep us in our five senses'.[102] But Saltykov notices that 'especially in front of Mr. Clerk, who has a proud air with him, the poor King cannot decide about which foot to rest on'.[103]

But this sympathy for the Indian royalty is strangely absent in the case of Bahadur Shah II, the last Mughal Emperor of Delhi. The negative perception starts with a royal procession entering the Red Fort, where Saltykov first saw him. The general disorderliness of it, together with the look of the Emperor, left him disappointed. Bahadur Shah was 'a withered old man with a severe aspect, sitting upright in a sedan-chair, under a canopy. . . . Twenty elephants followed immediately behind him confusedly as in a herd, some with gold-coloured flags, the others with timpanists', using their instruments with 'a sort of demoniac fury'. The Great Mughal 'held in his hand the hooked end of a gigantic hookah that one carried behind him. In the funeral brightness and in the smoke of torches, he looked like an embalmed corpse, as dark as a mummy, and decorated with tinsel'.[104]

This sort of satirical description of 'the last Mughal' continues. While describing his preparations for the presentation ceremony before the Emperor, Saltykov says that the reason why he was hurried by his host was that 'the Mughal . . . can undergo a ceremony only through the help of opium . . . and he can stay there only as long as the effect of the opium lasts'. He also 'had a haggard look. His eyes sometimes shone with a strange brightness and sometimes became dull as some tin. It seemed to me that he trembled'.[105] Saltykov's description of the court and the royal attendants and of his ceremonial presentation before the Emperor is also unappreciative. He states how while announcement of the empty titles of the Emperor was in progress, an emptiness reigned around the monarch too; how the servants were shabbily dressed; and how after offering three pieces of gold to the Emperor, he was dressed in a ludicrous accoutrement. He handed the Emperor three more pieces of gold in this comic dress to get a brilliant diadem of precious stones attached to his turban. And after he slipped a piece of gold in the imperial palm again, 'as patients do to doctors in England', a collar of pearls was wound around his neck, which turned out later to be nothing more than coarsely painted glass. Even the imperial robe was fake, made 'of velvet, imitating leopard skin and strangely decorated, in certain places, with bands of sable or some other light fur'. The Emperor's demeanour, while accepting these gold pieces with a satisfied look, was somewhat like an automaton. The culture of the court was debased too. For, when leaving the court Saltykov faced importunities to send a gold piece or two for the Heir Apparent who was not present due to some ailment, but would expect this gift, and also requests of greedy servants to part with another customary hundred rupees for them.[106]

One may compare this description with the vastly different portraiture of the Emperor by Austrian artist August Schoefft at about the same time, and William Dalrymple's comment on it, to wonder how an artist of the sensitivity of Saltykov was missing the depth of Bahadur Shah Zafar's character. In Dalrymple's words:

> The portrait of Zafar depicts a dignified, reserved, and rather beautiful old man with a fine aquiline nose and a carefully trimmed beard. Despite his height and surprisingly broad and muscular build, there is a profound gentleness and sensitivity in his large brown watery eyes with their unusually long lashes. As a teenage prince, Zafar had always appeared in his portraits as a slightly awkward and uncertain figure. . . . But . . . in his mid-seventies, . . . his bearing more regal. Yet . . . there remains in the expression of his dark eyes something unmistakably melancholic . . . Schoefft shows Zafar a little swamped under the brocade cloth of gold which adorns him, somewhat weighed down by the huge blood-coloured rubies and the strings of vast pearls. . . . It is a portrait of a man imprisoned by the trappings of his office.[107]

How to account for the different perceptions of the two artists? I think the key to any explanation is to be found in Saltykov's last quote about Zafar: 'This old man, whom I saw on the throne of

Delhi, was Bahadur Shah, descendant of Tamerlain'.[108] Possibly, Saltykov's dislike for the old person was inverted sympathy for the unworthy successor of the Great Mughals, one who could not protect the Empire.

REGARDING STEREOTYPES: THUGS, SUTTEE, BURNING OF CORPSES, AND *ANTARJALĪ*

Saltykov could not of course, entirely avoid the stereotypes of 'Orientalist' observation, though even in their depiction he always leaves an alternative possibility. The only exception perhaps is the representation of thugs, as we have seen in the comments by Wœrkens above.[109] Perhaps he was overly influenced by British perceptions while describing *Thugs* (or *Ṭhogīs*) as 'a sect which . . . follows the doctrine of killing as much of the world as possible to calm the anger of the Goddess Kali . . . '. For, he credits the English people for discovering 'three subdivisions of this sect spread all over India', on the basis of their mode of killing that had 'remained unknown during thousands of years', till they were discovered by the English people. He informs that one of the many stranglers he met in Lucknow confided in him 'with a smile of satisfaction' that he had strangled more than 600 persons in his lifetime. He was struck by his respectable air, cleanliness and even elegance, though he was 'sixty years old', and the love his wife and children had for him. He mentions another thug, a respectable old man of eighty-five years, who had died recently in this prison, and who had congratulated himself on having strangled 999 victims, and stopped there simply because it was a magic number. He tells grisly tales of misdeeds of other thugs; tells how the most notorious of them were deported; and how many were still held prisoners.[110]

Such influence by British colonial representation of 'thuggee' would not be surprising, if we remember the complex colonial discursive strategies through which the paradigm of religious murder in India linked thugs together with *antarjalī*, devotees throwing themselves from cliffs in Birkhala mountain over the Narmada River, or having their heads chopped off in the famous temple in Goalpara in Assam, or young women committing suttee, where in every case the Hindu goddess was presented as feeding on human death. [111] Actually, there is quite some controversy among historians regarding the extent to which 'Thuggism . . . is a myth invented by the British in order to extend their control over a mobile population, or to seize criminal jurisdiction in areas that had until then been in the hands of Mughal rulers', or the extent to which 'paralleling the way the colonizers constructed other concepts, *Thug* was the appropriation of an Indian word to give a meaning to a badly understood social institution'.[112]

Against this background one could excuse Saltykov for presenting just an eye-witness account with little or no embellishments or sensationalism, in only two pages, along with the rider that many prisoners held as thugs were pleading innocence. His linking the practice with Goddess Kālī can also hardly be faulted. A considerable body of literature on the so-called 'Thug mythology' referred at that time to the sanction for strangling without a drop of blood or unnecessary infliction of pain, coming down to them from the goddess, ever since she created two men and gave them two handkerchiefs to kill demons with, without bloodshed.[113] One account even gives a neo-Malthusian twist to it, where the battle-weary goddess left the task of executing the 'preventive check' 'upon the further propagation of demons' to two mortal persons.[114] Even the huge number of victims he mentions should be viewed in the context of a good number of publications, calculating the number of victims every year in terms of disappearance of 'hundreds of natives', creating 'no astonishment or alarm' as the thugs spared noticeable personages, and anyway human 'life in India is not of much account'. Besides, both a correspondent in the Thuggee Department, and a 'native newspaper' of 'great respectability', nearly, *Sumachar Durpan* (*Samācār Darpaṇ*) counted deaths in thousands in 1833.[115]

Saltykov also mentioned 'suttee' and *antarjalī* in a few places in his travels. But in these cases too, as in that of the Kālī Temple at Amber, a strong stomach and objectivity mark the accounts. For example, while describing a funeral procession carrying a woman on a stretcher at a village in 'Tritchinapoli' (presently called Tiruchirappalli), proceeding to 'the sound of drum and trumpet and accompaniment of songs', he remembers having been shown such a crematorium near the sea at Madras by Lord Elphinstone. But since he did not have any amateurish fascination for these things, he did not see this operation closely ('Mais, comme je ne suis pas particulièrement amateur de ces choses, je n'ai pas cherché à voir cette opération de près . . .'). Still we get the astounding information that, 'when the wind comes from the direction of the most highly rated of the piles, where they burn the bodies, we feel the smell of *mutton chops, lamb chops, as if we were walking past a kitchen*' [italics added]. Still more remarkable is the casual proviso that this was only concerning burning the dead; for 'here . . . they sometimes dare to burn the alive too'. Showing his difference still more, Saltykov admits to volition in 'suttee' in two places, Pudukkottai and Tanjore, but even more importantly, shows that there was sometimes dissuasion against it. In the first, the mother of the young king of Pudukkottai, a very sensible, good woman and loving mother, decided when her husband died, on 'burning with the corpse'. But through entreaties her well-wishers 'dissuaded her from it, by making her feel how much she was needed by her children'. In the second case, however, neither persuasion nor dissuasion worked. When the king of Tanjore died:

> His wife burned herself with an astonishing coolness . . . instead of putting herself on the funeral pyre of her husband, to be burned there over a small fire, she precipitated herself in a pit full of ignited matters which would consume her at once. She did it, after having taken leave of her ministers, and after having recommended her children to them.

Continuing his difference, Saltykov further adds that 'suttee' was not as endemic as believed. It was only 'among the high classes that this custom is practised', and it 'exists only on the territories of the native princes, being absolutely prohibited on that of the Company'. The East India Company also tried to suppress this practice at places not under their control.[116] To prove his points of the contradictory Company initiative and 'victim's' volition, he shows how Mr. Clerk, the Agent, rescued a girl of seventeen from being committed to 'suttee' in Amritsar in Punjab, 'in spite of the Brahmins, *in spite of the victim herself*' (italics added), thereby clearly hinting at volition.[117] If we compare these descriptions of 'suttee' with that of Heber,[118] mentioned above, the distinctiveness of Saltykov would stare the reader in the face.

The same difference informs Saltykov's description of *antarjalī* in Calcutta, which he witnessed on the banks of the Ganges during his regular walks. After relating how an unfortunate young, dying man had been brought in a palanquin in the hope of revival by the freshness of the air, his wild eyes and excessive thinness indicating the approach of death, Saltykov has no qualms in saying how, after a few days, he 'saw the sick young man, seated and apparently revived and I was surprised because the other day he was lying motionless and seemed almost dead', and how he helped him financially.[119] This story of revival is just the opposite of representation of *antarjalī* with the one given by Caleb Wright, a nineteenth-century amateur American anthropologist and traveller. For him it 'consists in pouring a large quantity of water down his throat; filling his mouth and nostrils with mud; repeating the names of the gods, and shouting, "O mother Ganges, receive his soul!". . . . Some are suffocated by filling the mouth and nostrils with mud; others are left where the rising tide will sweep them away'. Wright mentions 1900 such cases in just a month by the riverside in Calcutta.[120] The same attitude of objectivity characterizes Saltykov's description of burning of corpses. In the cremation ground, giving out 'a strong odour of kitchen', he 'saw two pyres in flames'; but though his black Mohammedan servant guided him, he 'could distinguish nothing human among the firebrands', and left the place.[121]

A painting captures the entire mood of *antarjalī*, corpse-burning and rituals by the riverside in a crematorium by the side of river Ganga. Here an old man, reclining on a litter, is being brought to the riverside, may be for *antarjalī*; another corpse with flowing hair, covered with a cloth and lying on a coir stretcher, is being entered into a brick structure, possibly for final preparations; hermits and ascetics of various descriptions, one with daubs on his bare body and forehead and others with their hairs in knots, look on; and a widow standing with her body and head covered with a white cloth, seems to be overseeing things. There is neither any burning pyre in sight, nor any 'suttee'.[122]

Clearly Saltykov does not approve of the practice of burning of copses in India, but the description of it, as of 'suttee' and *antarjalī*, suggest the presence of something more than what Serebriany would call 'strong stomach'. These are vestiges of hermeneutic-interpretive understanding.

OF ENGLISHMEN AND INDIANS

Cultural tolerance marks Saltykov's depiction of Englishmen in India and of Indians themselves. His occasional disparagement of English character comes more from a cultivated Frenchified artist and intellectual, rather than from a Russian nobleman. When he complains that 'the English people of India do not have the slightest conception of the combinations of lines, which make all my life',[123] one finds a distinct French echo of the charge of British obtuseness in art. And when Saltykov hints at British homesickness and xenophobia as the reasons behind the designing of their quarters as in 'home', he is definitely not speaking as a Russian, but rather as a continental European. One reason why offers of British hospitality during his travels annoyed him in spite of their advantages was that 'the English people live always as far from Indian cities as their business allows them, because they loathe the noise, the exhalations and the aspect of these cities', and 'want to avoid the contagion of the natives'. That is why in their parks 'they plant trees which offer a vague resemblance to those of Europe, and which remind them of home'.[124] To convey this urge, Saltykov also painted a English habitation at Ceylon.[125]

But when it was a matter of courage and guts, he extolled Englishmen and women in India. For example, he describes how in Calcutta, where 'the heat is hideous; the country is low and wet; there is no air to breathe, and all functions stop', the life of the English people was 'a constant fight against death'.[126] If the endurance of the English males deserved accolades, so did the pluck of English females. For, while he did not dare undertake the journey to Kanaur,[127] Gangotri and Jamunotri (the originating points of the rivers Ganga and Jamuna) in the Himalayas, some Englishwomen did go there. But he traces the courage of English women to the hardships of living in India. Though Saltykov thought their courage 'passes any idea', still after observing 'for a long time the manner of living of the fair sex in India' and what they could bear with in spite of being called weak he had no 'difficultty in believing' that they had really made the difficult journey.[128]

Saltykov's portrayal of Indians is also atypical among British, European and even some Russian Orientalists. We find none of the normal reproaches for the differences of Indians as in the travel accounts of William Hawkins, Edward Terry, Thomas Roe and others in the seventeenth/eighteenth century. We also find none of the European fantasizing of the licentiousness of Hindu—and in some cases even Muslim—women, as seen in the descriptions of Gouz, Ovington, Varthema, de Laval, de Mandelslo, Fryer and others.[129] Rather the passage below from where Marx quoted, hint at the gentle, honourable bearing of the Hindus. Even the tendency of the Hindu women to commit suttee is presented in an approving light. 'Even in the lowest class, Indians are finer and more skillful than the Italians. To the Europeans, they tender an extreme submission. . . . Nevertheless they are far from making themselves in the least bit despicable, because there is a certain calm nobility in their submission.'

Of course, Saltykov goes a little too far in claiming that these qualities compelled Englishmen to be 'fair to these Indians who are so docile, who, except any infringement with the laws of their caste, would suffer all that they would like to inflict on them without ever complaining'. But he hints that Englishmen are 'are struck by the staunch bravery of the regiments of Indian soldiers'. For, they know that the Indians would not brook any 'punishments which dishonor them in the eyes of their colleagues, and which maybe make them banished from their caste', and might commit suicide.

If these words, penned on 26 June 1841, sixteen years before the Sepoy Mutiny, are prophetic, then the linking of 'suttee' with the emotional nature of Hindus and the resultant suicidal trend is deeply insightful. 'Nothing is more common', says Saltykov, 'than suicide among the Hindus, without excluding the women, who often commit suicide lovingly. . . .' But the capstone of all this different representation is Saltykov's humility regarding his hermeneutic skills: 'these details . . . are the personal observations of a man in a new land who does not still speak the language of the country, combined with the narratives of the persons who inspired the most confidence in me.'[130]

The treatment of Indian women also partakes none of the stereotypes hinted above. Saltykov had a healthy interest in Indian girls, but never bordering on voyeurism, or never questioning their virtue. One remembers the highly romantic situation in the royal court of Gwalior where the charming fourteen year old cousin of the king was talking to him unseen.[131] Saltykov is not party here to what Teltscher describes as Roe's 'illicit game of peek-a-boo'.[132] It is not that the virtuousness of Indian women never attracted light banter from him, as for example, when he comments that 'pahārhī (Hindu) girls are virtuous, but little tempted, I suppose, because they are little tempting, being very dirty and very ugly. . . '[133] But this is a rare comment, to be placed beside his romantic interest, as on the streets of Lahore; when charming girls approached the king of Lahore one by one, and made presents to him; or when dancing girls indulged in their childlike freedom with the king; or when the intoxicating smell of dancing girls in the garden of Shalimar distracted him.[134] Once he refers to dancing girls offering themselves near his camp in Lahore. But he does it in poetic expressions of unfulfilled yearning. While 'sadly they look to see if we would call them, making graceful salutes with their fine arms', Saltykov's mild complaint is, it is 'forbidden to admit them to the camp', for, everything 'is formal here; we could imagine ourselves being in a convent'.[135]

In other cases Saltykov's description of Indian women dwells on their dignity and simplicity. As for example, when passing by a crowd in Fagu in the Himalayas he offered to make a sketch of an attractive woman,

> and suddenly she got loose from her group with an artless and grave air, and stood quite immovable for a quarter of an hour, as long as I wanted her to, and while I sketched her, everybody watched me doing it respectfully. The sketch finished, I gave to the model a rupee, which was accepted with a blush, but with a certain simple and primitive solemnity. They seemed to think that in making

the sketch, I was performing a religious act of my caste: because everything is caste in India.[136]

On one occasion, however, Saltykov's collector's zeal got the better of the refined intellectual in him, and led him to treat the hill women at Rampore in the Himalayas not too honourably. Perhaps in his passion for collecting 'curious women's ornaments . . . of common metals, but of antique and very strange forms', he crossed the limits of bargaining. His 'Indian companions acted as negotiators' and persuaded the women 'to yield their heavy jewels' to him, against their better judgement, through the lure of two rupees above the market value for them. The result of their agreement is best given verbatim:

Then, it was . . . necessary to enlarge the openings. The woman was laid down and a half-dozen of black and yellow men of the hillsides set to work, with pincers, slopes and axes . . . to remove these heavy ornaments from their arms and legs. By seeing them operating, one would believe to be witnessing a torture . . . you will be astonished by the smoothness of the legs and the arms of these women, . . . Sometimes they were not bad looking, with a healthy flush, because here, in these high regions they have a clearer complexion.[137]

It is a proof of Saltykov's relative freedom from racist feelings of superiority that he searched for resemblances between the hill people of India and people in Europe as well as in the south-eastern borders of Russia. The hill women in Almora seemed to resemble Russian peasant women.[138] At a place called Kheri, a few miles beyond Simla, the hill people seemed to him to have in them more of European, of Russian, Bulgarian, Finnish, or small-Russian stocks than Indians of the plains.[139] Similarly, at a place called Tchini-Gong, the last accessible post in India, beyond which lay the empire of China, there was already a beginning of the Chinese aspect and of the Tartars and of Tartaresses there, with the broad face of the 'Kalmouk' (Kalmyks), covered with cruel ornaments, like Schamanes of Siberia; and the 'strange resemblance of rustic buildings to the Swiss style' produced 'a singular impression' in him.[140]

But the people in the plains, in spite of their darkness impressed him with their simple lifestyle. While returning in a boat on the Indus, Saltykov reminisces about it:

I admire the manner of living of my Indians. They get up with the sun, light the fire, and sitting on the ground smoke the pipe of peace, and warm themselves, and, while conversing or singing in a monotonous tone, without rules, like birds, one of them crushes between two stones some wheat . . . with a little water. When the wheat is ground, he makes a dough with a little water, in the form of pancakes or chapattis. . . . He puts them successively on an iron plate placed over the fire, turns them over, and eats them. Then they drink some water and relight the pipe of peace. Sometimes they dare to cook, in an iron pot some rice or a sort of peas or lentils with onions, and add it to chapattis mentioned before, and the result is very good. [141]

Not completely free of the stereotypes of 'Orientalist' observation, yet sufficiently open to have independent views, Saltykov's panoramic and picturesque view of India remains a vastly under-explored resource, though it makes it possible to claim a distinctiveness and redemption for Russian 'Orientalism'. It is a pity that he is sidelined to such an extent in studies on Russian Orientalism.

NOTES

1. His name was spelt Aleksei Soltykoff when he published his works in French, and was turned into Alexis Saltykov in the Soviet era transliteration policy.
2. See Stacy, *India in Russian Literature*, p. 65; and L.B. Alaev, 'Predislovie (Introduction)', in A.D. Saltykov, *Pis'ma ob Indii* [*Letters from India*] (Moskva: Nauka, 1985), pp. 3–8, quoted in Elena Karatchkova, 'Ghost Towns and Bustling Cities: Constructing a Master Narrative in Nineteenth Century Jaipur', in Carol E. Henderson and Maxine K. Wesgrau (eds.), *New Directions in Tourism Analysis- Raj Rhapsodies: Tourism, Heritage and the Seduction of History* (Aldershot, Hampshire: Ashgate Publishing Limited, 2007), pp. 35–6.
3. Marx translates these words as 'More subtle and adroit than the Italians'. Here he is quoting from Saltykov's *Lettres sur l'Inde* (*Letters from India*) (Paris: Amyot, Rue De La Paix, 1848), digital copy by http://books.google.com retrieved on 10 January 2008, p. 61.

4. See Marx, 'The Future Results of British Rule in India', originally published in the *New York Daily Tribune*, 8 August 1853, excerpted in Iqbal Husain (ed.), *Marx on India*, with 'Introduction' by Irfan Habib, and 'Appreciation' by Prabhat Patnaik, sponsored by Aligarh Historians Society (New Delhi: Tulika Books, 2006), pp. 46–51, esp. pp. 49–50. Also cited in Karl Marx, *On Society and Social Change*, ed. with an introduction by Neil J. Smelser (Chicago: University of Chicago Press, 1973), pp. 138–44, especially pp. 143.
5. See Serebriany, 'Some Marginal Notes on India and Europe', p. 82.
6. See H.L.O. Garrett, I.E.S., *The Punjab a Hundred Years Ago, As Described by V. Jacquemont (1831) and A. Soltykoff (1842)*, tr. and ed. Garrett, Punjab Government Record Office, Monograph no. 18 (Patiala: Languages Department, Punjab, 1971), hereinafter Garrett, *Soltykoff.*
7. For the paintings see *Voyages Dans L'Inde et En Perse par le Prince Alexis Soltykoff*, Paris, V. Lecou, Éditeur, 10, Rue Du Bouloi, 1853, Paris: Typographie Plon Frères, Imprimeurs De L'Empereur, digital copy by http:// books. Google.com/, retrieved on 24 April 2009, pp. 12–299.
8. Kemp, *Bharat-Rus*, p. 212.
9. See *Voyages Dans l'Inde*; *Lettres Sur l'Inde*, 1848; and Alexei Dmitrievich Saltykov Knyaz, *Voyages dans l'Inde : Pendant les anees 1841–1942–1843, 1845–1846*, H. Gache editeur, 1841–6, Rue de la Victoire, 66.
10. The books referred to are Alexander Mackay, *Western India. Reports Addressed to The Chambers of Commerce of Manchester, Liverpool, Blackburn, and Glassgow, By Their Commissioner, The Late Alexander Mackay, Esq.*, ed. James Robertson, Esq., with a Preface by Thomas Bazley, Esq. (London: Nathaniel Cooke, 1853); and W. Knighton, M.A., *Forest Life in Ceylon*, in two vols. (London: Hurst and Balckett, Publishers, 1854).
11. 'Contemporary Literature', *The Westminster Review*, LXI (January and April 1854), American Edition (New York: Leonard Scott and Co., 1854): 158.
12. *Calcutta Review*, XLVI (1867): Article VII. –'From Simla to Chinese Tartary' author not mentioned, pp. 158–87, especially, 166–7.
13. From the Athenaeum: 'Life in Persia in the Middle of the Nineteenth Century', in *The International Monthly Magazine of Literature, Science and Art: Making of America Project, III* (April–July 1851), pp. 105–8.
14. Martine van Wœrkens, *The Strangled Traveler: Colonial Imaginings and the Thugs of India*, tr. Catherine Tihanyi (Chicago: University of Chicago Press, 2002), pp. 264–6.
15. Reginald Heber, *Narrative of a Journey Through the Upper Provinces of India*, vol. II (Philadelphia: Carey, Lea and Carey, 1828), pp. 13–14, quoted in

Elena Karatchkova, 'Ghost Towns and Bustling Cities', pp. xxxvi, 4, 27, and 33–5.

16. V. Jacquemont, *Etat Politique et Social De l'Inde du Sud en 1832: Extraits de son 'Journal de voyage, Avec une introduction de M. Alfred Martineau* (Paris: Society de l'Histoire des Colonies Françaises et Librairie Ernest Leroux), p. 35, quoted in ibid., pp. 34–5.
17. A.D. Saltykov, *Pis'ma ob Indii*, cited in Karatchkova, 'Ghost Towns and Bustling Cities', p. 36.
18. Ibid.
19. Heber, *Narrative of a Journey Through the Upper Provinces of India from Calcutta to Bombay, 1824-1825 (With Notes upon Ceylon.), An Account of a Journey to Madras and the Southern Provinces, 1826, and Letters Written in India*, in 2 vols., vol. II (London: John Murray, Albemarle Street, 1844), digital copy by http://books.google.com, retrieved on 12 January 2008, pp. 40–1.
20. Ibid., vol. I, p. 33.
21. Ibid., pp. 47–8.
22. See n. 85 of 'Introduction'.
23. Heber, *Narrative of a Journey*, p. 63.
24. Ibid., p. 102.
25. Ibid., p. 63.
26. Ibid., vol. II, p. 5.
27. See n. 12 of 'Introduction'.
28. James Mill, the Utilitarian debunker of Indian culture and Oriental scholarship, pilloried scholars like William Jones and Charles Colebrook for their efforts to unearth India's treasures, and attacked the entire body of Indian achievements in arts, architecture, woven manufacture, agriculture, literature, geography, history, philosophy, astronomy, grammar, algebra, form of government, fine arts, etc. See James Mill, *History of British India*, Book II, Chapters VII-X, 5th edn. with notes and continuation by Horace Hayman Wilson (London: James Madden, 1817/1858), pp. 1–164.
29. See V. Jacquemont, *Letters from India; Describing a Journey in the British Dominions of India, Tibet, Lahore, and Cashmeer, During the Years 1828, 1829, 1830, 1831, Undertaken by Order of the French Government by Victor Jacquemont, Travelling Naturalist to the Museum of Natural History, Paris*, 2nd edn., vol. I (London: Edward Churton, 26, Holles Street, 1835), digital copy by http://books.google.com, retrieved on 12 January 2008 pp. 241–4.
30. Ibid., vol. 1, pp. 178–9.

31. Ibid., vol. II, pp. 320–1.
32. See Saltykov, *Voyages dans l'Inde: Pendant les anees* for the pictures cited and analysed below.
33. Saltykov, *Voyages Dans L'Inde et En Perse*, vol. 1, pp. 199–200.
34. Ibid., pp. 12–13.
35. Ibid., pp. 13–14.
36. Ibid, pp. 89–93 and 95. Saltykov is here referring to Prince Dwarakanath Tagore, grandfather of the great Indian poet Rabindranath Tagore, and a prominent Indian entrepreneur. See Vladimir Ivanovic Pavlov, *The Indian Capitalist Class: A Historical Study* (New Delhi: People's Publishing House, 1964), p. 123; and Blair P. King, *Partner in Empire: Dwarakanath Tagore and the Age of Enterprise in Eastern India* (Berkeley and Los Angeles: University of California Press, 1976), pp. 129–30, passim.
37. Ibid., p.101.
38. Ibid., pp. 96–7.
39. A dentifrice made of roasted tobacco and copperas (ferrous sulphate).
40. See Rachel Fell McDermott, *Revelry, Rivalry and Longing for the Goddess of Bengal: The Fortunes of Hindu Festivals* (New York: Columbia University Press, 2011), pp. 26–7. Actually McDermott says, 'the number of Englishmen one attracted was considered the seal of prytige, the crowning touch of honour'. See p. 26.
41. Saltykov, *Voyages Dans L'Inde et En Perse*, vol. 1, pp. 96–7.
42. Environs de Calcutta, Octobre 1842, Voyages dans l'Inde: Pendant les années.
43. Saltykov, *Voyages Dans L'Inde et En Perse*, vol. 1, pp. 109–10.
44. Ibid., pp. 133–7.
45. Ibid., pp. 132–3.
46. Ibid., vol. 2, p. 286.
47. Ibid., vol. 1, p. 137.
48. Ibid., vol. 2, p. 131
49. Achat D'Armes À Delhi, *Voyages dans l'Inde : Pendant les années*, n.d.
50. Saltykov, *Voyages Dans L'Inde et En Perse*, vol. 2, p. 287.
51. Ibid., vol. 2, p. 289.
52. Ibid., vol. 1, pp. 164–6.
53. Une Rue de Lahore, *Voyages dans l'Inde: Pendant les années*, Mars, 1842.
54. See Narinder Singh Kapany and Kerry Brown, 'Introduction', in Kerry Brown (ed.) *Sikh Art and Literature* (London and New York: Routledge, 1999), p. 17.
55. Saltykov, *Voyages Dans L'Inde et En Perse*, vol. 1, pp. 154–5.
56. Ibid., p. 166.

57. Ibid., pp. 191 and 194.
58. Ibid., vol. 2, p. 281.
59. Ibid., pp. 55–7.
60. Ibid., fn. on p. 56.
61. See Intérieur Du Couvent de Condgeveram á 40 Milles de Madras Réunion Journalière des Brames en l'honneur deux Divinités Conservatrice et Destructive, Juillet 1841; Condgeveram, Ville Sainte Dans Le Carnatik Aux Environs De Madras, Lieu de Pèlerinage des Hindoux ; and Procession Religieuse Dans Les Galeries Du Couvent De Rameswaram, Juin 1841, in *Voyages dans l'Inde : Pendant les années.*
62. Une Pagode a Madura, Mai 1841, in ibid.
63. By 'Trimalnaïak' Saltykov is obviously referring to Thirumalai Nayak (*c.* 1623 to 1659), who took the lead in constructing the Vasantha Mandapa of the temple complex, after Arya Natha Mudaliyar, the prime minister of the first Nayak of Madurai (A.D. 1559–1600), took the initiative in rebuilding the temple after its alleged destruction by Muslim invader Malik Kafur in 1310.
64. Saltykov, *Voyages Dans L'Inde et En Perse*, vol. 1, pp. 70–1.
65. Jacques-Henri Bernardin de Saint-Pierre (1737–1814) authored *Études de la nature* (1784) (*Studies of Nature*), a hymn to a Creator God and a romantic novel *Paul et Virginie* (1788) (*Paul and Virginia*), whose Bengali translation 'Poul-Borjini' was much appreciated in those times, as also *Vœ ux d'un solitaire* (*Wishes of a Solitary Man*) (1789) containing his political views. Saltykov quotes him in the context of his novel *La Chaumière indienne*, in which a learned doctor came to India as part of an international society of scholars, seeking the truth through answers to thirty-five hundred questions asked all over the world. He had to perform many rituals to be free from his impurity and gain admittance to the priest, who resided in the Jagannath Temple at Puri, and get unsatisfactory answers. See Bernardin de Saint-Pierre, '*La Chaumière Indienne*', vol. 4 of *Études de la Nature*, pp. 261–315, cited by Binita Mehta, *Widows, Pariahs, Bayadères: India as Spectacle* (London: Associated University Press, 2002), pp. 114–17.
66. Saltykov, *Voyages Dans L'Inde et En Perse*, vol. 2, pp. 268–9.
67. Ibid., vol. 1, p. 13.
68. Ibid., p. 138.
69. Ibid., pp. 196–7.
70. Ibid., pp. 97, and 98–9.
71. See Procession la Déesse Kali, Calcutta, Octobre 1841, in *Voyages dans l'Inde: Pendant les années.*
72. Saltykov, *Voyages*, vol. 1, p. 163.

73. Ibid., p. 211.
74. Ibid., vol. 2, pp. 276–8.
75. Heber provides the statistic that out of 36 cases of murder during the preceding three months, seventeen were of children killed for their jewellery. See Heber *Narrative of a Journey*, vol. 1, p. 33.
76. Garrett, *Punjab a Hundred Years Ago*, p.120. Garrett adds in the footnote that Saltykov's description of the 'deotas seen in Bashahr to-day' is exact. Ibid.
77. Saltykov, *Voyages*, vol. 1, pp. 58–60.
78. Ibid., pp. 60–2.
79. Ibid., p. 64.
80. Ibid, pp. 62–3.
81. Ibid., pp. 64–6.
82. Ibid., pp. 66–7.
83. Ibid, pp. 77–8. The blue god with his nurse is really Lord Kṛṣṇa with his foster mother Yaśodā at Bṛndāban, a holy place of pilgrimage in Uttar Pradesh in India. By 'history of Adam' Saltykov means history of Lord Rama, here returning from Lanka (a South Asian country called Simhal by Indians before, Ceylon by the British, and now Srilanka) after defeating its demon king Rāvaṇa.
84. Ibid., p. 83.
85. Ibid., pp. 87–8.
86. Ibid., vol. 2, pp. 284–5.
87. See n. 88 of 'Introduction'.
88. Ibid., pp. 93–4. I call the translation bland because it misses much of the poetry of Saltykov's description. For example, 'et une nuée de cavaliers', has become 'a mass of cavalry', though the phrase 'a cloud of riders' would have better described the scene of riders on galloping horses throwing up a cloud of the dust with their hooves. Likewise 'je me crus transporté l'antiquité' would have been better conveyed by 'I believed myself transported to antiquity.'
89. Saltykov is referring to 'sahendaks or Circassian sahendaks', and the indomitable Circassian prince Khazi Guirey, who gave the Russians a lot of trouble. See Saltykov, *Voyages*, vol. 1, pp. 152–3.
90. My translation of this is 'To have under our eyes a similar spectacle, while Europe is plunged in a civilization as prosaic as that of China, and to see men in all their primitive poetry, such as one was on our premises with the Middle Ages, is not this quite interesting?' Ibid., p. 153.
91. Ibid., pp. 153–4.
92. See Max Weber, 'Prefatory Remarks' to *Collected Essays in the Sociology of*

Religion (1920), ed. Stephen Calberg with New Translation and Introduction (Chicago: Fitzroy Dearborn Publishers, 2001), pp. 155–6.

93. Saltykov, *Voyages*, vol. 1, pp. 154.
94. Garrett, *Punjab a Hundred Years Ago*, pp. 96–7; Saltykov, *Voyages*, vol. 1, pp. 157–9.
95. Saltykov, *Voyages*, vol. 1, p. 171.
96. Garrett, *Punjab a Hundred Years Ago*, p. 102.
97. Saltykov, *Voyages*, vol. 1, p. 160.
98. Ibid., p. 172.
99. Ibid., p. 162.
100. Ibid., p. 171.
101. Ibid., pp. 160, 167, 168.
102. Ibid., p. 176. Actually, the exact words in *King Lear* that Edgar says are not entreaties to the God, but admission that he has been possessed by five fiends: 'Both stile and gate, horseway and footpath./ Poor Tom hath been scared out of his good wits./ Bless thee, good man's son from the foul fiend!/ Five fiends have been in Poor Tom at once . . .'. Act Four, Scene I, *Complete Works of William Shakespeare* (New Delhi: Oxford IBH, 2005), p. 1099.
103. Saltykov, *Voyages*, vol. 1, p. 172.
104. Ibid., p. 224. Elsewhere he writes that his face was 'withered, gaunt and dark, as also were the hands; he had an aquiline nose, hollow cheeks, few or no teeth, and a sparse beard dyed reddish black, bordering on the purple. In the eyes he had surmé (surmā or kohl)'. Ibid., p. 227.
105. Saltykov, *Voyages*, vol. 1, pp. 225, 226.
106. Ibid., pp. 225–9.
107. William Dalrymple, *The Last Mughal: The Fall of A Dynasty, 1857* (London: Bloomsbury, 2007), p. 19.
108. Saltykov, *Voyages*, vol. 1, p. 227. Tamerlain (1336–1405) or Timur Lenk was a Transoxianan Turk, supposedly descended in the female line from Genghis Khan. He was a fourteenth-century conqueror of much of western and central Asia, and founder of the Timurid Empire and dynasty in Central Asia, which survived until 1857 as the Mughal Empire in India.
109. See n. 14 above.
110. Saltykov, *Voyages*, vol. 1, pp. 138–9.
111. Wœrkens, *The Strangled Traveler*, pp. 1–9, especially pp. 5–6.
112. Ibid., pp. 6–8. Also see Parama Roy, 'Discovering India, Imagining Thuggee', in *The Yale Journal of Criticism*, 9:1 (Spring 1996): 121–45.

113. See Colonel William Henry Sleeman, *Ramaseeana or a Vocabulary of the Peculiar Language Used by the Thugs, With an Introduction and Appendix, Descriptive of the System Pursued by that Fraternity and of the Measures which Have Been Adopted by the Supreme Government of India for its Suppression* (Calcutta: G.H. Huttman, Military Orphan Press, 1836), pp. 7–9; and Captain Leopold Von Orlich, *Travels in India, including Sinde and Punjab*, tr. from the German by H. Evans Lloyd, vol. II (London: Longman, Brown, Green and Longmans, 1845), pp. 144–5.
114. Edward Thornton, *Illustrations of the History and Practices of the Thugs, and Notices of Some of the Proceedings of the Government of India, for the Suppression of the Crime of Thuggee* (London: W.H. Allen and Co., 1837), pp. 55–8.
115. Sir John William Kaye, *The Administration of the East India Company, A History of Indian Progress* (London: R. Bentley, 1853), Chapter II, pp. 354–61, especially pp. 360–1.
116. Saltykov, *Voyages*, vol. 1, pp. 68–9.
117. Ibid, p. 161.
118. See n. 21 above.
119. Saltykov, *Voyages*, vol. 1, pp. 102–3.
120. See Caleb Wright, *Lectures on India* (Boston: Caleb Wright, 1851), p. 94; also see Caleb Wright, *Historic Incidents and Life in India* (Chicago: J.A. Brainerd, 1867), p. 100.
121. Saltykov, *Voyages*, vol. 1, p. 104.
122. See Saltykov, Les Bords Du Ganga Près de Calcutta, 1842, in *Voyages dans l'Inde : Pendant les années*.
123. Saltykov, *Voyages*, vol. 1, p. 199–200.
124. Ibid., p. 220.
125. 'Habitation Européenne a Simla', Mai 1842, in *Voyages dans l'Inde: Pendant les années.*
126. Saltykov, *Voyages*, vol. 1, pp. 93–4.
127. According to Garrett, Kanaur refers to the easternmost part of Bashar State and may be said to begin at the Wangtu gorge, 23 miles on the Simla side of Anin. See Garrett, *Punjab a Hundred Years Ago*, p. 11.
128. Saltykov, *Voyages*, vol. 1, pp. 188–9.
129. See Teltscher, *India Inscribed*, pp. 12–51, and n. 88 of 'Introduction'.
130. Saltykov, *Lettres Sur L'Inde*, Velor, 26 juin 1841, pp. 61–2 ; and Saltykov, *Voyages*, vol. 1, pp. 48–9.
131. Saltykov, *Voyages*, vol. 2, p. 284.
132. Samuel Purchas, *Hakluytus Posthumus or Purchas his Pilgrimes*, 20 vols. (Glasgow: James Maclehouse and Sons, 1905–7), iv., 375–6, quoted in Teltscher, *India Inscribed*, p. 42.

133. Saltykov, *Voyages*, vol. 1, p. 199.
134. Ibid., vol. 1, pp. 165, 171–2, 176.
135. Ibid., p. 161.
136. Ibid., pp. 197–8.
137. Ibid., pp. 212–13.
138. Ibid., p. 190.
139. Ibid., p. 197.
140. Ibid., p. 207.
141. Ibid., p. 233.

CHAPTER 5

Russian Orientalism *Par Excellence:* Vasily Vasilyevich Vereshchagin

What happens when a progressive Russian artist, critical of Europe's colonial- imperial wars, looks at Russia's own Orient? The paintings and writings of Vasily Vasilyevich Vereshchagin (1842–1904), provide a good answer to the question. Kemp has dismissed his writings on India as 'unspecialized travel literature', of a bygone era, emanating from Vereshchagin's two visits to India in 1874 and in 1882; though he was an important figure in the introduction of realism in Russian art, famous for his 'anti-militarist paintings'.[1] But Vereshchagin is too important in the history of Russian Orientalism, whether in Russia's near east or in India, to be dismissed in such an off-handed manner. First, he is the most complete classical type of 'Orientalist' in the Saidian sense, to have come to and observed India, and to have written about and painted Russia's near east and India, apart from providing the critical link between Russian Orientalism in Caucasus and Central Asia and in India. Secondly, despite his anti-war credentials, his voice is not only the most 'magisterial' among Russian Orientalists, but matches the most 'magisterial' examples of European 'Orientalism', if one examines his observations in Trans-Caucasia, and Central Asia, and the picture one gets of him from their joint travelogue, the Indian part written by Elisabeth Marie Fischer, his first wife, aide and companion on many expeditions and journeys to the Himalayas and India until the late 1880s. Finally, Vereshchagin's case shows the extent to which belief in European ideas of progress and reason can induce propagation of a civilizing mission which can be oppressive in the colonial context. These aspects of Vereshchagin's representation would, however, need a combined focus on both his oeuvre as an artist and on his travelogue in Trans-Caucasia and Central Asia. As a painter and artist a resurgence of interest in Vereshchagin has started after the works of Vahan D. Barooshian and David Schimmelpenninck van der Oye.[2]

THE PAINTER AND FIGHTER

Familiar Progressive Artist: Biography, Development and Achievement

Vereshchagin's story buttresses the identity of 'Orientalism' as power/knowledge in the context of colonial conquest even in Russia's case, partially through the difference between Vereshchagin's paintings and his travelogues, which apparently tell different stories. The difference is partly traceable to his biography. He was born in 1842 in a provincial town in northern European Russia to a member of the Russian gentry, owner of a fairly large estate containing some 350 serfs; and inherited Tatar blood from his mother's side. Barooshian says this aristocratic origin and the awareness of class divisions in his household and parental estate created complex psychological and ideological inputs for his development. Torn between a conscious ideological imperative to plead the cause of the peasant class as a sympathetic spokesman of its travails, and 'a subconscious desire' to gratify his mother's wish to see him as a 'famous, respectable military officer', his 'dual commitment, quite fruitful and even original in artistic terms, presented an ideological dilemma which he never quite resolved'. Vereshchagin was impelled to support the wars of the Russian State as a participant, to satisfy his mother's longing that he become an officer. But he condemned wars for their oppression of the common masses to whom he was emotionally wedded. Consciously aware of his primary mission 'as an artist', and never seeing himself 'as an officer' despite his active involvement in war, which contradicted his mission, he remained a split personality.

Vereshchagin was sent at eight to the Aleksandrovsky Junior Military School near St. Petersburg, and three years later, in 1853, to the Naval Cadet School at St. Petersburg. He was an outstanding student of his class. But bouts of seasickness during the two voyages to England and France as part of his naval training in 1858 and 1859 clouded his naval career. His artistic talent and promise was, however, spotted early and towards the last years in the school Vereshchagin began seriously honing it with the help of an art tutor. Later in 1860 he got a two-year stipend for studying at the Academy of Arts at St. Petersburg. But in 1863 he initiated a revolt against the Academy for its imposition of a particular artistic technique, anticipating a student's revolt there for emancipation of Russian art from sterile imitation of the masters. After this he left St. Petersburg to develop his artistic skills independently in the visually rich and inspiring Caucasus. Towards the end of 1864 he travelled to Paris on the strength of a bequest to complete his artistic training at the Ecole des Beaux-Arts or Jean Léon Gérôme's studio. In March 1865 he returned to the Caucasus to move about, see things and to make sketches of numerous ethnic types and their cultures and ways of life. Frustrated in his efforts after his return to Paris to found a journal for publishing his 'mass of drawings', he rejoined the Ecole at the end of 1866 to study under Gérôme and Alexandre Bidá.[3]

How did Vereshchagin stand as an artist? Ilia Repin, the leading artist of nineteenth-century realism in Russia, described Vereshchagin as 'a colossus, a great artist', 'a real Hercules', 'to a high degree an immense phenomenon in our life', 'a genius, a superman'. Even unsympathetic contemporaries could not deny him the status of a 'pioneer' in his time and an 'honorable place' in the history of Russian art and culture, because of the great power, 'artistic potentiality' and 'universal relevance' of his works. Barooshian claims that during the last quarter of the nineteenth century, his was the most compelling and famous voice of Russian art in the Western world, evidenced by his countless and well-attended exhibitions in Europe and America, and the profound impact of them upon the viewers of a 'genuine, real, and powerful talent . . . that knows no rest or fatigue'. In America of the 1880s and after, Vereshchagin's art led to the foundation of a new school.[4]

But Alexandre Benois considers Vereshchagin's work as very typical of the 1860s and 1870s, when realism in Russian painting was first making its presence felt. But 'unlike most of his fellow artists who came from the people and were cut off from "society" by their lack of breeding, Vereshchagin by his origin, education and social position, belonged to this "society"'. Benois thinks there are two reasons why Vereshchagin achieved the greatest popularity among painters outside Russia. First, because he belonged to the gentry, 'his art was more conscious and influential, and his preaching bolder'. Secondly, 'he treated Russian themes from the point of view of a man of Western culture'. Vereshchagin was, says Benois, 'a typical Russian nobleman, a man of broad views, of an open intellect, of an innate nobility of intentions, and absolutely alien to petty and narrow patriotism'. But these aristocratic qualities are not reflected in his works. In his view 'Vereshchagin was a European in his entire programme, in all his projects, but banal and "barbarian" in their execution'. This was because, while he could not get any insights into his art by mixing with his aristocratic companions, who were 'dense, unconcerned and perplexed in matters of art'; he could gain even less as an artist by mixing with fellow artists, most of whom were 'entirely absorbed in social problems and exhibited an absolute indifference to matters of purely aesthetic import'. Vereshchagin's visit to Europe also did not help, as he did not go with sufficient preparation to benefit from the works of the great masters. He remained more 'an ethnologist' than an artist, his 'oeuvre . . . poor in purely pictorial merits', because he 'was interested in ideas but indifferent to form'. However, Benois does not wholly dismiss his art. Though his pictures are 'poorly painted and childishly drawn', they are 'cleverly planned'. Many of his 'light and colour discoveries' have stood the test of time; and some of his 'Indian sketches are all fire and glow'.[5]

Subsequently, the *Soviet Encyclopaedia* pointed out the limitations of his paintings, though for the most part 'executed at the time of the events in which he was a participant'; and in his desire for full communication of the truth of these events, presented in thematic series, like the Turkestan Series (1871–4), the Balkan Series (1877–8 and 1880s), and a series on the theme of the Patriotic War of 1812 (1871–1904). It praised Vereshchagin's work for its 'democratic tendency', which drew him close to the *peredvizhniki*, or 'the wanderers'—a progressive art movement, and for the transformation that he brought about for the 'Russian battle-scene genre', replacing the previous romanticization of earlier battle-scene paintings with 'the genre of battles and history'. But allegedly, while containing 'philosophically profound insights concerning war', spurning 'the false heroics, conventions and parade-ground quality of academic battle painting', and depicting instead 'the cruel and bloody routine of war and the countless suffering borne by the people', his work did not reflect 'the true social nature of war'. So, while he opposed wars of conquest and colonial wars 'from a pacifist viewpoint', he did not throw light on the 'social conditions that bred war'.[6]

These 'limitations' did not, however, prevent the Soviet propaganda establishment from turning him into a friend not only of India but of all countries ruled by the colonial-imperial 'West'. The introduction to an 'official' album of Russian paintings on India proclaimed his desire, while in India, of producing a series of paintings describing the history of the British conquest of India, and mentioned as an example of his unfulfilled desire 'a painting of his entitled "A British Execution in India"', where the artist 'depicts the ruthlessness of the colonizers . . . to break the heroic resistance of the Indian people'.

Clearly, true to the 'friendship of the peoples' slogan of the post-1930 Soviet politics that made Nikitin a posthumous cultural ambassador for Russia, the album also tries to fit Vereshchagin in a 'curatorial' mould, showing how 'Vereshchagin did not see India as an exotic and backward country, but as a land of strong and courageous people, with a rich culture and a highly developed art'. Then it selects a few of Vereshchagin's paintings to claim that 'Vereshchagin left behind gallery of Indian portraits which are both national and deeply humanistic', inspiring 'affection for India and her people'.[7]

A BATTLE PAINTER WHO LOVED BATTLE BUT PREACHED AGAINST WAR

However, the image of Vereshchagin that emerges from his artistic and textual production in Caucasia, Turkestan and Central Asia, and during the wars, goes beyond the valorized image of an indefatigable opponent of imperialistic, colonial or other wars. True, Barooshian tells how his 'fearless nature found him in opposition to the Russian state, which he considered an instrument of oppression and violence'. It is also true that the Russian autocracy took Vereshchagin as 'one of the leaders of a conspiracy to overthrow the existing order'; and he was embroiled in controversies with military leaders in Russia and Western Europe, who suspected 'the revolutionary implications of his art and forbade children and the military to attend his exhibits'.[8] All these make plausible the extenuating circumstances of his participation in the conquest of Central Asia, and his presence in the Russo-Turkish War (1877–8), and the Russo Japanese War (1904–5) as an observer.[9] During the Central Asian conquest the reason was his penniless condition coupled with the knowledge gained through the Academy of Arts of an unusual opportunity that was available to serve as an artist as an orderly for General Konstantin P. Kaufman. Barooshian thinks this might have been a conscious attempt by the Academy to win Vereshchagin back either to itself or to military service. Kaufman was to become General of the Russian military forces in Turkestan and the new Governor-General of Turkestan in the Russian colonial conquest of Central Asia. Vereshchagin was supposedly an apt choice for the position. For, he defended Russia's conquest of Central Asia as a 'civilizing mission', and thought its benefits outweighed all Western misgivings about Russia's aggressive designs and the re-alignment in the balance of powers. Barooshian also cites Vereshchagin's firm belief that any firsthand experience of Asiatic barbarism would change the minds of 'myopic politicians' influenced by the fictional works of 'sentimental travelers'. Barooshian similarly explained Vereshchagin's readiness to go to Turkestan, or to join the staff of the Russian army in the Russo-Turkish War as a volunteer, as springing from his unfaltering commitment to modern progress. He showed how in July 1876, even though financially devastated by a swindle after coming to Paris, he still donated 100 francs when Serbia and Montenegro, encouraged by Russian Slavophiles, declared war on Turkey in an effort to achieve independence from oppressive Turkish domination.[10]

According to Schimmelpenninck Vereshchagin's decision was

occasioned solely by lure of greater comforts in painting. As he later told a friend, he 'had no passionate love for the East'. He 'studied in the East because' he was 'freer there . . . than in the West. Instead of a Parisian garret or some room . . . on Vasil'evskij Island [in St. Petersburg]', he 'would have a Kirghiz yurt. . . .'[11] But, as Barooshian points out, Vereshchagin's decision to join the wars was also occasioned by his compensatory psychological needs for heroics, patriotism and search for existential moments and situations to be captured in sketches and paintings. Regarding the first, there were at least three occasions when he actually fought and gave leadership: (i) during the defense of the Russian fortress in Samarkand in Central Asia against Muslim efforts at penetration after Kaufman's impolitic departure, from 2 to 7 June 1868 till his return; (ii) after Russian troops were encircled by a large number of Chinese troops and furious local population because of their over-reactive plunders; and (iii) during laying of buoys in the Danube for guidance to Russian torpedo boats as part of a torpedo-mining squad in Mali-Idjos in northern Siberia, when he was hurt by a ricocheting bullet. For the first two exploits he was awarded the Cross of St. George from an independent commission against his will, on Kaufman's recommendation, which he accepted, and the Cross of St. Stanislav from the State, which he refused. For the third gallantry he was awarded a golden sword by Grand Duke Nicholas, though he declined the offer. Finally, in the Russo-Japanese War he joined his Admiral friend on the battleship *Petropavlovsk*—the flagship of the Russian fleet in the Pacific—at his invitation, refused his request to leave it when it set out to sea to engage Japanese ships, and died when the ship was tricked into a mine bed, was exploded and sank with its crew of 700 souls.[12]

This indomitable urge to remain in the thick of battle cannot be explained simply by any pacifist mission. The explanations, backed by solid evidence, are: (i) though he treated war as a scourge, he was at the same time attracted to it; (ii) he regarded war as justifiable in special circumstances; and (iii) he valued it as a source of new, realistic sketches and paintings. Regarding the first Barooshian says in the context of his decision to join the Russo-Turkish war, that although he 'undoubtedly sympathized with the Slavic cause in the Balkans', he was also possessed, 'as he simply put it, by "a great desire to see with my own eyes a regular European war," and to "observe, feel and study people"'.[13]

The second factor, i.e. an admission of the liberating potential of war as a carrier of progress comes out from contrast between the central message of the Turkestan series, and Vereshchagin's most famous anti-war painting, which is a part of the series. Regarding his most famous painting *Apotheosis of War*, showing a 'pyramid of human skulls, some of which bear the marks of sabre blows', with ravens persisting 'in their futile efforts to feed on the skeletal remains', in the background of a 'once-blossoming landscape, formerly filled with gardens and other evidence of human creativity', now 'reduced to a wasteland', Barooshian finds, 'in the context of the Turkestan collection . . . a paradox':

> Vereshchagin disparaged barbarism and condemned war, but he justified war as a necessary evil—as part of the white man's burden—to eradicate barbarism. His support of war and of Russia's civilizing mission issued from his belief in the inevitability of historical progress through reason and science and in Russian cultural superiority to uncivilized peoples.[14]

The third factor, i.e. search for suitable material for paintings, sometimes took bizarre proportions. During the Russo-Turkish war two Turkish irregulars, soldier bandits (*bashi-bazouks*), known for their extreme cruelty were captured. Vereshchagin asked General Strukov, one of General Skobelev's aides, to 'hang the two bandits, because he had never witnessed such an execution', 'was much interested in the process', and wanted to sketch it. The request is said to have shocked the General who questioned Vereshchagin about his uncharacteristic thirst for blood. Vereshchagin felt frustrated when Skobelev changed his decision of hanging them after court-martial following Strukov's pleas. He sketched them before their release for a subsequent painting.[15]

This is why denigration of war from the perspective of the sacredness of life which touched an immense height of intensity in the poetry of Wilfred Owen (1893–1918) is sadly absent in Vereshchagin's painting. In Owen's self-avowed 'nonconsolatory elegies'[16] there is no 'exhilarating defiance of death', but a melancholic paean of life that is all the more poignant in the death dealing battlefield.[17]

Battle Paintings: Contents and Contradictions

This is not to suggest that Vereshchagin did not have sufficient paintings that brought out the worst aspects of war, including its barbarism and ugly and ignominious death. Actually his oeuvre also covered many other forms of inequality and oppression known in Russian, European or colonial societies. Thus one of his first paintings, *Boathaulers* (1866), which predated Ilia Repin's far more famous *Boathaulers on the Volga* by more than three years, sought to show that even after emancipation of Russian serfs in 1861, jobless and homeless Russian peasants from the villages were finding their life very hard, yoked to another form of slavery.[18] Though not always impartial, his anti-war paintings are diverse and truthful. One painting, *After Victory* (1868) shows two Uzbeks exploring the battlefield for dead Russian soldiers to behead them, contemplating a recent trophy with keen interest. *After Defeat* (1868) shows how amidst two piles of dead Muslim soldiers strewn outside the fortress walls, including a dead Russian in a white cap in the left foreground, a Russian soldier in the immediate foreground lights his pipe nonchalantly, and three Russian soldiers in the left background are conversing in complete obliviousness of the horror around them. The message is just not that apart from loosening the norms of morality and civilized behaviour, war cheapens life both for the victors and the vanquished. Schimmelpenninck thinks the artist was suggesting that 'East and West were actually not so far apart'.[19] The barbarism of war is also graphically brought out in *Presenting the Trophies* (1872) and its sequel *Rejoicing* (1872). In the former, in the courtyard of a magnificent palace, with the famous throne of Tamerlane seen between the second and third pillars, a small group of Muslim warriors have kept a number of blackened Russian heads for examination by the Emir of Bukhara, who has rolled off one from the stinking pile with his left foot, making a *mullah* cover his nose. In *Rejoicing*, in front of the decaying Shir dar Madrasa at Samarkand, amidst people of diverse social backgrounds assembled for thanksgiving, one *mullah* in the centre is holding up a pole, on which a Russian head is mounted, and is trying to whip up fresh religious frenzy in full view of the warrior chief on a gray horse in the right foreground.[20] *By the Fortress Wall: Let Them Enter* (1871) and *By the Fortress Wall: They Have Entered* (1871) tell a continuous story. The former shows long files of Russian soldiers waiting silently on tiptoes behind a fortress structure with sabres and rifles ready to take on advancing Muslim attackers. The latter shows the terrible tolls the assault on the fortress has taken on both sides, with rows of dead and wounded soldiers in the background and foreground, waiting to be carted away for mass burial or treatment; and a wounded man in the foreground trying with his upraised hand to catch the attention of three Russian soldiers standing on the ridge of the fortress wall, one guarding the Russian flag, two casually smoking their pipes. Still more different is *The Fatally Wounded Soldier* (1873), inspired by the experience of the defense of the Samarkand fortress. The wounded Russian has broken from the ranks of those defending the fortress and has dropped his rifle because of excruciating pain; and gripping his chest with both hands takes a few uncertain steps forward before the final collapse.

Two other paintings planned during Vereshchagin's participation in the Chinese border clashes—*Surprise Attack* (1871) and *Surrounded! They Are Pursuing* (1872)—valorize the undaunted courage, determination and patriotism of the common Russian soldier. In the former a small detachment of Russian soldiers camped in a valley and being observed secretly by Muslim scouts have come under sudden attack by mounted Muslim warriors; and in the second they have repulsed the assault, but are hardly in a position to ward off another attack. *The Forgotten Soldier* (1871) shows a Russian soldier lying dead on a slight slope in a background of river, plain and mountains, not sighted when the dead were collected and buried after battle. Two eagles and many ravens hover in the air above him and one raven has already alighted on his blood-stained chest, suggesting his fate.[21]

Many of the paintings of the Turkestan series, like the *Forgotten Soldier*, displeased the tsar and the Russian military and bureaucracy, as an affront to Russian army management. The tsar questioned Vereshchagin's patriotism in the context of *Surprise Attack, Surrounded! They Are Pursuing* and *By the Fortress Wall. They Have Entered*, giving him such an attack of nerves that he burned the pictures. He warded off all subsequent efforts to dissuade him from exhibiting these pictures abroad through academic and other allurements, causing calumny against him.[22] His paintings during the Russo-Turkish War too failed to please the tsar and the military-bureaucratic elites. *Alexander II at Plevna on August 30, 1877* (1878–9) which showed the tsar with his entourage sipping champagne with a confident air after having breakfasted on a small slope near Plevna at the time of his third abortive bid to take Plevna, together with *After the Attack: Dressing Station at Plevna* (1881), which showed thousands of Russian soldiers and even Turkish soldiers waiting to receive medical attention before tents having a capacity for five hundred, was accused of humiliating the tsar in the people's estimation. This was more so because another painting, *Before the Attack at Plevna* (1881) pointed out lapses in strategic planning. While the *Conquerors* (1878–9) showed Turkish soldiers stripping and denuding dead Russian soldiers of their uniforms and boots, *The Road of the Prisoners of War* (*The Road to Plevna*) (1878–9) told the opposite story of how after the Russian victory in December, thousands of Turkish prisoners of war were forced to march from Plevna to the Danube without adequate clothing and food; and how incommoded by the bitter cold they finally fell down to freeze slowly to death. A number of paintings critiqued the army top brass. In *All Is Quiet at Shipka* (1878–9), a three-piece painting, a hooded Russian sentry tries to protect himself against a blizzard with his rifle before finally succumbing, mocking General F. Radetsky's premature report to the military command that 'All is quiet at Shipka'. The even more critical *The Defeated: Funeral Service* (1877–9), portrays a scene in Telish in northern Bulgaria, of half of a Russian regiment killed and massacred because of a wrong command, and the conduct of a mass burial service by a priest assisted by a Russian soldier.[23]

VERESHCHAGIN AND THE TSARIST CIRCLE: TROUBLED RELATIONS

Predictably the tsar and his court did not take kindly to the paintings. The Grand Prince Alexander, later Tsar Alexander III in 1881, refused to see *The Road of the Prisoners of War* after seeing his courtiers' reactions. This made Grand Duke Vladimir, President of the Academy of Arts, criticize him for the 'impossible subjects' of his painting. Vereshchagin wrote in self-defence that his critics are 'concerned not so much with the universal idea of war as . . . with particulars'. He contended in another letter, that 'between festive paintings of war . . . and paintings of war as such, as it really is, there is a vast difference'.[24]

It was in this spirit that Vereshchagin drew one of his most popular war paintings, *Shipka-Sheinovo* (*Skobelev at Shipka*) (1883–8), where the message is, in Vereshchagin's words, 'in war, victory is only ten percent, and ninety percent is horrible mutilations, cold, hunger, cruelty, despair and death in its staggering manifestations'. General Skobelev is celebrating his decisive victory at Shipka, astride a white horse, followed by Vereshchagin and his staff saluting the cheering soldiers. Scattered are frozen Turkish and Russian corpses in the immediate foreground. While cheering troops are throwing their caps in the air, in the name of the country and the Sovereign, at the extreme left the frozen, raised hand of a dead Russian soldier mocks this victory.[25]

Vereshchagin's other paintings like the *Site of the Battle Fought on July 18 1877 in Front of the Krishin Redoubt near Plevna*, or the *Cannon*, etc., showed the gory, sepulchral aspects of war. *Captured with Arms? Shoot Them*, *Cart for the Wounded*, *Corner of the Turkish Redoubt Captured on May 30 but Abandoned on May 31*, *Interrogation of a Deserter*, *Interrupted Letter*, *In the Hospital*, *Picket in the Balkan Mountains*, *Picket on the Danube*, *The Night Bivouac of the Great Army*, *Letter Remained Unfinished*, *Letter to Mother*, *Spy*, etc., showed the travails, pain, loneliness and drudgery of soldiers in wars.[26] Barooshian rightly points out that the these paintings highlight 'the contradictory roles that Vereshchagin sought to play in his life; on the one hand his attachment to the military, his love of military action, his passion for objective scientific observation and knowledge of war, and on the other hand his condemnation of war and his genuine compassion for the sufferings of the ordinary people.' Like Tolstoy, he too 'condemned war but supported it patriotically when it served noble or just causes'. Grand Prince Alexander did not understand this contradiction. Hence his comment on a copy of the catalogue of Vereshchagin's Paris exhibition: 'either Vereshchagin is a swine or a completely deranged man'.[27] This also explains the hostile reaction of the Russian royal court to his 1880 exhibit of Balkan War paintings, which 'from the perspective of the Russian autocracy', were 'bitter reminders of its failed ambitions of military conquest; its military inferiority, economic backwardness, and diplomatic humiliation'. Together with 'his allegedly biased portrayal of the war . . . his refusal to accompany the tsar in his review', led the exhibit to be considered 'an assault not only against war but against the political order as well'.[28]

Moreover, Vereshchagin's art did not embarrass the Russian State and Church only through the war paintings. His *Trilogy of Executions*, beginning with the *Roman Execution* (*Crucifixion*) (1887), and covering *English Suppression of an Indian Rebellion* (1884) and *Execution of Conspirators in Russia* (1885), together with other biblical pieces raised thorny questions for both the State and the Church. This was not only because of the easily identifiable semiotics of crucifixion in all the paintings, but also because the third was clearly inspired by the public hanging of five members of the Russian revolutionary organization, *The People's Will*, who assassinated Tsar Alexander II.[29] Owing to the censor's ban Vereshchagin could never exhibit them. But the *Holy Family* (1884–5) and *The Resurrection of Christ* (1884–5) created quite a controversy in Vienna in 1885 and in Budapest in 1886, even before the exhibition. This induced Vereshchagin to give his first public talk before the Hungarians on the role of art in society, which was later incorporated in *Realism* and *On Progress in Art*.[30]

In *Realism* Vereshchagin defended his paintings that had come under attack, including *Alexander II at Plevna on August 30, 1877, After the Attack: A Dressing Station in Plevna, The Road of the Prisoners of War (The Road to Plevna), The Defeated: Funeral Service, Roman Execution (Crucifixion)*, and *Execution of Conspirators in Russia.* He claimed that the depiction of realities in them was either natural or based on personal observations. Regarding the first picture he called his critics naïve 'to imagine their Emperor parading on a fiery steed at a moment of danger when the battle was at its height'. Regarding the last he pointed out that 'Cannon-Fire in India was not at all to the taste of the British, whereas the Russians were full of praise for it'.[31] In *On Progress in Art* Vereshchagin justified his innovations by showing why blind imitation of the old masters does not serve any purpose.[32]

But neither these justifications nor Vereshchagin's last and patriotic series, the *Patriotic War of 1812* won him back to the good books of the tsar and the State. One reason behind this lies in the artistic limitations of the series. Napoleon, the leit motif in the series, comes out in the majority of the paintings as 'a troubled, tormented and indecisive man'. But this could not compensate for the exclusion of Tsar Alexander and General Mikhail Kutuzov from the series as subjects. The heroic resistance of the Russian people was described only in three paintings, *In Defeated Moscow (Arsonists or Shooting in the Kremlin)* (1897–8), *Wait! Let'em Come Nearer!* (1887–95), and *Captured with Arms? Shoot Them* (1887–95). Only a minor painting, *Bayonet-Charge: Hurrah! Hurrah!* (1887–95) is reserved for the Russian army, though the pyrrhic victory of the French army in *The End of the Borodino Battle* (1899–1900), also suggests the strong resistance of the Russian army. The pictures that show nonplused Napoleon in different moods are: *Napoleon I at the Borodino Heights* (1897); *Near Moscow Waiting for a Boyar Delegation* (1891–2); *Napoleon and Marshall Lauriston (Peace at All Costs!)* (1899–1900); *The Kremlin is Burning* (1887–98); etc. Similarly, *Return from the Petrovsky Palace* (1895), *Night Bivouac of the Grand Army* (1896–7), and On *the Road. Retreat, Flight* (1887–95) showed the bafflement and travails of Napoleon's grand army till its inglorious exit from Russia. But critics pointed out many loopholes in the narrative, like the portrayal of the defeated but not the victorious, 'lack of a tangible hero', and want of anything of historical significance for the Russian people. For these reasons Vereshchagin was even unable to sell the series in Russia.[33]

UNFAMILIAR 'ORIENTALIST' IN CAUCASUS AND TURKESTAN

How could the anti-establishment artist be the same man as the diehard supporter of Russia's expansion in the east? Here one needs to remember the circumstances in which Vereshehagin became a member of the Kaufman team. Ethnic classification became a tool of Russian rule in Turkestan after tsarist forces conquered the region in the 1860s and 1870s. The people of Turkestan, partly nomadic and partly settled townspeople and farmers, forming a compact society—though isolated geographically and culturally from the Russian core of the empire, almost entirely Muslim by religion, by language predominantly Turkic with linguistic ties to the Volga Tatars, and tied by religious bonds with the Ottoman Empire—presented two choices before Kaufman. One was the 'time-honoured formula of conquest, subjugation, administrative integration (siliianie) and conversion to Orthodox Christianity' that had characterized border-lands policy in the early eighteenth century. The other was the policy of ethnographic inquiry into the empire's peoples that Enlightenment had inspired and Empress Catherine actively pursued. The resultant policy of 'toleration and recognition of ethnic differences' informed the Kaufman administration's policy toward Turkestan subjects. As part of his modified Catherinian policy of applying a kind of European positivism to Turkestan, of understanding his subjects through ethnography, he searched for civilian specialists who could aid in this project. Vereshchagin, his 'artist-in-residence during the first years in Turkestan' was a prime choice.[34] Schimmelpenninck, however, thinks that in his decision of inventorying the newly-conquered area and appointing an artist for it, Kaufman was influenced by Napoleon's example in Egypt.[35] The centre of their activities, at least in the initial years, was the Tashkent branch of the Society for Amateurs of Natural Science, Anthropology and Ethnology. It sent many expeditions to map the geology and geography of Turkestan, and looked in 1871 and 1872 beyond mere collection of statistical data to include the 'past lives of the people and the description and study of their monuments' in their terms of reference.

As part of this huge textual production, Vereshchagin travelled to Turkestan 'on special commission' of the governor-general in 1868 and 1870, with complete freedom to create his own images of the territory, which included the people(s), the monuments and the conquest itself, and 'to present this visual picture to the Russian public'. Kaufman's foresight paid off. The Russian organizers of the Third International Congress of Orientalists in St.

Petersburg in 1876 asked him and other administrators of the empire's eastern regions for regional costumes and photographs and other evidences of 'the presence of live representatives of the Asian peoples belonging to the empire'. Kaufman more than complied. He sent personally selected artefacts, both dead and live (three natives), and other texts and images that would represent the real human face of his subjects to the Congress. Vereshchagin's artistic work benefited Kaufman's project immensely. In the Turkestan series, comprising more than 250 drawings and paintings, the overwhelming majority consisted of portraits of individuals attributed specific ethnic, though not individual identity, like *Uzbek Elder, a Kirgiz, A Sart Woman*, etc. In Moscow and Petersburg exhibits enthusiastic Russian crowds browsed this visual display of the empire's Muslim subjects.[36]

Kaufman's choice of Vereshchagin for this work speaks of his cleverness. Brower shows that the 'story of Vereshchagin's encounter with the Orient began with his break with the Academy of Arts and with its neo-classical artistic canons. His search for inspiration took him (like poets before him) to Caucasia,[37] and then to Paris to the art studio of one of the most famous Orientalist artists, Jean-Léon Jérôme'.[38] In the 'Introduction' we have shown how Russia's 'secondary orientalism' offered two choices of encoding her Orient: (i) 'forgetting all about the second-rate Russian Asia' and focusing on the 'real and alien (for Russians) "Orient"', and (ii) 'editing Russia's own East making it fit the generally accepted orientalist stereotype'.[39] Tlostanova thinks that Vereshchagin, who after Central Asia went to India and the Middle East, followed the first 'Orientalist' option.[40] But I think that traces of both the alternative ways are to be found in Vereshchagin if we go into his discourse on the east.

TRANS-CAUCASIA: FANATICISM, WILDNESS, DEVIANT DEGENERATION

Before we analyse Vereshchagin's representation of contemporary Caucasus and Central Asia, we should know where it stood at this historical juncture. Traditionally a 'paradigmatic anti-space, a nonspace' for the West, the quintessential border space, and 'no place',[41] cultural, linguistic, religious and ethnic hybrids of Zoroastrianism, Christianity and Islam', these two territories had developed 'their own unique and tolerant ways of dealing with this cultural multiplicity as well as the strategies of survival under various regimes'. On top of this they had been colonized 'not directly by the Western capitalist empires, but by the so called subaltern empires, or empires-colonies, like Russia, which itself was colonized epistemically and culturally by the West and thus, acted as mediators, as champions of Western modernity in these locales, albeit in a distorted form'.[42] It is in this context that we should find out just what Vereshchagin was in his depiction of these areas—a Russian Orthodox, a European positivist, a secular Russian, or a humanist cosmopolitan. But whatever he was, he plainly misread the multicultural texture of Caucasian society.

This is evident from his account of the Shiite festival of Muharram, in a town called 'Shusha' (Shushi),[43] in which avowedly the sufferings, sacrifice and martyrdom of the past Imams, and primarily of the first Imam Hussain, were remembered. Vereshchagin found the 'self-tormentation' of the Shiites in the procession on the tenth and final day of their mourning as nothing short of 'fanaticism and wildness'. Apart from repeatedly describing the 'performers' as 'fanatics', he also relates, with wry humour, how for want of other Muslim actors the role of the Imam's murderers was performed, somewhat unexpectedly and 'unsuitably', by Don Cossacks. The verbal representation is aided by three sketches, of a Persian, of a 'self-tormentor', and of a recumbent young Imam.[44]

If Muharram was wrong because of its masochism-sadism, two other sectarian deviations from Christianity too were criticized. But here a few words about these 'sectarians' may help us better to judge Vereshchagin as a Russian 'Orientalist'. As a Western authority on Russian 'sectarians' points out, on 20 October 1830, Tsar Nicholas I issued an edict which decreed that 'all religious dissenters (sektanty) who were classified as "especially pernicious" (including Dukhobors, Molokans and Subbotniks, but not including Old Believers) were to be relocated to Transcaucasia by either forcible exile or voluntary resettlement'. The legislation was a deliberate move to utilize the empire's periphery as a site to fence off sectarian Russians from Orthodox ones and 'to use communal isolation to resolve the perceived dilemmas of religious difference.' From 1830 through the 1880s, tsarist policy actively continued with the relocation of dissenters, in an effort to protect Orthodox subjects from the spiritually polluting infection by the heretics. As late as in the 1890s these non-conformists preponderated over all other ethnic Russians in Trans-Caucasia. 'The sectarian dominance of colonist communities', says Nicholas Breyfogle, 'inextricably linked popular spirituality with Russian colonialism. . . . Their segregation to the southern borderlands simultaneously altered the religious landscape of the tsarist empire in enduring ways'. Many of them resorted to a form of 'pacifist insurgency', which met with state repression.[45]

The difference of Russia's dissenter colonization in South Caucasus from the experience of the British in Rhodesia, the French in Algeria, and the Dutch and British in South Africa was that in the latter a numerically preponderant indigenous population remained after European conquest and resettlement; but in Russia the heretics and peasants, the sectarians, did not settle there with a colonial mission.[46] Besides, though these 'indigenous' Russian Christian sects and their different subsects broke away from the Orthodox Church to embrace different forms of theology and practice, they were distinguished by their Russian origin from 'imported' Western Protestant sects, and also from Old Believers, who looked upon themselves as true practitioners of Orthodoxy. Dukhobors, Molokans and Subbotniks were rather adherents of a certain part of a spectrum of religiosity, the hues and shades of their faiths and rituals often merging with one another. They came from similar spiritual roots in the Eastern Christian tradition; and were not always easily distinguishable in their day-to-day religiosity from Orthodox Christians. However, all of them were against the institutional Orthodox Church's insistence on mediation by priests in the worshipper's relation to The God, and on sacraments and icons, saints, relics, candles, and churches. There were, however, some real differences among them too. While the Dukhobors placed their faith in a strong oral tradition of psalms and hymns known as the 'Living

Book', in place of the Bible, the Molokans considered the Old and New Testaments as the sole source of religious authority. The Subbotniks observed some, if not all, injunctions of Judaism and chose the Talmud in place of the Bible. The Dukhobors and the Molokans also shared certain social and political viewpoints stemming from common religious beliefs, e.g. distrust of secular authorities of the state.[47]

But the Russian Orthodox lens through which Vereshchagin saw Muharram is applied to the 'Duchobortzis' (Dukhobors) too, whom he had met in 'Slavyanka', not far from Susha.[48] They had been exiled, Vereshchagin informs, from '*Rusia proper* on account of their indefatigable zeal in propagating their doctrines'; and had settled among the Armenians and Tartars.[49] In tune with the Russian State's fear of them, Vereshchagin, who disliked the ministration of any form of religious instruction to his children[50] got down to judging 'Duchobortzis' by comparison with the Orthodox Church:

> The main thought of their religion may be expressed in a few words—one God in three persons, viz. God the Father—the memory; God the son—the understanding; god the Holy Ghost—the will: the Trinity in Unity. *They have no sacred books, and do not recognize the Old and the New Testament, or the writings of the fathers of the Orthodox Church.* 'These books' . . . 'are . . . written by human hands and ... are imperfect.' Their conception of Christ is very obscure: beyond a confused notion that He is at once man and God, they have not the least idea how He lived and for what He suffered. The sources of their knowledge of Christ are their 'so called' Psalms of David [italics added].[51]

Vereshchagin next tells us that the Psalms 'could just not belong to him [David]', because after transmission for many generations through oral tradition they 'had been so corrupted as to make the most ridiculous nonsense'. However, he related the way they lived as a well-ordered group under their new governor; described their community life, their assets, etc.; and provided some important ethnographic data about them, apart from giving two sketches of a Duchobortzi man and woman.[52]

The 'notes' then relate the religious divisions and conflictual nature of another deviant Trans-Caucasian religious sect, the 'Molokanes' or Molokans, a group that did not live the orderly lives of the Duchobortzis, but had because of their religious divisions and conflictual nature split into several communities. Vereshchagin goes to the length of judging, as a Russian Orthodox, the most 'rational' among them. The 'pure Molokanes' are 'the most rational . . . as far as the observance of their customs is concerned'. This is because while holding the psalms of David in high esteem, they also 'recognize the Old and the New Testaments', and 'keep some of the festivals of the Old Testament like the Orthodox Church'. There was, however, some tension on this point, between 'pure Molokanes' and 'the Subbotnikes' who wanted 'to keep all the Jewish festivals', and other sub-sects who took 'an intermediate position between the Pure Molokanes and the Subbotnikes'.[53]

From the same Russian Orthodox lens Vereshchagin describes the 'Leapers', the third sub-sect of the 'Molokanes', as the most 'Oriental'. It is not only that the 'Leapers' organize their religion around their interpretation of the nature of the Holy Ghost, who 'manifests himself visibly in such a manner as to throw the devotees in transports'. The Leapers are also farthest removed from the dominant pattern of Russian Christianity, whether in their methods of expiation, or in their practice of heterosexual kissing in their prayer meetings, in which men take the initiative. The other 'Molokanes' are different too. Apart from making the women sit behind the men in the prayer meetings, as 'they are inferior to men in dignity', they also push 'the Christian dogma . . . that every sin of word or deed may be expiated by repentance', to its extreme limits. For, they deduce from this that one has to sin in order to be able to repent. Among the pure Molokanes there is no outward and visible sign of the process; and 'the happy one only heaves [a sigh]'. But the Leapers have the sign of boisterous expiation that involves men and women getting all the external marks of being possessed, and dancing and raving together. Vereshchagin's depiction of these dances and ravings has strong sexual overtones, made all the more suggestive by his pointers to the young age of the followers of this sect, and the constraining influence of Puritanism on them. Two sketches of a Molokane man and a woman complete the 'othering' of Trans-Caucasians from Russians as Europeans.[54]

Central Asia: Slavery, Pauperism, Russian Deliverance

If in the portrayal of Trans-Caucasian religious beliefs and ways of life Vereshchagin takes certain aspects of the Russian Orthodox Church practices as the only test of Russia's peripheral peoples' entitlement to Christianity, then in the depiction of Central Asia, he locates himself firmly in Russia as Europe. Anyway Vereshchagin's description as an 'otherness machine'[55] gets even more active in his depiction of Turkestan and other parts of Central Asia,[56] where he went as an attaché in 1867 to Kaufman.

The 'Orientalist' lens in the description of Central Asia comes out clearly in the subjects of the first chapter itself: slavery and slave trade in Turkestan; dancing boys dressed as girls; begging as a profession; and endemic opium eating among the people of Central Asia. We find Vereshchagin talking about the slave caravanserais and the slave trade; showing how chattel-slaves were priced and purchased; how they were sometimes lifted by force from the neighbouring lands of the 'Turcomans'; how the collection of slaves were otherwise determined by the vicissitudes of the neighbouring economies; and finally how Russia, in its civilizing influence, brought an end to the evil practice.[57] Here Vereshchagin is echoing the familiar argument of brigandage in the steppe and slavery in the backyard and Russia's civilizing mission as a rationale of Russian expansion.[58] Equally symptomatic of the 'secondary Orientalism'[59] in Vereshchagin's description is the reference to the 'public display' or 'tamasha' of 'dancing boys' or 'bacha', mainly 'before the fasts of the great festival of Beiram', which is also the season of weddings. He describes how a Sart trader took him aside to see the dressing of a 'batsha' as a girl, as a kind of privileged voyeuristic viewing; and how the side-glances and amorous gestures of the boy, dressed perfectly as and having the mien of a girl, after the dance performance, were taken with the most reverential admiration by the other Sarts.[60] The whole description has an unmistakably high dose of pedesasty, in a very uneasy echo of Chokhan Valikhanoff's reference to child abusing habits of the adult male population of East Turkestan and Semirech'e.[61]

Vagrancy and mendicancy also feature prominently in the description. 'Pauperism', notes Vereshchagin, 'is highly developed and organized in this country. The poor form a sort of brotherhood with a head, who is descended from the saint who gave the poor an organization and secured them in the possession of the land granted to them by the community. Anyone is free to take up his abode here and become a divana.' Pauperism is also a flourishing business, since the head of the brotherhood—'Tiura', literally 'lord of the poor'—lives in style, collecting his dues from subordinates, giving judgements and settling differences. Pauperism arises from the social allowance for idling in the Orient. 'Anybody', says Vereshchagin, 'who prefers a vagabond life to labour can become a divana, or licensed beggar'. The new entrants are given a 'special red uniform', rags for begging, and living space in the dorms of the 'kalendarkhan' (asylum for the poor). After marriage they get separate houses in the 'kalendarkhan'.[62]

Opium eating is closely related to vagrancy and mendicancy. It is not only because nearly 'all the divanas are confirmed drunkards [and] nearly all are opium eaters'. It is also because 'the kalendarkhan is not only an asylum for beggars, but also something of a café restaurant and a club', where anybody can come for a smoke of 'nasha', or a 'draught of Kuknar'.[63]

The critique does not stop here. Vereshchagin found the houses and schools of 'Tashkend' (Tashkent) and the entire educational system hopelessly archaic and backward. The houses were of clay, and without proper windows. But in this fallen-out-off time place the civilizing influence of Russia had already made the wealthier householders 'substitute panes of glass for the lattice work covered with oiled paper which used to serve them as windows'. But even then, 'these windows all look on the court, probably many years will pass before the natives venture to make their windows look on the street'.[64] The educational system was also hopelessly Oriental, archaic and untouched by the winds of European modernity. It is not only that the schools, from the elementary to the higher were linked to and controlled by the mosques, the curriculum too contained very little worth learning, because of the monomaniac preoccupation with tradition and religion. Education meant 'expounding the Koran and the commentaries on the Koran composed by the numerous company of Mussulman saints'. Regarding the 'merest rudiments' of 'real education', the *mullahs* (teachers) were 'as deficient as their pupils', though this did not 'prevent them from looking upon themselves and being looked up to by others as great masters'. An example was provided by a *mollah*, 'a venerated man of leaning, and mentor to all the mullahs of Tashkent, a veritable "lamp of learning".' Vereshchagin learned from him that he had got his learning from his father who in turn had studied in Bokhara (Bukhara). 'As he spoke', notes Vereshchagin with deep sarcasm, 'my companion made a solemn gesture towards the south-west, as much as to say, 'There at that brilliant focus of learning and civilization'. He mocked Bukhara as the 'fountainhead', studying where gives, 'an intimate acquaintance with this world and the next'.[65]

The 'secondary Orientalism' and 'secondary Eurocentrism' implicit in this derision does not remember that even in the mid-eighteenth century German and Dutch experts were beseeched to set up new centres of learning in Russia; that the Moscow University in and after 1755 consisted solely of German experts, and during the reign of Empress Elizabeth, of French scholars; and that the most prestigious school in St. Petersburg was run by Jesuits and imparted education in Latin and French.[66] One could even have pointed out that Aleksandrovsky Junior Military School in Tsarskoe Selo, Vereshchagin's first school, trained Russian aspirants to high office in French, German and Latin, together with Russian.[67]

All these vices seemingly disentitled Central Asians to any right to have their own territory. Vereshchagin uses the heterogeneous population of Tashkent to search for the logic of a mass Russian influx and a new Russian settlement. The land 'lately conquered by Russia', writes Vereshchagin without a shred of uneasiness, is inhabited by 'Sart' townspeople, 'Tadshiks', 'Usbek' (Uzbek), 'Kirghiz', 'Kuramasses', 'Turcomans', 'Nogais', 'Kashghars', 'Afghans', 'Persians', 'Arabs', 'Jews', 'Hindoos', 'Gypsies', and lastly Russians.[68] Quite expectedly the mixed populations of Trans-Caucasia and Central Asia are treated differently. Vereshchagin has sympathy for the Dukhobors/Molokans, 'removed some thirty-five or thirty years ago by order of the Government', and 'now permitted to return to their homes'. He is sure that 'if land enough is assigned to them many will leave Transcaucasia, where they are unable to make themselves at home' and feel out of place among these 'giant mountains'.[69] By contrast Central Asia is marked out for Russian expansion and colonization. The first argument is familiar enough, namely, the benefits from Russia's civilizing mission. Its first impact has been the decreasing force of slave trade in Central Asia under Russian influence: 'That the cleansing of this foul cesspool has begun, thanks to *the interference of Russia, is at any rate a matter of congratulation* . . . [italics added].[70]

Vereshchagin reminds that abolition of slavery would cover 'that other class of slaves, who are not called slaves in any textbook, but yet whose slavery is the most terrible of all,—the mothers, wives and daughters of the Barbarians of Central Asia,—do they not also already feel the slow but sure influence of the laws and civilization of the Caffirs [kafirs, infidels] upon their position and destiny?' Vereshchagin is certain that they surely do. For, he has heard how his 'Asiatic' landlord resents being prevented from beating his wife—'his property, his lawfully acquired chattel slave'—by her threat 'to go to the Russians'; and knows how embittered he is by 'this apostasy and the authors of this discord'.[71]

If anyone thinks that it was to correct the civilizational lag of Central Asia that Vereshchagin wanted Russia's intervention in Central Asia, s/he should be in for some shock from Vereshchagin's exploration of the heterogeneity of the demographic profile of Tashkent for the possibilities of Russian infiltration that it offered. He first mentions, in a rueful tone, that the presence of the Russians in Central Asia was even then meagre. He adds with some pride that 'their predominance, which is an indisputable fact, rests upon the fear which the nations have of their uniform, victorious arms and the great superiority of European civilization to the semi-barbarism of the peoples of Central Asia'. But then he seems unhappy that 'soldiers, officials or merchants' were almost all the types of Russians who were present in Central Asia. He shows in simple enough imperialistic terms what types of non-Russian influx was anyway brewing force in Central Asia, and what should be the best policy to manage it, without any trace in it of his famous concern for colonial subjectivity:

> Colonists have not yet appeared in the land of Sarts, Usbeks and Kirghiz; but they are already slowly but surely approaching Syr-Daria; and the time is not very distant when the country folk of South Western Siberia will knock at the doors of this new Russian province. The *colonization of Central Asia by Russia no doubt presents serious difficulties; in the first place land must be acquired, taken from the natives* and assigned to Russians; and this is no easy matter. Nevertheless this problem must be solved, with due regard to the requirements of justice, and that as quickly as possible. *On its solution depends the future of Russian supremacy in Asia, and the welfare of the peoples who have already submitted to us, who,* when all is said, *have much to gain from the establishment of Russian rule* in Central Asia than from a return to their former slavery. The overthrow of the Russian rule would be the signal for the commencement of those civil wars, of that violence and robbery and perpetual injustice, of which hitherto the history of Central Asia has consisted under dynasties and in all districts . . . [italics added].[72]

Few Western Orientalists, even of the most 'magisterial' school, have defended the imposition of European rule in any part of the East in clearer terms. But the question is, since annexation of Central Asia was already very far advanced, what other form of Russian 'colonization' was Vereshchagin talking about, which presented so many 'serious difficulties'? The key to his mind may lie in the meaning of the word 'colony' given by the *Oxford English Dictionary*, as 'a settlement in a new country . . . a body of people who settle in a new locality, forming a community subject to or connected with the parent state; the community so formed, consisting of the original settlers and their descendants and successors, as long as the connection with the parent state is kept up'. Clearly, Vereshchagin had in mind this meaning of the term, by which even British rule in India was not fully colonial. For, until Russians set themselves 'deliberately and systematically to colonize the country, Russian Turkestan . . . will be Russian in name only'. And unless 'the government procures land enough to plant a numerous Christian and civilized population among the uncivilized Mahomedan population, Syr-Daria will belong to us only in the sense in which India belongs to England, i.e. we must make up our minds that sooner or later the natives will rise and turn us out'. He compared the Russian position in Turkestan with 'that of France in Algeria; the only way to prevent the people from constantly rising against us is to colonize the country'.[73]

These words make it clear that Vereshchagin wanted Central Asia to go the way of Americas, Canada, Australia and New Zealand, 'lands of original settlement', where the settlers formed stable local communities with varying amounts of links with the parent state, and had no thought of returning. These are the words of a colonialist, not of a friend of the oppressed. Do Vereshchagin's paintings say any different story?

MESSAGE OF 'ORIENTALIST' ART: INFERIORITY OF RUSSIA'S ORIENT

I do not think they do, in spite of Kemp's drumming of Vereshchagin's opposition to colonial wars and the execution of mutineers in the Sepoy Mutiny by the British authorities in his painting.[74] This is because of the dominance of 'Orientalist' stereotypes in his sketches and paintings in Trans-Caucasia, Central Asia, other parts of the East and India, and of a 'secondary eurocentrism' in his ethnography. The sketches in Trans-Caucasia include a 'Persian', a 'Muslim Self-Tormentor', a 'Young Imam' sleeping on his podium at Sushi, and a 'Duchobortzi' and 'Molokane' man and woman. Those of Central Asia are far more diversified. They contain—at Turkestan, sketches of a 'Slave Dealer', 'Chorus of the Divanas', and 'Opium Eaters [at the Kalendarkhan]'; at Tashkent—ethnic types, like an 'Afghan', a 'Nogais', an 'Arab', a 'Jew' and a 'Jewess', a 'Jewish Youth', a 'Hindoo [Hindu]', Mahomedan [Mohammedan]', a 'Hindoo Fakir', a 'Gipsy [Gypsy]'; and near the Chinese Frontier, at the places of Khojakent-Buka, a mixture—of a 'Villager of Chodsagent', a 'Chinese Girl', a 'Kalmuck (Kalmyk) Officer', and a 'Kirghiz Falconer'.[75] It was a perfect gallery of ethnic types, displaying all the stereotypes of Oriental mentality and social behaviour. A few of them convey Oriental indolence, and a few others depict Oriental lasciviousness and child prostitution. In 'The Selling of a Child Slave', a masterly treatment of chiaroscuro, a wealthy Turkestani merchant's lust, a child slave's innocent helpless nudity and a slave dealer's monetary greed fight for attention.[76] A dominant ethnographic-Orientalist orientation is also evidenced by other paintings: *At the Door of a Mosque, Beggar Ninety Six Years Old, Entrance to a Temple in Nikko, In a Boat, Japanese Woman, Monastery in a Rock Ladakh, Moslem Servant, Sinto Temple in Nikko, Sowar the Messenger of the Government, Zyrian, The Doors of Tamerlane, Two Hawks Bashibazouks*, and the famous *Uzbek Woman in Tashkent*, among others.[77]

In the post-Soviet times the appraisal of this 'Orientalist' gaze has been both positive and negative. Starting with positive appreciations, a modern American expert on Central Asia says that 'Vereshchagin portrayed an Asian Russia that was both exotic and entrancing, a world of fierce hand-to-hand military engagements, ambushes and sieges, despotic khans, sun-draped courtyards, mosques and minarets . . . an exotic Orient designed to correspond with European views of the orient in general.'[78] Alex Marshall makes light of the fact that 'he has been dismissed by some as a banal, racist and arch-imperialist genre painter (particularly by most modern Uzbek historiograpers)', as Vereshchagin's views of war and humanity are complex and ambiguous.[79] Similarly, after maintaining that Kaufmans' 'impulse toward rigorous ("scientific") description coexisted with a will to exoticize Central Asia', Adeeb Khalid links Vereshchagin's painting in Turkestan with the second aim. He shows how, 'During two stays in Turkestan, Vereshchagin painted and sketched numerous scenes of local life that illustrated the fanaticism and barbarity of the newly conquered territory: dervishes with irrationally dilated eyes, battle scenes with pyramids of (Russian) skulls, and slave auctions all served to fix the otherness of Central Asia . . . well beyond Russia.' Khalid shows how, with the illustration of Eugene Schuyler's two-volume travelogue *Turkistan*, perhaps the most substantial work on Central Asia to appear in English in the 1870s, 'Vereshchagin's vision . . . became the standard view of Central Asia in Britain and the United States as well'.[80]

Critiquing Vereshchagin's famous Turkestan series, Caucasian scholar Anaita Khudonazar has shown how *Uzbek Woman in Tashkent.* (1873) demonstrated one aspect of Central Asian barbarian customs. It 'shows a dark figure walking on a sunlit street with face and body completely covered with a black veil', and '[l]arge shoes and side pockets hiding the figure's hands complete its visual seclusion, intensified by the bright wall behind her'. Vereshchagin was not only introducing the Russian and European public to the empire's Orient with such paintings as *Opium Addicts*, *Bacha and His Admirers* (or *The Selling of a Child Slave* referred to above), *After Victory*, *Dervishes*, among others, but also the 'most savage elements of the Central Asian lifestyle'. Though regarding *Opium Eaters* and *Bacha and His Admirers* Schimmelpenninck stresses mainly on the 'objective approach, utterly devoid of moralising disapproval or clichéd exoticism', and even suggests that Vereshchagin hinted that 'Asians were no more predisposed to the vice than others',[81] it is clear that Turkestan series is now hurting new Central Asian sensibilities.

Proving Vereshchagin's definite adoption of Tlostanova's first option for Russia's secondary 'Orientalism', his portrayal of these ethnic types as documentation of inferior races that would help the European Russian's efforts to properly assess *his* (use of sexist pronoun is conscious) suave identity is not confined to sketches and paintings in Trans-Caucasia and Central Asia, but extend to his sketches in the Himalayas in both the volumes of the travels. In the first, the reader sees a *Fire-Worshipper*, *A Youth of Sikkim*, *A Woman of Sikkim*, a *Bamian Merchant*, a *Bouthian (woman)*, *Lama Disguised As a Deity*, *Lama Wearing Mask*, *Young Lama*, and *Changshed* (the chief minister of the king of Sikkim').[82] In the second Vereshchagin offers sketches of *A Cashmere Woman*, a *Shiite Mussulman*, *The Wife of Five Husbands*, a *Guide*, *Girl of Ladakh*, *Natives of Ladak*, *Sayce* (*Groom*), *Dancing Girl of Cashmere*, *Official of Thibet*, etc.[83]

Why should the 'Orientalist' depictions of these ethnic people necessarily indicate that they were inferior to the Russians? The answer may be found in just one comment from Vereshchagin, below the sketch of a Hindu, apparently a 'baniya' (trader), in which he differentiates the 'Hindoos of Tashkend', from the Jews, though both of them share the same 'eagerness to scrape money together by every possible means'. It is that 'where the Jew in the hour of danger buries his gold and his treasure and runs away without looking back, the Hindoo quietly sits on his strong box and awaits his death'.[84] The clever timidity of the Jews and the fatalism of the Hindu, both effeminate, obviously set them off from the virile Russian male.

The perception of inferiority of the Orient in his art is not negated by his paintings of the Russo-Turkish War of 1877–8 and the fields of corpses that it produced, though they 'caused disquiet at the imperial court';[85] or by the fact that Vereshchagin did not share Dostoyevsky's panegyrics of General Skobelev's heroism in that war; but rather blamed him for the senseless killing of Turkish soldiers without taking them as prisoners of war.[86] This is because finally he supported Russia's war in Samarkand from the point of view of its civilizing mission. This makes his concern for the sufferings of Indian mutineers not above dispute. As Tlostanova so aptly comments:

> Often the negative characteristics associated with Orientalism were projected by the Russians onto the interpretation of other empires while the native material was not coded in the orientalist terms. Vereshchagin 'defended' Samarkand from the local revolting people but turned overnight into the defender of the Indian peasants against the British colonialists.[87]

This reference to binary 'Orientalism' helps my argument below that despite Vereshchagin's choice of the execution of the mutineers as a subject, his Orientalist paintings in general, ethnographic sketches and—in the Indian case—his behaviour as a traveller, equally show him as a European encoding himself in the context of Indian and Asian backwardness and non-modernity. Of course, unlike his East European oeuvre Vereshchagin does not garnish his paintings and sketches in India with written records. But here we are taking the liberty of using his wife's travelogue as the revealing text for many genealogical and textual reasons. First, the continuity between his depiction of Trans-Caucasia and Central Asia and his wife's portrayal of India is explained by the fact that in a book written in his name, his wife's accounts of their travels in India occupy a huge space in both the volumes. The continuity is made explicit by Vereshchagin at the end of his narrative of journeys to Trans-Caucasia and Central

Asia, where he says that after leaving Central Asia in 1870, as 'soon as these pictures were finished', he started off for India with his wife, 'who made notes, while I visited India and painted'. The delegation is unconditional in the words: 'Here I hand over to my wife'.[88]

In the light of the above observation, by the most conservative interpretation, the Indian travelogue[89] represents a mutually agreed division of labour. At the least it indicates that Vereshchagin was not in disagreement with her portrayal of him in her notes. For, the ease and frequency with which Mrs. Vereshchagin uses the plural pronoun 'we', suggest that Vereshchagin approved of her depiction. Besides, it is impossible that in their constant company on the mountain paths she did not compare notes with him. I now turn to her travelogue in some details as it gives us an intimate observation of the artist and his transformation in Europe's Orient.

EUROPEANS IN THE WILDERNESS: VERESHCHAGINS IN THE HIMALAYAS

The contents of the Mrs. Vereshchagin's memoirs in the second part of volume I and the first and longest part of volume II of her travels in India may show quite clearly that Vereshchagin's 'secondary Orientalist' lens extended beyond Russia's East to the eastern parts of the Himalayas, which they explored at the inopportune and inhospitable time of January in 1874,[90] Vereshchagin appears here not as a 'social critic', a declassed artist, feeling deep empathy for the subalterns in India suffering under the impact of oppressive British rule, but as a man who was thoroughly enjoying himself in a perfectly 'virile' way both as an artist and as a 'man'. All through the way he is shown by his admiring wife to be shooting game, taking dangerous steps, and treating the 'natives' in a way that somewhat belie the social message of his paintings.

The Artist and his 'Energetic Measures'

Throughout the travelogue we find Vereshchagin resorting to, in his admiring wife's terms, 'his energetic measures', 'his violent remedies' to force the 'natives' to go with them as bearers, or to mend their ways of intransigence. The renowned 'artist at war' is in India rather seen to be at odds and at war with the physical and human obstacles, and fighting them with virile 'energetic means' and giving the effeminate Indians the treatment they deserved.

The overbearing attitude towards the men of the hills is evident from the very start of the journey, once they determinedly started their ascent to 'Djongri', on their way to Mount Kanchenjunga from 'Pemiontsi', in the deadly cold of January. Vereshchagin 'persisted in making studies from nature of the very highest summits of the mountain chains' against the reluctance of the coolies to undertake the rather painful journey, and decided to venture the ascent without their help. But after arriving at the 'Mount Leptcha' they found themselves not only at the mercy of the furious elements, but unable to walk without the assistance of the coolies in their coldness, hunger and exhaustion. Vereshchagin accordingly first sent back their huntsman, and then the last remaining bearer, to search for the coolies with orders to bring cushions, wrappers and provisions. These people returned after the inevitable delay caused by the inclement weather with the things and even bodily carrying Vereshchagin, who had ventured down in desperation. But still their chief was told that Vereshchagin, 'would have been glad to box' his ears. Besides, after Vereshchagin completed his studies of snow, physically supported by two coolies, and desiring further ascent found even the coolies in shoes adamant about not going further, he threatened them with confiscation of their wages. And Mrs. Vereshchagin wrote with obvious approbation about how the '*fine Indians* come trooping up one after another, and *behold for the first time in their life a mass of snow*' [italics added].[91]

It is strange that in the only page devoted to the Indian travelogue in his famous biography Barooshian refers uncritically about not only to the risks Vereshchagin took for making sketches of the 'changing shadows and the effects of lights' at these heights, but also to the prowess of the artist in bettering the 'weary entourage' in scaling the heights amidst the snowstorm, which had lagged behind him. Later the role of the servants in saving his life is mentioned, but not his ungrateful aggression towards them.[92] As one reads the second volume of the travelogue, one notices how

Vereshchagin changes from the intent to 'box' the ears of the natives to actual 'boxing' quite often, and sometimes takes harsher steps. Mrs. Vereshchagin writes with approbation how on their way to 'Cashmere-Ladak', the laziness and boozing of bearers, coupled with the cheek of a 'a one-eyed man', to pester Vereshchagin for money made Vereshchagin give 'him and his comrade a sharp box on the ear'.[93] From this point we see the Vereshchagins frequently changing their bearers to get over the problem of recalcitrance and using various oppressive tactics to compel them to follow their trail. At a halting station near Leh, capital of Ladak (Ladakh), he outwitted all the coolies who were running away after a hot chase 'in a great fit of rage' to catch them all, to the last 'shameless wretch'.[94]

One could show this behaviour as caused by the irresponsible and whimsical attitude of the bearers who had not kept their part of the bargain, were it not the case that Vereshchagin was very often forcing the local people to do their bidding. For example, near a salt lake at a place called 'Tso-Moriari', he forced 'one of the tallest and strongest' of the men 'to sound the depth of the water' after tying a rope round his waist, though 'the moment he left he was out of his depth', and had to be quickly pulled out, lest he died. Besides, Vereshchagin was forcing local people into unwelcome work. For, as admitted by his wife, every time securing new bearers after discharging the previous set could not be done without 'some trouble, because . . . *natives dislike that work*' [italics added].[95] One is not left guessing for long about what 'some trouble' really meant. For, at a place called 'Lio' in the province of 'Spiti', it involved collecting 'all the old men, who, convinced that they need not fear being pressed into the service, had remained in their houses', to emotionally blackmail the sons to appear immediately 'in order to set them free from the burdens and to carry the things themselves'.[96] This tactic of taking the old men of the village hostage, to force younger men of the village to come forward to work as bearers, was repeated at a place near 'Sungen' at Spiti, where Vereshchagin set up, at a large village, '*a regular hunt for the men, who ran on all sides like goats, collected the necessary number*, most of them being old people, who were as usual voluntarily relieved by their sons or relatives' [italics added]. It caused Mrs. Vereshchagin's momentary uneasiness with her husband's behaviour. 'This plan', she admits a little bashfully, 'though it cannot exactly be called humane, may be recommended as almost *the only efficient way* to the traveller in this country who is left in the lurch by the bearers' [italics added].[97] A little before this hunting expedition, this only efficient way, induced Vereshchagin to use a revolver to threaten one of the 'rogues', who had given Vereshchagin the slip, and succeeded in making his escape, making other bearers follow suit. This time the only extenuating factor that Mrs. Vereshchagin could think up was that the pocket revolver was '*certainly very small* and *the bullets only about the size of grains*' [italics added], though 'the threat did its work', and they continued their journey 'without further misadventures of this sort'.[98] Her further justification was that all these 'energetic measures' were necessitated by the process of securing porters and provisions in the more inaccessible parts of the Himalayas. So on their way back, when the roads became level and all their necessities could be obtained 'without bickering or quarreling', she hoped that these 'energetic measures' could now, *to the advantage of both sides*, be dispensed with' [italics added].[99] But her hopes were belied, as after passing 'Rampoor', Vereshchagin had to apply them for mule-drivers who were running away leaving their mules behind.[100]

Besides, it was not the bearers alone who were recipients of such 'violent remedies'. The *lombardar*, or village magistrate, at Rampore was held captive after he failed to provide them with the necessary provisions and the promised mutton and 'black game'.[101] A little before, the local lombardar at Tchimri, got rebuked for asking for tips for his normal services. Vereshchagin 'bestowed a blow on the lombardar instead of the gratuity expected of him'. As a result the promised horses, after much pretence that there were none at hand, were brought around, but again started disappearing 'one after another . . . behind the bushes and trees', till the artist's 'energetic interference' put 'everything to order' again [italics added].[102] Another *lombardar* of the station of Pengong, at the furthest limit of their journey along the Tibet border, was subjected to similar treatment, for refusing to give expected exchange for Kashmiri rupees from the coolies. He was boxed till he agreed. This must have, however, embarrassed Mrs. Vereshchagin's civilized sensibilities. For, she wrote that 'I must relate this incident although we are somewhat ashamed about it'.[103]

Apart from coolies and lombardars, one of the women travelling with them with yaks for milking, was subjected 'to one of his violent remedies', for pinching some milk, though the woman 'took it very good-naturedly'.[104] Likewise, the groom for the horse 'received a box on the ear for negligence of the health of a horse';[105] two other grooms got boxes on their ears for 'begging on the roads to buy things while keeping the wages received sewn into their rags'. Physical violation was justifiable because Vereshchagin gave some rupees to his tour manager, to 'buy their provisions for them, even against their will'.[106]

All these incidents of physical violation did not, however, prevent the couple from believing that they were a lot more even handed and superior in their treatment of the natives than the British. At Simla a large group of Englishmen had arrived just before them and one of them had severely manhandled the local *lombardar*, 'because he had not provided him with milk, till he was covered with blood'. Mrs. Vereshchagin complains that 'Englishmen, especially the officers, behave in such an arrogant manner towards the natives, and handle them so roughly that *all the "energetic measures" of my husband were mere trifles in comparison*'. [italics added][107]

This behaviour from the famous anti-colonial artist in India, would be inexplicable unless we remember the tension Barooshian points to in Vereshchagin between the 'conscious need to serve the peasant class as a compassionate exponent of its travails', and 'an unconscious desire to satisfy his mother's wish that he become a famous, respectable military officer';[108] and the Oriental setting of his activities which subdued his superego.

MRS. VERESHCHAGIN'S HIMALAYAS

Superstitious and Competing Religions

The irrationality of religions in India and their inferiority to Christianity has for a long time been one of the recurrent themes of European 'Orientalism'. In Terry's brilliant reduction: 'the summe is that both Mahometans and Gentiles (Hindus) ground their opinions upon tradition, not Reason'.[109] In Mrs. Vereshchagin's accounts of 'Cashmere-Ladak' too, the most important themes are the superstitions of the people; their religions; polyandry; transmigration of Buddhist souls, and the tradition-bound life and activities of the Buddhist *lamas*. Although Buddhism gets some preferential treatment compared with Islam and Hinduism, the *lamas* do not. Much of her memoirs are taken up with their non-spiritual and superstitious ways. If Vereshchagin looked askance at the deviant, sectarian and fallen faiths of Trans-Caucasia and Central Asia, then his wife, chose Islam, Hinduism, and Buddhism in the hills for not so oblique banter. And the sketches by Vereshchagin show that the scorn is shared. Revealingly, 'Mussulman Shiites' are the first objects of attention not only in the first volume written by Vereshchagin, but in parts of the first and the whole of the second volume written by Mrs. Vereshchagin too, who finds them in the places of Dras and Tashgan, and looks with expected irreverence at the religious beliefs of these people, who 'resemble Jews in the types of their faces'. But the kind of relationship between the religions in the mountains that she depicts does not seem to accord with India's long history of inter-faith tolerance. Let us turn to the superstitions first. Seeing on 'a bush in the neighbourhood of the village hung a lock of woman's hair and an offering to the divinity', Vereshchagin jokes that 'the hair must have been offered to the god by some man who had obtained the trophy in a fight with another'. Mrs. Vereshchagin informs that the Muslims who live there are no 'less superstitious than the Buddhists', as they too wear amulets 'sewn onto their garments'. Only, while 'the Buddhists obtain their little bits of paper inscribed with prayers and curses from Lhassa in Tibet', the Shiites get theirs from local *mullahs*, one of whom, busy in the 'distribution of heavenly favour', gave them a 'a glance of great disfavour'.[110]

After this exercise in rationality Mrs. Vereshchagin turns to her confident account of inter-religious relations in India. We are first treated to this insightful observation that in India every stronger religious sect preys on the weaker and 'absorbs' it. 'Buddhism, driven out of the valleys, found a retreat in the Himalayas, where it was driven back further and further in the mountains by Brahminism and Islamism'. In the Himalayas too the Muslims of Kashmir 'of the Sunnite sect absorb' the Muslims of the 'Shiite sect on the borders of Ladak'. The Shiites 'in their turn absorb the Buddhists who dwell next to them'. This insightful account of absorption in turns is obtained from no less an authority than the local elder or 'tikodar' at Dras, who has told her that in the three conversions that had taken place in the last eleven years, all were from Buddhism into Shiite Islam. But Sunnite Islam, 'the most vigorous and aggressive' among the faiths, 'finds proselytes among the professors of all the religions, and absorbs (in a spiritual sense) the Shiites that come into contact with it', and will finally conquer it. At that point however, the Shiites were predicted to be able to maintain their ranks by finding 'proselytes among the Buddhists. . . .' That Buddhism was not disappearing faster though being driven to the mountains was because Tibet, one of the strong centres of Buddhism was 'not far off on the one side, and the great Buddhist people of India give them a strong moral support on the other'.[111]

Buddhism faced other challenges than loss of followers. Unaware of the long history of interpenetration of Buddhism and Hinduism and creation of common deities in Buddhist Tāntrism as well as influence of Buddhist Tāntrism on Hinduism[112] Mrs. Vereshchagin wonders at the influence of Brahminism on the pictures of deities in a monastery at Shergol, particularly on that of 'the god of War on a white horse, and various other deities with numerous heads, hands and feet'.[113] She seemed to think that in some parts of the Himalayas the influence of the Brahminism on Buddhism was even greater, almost threatening its existence. At the station of Sungen in Spiti the 'features and the customs' of the Buddhists resembled those of the Hindus, since while 'the temple is certainly Buddhist', the 'Brahminical additions' indicated that 'the natives would soon completely go over to Brahminism'.[114]

Superstitious Buddhism and Mundane *Lamas*

Though Mrs. Vereshchagin started with the gentle nature of Buddhists, holding it responsible for the retreat of Buddhism in the face of onslaughts by the two principal sects of Islam, subsequently her views on Buddhism depended on the way the *lamas* received them. Initially her husband gained an entry to a monastery, to draw 'the interior and the exterior of the temple, which he would never have been able to do with a Hindoo temple'.[115] Of course, at another monastery at Pemiontsi, the monks did not receive them 'very cordially', and looked at them 'all the time with distrust', with only one saluting them, while others 'laughed at us openly during our visits'.[116] But near a Buddhist 'temple' at Tchangatchelling, with rain pouring down hard and the bearers long in coming, the gesture of the 'oldest of the *lamas*, the abbé' in giving them shelter for the night in the temple made their religious tolerance 'astonishing', particularly compared to Hindus, 'who curse as a profanation, not only the entrance of an unbeliever in a temple, but even approach to their divinities. . . . ' But neither the permissiveness of Buddhism nor the kindness of the chief *lama* could stop her from making fun of the *lama's* superstitions for putting them up not in the upper temple, 'where the evil gods who live in it would not tolerate us, but in the lower temple', and of the ailing *lama's* recovery from his illness after taking drinks from the bottle of port wine they had presented him. The friendly *lama* was also not spared derision for telling them about his dream that 'the divinities of the temple were irritated' against them for the absurd reason that 'we roasted our meat raw, instead of giving it a preliminary cooking'.[117]

At a religious festival at Pemiontsi the devotees' practice, while offering sacrifices to the gods, of closing 'the apertures of their noses with a veil, so that their breath may not contaminate their offering', and a mask dance that was part of the festival came in for special banter. The dance in which two old clowns with masks of a man and a woman presented themselves, and the *lamas* also wore masks to amuse the spectators, provoked Mrs. Vereshchagin's comment that their 'jokes and attitudes, as well as some points in the play' were 'somewhat indecent', though 'this evidently suits the public taste'. Everything, including the *lamas*, the deities, the audience, and their conception of the divine, came in for derision, including the *lamas*' 'ample dresses of silk, with sashes to match, rolled around their chests and their waists', but 'ordinary, soft, heavy shoes'; and their facemasks of 'stags, pigs and even human faces', things that only the natives could stand. In true 'Orientalist' style she refers to the monstrous gods of Mahāyāna Buddhism: 'But what faces! Eyes staring out most frightfully, enormous teeth, &c. The deities . . . to judge from the masks, which are supposed to resemble them . . . must be very hideous and terrible looking; and that is what the natives like.'

Mrs. Vereshchagin could not also desist from 'Othering' the folk-pantomime depicting the ubiquitous message of fight between good and evil that is the stuff of all folk-forms, and conveying standard Buddhist concerns with violence, disease and death. The dances in the pantomimes and their gestures were crude, even while depicting the fight between 'good and evil spirit'. 'A puppet representing the Devil comes on to the stage', followed by 'ambassadors from all countries', who gave the devil a chase and caught him as he was 'hiding himself' to elude them, finally making off 'towards the sea'; and killed him. Since the puppet was made of rice, the audience could 'satisfy at the same time their hunger and their anger against the Devil', throwing the head 'to the gods as offering'. But the Devil had a reincarnation and began his tricks with human beings. Mrs. Vereshchagin's hermeneutic deficiency comes out in the following comment:

> It is rather difficult for us to follow the play, for every time we interrogate the interpreter he answers, 'The good spirits are complaining that there is war so often, and that there is so much disease and death among the mortals.' . . .We had the honour of being the first Europeans who ever were present at this fetê, which, indeed, we found of slight interest and very fatiguing.

Obviously she could not understand the central message of Buddhism played out in the pantomime even with the help of the interpreter. Possibly being the artist he was, Vereshchagin did not share her views here. For, while she returned home the same evening, he came back in the next morning, seeing a repeat performance where 'a war dance had been introduced', and painted sketches of the masked lamas were shown. Mrs. Vereshchagin's contempt for the play was also possibly influenced by the subaltern status of the actors too. She points out that one of the main actors in the pantomime was 'an old man with one eye, of whom we were in the habit of buying eggs'.[118]

If the fête at Pemiontsi was not sombre and sacral enough, then another fête at the monastery of Tassiding, with its miracle of subterranean waters, and other rites was frivolous. True to Teltscher's mention of the attitude of 'compare and contrast' in European 'Orientalist' description of India,[119] Mrs. Vereshchagin refers to a rite, 'very odd', though 'considered quite natural here', of approaching the god by crawling on their bodies, and circling the temple in this fashion. Her reservation, even after a single viewing is that the 'procession always begins solemnly, but it finishes less devoutly with jokes and laughter'; and in the evening 'peasants assemble in front of their monuments, and . . . *sing like children*', probably 'somewhat under the influence of murwar' [italics added].[120]

The application of the binary of adult/child—so typical of postcolonial theory—to the local Buddhist rites logically leads to banter at the miracles. At the monastery of Tassiding a vessel of water sealed the year before was opened to see if the quantity of water kept in it had increased. If it did, it foretold a prosperous year; if it did not, it augured evil.[121] At another old monastery, the miracle was of 'cymbals . . . kept under the ground which when taken in the hands clash one against the other'. A few hours' journey from there, in a grotto, normally dry, some warm water with high curative properties could be made to appear by saying 'prayers and charms'.[122] Mrs. Vereshchagin haughtily puts these miracles on par with a mundane happening in their team, concerning a 'servant (tchaprassi) of high Thākur caste, who did not touch any food or articles used by them, but finally decided to drink water drawn by their 'bisti (water carrier)', since 'the distance of the spring is too great'.[123] This banter does not, however, remember the extent to which Russian Orthodox Church took biblical miracles in the New Testament not symbolically, but often literally.[124]

The Buddhist doctrine of transmigration of the souls of *lamas* is also passed off as superstition. At Tomlong in Sikkim Mrs. Vereshchagin talks about the monastery where the Koupgenlama, the greatest of the *lamas* in the kingdom, lives. She says satirically that he 'is immortal, for each time that he dies he is born again'. So are the three other *lamas* who founded the kingdom of Sikkim. Dobdi-lama, the first, lived in Jaksun; the third stayed at Tchangatchelling. The second, the *lama* of Tassiding, became the chief *lama* at

Pemiontsi after coming back to life. 'Lately, he has been born again as the king's son'. The king, unwilling to live 'separated from him', made him come and live near him and appealed to the Dalai Lama of Tibet for permission of his marriage, and for building a monastery for him near his royal palace. When the king died with no other son and heir, the chief *lama* of the new monastery mounted the throne.

Mrs. Vereshchagin comments with scarcely hidden banter that 'this was not done without some difficulty, as this was the first time the temporal government had been in the hands of a priest'. She also informs us that this *lama*-king was the predecessor of the present king, and he had his present reincarnation in a poor family, living quite happily not far from the monastery, in Tomlong in winter, and in Pemiontsi in summer 'in the quality of Koupgenlama, or superior *lama*'. He is so deified that none but the highest *lamas* and his own servants had the privilege of seeing him. Even they had to genuflect on seeing him as one does before a deity; and those who met with him accidentally threw themselves on the ground to stop their eyes from seeing him. But Mr. Vereshchagin chatted with this holy man, when he painted in the monastery. Mrs. Vereshchagin is not ready to agree with the divinity of this 'young man of nineteen years of age, with brown hair and a wide and rather stupid face', sitting on 'a large old armchair, which is like Pope's throne', and talking quietly, 'often interrupting himself'. She makes fun of the fact that the belongings of immortal *lamas* are restored to them eight years after reincarnation.[125]

If the most exalted Sikkim *lamas* could be treated with this irreverence, then it is easy to imagine the probable lot of other ordinary *lamas*. Predictably enough Mrs. Vereshchagin depicts them as ignorant, mundane, and lacking in spirituality. Proving Sardar's diagnosis that 'what is essential to the Orientalist vision is the desire not to know',[126] she classifies the Buddhist clergy 'into two sects, the red and the blue, according to the colour of their vestments', among whom discord is perpetual. 'In some provinces the red predominates, in others the yellow. In the kingdom of Sikkim the red are the most numerous'.[127] It is strange that the inanity of the distinction, which almost matches some famous distinctions in English satirical literature, like those between 'Tramecksan' and the 'Slamecksan', and the 'Liliputs' and the 'Blefuscus' in *Gulliver's Travels*; the 'Blues' and the 'Buffs' in *Pickwick Papers*; or between the 'Tweedledum' and the 'Tweedledee' in *Alice in the Wonderland*,[128] did not warn her to look beyond the colour of attire at more substantive divisions between schools of Buddhism.

In Mrs. Vereshchagin's estimation the *lamas* were timid; not above greed for worldly things; not much interested in their spiritual duties; and xenophobic. Their timidity was proven by the sudden tendency of the *lamas* of Tassiding to avoid the society of the Vereshchagins. The reason was that their major-domo Lodi, a convert to Christianity, had come here before, with his missionary to preach Christianity among them. The *lamas* feared that he had come again with another Christian priest to 'try his chance'. And they could think of no better way of escaping than to 'hide themselves'.[129] Regarding love for worldly things even the Koupgenlama was not free of it. At the time of their departure from Sikkim they made a present of a looking glass to him. But the 'holy man probably expected more, for he asked our messenger if that was all'.[130] Their non-spiritual ways were revealed at the monastery of Hemis in Kashmir, where fifty monks lived with a large number of pupils. Though there was 'ample opportunity here for a life of contemplation . . . the desire to satisfy the wants of their lower nature seems to have obtained the upper hand'. At their arrival 'the *lamas crept out, like rats out of their holes*', gazing at them '*with wild and unfriendly eyes*'; and 'only the eldest of them', was '*more communicative*' [italics added].[131]

Not caring to inform why the *lamas* cared only for base needs, she somewhat self-contradictorily denigrates the parasitic nature of *lamas* at the chief monastery at Ladakh. The hundred *lamas* and their numerous pupils, had only two occupations, 'to eat and to pray, to pray and eat', as a result of which when 'the gifts of the believers fail, they seem to live in a very poor way'. The prayers of the *lamas* do not redeem them because of the nature of their prayers. In the yard spanning 'the whole length of the convent, are high poles, on which are hung pieces of white stuff inscribed with prayers'. She mocks that the 'wind blows these prayers to and fro and wafts them to heaven'.[132]

The non-spiritual *lamas* were easily softened by gifts of wine. On their downward journey to Ratlam, they met a *lama* 'who was at first very churlish and uncommunicative', but became so energetically garrulous after a gift of a bottle of brandy that it was difficult to stop his babble or get rid of him.[133] There is here a clear continuity between the two volumes. If in the first the progressive artist was judging the sectarians of Caucasus from the point of view of Russian Orthodoxy, then in the second volume his wife was trashing Buddhism from the same perspective.

Polyandrous Women of the Hills

Eastern women and their sexuality being one of the most dominant archetypes of European 'Orientalism', it does not seem surprising that women and polyandry in the hills should attract Mrs. Vereshchagin so much. She finds evidence of the custom in the station of Tchargol, near the village of Karbu, where Vereshchagin painted an ugly old woman 'who had no less than five husbands', and in the village of Hemis. Unlike Russian generals, who were disappointed with their 'second-rate' Orient, where the 'women were not beautiful . . . and exotic enough' and were put down by 'the gap between the Oriental European fantasy and the reality' of a plain woman,[134] Mrs. Vereshchagin has plain disgust for the 'rather stout' woman, with her grey uncombed locks, fluttering round her head in great disorder, and wearing 'a hood on which was a large turquoise, a dress of black stuff woven by herself, and a goatskin over her shoulders'. She is surprised that a woman as coarse and unattractive as her was desired by five men and could keep them loyal to her bed. She delves into the social and economic reasons behind the locally endemic custom, where a family of several brothers marries one woman; but the rights of the eldest brother, the head of the family, 'come first, then those of the second brother and so on'. There can be an exception to this rule only when 'the wife buys her freedom from the oldest brother with a horse, a cow or something of the sort, with his . . . consent'. But since this necessitates that the preferred younger husband should build a separate house and set up his own household all by himself, this is a rare occurrence. She finds the chief reason behind this custom to be poverty, high bride price, and 'saving for the family by having one wife among them'.

As an amateur social scientist Mrs. Vereshchagin finds that Indian women with multiple husbands are naturally 'overworked and age very quickly'; she notices 'a few pretty natives', and wonders how harmful polyandry would be to their good looks. The reason behind the 'unpleasing appearance' of 'the older women, and especially of the very old ones' is 'the excessive amount of work they do. What a strain must be placed upon their strength by the rearing of their numerous children?'[135] The last sentence clears the point that by excessive work Mrs. Vereshchagin is not just meaning excessive pressure on her normal sexuality but the duties of mothering too.

But loss of looks and ageing were not the only effects of polyandry amongst Indian women. One more serious loss of a polyandrous woman was of the romantic aspects of their conjugal life, where they stood in very bad comparison with European women. As she asked herself, 'under such circumstances can there be any coquetry or jealousy which reigns among our European women, who have only one husband?'

After clarifying European women's superior position, in matters of coquettishness and jealousy Mrs. Vereshchagin searched for this jealousy only among those who under polyandry could experience it—the brothers and co-sharers of the woman's body. But she seemed genuinely surprised at seeing little traces of it, when they replied, 'How could that be possible? One cannot imagine such a thing.' So she coaxed out the shamefaced admission, that in recent years 'quarrels on this account had taken place', and had been decided by 'an English sahib (gentleman)', though 'they appeared to regard it as particularly disgraceful'. Anyway, in her view, the worst hit by the custom were of course the women, and 'one or two women of each family go to a convent and the daughters of poor parents are obliged to make up their minds to single blessedness'.[136] However, she does not seem to know that polygamy continued in Russia up to the seventeenth century, leaving even less scope for womanly 'coquetry or jealousy' for Russian women in those times.

But apart from polyandry the incapacity of hill women to dress fashionably according to European tastes marred their looks. They stuck 'a bright coloured flower into their thick locks', painted 'thickly their noses and cheeks with red colour', and used 'lard very freely for their hair'. She praises their costume, but mainly because their head-gear resembled 'the Italian fashion'.[137] In the case of women of Rampoor, endowed with a pleasing appearance, hard labour and bad dresses further marred their looks: 'they soon look old on account of the hard work they have to do and the nose ring which is the fashion here gives them a disagreeable expression'.[138]

The 'Depraved' Natives in the Hills

In standard 'Orientalist' tropes Indian women are known for their mysterious sexuality, but men for their negative qualities of pusillanimity, depravity, cunning and cowardice. This is because Oriental males have to serve as effete foils of the troublesome women whose sexuality the Western man fantasizes about.[139] Mrs. Vereshchagin too found the men wily and deceitful. Since they 'demanded an enor-mous price for all they brought', the Vereshchagins were forced to buy of them only 'those things which were absolutely indispensable. . . .'[140] The bearers were no better. Their chief, 'was an old wolf'. Though he knew his business well, he 'was not devoid of cunning'. His nephew, a handsome young man, 'a future sirdar', and the carrier of their paint box, was not human enough as he had 'made fun of their distress' on the top of the Mount Leptcha'. The huntsman, was a drunkard and 'very likely he was not capable of shooting even for fun at a living creature'. The bearers were generally 'agile, rough and not perfectly honest'. The Boutthias were the most courageous among them and most diligent; while the Leptchas had the best manners and temper.[141]

That Mrs. Vereshchagin fully shared her husband's perceptions of their cultural backwardness, does not need much showing. Just as Vereshchagin mocked Central Asians for speaking of Bukhara as a centre of learning with unreserved, if undeserved, awe,[142] his wife laughs at functionaries of the kingdom of Sikkim for speaking of Tibet with an inexplicable deference, as if 'of an earthly paradise', although the Vereshchagins 'know perfectly well that it is a rude country with few attractions'.[143]

Mrs. Vereshchagin could not also help despising the natives because they lived at the subsistence level. She found that not only did the servants of Changshed, the chief minister of the King of Sikkim, kept continuously coming to them 'to sell various objects belonging to their master, and which the minister was ashamed to offer us himself', but they hankered even after things that were at best refuse, if not garbage, like 'empty oil flasks, bottles of wine, and even tin biscuit boxes'. The natives were also inordinately greedy for all things manufactured in the West. When at the time of their departure they were making presents to the hosts, even the venerated Koupgenlama was expecting something more than the present they gave him; and the chief minister 'was *waiting like a child* for the present which he expected would be given him' [italics added].[144]

From her superior position she not even set much store for the genuine human emotions of the natives. Onward their way from the river Sutlej they procured a small sheep, dear pet of a woman and her son, in a village, through coercive persuasion by the village headman. But when they wept bitterly at the loss of the pet she only 'doubted whether the money they received in stead of it consoled them'.[145]

Who in India Doesn't Like Being Seen as a European?

From their inflated sense of superiority the Vereshchagins cannot imagine that each and every Indian does not prefer a European identity to that of an Indian. This came out from their analysis of the behaviour of Lodi, their tour manager, a person thoroughly trustworthy, whom they missed during their misadventure on the top of the Mount Leptcha. [146] But when he showed feelings for his Indian roots Mrs. Vereshchagin was incredulous. Lodi was extremely Europeanized: a 'Leptcha . . . a young man, dressed like a European and a European in many of his ways, but Mongolian in complexion and features'; 'a converted Christian, whose work was preaching the gospel . . . in the service of the missionary of the district';[147] and a man with good persuasive skills in con-version.[148] But when at the station of Sungen a woman came all the way from Spiti in search of Lodi, whom she mistook for her lost brother, 'who had gone away a long time ago with a European and had never come back'; and inexplicably enough Lodi cried at her inconsolable grief, Mrs. Vereshchagin was sure that 'it was more with anger because he had been taken for a native, when he not only wore the dress but imagined that his features were like those of a European'.[149]

Wondrous Western Quackery *vs.* Eastern Charms

The feelings of superiority that accompany 'secondary Orientalism' sometimes took comic proportions, like when the couple turn into quacks, and with Western wine and cosmetics cure chronic Eastern diseases. We have already seen how the couple was convinced that they failed to ensure a full cure of a *lama* from his terminal disease with their port wine just because he had already resigned himself to it.[150] But even then Vereshchagin helped the *lama* to get well once again with 'another bottle of port wine he had asked for'. His wife was meanwhile curing the goiter of the same *lama's* wife with a 'pot of pomade ordered from Darjeeling.[151] Besides, in Tomlong not only the personal servant of the Koupgenlama but many other people come to them for cures, including a *lama* wanting a cure of his worms. They gave him 'some drops of liqueur of mint'. Apart from the *lama's* testimony that 'they did him good', they had the confidence that anyway 'our medicine could not do him less good than the charms . . . which the priests make use of here against all diseases'. *Lamas* could be subjected to this quackery not only because of their abject poverty, which made them sell not only articles of their clothing and other objects, but even higher signifiers of their culture, including a magic seal blessed by the Dalai Lama.[152]

White Goddess and a Deceitful Insignificant King

Mrs. Vereshchagin's self-image of a white goddess treading in the hills is traceable to her consciousness of being a wonder among natives. That is why she treated the *lamas* in this half-jesting half-despising manner, though she had already noticed that 'in this part of the country the clergy enjoy great consideration'.[153] She notices while they were passing Darjeeling in the eastern Himalayas, that she 'excited much curiosity' among the Boutthias, the original inhabitants of Darjeeling, as 'until then not a single European woman had passed through that country'.[154] Later, we see her saying, in the western Himalayas, 'I continue to be an object of interest to all the ladies of this country. . . . It is impossible to give them greater pleasure than by letting them feel the garments [of mine] and examine the quality of the stuff'.[155] This feeling of being a representative of a superior race and culture persists when she recounts somewhat theatrically the presentation of her and her husband to the king of Sikkim, where besides the population of Tomlong, people from all around came 'to see *the novel spectacle of a European lady presented to the king of Sikkim*' [italics added]. From this exalted position she viewed the two rows of soldiers—'wearing on their heads those inevitable baskets, in which they look more like shepherds than warriors'—through whom they pass.[156] It is from this feeling of white superiority and consciousness of being the citizen of a great power that she brings out the comic aspects of the unimpressive, theatrical court and the meagre resources of a little mountain kingdom and its king, and his arrogation of equality of status with European monarchs, in words that do not remind one of the famed empathy of the Vereshchagins for subjugated nations, the 'Other' of European colonialism. She suspects that 'the throne covered with silk drapery' that the king sits on, is nothing but 'cushions as well as the silk hangings', covering up 'some old box . . . *We do not know for certain, but such is our supposition*' [italics added]. The young and physically unimpressive king was also without manners, as he did not salute them, either because 'etiquette forbids him', or perhaps because 'he was shy'. He was also naïve enough to ask them about 'the health of the queen of England and her ministers'.

Mrs. Vereshchagin's aristocratic manners do not prevent her from stating that both of them were deceived by the 'perfect mountains of presents' that the servants threw at their feet. Vereshchagin had prepared beforehand two sets of presents for the monarch, depending on what they received first. 'The first lot of various trifles' was kept ready to offer the king if the royal presents were also 'small and insignificant'. The second lot, intended to match the king's munificence with his gifts, mainly consisted of a gun bought in Calcutta. Taken in by the huge quantity of the royal gifts, he presented this gun also and showed the king how to operate it. But going home they found the king had given them a 'basketful of oranges, some packets of bad rice, and butter, the latter for the most part already rotten to greenness . . . some sheep, chickens, . . . and a very bad Thibet pony'. They realized that 'Our gun was of much more value than all these put together'.[157]

In this act of deception the king was of course no worse than other people of the hills. In the eastern Himalayas they had already found out about the crafty villagers. 'We received', says Mrs. Vereshchagin, 'a great many presents from the natives . . . but we soon remarked that the principal cause of the prodigality of presents was nothing other than our readiness in giving money. We left of sowing rupees, and immediately ceased to reap the presents'.[158] But they seemed to know that one cause of the poor quality of the royal presents was the poverty of the little king and his kingdom.

A 'Takour', a Dog and the Subordination of the Orient

It is against this superiority of a white man as god that Mr. and Mrs. Vereshchagin reacted to the 'pigheaded' efforts of a servant (tchaprassi) belonging to the high caste of Thakur, at maintaining his ritual purity, while preparing his food, away 'from the infidel and defiling observation of not only us but of our people'. She seemed very happy when once a roving, inquisitive cow sniffed at the preparation, and spoilt the broth of this man. She was also happy that the cow being a sacred animal the tchaprassi could do nothing to the offending animal except having 'recourse to fair words'.[159] The frequency with which she mentioned the 'pigheaded belief of the tchaprassi in the superiority of his caste', suggests that their own racial vanity was hurt. Finally, when once she chanced upon the place where he was cooking his daily meal, and the tchaprassi threw away all his food that 'had been polluted by our presence and extinguished the fire', her husband resorted to his now familiar 'energetic measures'. She relates with satisfaction how he flew 'into a passion at his impudence, and to his great alarm' not only seized 'his cauldron in his hand', but threw it 'over the wall of the monastery, telling him that he will follow it himself if he *attempts to show his pride so insolently*' [italics added].[160]

If the fall of a Thākur could be seen with unmixed pleasure, the matter was not so uncomplicated with a Tibetan dog that they had bought at a place called Sakti, and had named him after the place. The master of the dog had sold him on the condition that he would not be kept on leash, 'because, however strong and thick it was he would be sure to bite it through'. This dog had not been held on a rope during their whole journey.[161] But when they were returning home to Russia they had to keep it in a cage in their mail coach. They loved the fiercely independent-minded dog, but when he broke a tooth and bloodied his mouth by trying to cut the iron grating with his teeth Mrs. Vereshchagin could not help making this comment: 'I suppose as a clever dog he wanted to make comparisons between an iron grating of English workmanship and the hairy ropes of Ladakh. The comparison could not have been favourable for the latter'.[162]

There could possibly not be a worse allegory for the post-Sepoy Mutiny India; more so, coming from the wife of an artist known for a painting which became iconic of artistic protest against colonialist war, in spite of some controversies regarding its authenticity.[163] A critic of Barooshian has praised him for helping to restore Vereshchagin's 'oeuvre to a more universal appreciation'.[164] This appreciation is not, however, possible only through his pictures, or through 'writing a hagiography that fails to probe the less obvious aspects of Vereshchagin's life, to place him properly in his times or to take a more critical look at the painter's self-satisfied moralizing'.[165] For this critical look E.K. Valkenier advises future researchers to focus on 'Vereshchagin's selective treatment of British and Russian colonial rule'; and to compare the 'gory depiction of the impending execution' of Indian mutineers with 'a similar pictorial language applied to Central Asian Khans who delight in displaying the severed heads of Russian soldiers'.[166] To me, however, another useful lens would be to look into the travelogues of the Vereshchagins, and the reflection of the artist in both. While considering Vereshchagin as 'Russia's Orientalist painter *par excellence*, using the adjective in the traditional art historical sense', and suggesting that 'Looking at his work is the best way to consider how a nineteenth-century Russian artist saw the East', Schimmelpenninck posits that his views of the Orient were best expressed in the 'two Turkestan tours in the late 1860s'.[167] But there is a thread of continuity between them and the Himalayan tours that is not sufficiently recognized.

NOTES

1. Kemp, *Bharat-Rus*, pp. 211 and 213.
2. Vahan D. Barooshian, *Artist at War* (Gainesville: University Press of Florida, 1993); and Schimmelpenninck, 'Vereshchagin's Canvases'.
3. Barooshian, *Artist at War*, pp.1–17; Schimmelpenninck, 'Vereshchagin's Canvases,' pp. 186–90; *Great Soviet Encyclopaedia* (London: Collier Macmillan Publishers, 1983 and New York: Macmillan Inc., 1983), vol. 4, p. 599 d.
4. Ibid., 'Introduction', *Artist at War*, p. xv.
5. Alexandre Benois, *The Russian School of Painting*, tr. from the original Russian by Abraham Yarmolinsky, with an Introduction by Christian Brinton, with thirty-two plates (London: T. Werner and Lawrie Ltd., 1916), pp. 128–31.
6. *Soviet Encyclopaedia*, pp. 599–600.
7. Vereshchagin et al., *Artists Look at India* (a collection of Russian paintings on India starting with Vereshchagin) (Moscow: State Fine Arts Publishing House, 1955), p. IV.
8. Barooshian, *Artist at War*, p. xvi.
9. *Soviet Encyclopaedia*, p. 599d.
10. Barooshian, *Artist at War*, pp. 20, 56–7.
11. Andrej K. Lebedev, *Vasilij Vasil'evich Vereshchagin: Zhizn' i tvorchestvo, 1842–1904* (Vasilij Vasil'evich Vereshchagin: Life and Work 1842–1904) (Moscow: Iskusstvo, 1972), p. 14, cited in Schimmelpenninck, 'Vereshchagin's Canvases', p. 191
12. Barooshian, *Artist at War*, pp. 23–5, 31–2, 62–79, and 150–3.
13. V.V. Vereshchagin, *Vassili Vereshchagin: Painter–Soldier-Traveller: Autobiographical Sketches*, vol. 2, trs. from the German and the French by

F. H. Peters (London: Richard Bentley and Son, 1887), p. 215; and V.V. Vereshchagin, *Izbrannye pisma* (Moscow: Iskusstvo, 1981), p. 52, both quoted in ibid., p. 60.

14. Ibid., pp. 45–6.
15. Ibid., pp. 74–5.
16. See Jahan Ramazani, 'Wilfred Owen', in *Poetry of Mourning: The Modern Elegy from Hardy to Heaney* (Chicago: University of Chicago Press, 1994), pp. 69–70.
17. See for example, Wilfred Owen, 'A Terre (Being the Philosophy of Many Soldiers)', in Jon Silkin, *The Penguin Book of First World War Poetry* (London and New York: Penguin Books, 1996), pp. 201–3.
18. Barooshian, *Artist at War*, pp. 17–19, and plates 1 and 2.
19. Ibid., pp. 26–9, figures 2 and 3; Schimmelpenninck, 'Vereshchagin's Canvases', p. 197.
20. Ibid., pp. 35–7, figure 5 and plate 3.
21. Ibid., pp. 39–44, plates 5 and 6, figures 7, 8, 9, and 10.
22. Ibid., pp. 49–53.
23. Ibid., pp. 65–73, figures 12, 13, 14, 15, 16, and 17.
24. Ibid., pp. 81–6.
25. Ibid., pp. 86–7, plate 11.
26. See Vasily Vereshchagin, *Oil Painting Reproduction from Tamsquare Art*, http://www.tamsquare.com/artist/Vasily-Vereshchagin/—visited last on 25 May 2008.
27. Barooshian, *Artist at War*, p. 87.
28. Ibid., p. 94.
29. Ibid., pp. 98–105; figures 18–20.
30. Ibid., pp. 107–14.
31. V.V. Vereshchagin, 'Realism' (1895) in Khudozhnik 1891, No. 1, 20–4, tr. Robert Russell, with notes by Alexey Makhrov and Robert Russell, Russian Visual Art Criticism, 1800–1913, Primary text in Translation, www.hrionline.ac.uk/rva/texts/ver/verbib.html—visited on 29 December 2009, pp. 6–12.
32. V.V. Vereshchagin. 'On Progress in Art' (O progresse v iskusstve), in F.I. Bulgakov, *V.V. Vereshchagin i ego proizvedeniia* (St Petersburg: Tipografiia A. S. Suvorina, 1905), pp. 133–6, V.V. Vereshchagin, *Povesti, ocherki, vospominaniia* (Moscow: Sovetskaia Rossiia, 1990), pp. 208–11, www.hrionline.ac.uk/rva/texts/ver/verbib.html –, visited on 29 December 2009.
33. Barooshian, *Artist at War*, pp. 124–42, figures 29, 24, 30, 25, 27, 28, 29, 31, and plates 15, 16, 13.

34. See Daniel Brower, 'Islam and Ethnicity: Russian Colonial Policy in Turkestan', in Daniel Brower and Edward. F. Lazzerini (eds.), *Russia's Orient*, pp. 115–25.
35. Schimmelpenninck, 'Vereshchagin's Canvases', pp. 180–1.
36. Brower, 'Islam and Ethnicity', pp. 125–6.
37. For an account of such poets, see 'Romanticism: The Caucasus of Pushkin, Griboedov, Lermontov', in Sahni, *Crucifying the Orient*, pp. 33–69.
38. Brower, *Islam and Ethnicity*, p. 126.
39. Tlostanova, 'The Janus-faced Empire', pp. 1–3.
40. Ibid., p. 2.
41. For another such 'no place' in the 'kresi' of Poland, on the periphery of Russia and undergoing a similar colonization into a homogenous mould from its previous multi-cultural fabric, see Kate Brown, *A Biography of No Place: From Ethnic Borderland to Soviet Heartland* (Harvard University Press, 2005).
42. See Madina Tlostanova, 'Life in Samarkhand: Caucasus and Central Asia vis-à-vis Russia, the West and Islam', *Human Architecture: Journal of the Sociology of Self-Knowledge*, 1(Fall 2006): 105–16, especially, 106–9, www.highbeam.com/doc/1P3-1559750411.html—retrieved on 10 May 2008.
43. It is the capital city of a geographic region in present-day south-western Azerbaijan and eastern Armenia, extending from the highlands of the Lesser Caucasus down to the lowlands between the rivers Kura and Aras. See '1865 Caucasus Molokane and Leapers: Eye-witness Report, by Vassili V. Vereshchagin', www. molokane.org/books/Veresehchagin/1887.html; and en.wikipedia.org/wiki/Karabakh—visited on 11 December 2009.
44. See Vassily Vereshchagin, 'A Religious Festival of the Shiites', in chapter I, 'Notes of a Journey in Trans-Caucasia', in *Vassili Vereshchagin: Painter–Soldier-Traveller: Autobiographical Sketches*, vol. I, translated from the German and the French by F. H. Peters, in two Volumes (London: Richard Bentley and Son, 1887), pp. 38–54. For the ethnic sketches see pp. 41, 51.
45. Nicholas Breyfogle, *Heretics and Colonizers: Forging Russia's Empire in the South* (Ithaca, N.Y.: Cornell University Press, 2005), pp. 1–2.
46. Ibid., pp. 5–6.
47. Ibid., pp. 8–12.
48. In 1863 Vereshchagin visited the Dukhobor and Molokan village of 'Slavyanka', 'Elizavetpol Governante', founded in 1844 by Dukhobors relocated from Sloviansk (Donetsk Oblast, Ukraine). See '1865 Caucasus Molokane and Leapers'.

49. Vereshchagin, 'Notes of a Journey in Trans-Caucasia', p. 55.
50. Barooshian, *Artist at War*, p. 143.
51. Vereshchagin, 'The Duchobortzis', p. 58.
52. Ibid., pp. 59–75; for sketches pp. 59 and 61.
53. Vereshchagin, 'Notes of a Journey in Trans-Caucasia', pp. 76–8.
54. Ibid., pp. 77–80; for sketches pp. 77 and 79.
55. I am borrowing this term from Sara Suleri, who says in her autobiographical novel that she had 'lived many years as an otherness machine, had more than my fair share of being other . . .' See Sara Suleri, *Meatless Days* (Chicago: University of Chicago Press, 1991), p. 105.
56. Vereshchagin, 'Notes of a Journey through Central Asia', in *Vereshchagin: Painter–Soldier-Traveller*, vol. I, pp. 99–206.
57. Vereshchagin, 'Notes of a Journey through Central Asia', pp. 99–105.
58. See n. 34 of 'Introduction'.
59. See n. 21 of 'Introduction'.
60. Vereshchagin, 'Notes of a Journey through Central Asia', pp. 105–6.
61. Captain Valikhanoff, M. Venukoff et al., *The Russians in Central Asia*, p. 49, cited in Palat, 'Tsarist Russian Imperialism', p. 186.
62. Vereshchagin, 'Journey through Central Asia', pp. 111–13.
63. Ibid., p. 118.
64. Ibid., pp. 121–5.
65. Ibid., pp. 126–8. In Russian Orientalism comparing Bukhara and St. Petersburg about anything was anathema. N.V. Khanikoff, *Bokhara: Its Amir and its People*, tr. from the Russian by Baron Clement A. De. Rode, London, 1845 cited in Palat, *Tsarist Russian Imperialism*, p. 185.
66. See Sahni, *Crucifying the Orient*, pp. 12–13.
67. Ibid., p. 13.
68. Vereshchagin, 'Journey through Central Asia', pp. 130–44.
69. Vereshchagin, 'The Molokanes', pp. 94–5.
70. Vereshchagin, 'Journey through Central Asia', pp. 102–3.
71. Ibid., pp. 104–5.
72. Ibid., pp. 143–4.
73. Ibid., p. 145.
74. Kemp, *Bharat-Rus*, pp. 213–14.
75. Vereshchagin, 'Journey in Trans-Caucasia', pp. 41, 49, 51 59, 61, 77, and 79; and 'Journey through Central Asia', pp. 101, 115, 117, 136, 138, 139, 141, 143, 151, 181, 183 and 197.
76. See Barooshian, *Artist at War*, pp. 37–9.
77. Vereshchagin, Oil painting Reproduction from Tamsquare Art; for other Orientalist paintings of Vereshchagin, dealing with Caucasian and Central

Asian Culture and available online, see 'Vereshchagin en Asia: Dias del futuro pasado', http://www.futuropasado.com/?p=1021 - 29k, visited last on 25 May 2008.

78. See Alex Marshall, *The Russian General Staff and Asia 1800–1917* (Abingdon, Oxon: Routledge, 2006), pp. x-xi.
79. Ibid., p. xi.
80. Adeeb Khalid, 'The Making of a Colonial Society: The Russian Conquest', in *The Politics of Muslim Cultural Reform: Jadidism in Central Asia* (Berkeley: University of California Press, 1998), p. 57. n. 30.
81. *Caucasus and Central Asia Newsletter*, The Caucasia and Central Asia Program at the University of Berkeley, California, Issue 9, Spring 2006, http://socrates.berkeley.edu/~bsp/caucasus/, last visited 19 May 2008, pp. 2–3, and 7; Schimmelpenninck, 'Vereshchagin's Canvases', pp. 195–7.
82. *Vereshchagin: Painter–Soldier-Traveller*, vol. I, pp. 213, 221, 223, 227, 233, 263, 267, 287, and 291.
83. Ibid., vol. 2, pp. 19, 21, 27, 65, 69, 71, 91, 103, and 109.
84. Vereshchagin, 'Journey in Trans-Caucasia', p. 142.
85. Marshall, *The Russian General Staff*, p. xii.
86. Sahni, *Crucifying the Orient*, p. 83.
87. Tlostanova, 'The Janus-faced Empire', p. 3.
88. Vereshchagin, 'Journey through Central Asia', vol. 1, pp. 205–6.
89. See 'India', by Madame Vereshchagin, in *Vassili Vereshchagin: Painter–Soldier-Traveller*, vols. I and II.
90. Madame Vereshchagin, *India, Part I: The Eastern Himalayas*, vol. 1, pp. 236–8.
91. Ibid., pp. 241–6.
92. Barooshian, *Artist at War*, p. 55.
93. Madame Vereshchagin, *India, Part II: The Western Himalayas—Cashmere Ladak*, vol. II, p. 10.
94. Ibid., pp. 39–40.
95. Ibid., pp. 61–3.
96. Ibid., p. 86.
97. Ibid., p. 93.
98. Ibid., p. 87.
99. Ibid., pp. 95–6.
100. Ibid., p. 106.
101. Ibid., p. 105.
102. Ibid., p. 49.
103. Ibid., p. 58.

104. Ibid., p. 70.
105. Ibid., pp. 75–6.
106. Ibid., pp. 90–2.
107. Ibid., pp. 107–8.
108. Barooshian, *Artist at War*, p. 3.
109. See Purchas, iv. 40, cited in Teltscher, *India Inscribed*, p. 17.
110. Madame Vereshchagin, *India, Part II*, pp. 13–4.
111. Ibid., pp. 20–2.
112. See for this Benoytosh Bhattacharyya, *An Introduction to Buddhist Esoterism* (Delhi: Motilal Banarsidass, 1989), pp. 109–64.
113. Madame Vereshchagin, *India, Part II*, p. 22.
114. Ibid., pp. 88–9.
115. Madame Vereshchagin, *India, Part I*, pp. 222–3.
116. Ibid., p. 235.
117. Ibid., pp. 258 and 262–4.
118. Ibid., pp. 264–70.
119. See Teltscher, *India Inscribed*, pp. 12–34.
120. No meaning is given of the word; must be some alcoholic drink.
121. Madame Vereshchagin, *India, Part I*, pp. 276–80.
122. Ibid., p. 255.
123. Ibid., p. 276.
124. See 'Dmitrii Bogdashevskii (1861-1933): His Hermeneutical Approach', in Alexander I. Negrov, *Biblical Interpretation in the Russian Orthodox Church: A Historical and Hermeneutical Perspective* (Tübingen: Mohr Siebeck, 2008), pp. 196–7.
125. Madame Vereshchagin, *India, Part I*, pp. 294–6; also see pp. 272–3.
126. See n. 12 of 'Introduction'.
127. Madame Vereshchagin, *India, Part I*, p. 273.
128. See Jonathan Swift, *Gulliver's Travels*, ed. Peter Dixon et al. (Harmondsworth: Penguin Books, 1976), part I, 'A Voyage to Lilliput', chapter IV, pp. 81–6; Charles Dickens, *Pickwick Papers* (London: Chapman and Hall, 1868), chapter XIII, pp. 88–9; and Lewis Carol, *Alice in the Wonderland and Through the Looking Glass* (Kolkata: Rupa & Co. by Arrangement with Collins, 1984), Chapter IV, pp. 177–91.
129. Madame Vereshchagin, *India, Part I: The Eastern Himalayas*, p. 274. Note that like the coolies in the region the *lamas* also hide themselves, fearing capture.
130. Ibid., p. 300.
131. Madame Vereshchagin, *India, Part II*, p. 31.
132. Ibid., p. 46.

133. Madame Vereshchagin, *India, Part I*, pp. 284–5.
134. Tlostanova, 'The Janus-faced Empire', p. 2.
135. Madame Vereshchagin, *India, Part II*, pp. 26–31.
136. Ibid., p. 31.
137. Madame Vereshchagin, *India, Part I*, pp. 220–3.
138. Madame Vereshchagin, *India, Part II*, pp. 103–4.
139. Teltscher, *India Inscribed*, p. 51.
140. Vereshchagin, *India, Part I*, p. 236.
141. Ibid., p. 249.
142. See n. 65 above.
143. Madame Vereshchagin, *India, Part I*, p. 298.
144. Ibid., pp. 299–300.
145. Madame Vereshchagin, *India, Part II*, p. 97.
146. Madame Vereshchagin, *India, Part I*, p. 246.
147. Ibid., p. 229
148. Ibid., p. 274.
149. Vereshchagin, *India, Part II*, p. 92.
150. Madame Vereshchagin, *India, Part I*, pp. 262–4.
151. Ibid., p. 269.
152. Ibid., pp. 296–7.
153. Ibid., p. 252.
154. Ibid., pp. 231–2.
155. Madame Vereshchagin, *India, Part II*, p. 35.
156. Madame Vereshchagin, *India, Part I*, pp. 290–1.
157. Ibid., pp. 292–4.
158. Ibid., p. 255.
159. Ibid., pp. 254–5.
160. Ibid., pp. 270–1.
161. Vereshchagin, *India, Part II*, pp. 49–50.
162. Ibid., p. 111.
163. Vereshchagin's series of three pictures of execution generated considerable controversy among art critics. His picture *Blowing from Guns in British India* or *Cannon-Fire in India* showed sepoys tied to the barrels of guns and about to be executed. Critics argued that such executions were typical of the Sepoy Mutiny of 1857, but the victims in the painting were modern soldiers of the 1880s and the painting sought to present itself as an impartial record of a real event. Vereshchagin took considerable pains to prove that 'not only was this form of execution . . . used widely during the above mentioned rebellion . . . but it was also used by the British

authorities in India for many years both before and after the Sepoy Rebellion in 1858'. See Vereshchagin, 'Realism', pp. 6–12.

164. John E. Bowlt, 'Review of Barooshian's *Artist at War*' in *Russian Review*, 53: 4 (October, 1994): 572–3.
165. Elizabeth Kridl Valkenier, 'V.V. Vereshchagin: Artist At War', *Slavic Review*, 53: 2 (Summer, 1994): 552–3.
166. Ibid.
167. David Schimmelpenninck van der Oye, 'Vereshchagin's Canvases', p. 182.

CHAPTER 6

Minaev, the Russian Exemplar: Academic Indology and the Diaries

Ivan Pavlovich Minaev (1840–90) is the only Russian traveller who had deep contacts with the Russian Orientology taking shape at the onset of what Tolz calls the second phase of the Oriental Renaissance. He is also ranked highest among Russian Orientalists by pre-Soviet and Soviet Indologists, as by many Indian scholars. and honoured as 'the founder of the Russian school of Indology and Buddhist Studies'.[1] But Morrison squarely places him among those Russian intellectuals and administrators for whom together with the 'interest in India as a potential field of conquest', Asia in general and India in particular was seen 'as playing a crucial role, political and moral, in the working out of Russia's destiny'.[2] Is there then a significant difference between the academic Orientalism and private observations of Minaev—of the sort exemplified in Vasily Vereshchagin's oeuvre? To answer this question we need an acquaintance with Minaev's academic Indology, its place in Russian 'vostokovedenie', and the consonance of this Indology with his views on India, as expressed in his diary notes. This is because it is for the first time we are dealing with a serious Russian academician who could give a historical-hermeneutic look at India's culture, beyond even Lebedev and his other predecessors, who as travellers and artists lacked the cognitive ability of exploring India's ancient tradition and interpreting the present in its light. Minaev had the requisite competence for doing so. But the researches in his travelogues directly or indirectly aided the national interests of the Russian State in India, explaining, at least partially, his exalted place in Russian Oriental studies and leaving room for some suspicion that he is a little more favoured over many of his predecessors because of the perceived practical value of his researches to the Russian State.

MINAEV'S BIOGRAPHY AND ACADEMIC DEVELOPMENT

Born on 9 October 1840 in Tambov, to an officer of modest means, Minaev completed his secondary education in Tambovsky School in 1958. He then enrolled in the Faculty of Oriental Languages of the St. Petersburg University, and passed out in 1868 from the Sino-Manchurian Department. A student of the renowned Sinologist V.P. Vasilyev there, and then of A. Weber, T. Benfey and F. Bopp at Germany, Minaev was primarily a Sanskrit scholar, but equipped in ethnography and geography too, besides being a talented socio-political commentator. Bongard-Levin and Vigasin judge his scholarship, espicially in his specialty area of classical Indology, as impressive, comprising Vedic literature, the edicts of Aśoka, Jaina texts, Pali language and its grammar, and the Prākṛt languages, the teaching of which he first introduced in Russia. It was, however, Minaev's Buddhist studies which made him famous. Immediately before his appointment as Reader in the Petersburg University in 1869, he wrote a dissertation on the *Pratimoksha-Sutra* of Buddhism; and in 1871 defended his doctoral thesis, 'Essay on the Phonetics of the Morphology of the Pali Language'.

THE OEUVRE

Minaev's linguistic-Indological works consist of: (i) *Pali Grammar*, an authoritative contribution by him to the field; (ii) *Declensions and Conjugations of Sanskrit Grammar*; (iii) 'Essay on the Most Important Monuments of Sanskrit Literature' (1880), one of the first books giving a detailed history of Sanskrit literature in the Russian language; (iv) *Indian Tales and Legends, Collected in Kumaun in 1875* (1876), containing translations of 47 tales in 'Pahari language', and 23 legends, supplemented with historico-geographic notes and ethnographic information about sub-Himalayan Kumaun; (v) literary comments on the subject of folk-tales contained in *Indian*

Tales (1874); and some Jātaka stories retold, concerning the many reincarnations of Buddha (1871 and 1872). Minaev's Buddhist treatise *Buddhism: Investigations and Materials* (1877), sought to offer a 'critical examination' of 'the history of ancient Buddhism, its institutions and its doctrines, organization and basic religious and philosophical conceptions . . . and . . . the heretical doctrines and splits in the internal organizations of Buddhism', apart from reproducing ancient Sanskrit manuscripts having great influence on the history of Buddhism. After his untimely death some portions of the existing materials were brought out together under the title of *Materials and Notes on Buddhism* by his illustrious student S.F. Oldenburg. Minaev's interest in historico-geographical studies is reflected in his early work, *Geographical Studies of Mongolia, Information about the Countries on the Upper Reaches of Amu Darya* (1879); translation of *Travels of Marco Polo* (1902) from French; a short article 'Forgotten Path to China' (1889); and *Ancient India* (1881), essentially a re-look at the geographical places and facts mentioned by Nikitin. An article 'Russian Thoughts about India in Ancient Times' (1884) was a kind of sequel to *Ancient India*.

Bongard-Levin and Vigasin, and Kemp point to Minaev's studies of the Vedas in his early twenties, and his attempts, together with his study of Pali literature, to set the Vedas into chronological order. Arguing that nagging illness and frustrated ambitions made him lower his sights to concentrate on Buddhism and philology, all praise his steadfast pursuit of the historical approach, evident in the words: 'In portraying the destiny of a religion we must discover the laws determining its development', because 'the essence of any spiritual development . . . can be understood only when this process is traced back to the beginning. . . .' Kemp thinks that this historical approach turned the emphasis of his studies from theological doctrines to the exploration of social and political conditions in which the mix of mythology and dogma generated them. This is why he looked at general tendencies of continuities and discontinuities within religious sects in India; and did not isolate the Vedic religion, Buddhism and Jainism in his studies, due to the importance of 'the genealogical connection between religious doctrines . . . and their mutual historical relationship that gave rise to various trends.' They contend that Minaev recognized no boundary between ancient and modern times, as answers to many of India's present day questions could be found in its ancient history.[3]

MINAEV AND THE DEBATE ABOUT ARYANS

Minaev's deep sense of debt to the Eastern and particularly to the Indian civilization comes out from his 'Introduction' to *Pali Grammar*.[4] Here he does not simply echo the familiar points of Sanskrit being one important branch of the common hypothetical Indo-European language, and of its similarity with Russian/Slavonic, as belaboured by Anton, Adelung, Uvarov, Petrov, Kossovich and the Slavophiles. Rather, he combines his knowledge in comparative philology and linguistics to add a few very original points to the current theories of the origins of the speakers of Sanskrit, the Aryans. At a time when, before the discovery of the more ancient Indus Valley Civilization, the 'discovery' of Sanskrit was appropriated in the 'Orientalist' efforts to establish the superiority of the European races, the common linguistic features of Sanskrit with many European languages became a useful ploy to argue the European origin of the Aryans. Sahni sees a subtle interplay of racism and social Darwinism in this theory, which was later emulated by the Russians too.[5] In India Dayananda Saraswati offered his counter-argument in *Satyarth Prakash* (1882) about the Vedic Aryans being a primordial and elect people, who had migrated in the beginning of the world from Tibet—the first land mass to resurface from the oceans—towards the Aryavarta, or the territory covered by modern Punjab, Doab, and the Ganges basin.[6]

Minaev sought to approach the issue through the path of philology and linguistics. For, the 'explanation of a series of grammatical phenomena by the analysis of the forms of language, the laws established for the different transfers of one sound in various languages, [and] the examination of the vocabulary according to results afforded by the scientific method' made it certain that there was a single body of people in the antiquity which spoke the primordial source of today's Indo-European dialects. He examined the reigning hypotheses and 'ingenious conjectures' about 'where this people primitively dwelt', to project Asia to be their original abode. This was not only because 'the most ancient traditions respecting the human race, as well as the Semitic conception of a golden age are localized in India'. More importantly, after the discovery of Sanskrit, and the knowledge of the geographical details in the first chapter of the recently discovered *Vendidad* (*Zend Avesta*), the question of the natal home of the Indo-Europeans was firmly settled in favour of Asia. For, the 'most ancient monuments of literature' were located here; and, besides, 'it is thence or from the bordering countries in which the first Indo-European songs are even to this day preserved as sacred things, that European nations too must needs have issued'.

The detractors of the 'Asiatic origin of the European nations' adduced two arguments to prove Aryans' European origin: the lack of commonness between the names of flora and fauna in Asia and Europe; and the near-impossibility of 'the existence of aborigines upon the heights of the Pamir'. Minaev regarded none of them as relevant. More important was 'another order of facts'. First, 'in certain legends, some reminiscences were found of successive immigrations of Aryans into India' from places in Asia. Secondly, in the backdrop of uncertainty about the first point of departure of the Indo-Europeans, the crucial place would be where they had lived for the longest time in common, as evidenced by traces of common language, cosmological conceptions, and rudiments of domestic organization. That 'the Aryans of Asia . . . still lived a common life, a long time after the greater number of European branches had become detached from them', was provable by many things. The first was the commonalities in the vocabulary and grammar of the ancient Bactrian and Sanskrit. The second was the common mythologies, religions and popular legends of the Iranians and the Hindus, both betokening 'a period of life which is common, which has probably endured longer than among the other nations'. Minaev showed how a mass of identical words referring to worship or names of heroes regarded as sacred in both 'Vedic hymns' and in the 'fragments of the sacred writings of the ancient Bactrians' that are still available, clearly indicate that 'at a distant period, during the pre-historic unity of the two Aryan races (the Iranians and the Hindus) the religious conscience enlarged itself, and that the mythological conceptions regarding the universe, were, up to a certain point systematized'. He shows it through the linguistic and mythological similarities in which Zarathrustra (Zoroaster) fought Agromaniyu and Śākyamuni combated with Mára. Minaev points out that the principle of evil Zarathrustra fought was named 'maiyo', mortal serpent in *Avesta*, and 'derived from the root 'mar'—to die—with the suffix 'ya'. In Sanskrit the word 'Mára', the demon who troubled the Buddha in early Buddhism, has also the same root.

Finally, to establish the Asiatic origin of the Aryans, Minaev refers to the 'confused recollections of an extra-Indian origin' not only in the Brahmanic accounts of the Hindus, but also in the later Buddhist writings, and in the legends of the genealogy of the Śākya kings. These refer to: (i) their conception of the extreme north as a sacred country; (ii) their placing of the seat of the gods and the good 'in that direction' and at Uttarakuru (Ottorokarra of Ptolemy); and (iii) the fact that 'in the ancient monuments of Indian literature, the years are reckoned by winters . . .'. He quotes Jātaka and Pliny to make his point that the river Sídá that Buddhism refers to, conveying the 'obscure notion of a distant cradle', was the same as 'the Jaxartes, the Silis of the ancients'. Likewise, the frequent references in the *Ṛgveda* to the countries to the north-west of India and the paeans sung by the singers to the river Sindhu (Indus) and the rivers falling into it, indicate that 'It is in the eastern Kabulistan (Afghanisthan) and in the Punjab, as far as the Saraswati, where the hymns were composed. Thence the Aryans spread themselves gradually towards the east end and to the south of the Vindhyas'.[7] So finally the origin of the Aryans was located in north-west India.

Scholar of Pali and Buddhism

Much of Minaev's reputation as a Buddhist scholar depended on his mastery of the Pali language as also on his discovery and possession of important Pali manuscripts. In Bongard-Levin and Vigasin's estimation his contribution lies in the following areas: (i) cutting his solitary way through a great number of manuscripts stored carelessly without inventory in royal libraries in Burma; (ii) not only stressing the great role of Buddhism in unfolding the cultural and historical development of the East, but making 'wide use of Buddhist material in his studies of folklore, literature, religion and language', and (iii) strengthening the ever growing efforts of the West to make use of Buddhism in exploring the 'depths of the spiritual culture of the Orient', in the context of the appearance of many earlier unknown Buddhist works in the 1870s and the 1880s. In the backdrop of the contemporary interest in the historical legacy of southern Buddhism—the Theravada School—European Orientalists were churning out ever new researches. Once the Pali works on the Hīnayāna school of the south, were supplemented by newly-found relics of northern Buddhism—Mahāyāna—through the discovery of Nepalese Buddhist manuscripts, Tibetan historical and religious literature, and inventorying of Chinese Buddhist canon (*Tripitaka*) by European and Japanese scholars, European Buddhist researchers were presented with a new problem. The Mahāyāna texts forced them to revise many of their beliefs about the original teaching of the Buddha, about the trajectory of the development of the canon, and the evolution of Buddhist metaphysics in different schools of thought, both in its natal home in India and outside. Avowedly, 'all the above aspects of Buddhist studies were reflected' in Minaev's works, placing him at par with great nineteenth-century scholars of Buddhism like E. Burnouf and Emile Senart of France, H. Oldenberg of Germany, T.W. Rhys Davids of Britain, and Hendrik Kern of Holland. Minaev supposedly exploded the view that once Buddhist religious-ethical teaching emerged, it almost remained unchanged, and *Tripitaka* remained its final book, complete and definitive. He rather presented Buddhism as a 'broad historico-cultural and social phenomenon', which helped shape many aspects of the cultural life of the Eastẹrn nations, and sought to relate actual events in the history of Buddhism to certain watersheds in the political history of India. It is claimed that from his analysis of Pali, Sanskrit, Chinese and Tibetan texts, the Buddhist Councils, taken in conventional wisdom to be general all-India councils settling questions of metaphysics and religion, are proven to be regional sectarian meetings preoccupied with deciding community affairs of particular sects, a view later substantiated by French scholar Louis de la Vallée Poussin.

Bongard-Levin and Vigasin show that this evolutionist view questioned the dating of the *Tripitaka* prevalent in his day and contended that neither the *Vinayapitaka* nor the *Suttapitaka* had assumed their canonical shape during the First Council. To make this point Minaev added the available evidence of literary works to that provided by the Bairat inscriptions of Aśoka, and the sculptural-architectural evidence of the bas-reliefs of the famous Bhārhut Stūpa. These suggested the existence of quite a few canons differing from the Pali Theravada one, the history of which could only be reconstructed from a comparative analysis of the 'separate religious doctrines' of Buddhism and their gradual development. For example, the Mahāyāna school was the repository of the oldest teaching of the Buddhists, though not preserved in the canons. So Minaev focused on little-discussed works, the still unexplored Jātaka tales and on physical relics as texts. The second phase of Minaev's study of Buddhism started with the publication in 1889 of the poems of the seventh-century preacher and philosopher Śāntideva, the *Bodhisattva-caryāvatāra*, actually a compendium of the philosophical schools of the Mahāyāna. While the first phase of his research had concerned itself with the history of Buddhism and the Buddhist community, the second was veering towards its philosophical content.[8]

Considering the high esteem Bongard-Levin and Vigasin's book enjoys even among non-Soviet scholars,[9] the fulsome terms of their praises for Minaev underscores his place in Soviet, even if not European Indology. European Indologists faulted his scholarship for many reasons. When the French translation of the book *Buddhism* (1887) first appeared in 1894, Rhys Davids contested all the claims of Minaev to original research.[10] He not only challenged Minaev's thesis regarding the role of the Councils in Buddhist theological development, but questioned his methodology too, which belittled the well-grounded knowledge about the Councils and the 'holy personages' who held these councils, without any concrete evidence of the different trajectory of the development of the Buddhist doctrine that he hinted at. Rhys Davids called the reliance that

Minaev placed on the Buddhist sculptures and Aśokan inscriptions after rejecting the literature as misplaced. He claimed that the concluding chapters in the book dealing with the eighteen schools in which Buddhism was divided in the pre-Aśokan days contained nothing new, as these traditions were available in easily accessible translations. Even the Pali bibliography of Buddhism, discovered by Minaev in Burma, and coming as an appendix after these chapters, had 'appeared already *in extenso* in the journal of the Pali Text Society'.[11]

The critique may have seemed spiteful toward the greatest Russian Indologist of the second half of the nineteenth century,[12] had a nagging suspicion not remained that he was a little blown out of proportion. For, it is not only that many Western books of research on Buddhism do not so much as mention his name,[13] but many Russian experts also do not do it. Serebriany does not miss him among the Russian Orientalists ignored in Halbfass' *India and Europe*.[14] The 'grand Russian project' of *Bibliotheca Buddhica*, a collection of Mahāyāna texts, that he describes as the supreme example of 'international and interdisciplinary cooperation', started and edited by Minaev's student, Sergei Oldenburg,[15] gained four, even if brief, mentions in the great Dutch expert Jan Willem Jong's philologically oriented but comprehensive study of 500 Buddhist scholars in Europe and America.[16] But there was no mention of Minaev. Of course, one of the most definitive commentaries on Śāntideva's *Bodhisattva-caryāvatāra* gives him not only the credit of being the first scholar to have translated this text, but also avers that Louis de la Vallée Poussin's more advanced commentary had the benefit of his earlier research.[17] Still it becomes difficult to explain the enormous prestige that Minaev enjoyed in the erstwhile Soviet Union compared with many other Orientalists, if we do not take into account the value he had for the Russian State as its cultural ambassador. If Scherbatsky's book *Buddhist Logic* (1930–2) judged by D.N. Shastri as 'the most eminent work on Buddhist philosophy to appear in the last 250 years', was 'hardly mentioned in Soviet writing on Buddhism',[18] what was so special about Minaev? Part of the explanation may lie in the extreme importance accorded to his *Diaries* and its special brand of Indology.

POWER/KNOWLEDGE IN/AND THE DIARIES

Interest of the Russian State in the Diaries

The three journeys Minaev made to India with support from the Russian Geographical Society in 1874–5, 1880, and 1885–6, which generated the *Diaries*, are passed off as exclusively academic, on the ground that during the first trip he also visited Ceylon and Nepal; and during the third Burma too, all important places for studying the history of Buddhism. An Indian scholar, of Indo-Russian relations vouches for this.[19] Some Western experts on the USSR of course try to see more in the visit than just academic intent. Morrison points out that in his very first diary Minaev wrote that detailed knowledge of India—Britain's wealthiest and most significant overseas possession—was necessary for competition with her in Asia.[20] Marshall informs that Minaev made these research trips to India because besides Indology he was also 'deeply involved in helping resolve Russia's Asiatic policy throughout this period, studying contemporary events alongside the ancient history of his area of expertise'. He also refers to recent archival research that has shown how 'this undertaking also included previously unsuspected links with the Russian War Ministry'. Allegedly, after his trips to India Minaev had repeated meetings with both L.N. Sobolev of the General Staff's Asiatic department and with Chief of General Staff N.N. Obruchev. He also met with Governor-General Kaufman, who had already sought his opinion about the Indian Nāmdhārī sect, in connection with the Gurcharan Singh Mission of 1879. Marshall also mentions that General Kaufman tried to depute one of the topographers on his military staff to accompany Minaev on his first trip to conduct surveys around Peshawar. What is more important, the Military Scientific Committee of the Main Staff is meanwhile said to have communicated to Minaev a set of questions on a number of points which had appeared to the General Staff to have strategic significance. These included 'the attitude of the Sikh states' to British rule in India, 'in view of the envoys recently received in Turkestan and information gained by General Stoletov in Kabul'; 'the situation in the north-east (Burma and Assam)'; and the mental state of India's native rulers, in particular 'the sovereigns of Gwalior and Indore' (in modern Madhya Pradesh). Marshall concedes that although Minaev provided the Staff with 'little information of long-term value', he did provide insights into some of these aspects of British rule in India.[21] Post-Soviet Russian Orientalists have not sought to refute all these charges, though in the 1980s, Soviet Indologist N.A. Khalfin looked back to contemporary British fears of a 'hypothetical' invasion from the north, particularly after the joining to it of Central Asia, as unfounded. He cites the lukewarm responses by tsarist authorities to a host of missions between 1860 and 1887 from India seeking Russian intervention to buttress his point that let alone contemplating an invasion against India, the 'sober-minded politicians in St. Petersburg' did not even seek to take advantage of India's post-1857 grouse against English domination. This was evident from the short shrift given to diplomatic missions from various parts of India between 1860 and 1887, from native princes as well as religious rebels, requesting Russian intervention for their causes.[22] But conclusive documentary evidence regarding Minaev's complicity in intelligence gathering for the General Staff has since been provided by P.I. Shastitko, Purabi Roy and Alexander Morrison.[23] Interestingly, while seeking to exculpate the tsarist authorities, Khalfin too corroborates the fact that in the course of examining the 'political credo' of Gurcharan Singh and the Namdhari sect, General Kaufman confirmed their anti-colonial credentials and Gurcharan Singh's affiliation to them from Minaev.[24]

The Diaries in Soviet Eyes

Minaev's *Diaries* got so much importance in Russia that a few more words about them and about how Soviet Indologists viewed them may be opportune. Minaev turned the first diary into a book *Sketches of Ceylon and India: From the Travel Notes of a Russian* (St. Petersburg, 1878, parts I and II). He died before completing the job. Work on it was begun by his niece under the auspices of the Geographical Society of the USSR towards the end of 1920, but could not cross the preparatory stage. It was taken up again after the end of the Second World War, to celebrate the 110th birth anniversary of Minaev in 1950 by Barannikoff, who did most of the editorial work. After his death, his colleagues, N.M. Goldberg and G.M. Kotovsky of the Institute of Orientology, Academy of Sciences, USSR prepared the final text for the press.[25] Bongard-Levin and Vigasin regard the 'appearance of the book' as 'a notable event not just in Russian, but in West European Indology also'.[26]

Soviet Indologists were of course not always happy about all of the observations of Minaev in his *Diaries*. Kemp mildly complains about 'inconsistencies in his remarks', indicating his conflict of mind and despondency, which he did not revise for publication.[27] The later editors of his *Diaries* too seem perturbed by these inconsistencies and contradictions, most of which relate to his concern with Indian religions and their Indological importance (anathema to the current Bolshevist reductionism), his eclecticism, adherence to 'reactionary views of a few idealists—historians who considered religion to be the basic motive force of history', and 'observations . . . devoted to themes tainted in one sense or other with religious colouring, beginning with the description of Buddhist monasteries and ending with Hindu-Moslem relationship. . .'.[28]

Not bothered about how a leading Buddhist scholar could avoid writing about Buddhist monasteries in a book on Indology, the editors seem relieved about the reappearance of Minaev's materialistic leanings in the pages of *Ancient India* and of his researches on Buddhism. They were unhappy with Minaev's words, 'up till now all communities of Asia were forged together by religion; in this bond of union alone they were finding their peace'.[29] Kemp seeks to present Minaev's concern with religion as an aberration, caused by the 'peculiar and profound influence' his 'academic interests' had on his 'personal attitude to life'; by the 'direct contact with India and his fieldwork there'; and by 'his intellectual and emotional experiences',[30] as if the Continent of Circe had at least temporarily held the scientific Odysseus in its oriental thraldom.

Why the Soviet Indologists tolerated these aberrations can be explained by a close look at the contents of the second and third *Diaries* (the first, *Sketches*, is unavailable in English translation) which makes it plausible that Minaev might have been looking at aspects of British India that might be valuable to the Russian State. Let us look at these pieces of information in the *Diaries*.

Diaries: Charge of Espionage, Revealing Contents

Even a cursory glance at the *Diaries* shows that the types of questions which the Military Scientific Committee of the Main Staff asked Minaev to seek answers to in India, are the ones he is raising with patient regularity and persistence in social gatherings, individual interviews, and even during Indological discussions with Indian scholars. Gathering information on them, for whomsoever it was done, was clearly one of the objectives of the journey. Significantly, Minaev was aware that because of his inquiries or otherwise, at least some people did suspect him of espionage. A *talukdar* (member of landed gentry) of Hyderabad did not believe that the object of his visit was academic.[31] Minaev was relieved that at a place called Panchmora, two judges and the chief justice 'made fun of the suspicion of the British'.[32] But three days later he discovered behind 'the seeming cordiality of the British, . . . a strong feeling of annoyance', reflected in the boasting of a 'somewhat stupid' principal of a college at Indore at a dinner hosted by a British bureaucrat that 'the Secret Police in India headed by his son-in-law keep a very close watch over the . . . Russians'. Minaev says petulantly that his 'reputation of being a spy has been conclusively established here'.[33] He mentions on the last day of the second trip that the police had interrogated Jitesh Ram, friend and fellow Indologist, 'as to why the Russian Sahib would be coming to him'.[34] Even during his third trip a judge from Arra in Bengal Presidency (now Bihar) told him 'point blank that the Government would keep watch' on him.[35] It is strange that while so sensitive about such suspicion, Minaev requested on his way to Quetta (presently the provincial capital of Baluchistan in Pakistan), Sir R.B. Sandeman, colonial British Indian Officer, creator of British Baluchistan, and at that time agent to the Governor-General in Baluchistan, to get him 'an account of the military road', only to meet with the rebuff that it was a closely guarded secret with the army.[36]

Let us look at his queries classified under the following sub-heads.

Mental States of the Native Royalty and the Russian Factor

Minaev did want to find out the disposition of the threatened native princes, including the Nizam of Hyderabad, a thing that

Military Scientific Committee of the Main Staff asked him to explore. He gathered from an unidentified fellow Russian that 'Salar Jung (of Hyderabad) was very much displeased with the British',[37] and from one Major Ronaldson came to know that the reason was the taking away of Berar (part of the Central Provinces). Berar had been taken for money, but was not returned even after the debt was paid off.[38] He notes at Hyderabad that in contrast to British India the people were loyal to the government,[39] and that contrary to British perceptions, 'the people in Gwallior prefer their own lot to that of the British subjects', because of lower taxes, though 'Europeans do not get those comforts which await them at every stop in British India'.[40]

To his evident disappointment not all the native princes or their chief functionaries were, however, yet prepared to think of opposing British rule in India. Sir Madhavan Rao at Baroda, whom Minaev scoffs at as 'the most interesting *thing* in Baroda' (italics added), gets sharp barbs for his views that: (i) The 'existing relationship of the British with the natives was extremely beneficial to India'. (ii) The 'British are keeping themselves aloof from the natives and are not striking roots in India. The natives in consequence are preserving their originality'. And (iii) 'British rule was . . . necessary for . . . uniting India. Drive out the British and Indians will scatter in different directions and begin to antagonise one another'. Minaev's discomfiture is evident in the following quote:

> His words meant: thank god, the British are keeping aloof; thank God, the Indian climate is unbearable to Europeans, else they would have occupied the whole of India, and turned India into Australia. But now it is not difficult to drive out the British. Indians send up their prayers to the sun for nothing; the sun has done a great service to them.[41]

Also frustrating was that even those officials in the native administrations who were nursing rancour against the British were passive in their grouses. A clerk-turned-talukdar of an independent principality had become an Anglophile with a vengeance, hating the British all the same, as his imitativeness had not obliterated from his mind 'the memory of how Sahiblog used to order him in the past'.[42] But Minaev has no interest in this passive hatred.

Minaev was as critical of native rulers' submission and loyalty to the British rule, and their blind imitation of European and particularly British ways, as of the British strategy which inculcated in them this loyalty. This explains his vitriolic words against the Raja of Alwar in Rajasthan, whose English upbringing explained the obvious 'signs of British influence' in the city; as also against another Anglophile king of Ratlam in Indore. The Raja of Alwar had adopted only the outward marks of Western modernity, dressing himself 'in European style'. But his English education had not dissuaded him from 'marrying twice'. 'Gun fire and the sound of "God Save the Queen etc."', marked his return to the town. While granting Minaev a visit he entered his office without attendants, revealing a measure of Westernization. But Minaev's dissatisfaction after the visit is plain. After informing that this 'ruler of the new generation is an alumnus of the Ajmer College', he wonders what they taught the native princes in these colleges. He is nearly sure that 'very little is taught and in any way not statecraft. To cultivate the latter in the young wards is not at all in the interest of the British Government'. The college is berated for the 'empty handedness and want of education' of the trustees as of the Principal, who had wormed his way up to the post by 'working out for himself a literary name, carving out many new books from old ones'. On top of that 'Captains and Majors, Residents and Agents, people for the most part not blessed with brilliant education' had arrogated the 'task of educating the young rulers'. The curriculum of princely education too, while being poor in quality, alienated the recipients from their motherland. For, while 'the young Raja speaks English very badly, is not strong in science, and has a passion for brandy, polo, badminton, cricket, hunting and so on', the teachers out of their narrow patriotism, and 'actuated by low pharisaical religiosity . . . engraft unbelief on the minds of their wards, and corrupt them so that they look upon their own motherland with contempt', turning them into 'these prince apes'.[43]

All these signs had probably convinced Minaev that not much resistance was possible even from the native states. His observation in Ratlam, 'that discontentment is not active received further confirmation here'.[44] At Gwalior he notes, 'In independent states, where the Resident means everything, each and every sahib is looked upon with timid hostility by the inhabitants'.[45]

This sorry situation led Minaev to believe that all acts of justice meted out to native princes by the British were motivated by the Russian factor. Even return of the Gwalior Fort to Scindia, 'a policy of concessions to, and conciliation of, the natives', was occasioned by 'apprehension of open hostilities with Russia'. Along with the Burmese War even this was dictated by British calculations about Russia. 'It appears', said Minaev, 'that in India nothing in the nature of a more or less big job is undertaken without its having something to do with Russia'.[46] In Britain's annexation of Burma against the will of the natives for the overt reason of 'securing new markets for their goods and new positions for their officials', the ultimate goal was engaging Russia. 'They are expanding the army in view of the coming clash with Russia. . .'.[47] Anyway, Minaev saw little chance of native princes mounting a challenge to British rule. 'The Scindia is not strong. . . . The Nizam is also placed in similar circumstances. Only Nepal is independent. But will it be able to do much?'[48] The last question leaves no doubt about his concern for Russia's interests in India.

Who Were For and Against Russia and the Afghan War?

Minaev was also inquisitive throughout the *Diaries* about the attitude of the different sections of the Indian people towards Russia, trying to figure out among whom Russia was most popular/unpopular in India. For this he not only questioned a wide cross-section of Indians but also browsed the reporting about Russia in the elite English and mass vernacular press. In one of the very first entries in the *Diaries* of the second journey he asks the English Registrar of the Bombay University, whether 'in India, public opinion was very antipathetic to Russia', and notes the disappointing affirmative answer. The explanatory notes by the editors clarify that here he was speaking about 'the opposition of the British officials and military circles'.[49] He learns from the Principal of the Elphinstone College in Bombay that this antipathy was particularly marked in military circles',[50] and that the reason behind the hatred among British officials of Bombay for Russia was that 'in Bombay there were very few people belonging to *the liberal party*, [of Britain] about 5 people, and they were accused of lack of patriotism' [italics added].[51] Even during his third trip he came to know that in 'military circles everywhere in India there is ill-feeling against Russia'.[52] This extreme concern about the attitude of the British military and bureaucracy must have arisen from a desire to gauge their level of commitment in the event of a possible Russian foray in British India. This is why he notes the bragging of a planter in Prome in Burma that they wanted 'the arrival of the Russians in India; not one of them shall go back', with the comment that this was 'the distorted expression of the opinion of *unofficial India*, that India which is in direct opposition to *radical India*' [italics added].[53]

One can ask what Minaev means by this '*unofficial India*', which was never in a position to challenge Russia in these terms, having 'neither wealth nor importance', and not commanding 'any respect in its native land', paid heed to only 'when the question concerns British trade?' Was he meaning rural India, possibly dominated by Muslims? Otherwise the words, 'Unofficial India, considering itself to be the offspring of the conquerors stands on its prerogatives like an aristocrat and does not want to lose them',[54] have no meaning. The words, it is 'traditionalist, native and feudal—where it is different from *radical India*, and it was a bulwark for the British, given the pro-British attitude of the rural commoners', make the meaning even more probable, as do the words that 'official India' actually looks upon the growth of political ideas amongst the natives not without satisfaction'.[55]

Radical India obviously meant the more politicized urban intelligentsia, particulary of Bengal,[56] a meaning strengthened by Minaev's frequent mention of the 'kindness of the Bengalees' towards him, which was 'extended to the Russians and not to me personally'. Bengali men of letters like Haraprasad Shastri, Haridas Shastri, etc., convinced him about the great 'amount of curiosity' of Bengalis for Russians, and in a manner of return of favours he criticized British white racism directed against the Bengalis, 'for their dark skin'. Bengalis were good not only for liking Russians, but also for opposing the annexation of Burma and the war, which meant nothing but new taxes.[57] The ultimate virtue of love for Russia could even allow 'a madcap' from the Asiatic Society, trying to sell his overpriced books to him, because he painted a bright picture of Russia's future in India, 'and called the Russians the future rulers of India', from his reading of newspapers.[58]

Minaev was also inquisitive about how much and through what sources common people knew about Russia, and what was their attitude to her. He was not at all happy that the only information Indians were getting about Russia was filtered through biased British representations, 'calculated to undermine the credit of Russia and to lower her in the eyes of the population'.[59] He was not happy either that so many people were ignorant of Russia, starting from one of the younger sons of Salar Jung,[60] an Afghan in the service of Nizam,[61] to a bookshop owner who admitted that 'what he knew about Russia was through British sources and regarded Russia as a barbarous and despotic country'.[62] While going from Bombay to Calcutta during his third trip, he engaged a Hindu pleader and a Muslim merchant into conversation about it. The latter, in spite of having trade with Jedda (a city in Saudi Arabia), was completely ignorant about Central Asia and Russia. He thought Samarkand to be 'under the Chinese rule', and did not have 'the remotest idea about Russia'. The Hindu pleader 'had read about Russia', but knew 'that the country is a despotic one . . . unjust to its own subjects at home', and unlikely to be 'just to the people of a foreign land'.[63] These confirmed the views of a fellow Russian that 'the natives knew little about Russia, and whatever they knew they did only through the Britishers'.[64] But at Nasik he found that while the 'discontent of the rural population' against the British was 'even stronger than amongst the educated', the natives 'do not share this hatred towards Russia', having rather 'sympathy towards Russia', and the government, 'suspecting the educational classes fall into an error of exaggeration. Among the insignificant educated minority no sedition—rumours apart—is observed. Nor can there be any'.[65]

Minaev was uneasy with Russia's image of 'secondary modernity'. That is why he disliked the observation of a spiritualist named Ware Edgar that 'a new world religion must be conceived either in India or in Russia':

I asked him why he supposed this should be in Russia . . . from further talks it became clear why. We are less cultured. That is so, but our political ideas are beginning to grow stronger. And at those places where this crying evil of the day has taken possession of the minds of people, there is no place any more for religious tendencies.[66]

If we read this statement with his earlier comment that an Indian is an eternal mystic,[67] Minaev's sense of difference between Russia's advanced, even if secondary, modernity and India's traditionalist core becomes obvious.

Minaev notes in his *Diaries* any talk of an Indian relating to the possible extension of Russian empire to India, whether in a word of welcome, a prophecy, a reasoned judgement, British propaganda, local press coverage, or anything else. At Agra, after a cordial reception, he asks the son-in-law of the Nawab, 'why these people received me with such pleasure'. With gratification he notes his answer that 'Everyone in India believes in the advent of the Russians, and hates the British for the burden of taxes. The Russians are regarded as mighty'.[68] He also records 'a popular belief, a kind of prophecy' in Delhi that 'the British rule must come to an end in one hundred and twenty-five years'. Its supposed ground is that 'the British talked about the possibility of Russian invasion so much and so long that the Indians came to believe them'. Seeing 'what a fascination the natives have for the might of Russia they (the British) have started to assert something else', and have been 'trying to convince the natives that Russia is weak', and too 'harassed by her internal troubles', to pose any threat.[69]

A meeting with a Muslim notable at his palace in Ratlam generated the realization that Russia was welcome in India because of the Indians' search for respite from the elitist and snobbish detachment of English rule: 'Contemporary Britishers do not know India, do not strike deep roots here and do not have any attachment. The people await Russian invasion. The British themselves have enlightened them in this regard'.[70]

This realization was confirmed by an interlocutor in a dinner party in Lahore that India was the 'most vulnerable place' for England, and others' silent agreement on this point,[71] as also by the revelation of a Gujarati trader on the penultimate day of his departure in the second trip, that the accumulated grievances of the people, coupled with the possibility of Russian help, had made the situation fertile for a repeat of 1857. While 'people were grumbling against land laws, taxes and irresponsibility of the British officials', the appearance of Russians on the border of Afghanisthan, coupled with a possible 'general treason by the native army', boded ill for British rule.[72] All this convinced Minaev that the Englishmen in India were afraid of a potential invasion by Russia, though they did not admit it.

As part of his efforts to learn about the Indians' attitude towards Russia, Minaev wanted to ascertain from all sections of the Indian population what they knew about the Second Anglo-Afghan War (1878–80), how they viewed it, and on which side their sympathies lay. These included students, merchants, common people, European acquaintances, British civilian and military officials, functionaries of native states, members of different religious denominations, and fellow Indologists. One gets an impression that while he was deeply concerned about Britain's and Russia's chances in the war; he was trying to map the entire spectrum of Indians' opinions on British policies on Afghanistan. It turned out that the common people had no idea of the Afghan War. But 'the educated classes sorrowfully apprehend the increases in taxes' because of it. He questioned one bookseller about 'who was right and who was at fault' in the war, to get the answer that 'it was his duty to defend his own master'.[73] Three students who came to meet him said that they 'did not know the truth about this War because the government would not disclose full information'.[74] At a dinner he knew from his 'interlocutors their conviction that a war between Russia and England was inevitable', as forces 'were being mobilized in Afghanistan in large numbers'.[75] But to his chagrin he found that when the War came up for discussion, references were indirect and oblique, as when a lady spoke about the Bhil uprising and expressed her desire that 'the troops should not be removed from Secunderabad' for deployment in this war.[76] Minaev's eagerness for Indians' attitude toward the war is evident from the haste with which he engaged Rustomji Noserwaji, Parsi official in the Nizam administration, as also a British Major into a discussion about it just after introduction.[77]

The Major said that the 'Afghan War is being prosecuted not for the safety of the Indian borders, nor for the sake of India, but for Britain's benefit and that with India's money'.[78] But many Englishmen did not share the Major's views. Minaev notes with disapproval: 'Here, as elsewhere in India, majority of the British population have strong conservative beliefs. Indeed only the women wish the end of the war, but from what they hear from their husbands they express their apprehension that troops may be withdrawn from Afghanistan by the liberal ministry'.[79]

Minaev broached the subject also with Indian academicians. He 'touched upon the hatred which is at present noticeable among the Britishers toward Russia' with Mahadev Moreswar Kunte, to know that the 'natives do not share this hatred'. Minaev did not of course fully believe him, and his 'Orientalist' position is clear in the words, 'it is very difficult to ascertain the real feeling of the natives. Either they do not speak out their minds or they do not speak the truth'. But he notes his view that the natives 'regard the Afghan War with extreme apathy'.[80]

The next feedback came from Kashinath Trimbak Telang, who judged the Afghan War as a 'senseless' war, there being 'no necessity for starting it', though 'India will be saddled with the cost'.[81] Just two weeks before Minaev left India after his second trip, he heard at an evening meeting at the house of Jitesh Ram that the Afghan War 'was being desperately condemned, where: "Men will be killed, money and even kingdom lost".'[82] He also learnt from (Mahamahopadhyay Pandit) Mahesh Chandra Nyayaratna (Bhattacharyya), that people were unhappy with the 'Afghan affair' for 'swallowing a lot of money' and imposing ever new taxes on them, only for 'strengthening the [British] frontier' at their cost.[83]

It was apparently heartening for Minaev that apart from academicians even incurable Anglophiles like T.M. Rao thought the Afghan War 'to be unjustified' and said his 'sympathies are with the liberal ministry'.[84] Minaev talked a merchant into the topic, who said that 'even assuming the best possible outcome of it [for the British], annexation of a poor country like Afghanistan could not in any way be profitable'.[85] He gathered from the soldiers starting for Europe, for the Malta Island and that they were also not well-disposed towards the war.[86]

Minaev even tried to find correlations between religious affiliations of Indians and their attitude to the Afghan War. He noticed that the Muslims at Aurangabad were 'closely watching the Afghan War, and are confident of the success of the Afghans', though the 'Hindus regard it comparatively indifferently'. 'Sympathy for the British' was not noticeable among the common people at a town near Ellora, though regarding the outcome of the war 'confidence in their success was complete'.[87] Among the other religious denominations the Sikhs were lukewarm, as 'the Afghans are Muslims'. Minaev met a Pathan who was highly sceptical of British victory in the war. But the 'Hindus view the Afghan War differently. They, just like the Sikhs, do not have any sympathy for the Afghans.'[88] During a dinner with a native aristocrat at his palace in Ratlam Minaev came to know that in the backdrop of discontent 'everywhere in India' the Afghan War had proved 'a colossal political blunder' for the British, as the 'Afghans are now the enemies of the British for all time to come', though they should have been their friends.[89]

But even the solid support of the Muslims of all classes and groups for the Afghans did not seem sufficient to Minaev for the possibility of a flare up against the British: 'Muslims are on the side of the Afghans. But they too, like the Hindus, believe in the inexhaustibility of British resources. This belief saves the British from their ultimate downfall'.[90]

All this increased Minaev's mental reliance on the Russian factor. In his third *Diary*, aboard a ship cruising along the Red Sea, he learnt from Sir Sandeman himself that Indians would have reacted less at this time to a Russian intervention in the Afghan War; as 'the natives are convinced that Russia will take Hirat'. Their mood was 'much more conciliatory'. Minaev, however, disliked the myth of British invincibility. Sandeman was sure that Britain would win the war as troops were ready to be dispatched there in the spring; in spite of the fact that Russian troops had already reached Khorasan. 'The British naively believe', Minaev wryly comments, 'that Russians will be defeated there and a catastrophe will follow'.[91] Curiously enough he reports a suggestion about the division of Afghanisthan between Russia and England made by Sir C. McGregor and General Roberts without comments.[92]

All this puts Minaev's concern about Afghanistan or Burma in a somewhat dubious light. While Minaev reports Sir Alfred Lyall's opinion on this point that 'England has reached her natural limits in the east as well as in the west: on one side the rock of the Chinese empire and on the other, Russian: the days of Afghanistan are numbered, it must collapse', the tone is of only half sympathy for the poor country. Of course, he laments that Afghanistan, fated to be 'crushed . . . will crumble by the impact of western civilization. The same thing happened to Burma'.[93] But the other half of the feeling is definitely the suggestion that the mighty Russia standing as a rock of resistance may change the game yet.

Discontents against British Rule and its Significance

Minaev's pursuit of queries suggested by the General Staff is evident also in his routine inquiries into the feelings of a wide section of the people of India, including students, other educated sections, the common people and the peasantry, and even resident Englishmen regarding: British rule in India generally; the possibility of a repeat of the 1857 uprising; the attitude of these people towards the recent Anglo-Russian war over Afghanistan; and, in the third *Diary*, towards the overtaking and annexation of Burma. Sometimes he even provokes Englishmen into admitting the degree and extent of the antipathy towards the British in India as is seen in the following quote:

> Peterson in course of his conversation *blurted out* that in India the educated classes are not quite contented, but not so the ordinary people. I think it is quite probable; the riaiya [etymologically of Arabic origin and meaning peasantry] do not know and quietly suffer the Ingrizi Raj [English rule]' [italics added].[94]

Minaev also delved into the most potent causes of the disaffection of educated Indians with colonial rule. He says ruefully that despite suspicion of the British authorities and the Education Department about college students, they are 'independent but loyal', and 'serve more willingly under the British administration than under native'.[95] But talks with Telang, a local Brahman at Panchmora near the Ajanta caves, and 'a stupid boy named Radharaman', at Allahabad bucked him up. Telang found Englishmen's 'notion that in India the educated classes alone are discontented', as 'entirely false'. Rather starting with cultivators, everyone was discontented, though their discontentment had not yet 'reached an active stage in the process of its development'. Existence of 'strong though not active dissatisfaction with the British Government' was testified to by Telang, the editor the *Deccan Star* and friend and follower of the famous revolutionary Vasudeo Balwant Phadke (1845–83), by the Panchmora Brahman and even by Rādhāramaṇ. Sources of discontentment were: high rates of taxation; ban on exploiting the forests; introduction of widow remarriage; press laws; taxing of salt, prohibition of making of salt from seawater and of gathering of leaves and brushwood from the forests; the frittering away of the Famine Funds (Famine Insurance Grant created after the terrible famines of 1876–8 in Bombay) to defray the costs of the Afghan War; the high taxes paid by Kunbis; and removal of import duty which affected both the mill owners and the poor. Students were dissatisfied because of the pittance they received in government jobs after completion of their grueling studies.[96]

Minaev went into the discontentment of the local people towards the British in Maharashtra and its reasons in greater detail, possibly because he was impressed by the rich history of resistance in Maharashtra to British expansionism during the Indian uprising.[97] Immediately after denigrating the decadent ways of the royalty in the native state of Alwar in Rajasthan, he reminds that in 'Maharashtra the legend about the past glory is still fresh', and that Nana Sahib is remembered not as 'a cruel-hearted bandit, but as a national hero'. There were many disaffected groups which made the socio-economic situation in Maharashtra different. These were: (i) the once powerful and rich Deshmukhs (titular landed gentry of Maharashtra), 'impoverished and shorn of importance . . . spending their last days in Poona in mansions, which once sparkled with luxury but are now dirty and half in ruins'; (ii) Brahmins who 'looked upon the activities of the present government with repressed spite' for the same reasons; (iii) other groups, not similarly privileged before, but motivated by 'local Maratha patriotism' that found expression in literature, songs, etc., which brought back 'the grandeur of the times of the Peshwas and different family chronicles, etc.'. Minaev was not sure if their grouses would translate into 'anything more serious in the political field', in the backdrop of the severe punishment meted out to Phadke, which showed 'that attempts at revolt are premature here'.[98] But still the British had no faith in the loyalty of the native population. 'In the land of the Marathas the entire population and mainly the Brahmins are declared suspects'.[99] A Jain priest complained before him that 'the Christian commandment "Thou shalt not kill" was not observed in the case of animals and black people'.[100] Yet, Minaev was sure that the British had little reason to apprehend a repeat of the 1857 mutiny. As he noted just a fortnight before his final day of the second trip at Bombay, the 'general discontent among the masses', had not infused among the masses any revolutionary intent 'in the fullest sense of the term'. Rather, 'slight concessions from the side of the Britishers would reconcile the natives with the British Empire, which is accepted by practically all the educated people as something necessary'. The meekness of the people and their submission to the wishes of every Sahib made a mutiny unthinkable.[101]

Discontent among the natives was particularly acute in the Presidency of Bengal. A judge from Arra (now a town and a district in Bihar) had told him that in Bengal 'plots are being hatched constantly; these do not lead to serious outbursts only because the Government keeps a vigilant watch over the natives'.[102] Minaev found that contrary to Hyderabad, in British India 'everyone is displeased, but rebellion is a long way off'. For, people 'are so thoroughly convinced about the might of the British, that at present they are not going to risk a revolt against them. Their mood is bound to undergo a change as soon as they realize that Britannia is not as strong as they imagine her to be, and that her power has been dealt a mighty blow'.[103]

Typically of St. Petersburg's post-1860s proneness to represent 'fanaticism' as a general characteristic of Islam,[104] Minaev does not trace the grounds of dissatisfaction of the Muslims to lack of development, but to their religious intolerance. As he puts it, 'on account of their religious concepts they cannot reconcile themselves to their subjection to a Government of alien faith'. Going one step further he says: 'At heart every Muslim in India is a rebel'.[105]

Minaev tried to find out the reasons of the discontentment against British rule even from resident Englishmen. In a voice to be echoed later by Rabindranath Tagore and Hannah Arendt,[106] he also blamed the distant, impersonal, bureaucratic rule that Britain introduced in India as one of the major sources of dissatisfaction. He notes his English host's view in a post-dinner chat that 'people of England bother very little about India and pass orders on Indian affairs from there'.[107]

The role of newspapers in spreading this discontent was determined by the nature of this partly modern, but largely Oriental society. Even though the 'development of the native press' was exerting 'influence over the opinion of the native society', the spread of revolutionary nationalism was not merely a result of 'print capitalism'.[108] 'Vernacular papers preaching discontentment', says Minaev, 'do not have subscribers, but they reach the villages. In the evenings cultivators gather under a tree, a newspaper is read out and they listen to it. From time immemorial Indians have loved to hear recitation. But formerly they used to listen to the *Mahabharata* and now they listen to political [news]paper.'[109] But even in this premodern society, colonial rule had left the majority of Indians dissatisfied and nationalistically aroused. Towards the end of the third trip Minaev referred to the 'Black Hole and the Kanpur brutalities' as 'testimony to the amount of hatred the British are capable of inspiring against themselves'.[110]

Burmese War and the North-East

Like the Afghan War in the second *Diary*, the Burmese War and its aftermath was the object of questions in the third. Instances of local opposition to it were recorded by Minaev with the same tenacity, making this *Diary* one of the earliest authentic documents of the spolia-tion of Burma by the British, against official British history, which had even invaded children's books.[111] Minaev was certain that the occupation of Burma had Russia in mind:

> They are seeking an alliance with China and capturing Burma. The blow is calculated to defeat two opponents—France, and indirectly Russia. They want to outrun France and reach the markets of south-western China sooner. Besides, they think that the fact of China being in the neighbourhood will facilitate

closer contact with her and this will surely be of very great advantage in their fight with Russia.[112]

The deep animosities Minaev bore towards England and the English and his complexes about Russia's 'secondary modernity' might have induced him to do fact finding for the General Staff. The next section brings this out.

NON-RUSSIAN WESTERNERS AND ENGLISHMEN

True to his 'secondary Orientalism' Minaev suffered from deep feelings of anxiety about the superiority of the Englishmen and Europeans to Russians. In the very beginning of the second *Diary* he takes exception to the bragging of an Australian fellow-passenger on the ship, 'who could not boast of much elegance of manners', that in any war England 'can cope with ten countries like Russia'. An American passenger also gives umbrage by describing Russia as 'a stupid place', though after Minaev disclosed his nationality, he 'showered apologies'.[113] But the lingering rancour is reflected in his opening observation during the third visit to India that 'the Britishers as a race' are 'not handsome', 'particularly the ladies'. The latter's ugly faces 'unshapely figures', and the unseemly dresses of both males and females make him wonder how they would have looked with their 'bizarre attires', had they been whisked away from their midst to the 'Italian boulevard in Paris'. The swaggering men were comic in their 'striped flannel', rolled-up trousers, yellow shoes, and 'some kind of a curious covering in the shape of a skull-cap on his head', or 'in a pink shirt and tobacco coloured jacket'. Women were worse. Because of 'their lack of beauty and affected manners', one could not 'think of any attire which would become them'. Their howling and yelping while 'dancing away waltzes and polkas' made them even less appealing.[114]

One is instantly reminded of the racist depictions of Russians in the seventeenth, eighteenth and nineteenth centuries by the British, the Germans and the French where Muscovite notables were criticized for manners like 'those of savages', uncivil behaviour towards women, dirtiness, 'long, cumbersome garments . . . unkempt hair . . . and matted beards'.[115] Was Minaev just getting his own back against

Westerners? But the assertion of Russian superiority could not be kept up long enough, and the self-confession of racial inferiority crept in when in the very next entry in the *Diary* he shows how 'concert, recitation of verses, etc., on the deck, ending up with dances', though badly executed, exemplified 'excellent manners of the British'. For, if Russians 'arranged something like this on board our own ship, there would have been noise and uproar and we would not have escaped biting criticism'.[116]

The mood, however, was not consistent. After looking at his co-passengers in the ship *Pemba*, on his way to Rangoon from Bengal, Minaev found that the 'society on board the ship', consisting of 'some Rangoon-based roving actors', was 'extremely vulgar', and wondered how they perceived themselves as 'the civilizers', while making 'room for themselves in a country given over to plunder and loot'.[117]

The blow-hot-and-blow-cold about the British continues through out the *Diaries*. In the same vein that Tagore later castigated the 'dinner giving societies' of the British[118] Minaev makes fun of the interminable dinner parties and monotonous balls that the British give and the inanity and listlessness of the conversations there.[119] Like Tagore he wonders 'What do Britishers talk about at dinner?' Then he suggests himself that apart from 'the events and affairs at home', the main topic is 'spiteful and unwitty remarks about natives'.[120]

This complex about the British also rubbed on Anglophile natives. Minaev derided the head of the police of Aurangabad and his shockingly 'blind imitation of the English way of life',[121] and a 'clerk in the service of British Government', who was 'transformed into a Talukdar in the territory of an independent Raja', and started behaving like a 'real collector of the British variety'. He had 'even a black "Mem Sahib" [honorific address for European females]'; and travelled 'with his lady just like some European Sahib'.[122]

Anxieties about Russian inferiority were directed at more serious people. A German Orientalist named E. Forchhammer, 'well known among the British as an archaeologist and scholar of the Pali language', was first described as a mean, arrogant pretender simply because he received Minaev very badly at his home. Though after he made amends and showed him his photographs of Arakan inscriptions, he became merely a fool,[123] who 'had not made important discoveries', though 'a few of the details are interesting and of course not without their significance for the history of Buddhism in these countries'.[124] But finally he became not only a 'doddering fool and an unadulterated ignoramus', but a cheat of the highest order, because he had declined to show him a manuscript, whose name he could not recall, but still he assured him 'that he was making it ready for publication, and he was saying this about *Kesadhātuvamsa.* Professional rivalry may have been operative here, leading him to note in his Diary 'Oh, the queer fool! You are stealing the fruit of my labour'.[125] Similarly Charles George Adams, another Indologist, who had translated his *Pali Grammar* also 'turned out to be a veritable ignoramus'.[126] And German informants who informed him that 'the Viceroy would be staying on board the ship' in which he was travelling, are described as 'the German rascals'.[127]

SPARSE INDOLOGY IN THE *DIARIES* AND 'ORIENTALISM'

INDIAN INDOLOGISTS

The analysis of the contents so far shows that Minaev's *Diaries* have been excessively valorized as the key to his Orientalism. It also puts before the scanner the Soviet Orientalists' view that Minaev was mainly concerned with matters of classical Indological interest in India in his *Diaries,* since they do not devote too many pages even to his Buddhist concerns and his over-hyped meetings and interactions with Indian Orientalists.[128] Much more of the contents are devoted to questions of politics and international relations in a colonial setting. But even in the limited pages concerned with Indology we get ample scope to support Said's view endorsed by Ronald Inden that Orientalist discourse poses 'as a form of knowledge that is both different from and superior to, the knowledge that the Orientals have of themselves'.[129] An analysis of his Indological notes in the second and the third diaries is necessary to definitely address these points.

The researches in the religions' transformations in India are not all that deep. After discussions with eminent historian and Indologist Professor Bhandarkar (1837–1925) about the Brahmo Samaj, what Minaev said about its differences from the Prarthana Samaj[130] are both ordinary and confusing. He says that the 'Brahmos do not recognize the Vedas as "the book of revelation", or "infallible books"', not remembering that they also professed a 'textual Brahmanism' based on the Upaniṣads, as 'infallible books'.[131] He informs that the Arya Samaj was different from the 'Prarthana Samaj', insofar as it acknowledged the infallibility of the Vedas, 'but at the same time in its congregations it devotes attention chiefly to social problems'.[132] He visited one 'Prarthana Samaj' and, reminding us of Teltscher's point on 'compare and contrast', typical of 'Orientalist' travelogue, remarked that their service and the 'whole ceremony was on the pattern of the Unitarians'.[133] His comments on the Theosophical Society were also not much informative, except cryptic comments such as, it is 'not altogether spiritual. Blavatskaya calls herself a countess',[134] or that 'many Brahmans, particularly of the South belong to the Masonic Lodge'.[135]

Minaev did not think too highly of Indian Indology or Indologists, though Soviet Indologists make much of his meeting with them. Textual analysis shows that he did not take too kindly to their critique of European Orientalists, and somehow identified with the latter. Kunte's scholarship in Ceylonese Buddhism, including *Lalitavistara*, is belittled as he, 'like many native scholars, looks upon European Orientalism with disdain'. Unlike Professor Bhandarkar and Shankar P. Pandit, both of whom were 'men of great tact', Kunte 'said plainly that European Orientalists were superficial'.[136] He judges the teaching of Kālidāsa's *Raghuvaṁśam* in a temple at a town named Rowza near Daulatabad in Maharashtra as very poor: 'One of the six pupils read a shloka hurriedly and then began to interpret the same in Sanskrit, apparently with sentences learnt by rote'.[137] At Ahmedabad in Gujarat he notices that, 'Brahmans had no discussion but merely recited "verses of a special kind" in sing-song voice'.[138] British scholarship on Buddhism was also poor, and Ware Edgar, whom he met, knew 'little about Buddhiṣm', though 'evidently he has done a lot of thinking about religion'.[139]

Burmese Monks

Minaev did not think that monks in Burma too knew much about Buddhism either. At Prome, he visited the Say-Hlot Troya daw Kyoung, known after the famous old monk Muninda, and after that the Thum That monastery, where he noticed that the chief monk named U-mhe 'was all the time murmuring something and counting his beads with his fingers'. After asking him what he was reading he knew that the words began with 'Sakhyadhamma' [*sic*]. He scribbled the words in his notebook to find later that only 'the beginning was fairly correct. Evidently, the monk did not understand anything of which he was reciting'. He had not also 'heard about Subhūti and Suma gala', and his 'knowledge of geography was limited'. A man whose 'mind does not travel beyond the words he repeats without understanding their meaning', passed off as a monk.[140]

Another monk at the Myothit Atwinwoon Minkyoung monastery was ignorant enough to claim that Buddhist text '*Lalitavistara* was the same thing as *Buddhavamsa*', and was proud to be the only person in Mandalay who could talk in Sanskrit.[141] At the Tah tha bine Sayadaw Gyi Kyoung monastery too, where the great 'Mālāla kara-saddhammavamsa-atulapavaradhamasenāpati-mahādhammarājaguru'[142] lived, the level of Buddhist or Pali scholarship was not sufficiently high. He was 'sitting on a platform on the verandah . . . reading some printed work'. About ten monks assembled around him were speaking Pali either very badly or unintelligibly, and were asking 'silly questions about Buddhists in Russia'.[143]

Maung Po Hmin was another renowned monk who also knew very little about Pali literature; he was kind 'but not well informed'.[144] So, while reminiscing about his impressions of Mandalay, Minaev admits blandly, 'honestly speaking, I could not recall the name of even one single monk of learning'.[145] An old monk who wanted to befriend him because he wanted to be spoken about to the Czar asked him if he was a Buddhist. Minaev's reply, starting with the words, 'Adopted the three vows but not pabbajito',[146] conveys that he knew more about Buddhism than the monk. From his questions about Buddhists in Russia, their dresses, and literature, he realized that 'like all Buddhists of the south he has no idea whatsoever about the Buddhists of the north'.[147] At Moulmein a monk of a particular sect called himself 'a hermit' in English, but could not translate the word properly into Burmese, and chose the word 'Jatila', to describe himself. Minaev protested, 'But Jatilas[148] are not Buddhists'. But the hermit 'insisted that "Jatila" and "Hpungi"[149] were one and the same thing.' [150]

That Minaev had a stereotype of Buddhism and Buddhists in his mind, leading to a feeling of unease at the sight of local Buddhist sects, becomes clear from his reaction to the likeness of 'a wandering Tibetan monk' bought in Darjeeling, which he calls 'a type of Buddhist apostle amongst a savage people'. 'His features, costume, and all the accessories of his attire', with 'skulls, strings of beads, mass of diverse things and objects, precious stones, amulets, talismans, etc.' tucked in a bag, and his 'floating dance and wild tune', instilled 'in the spectator some sort of mysterious trepidation'. Minaev thinks that ancient 'preachers of countries behind the Himalayas', were always 'first of all sorcerers possessed of supernatural powers'.[151]

One would be reminded here of the unease of Vereshchagin when seeing the sectarians in Trans-Caucasia.[152] The Tibetan monk was deserved by his people. They 'have a clever look', knowing 'on which side their bread is buttered. Their treatment towards Europeans is marked with complete absence of servility'. These words, betokening 'secondary Orientalism', logically lead to lack of faith in their Buddhism, and resultant doubt about 'whether any of them obeys the ten commandments'. This denigration of the alienness of Tibetan Buddhism with its 'external appearances' that 'must excite wonder in everybody's mind', does not, however, prevent him from tracing the influence on certain 'mudras' of Tibetan Buddhism of early Christian images'.[153]

'Curatorial' Pilgrimage

Other Indological information in the *Diaries* is a tourists' eye-view of religious India, like the visit to an 'uninteresting temple on Parvati hill', near Pune, and importunities of 'greedy Brahmins',[154] and un-instructive records of other places visited. Going to the 'temple of the Satnamis', Minaev learnt of 'a very interesting sect which does not worship idols', but 'recognizes a number of prophets and among them Jesus Christ and Muhammad'. He named their scripture, with a faux pas, as 'Kulatattarupa or Taratama', and[155] their 'leading preceptor' as 'Nilajanand Swami and also Shri Dhanudevichandraji'.[156]

Even records of visits to Buddhist caves and monasteries contained nothing novel or enlightening in their description, as at Karli, near Lanauli in the Bombay province; Kanheri caves near the shore of the bay of the Arabian Sea opposite the town of Thane; Pandu-Lina Hills and Chamara Lina caves (Jain cave temples) near Nasik; and the famous Ellora and Ajanta caves.[157]

Buddhist *stūpas* and monasteries of Burma are better covered, like the Shwe-Zan-daw, the 'Stupa of the Golden Hair', which had different kinds of structures including 'pillars with inscription, i.e. a day, and an animal—the symbol of that particular day—painted on them in alphabet, as if indicating the person who was born on that day to go there and offer his prayers and bring sacrifices of flowers and so on'.[158] Another monastery called Ku-tho-day-paya contained big tablets to spread the three *piṭakas*, distributed over the three courtyards in such a way that the text spilled over from one courtyard to another. The monastery's courtyard was littered with tablets of the entire *Suttapiṭaka*, *Abhidharmapiṭaka*, *Vinayapiṭaka*, and portions of other religious treatises like *Bhikkunī-pācittiya*, *Vinayamahāvagga*, *Cullavagga*, *Parivāra*, *Indriyajātaka*, and the entire treatise of *Paṭṭhrāna*.[159]

The most positive point about the Indological content of the *Diaries* was perhaps the 'curatorial'[160] urges of Minaev, though here one objective was pointing out the neglect of the British towards conservation of Indian heritage. Both Rowza town and Aurangabad were in ruins, the latter more so, and 'abundance of tombs' made it look like a 'deserted cemetery in ruins'.[161] Great monuments of Lucknow were in disrepair. 'Chattar Manjil at Allahabad was turned into a club'.[162] British Indologist and historian Grant Duff[163] is criticized for his lack of 'curatorial' care, and destroying 'Maratha chronicles and family archives', after using them, though they 'included many local chronicles and important documents'.[164] Ancient monuments in the Gwalior Fort were not being preserved by the British with due care, with 'temples and palaces turned into provisions stores and ordnance depots by the British'.[165]

The 'curatorial' fervour and its attendant critique of British colonialism regarding conservation occur also in the *Diaries* of the third trip. At Mahāmuni Paya in Burma everything around was 'in a state of desolation and decay. The tanks on the east have become mouldy'. In the king's library looted by 'dacoits', 'a mass of palm leaves is strewn all around the building . . . amongst these sheets writings in Singhalese characters . . . and also some sheets containing archaic alphabet written in ink. These manuscripts probably belonged to the library long since, i.e. even before Mandalay was built'. Even the resident monks did not know about the treasures that were lost. There remained more than twenty chests, on each of which 'an inscription about the *Piṭaka* or the section of the *Piṭaka* was preserved. Slightly better chests, that is, decorated or gilt ones were carried away by the dacoits. . . .'[166]

Minaev's 'curatorial' impulse was mixed with his pride in his unrivalled knowledge of Pali and his sense of superiority over British scholars. Finding in the library of the former King of Burma after its annexation by the British, one chest with hundred manuscripts 'in disorder', including 'all the *Piṭakas* complete with commentaries . . . all gilt edged . . . and a few of them encased in golden boards', and many other manuscripts, 'in a terrible state of disorder with many odd sheets in them', he started listing the Pali and Burmese manuscripts'.[167] Thereafter he listed manuscripts found in another library opened in the palace under the management of a British Royal Artist turned Colonel. As he notes: 'Sorting out these books by me had an effect. The Britishers became fussy. It was a shame to them that they had no scholar with them who could decipher Pali.' Also ego-boosting was the fact that 'the eldest son' of the 'ex-librarian of the dethroned king' wanted to learn Pali from him. In his words, 'Here I have the reputation of a great scholar. Monks talk about me. . .'.[168]

This small manifestation of self-importance does not detract from Minaev's 'curatorial' enthusiasm. He inspected a few more libraries in Burma, to finally strike gold in the real library of the king, then 'under the management of the Prize Committee'. His sense of achievement and exultation after finishing 'the examination of manuscripts' at this library is genuine. After painstaking inventorying for twenty hours in four days, his ecstasy about the total collection is manifest in the following words:

> I had not the opportunity of seeing such a quantity of Pali manuscripts collected at one place at any one of the European libraries . . . . Not all the manuscripts are in Pali language. One [chest] is almost exclusively filed with Burmese translations. . . . The library is rich with works on grammar. . . . I do not know the wealth of the library. . . . The most important collection of Buddhist literature is here. I shall not be in the least surprised, if a closer scrutiny of this collection reveals works completely unknown to European scholars even by name.[169]

Of course, the sense of being the only expert around did not leave him. While gaining a difficult entry into the king's library at the palace he notes with obvious distaste the condescending words of the man giving permission that 'that they had some plan with regard to it', with Dr. Forchhammer in charge. While cataloguing the wealth of Burmese and Pali manuscripts in the library, he hinted again at his own superiority as a Buddhist scholar: 'The knave of a clergyman, Colbeck, invaded me while I was working. Not knowing a word of Pali he is going to make an inventory of these books'.[170]

Western feelings of superiority inform Minaev's depiction of Indian Indology as sub-standard. His description of Indians too sometimes reflects the classic 'Orientalist' stereotypes. The 'greedy Brahmans' on Parvati hill.[171] are followed by meek and mystic students, the majority of them 'Brahmans',[172] at the Deccan College, their docility making 'no surveillance over them needed', there being 'no waster among them, or rarely so'. Apparently, they lacked the virile exuberance of their Russian counterparts. In Minaev's words, 'I should like to see what would happen in the dormitories of our universities under such circumstances'.[173]

Because Indians are essentialized as the 'spiritualist' foil of the materialist Westerners in typical 'Orientalist' literature, considerable exposure to Western rationalism seems not to have diminished the mystic core of the students. The rooms of students at the Deccan College were full of English books, by Spencer, Darwin, Mill, and J.W. Draper, 'but along with them also the *Theosophical Journal* published by Madame Blavatskaya', proving an Indian to be 'an eternal mystic; he continues to admire Spencer and at the same time is devoted to spiritualism'.[174]

The 'Orientalist' blinkers in observation of Indians come out in the description of the interior of the mirror monastery Mhan-Kyoung inside the Atumashi temple. There 'mirrors behind the sacred statues', 'vases of European make, glass chandeliers and candelabras [presumably of European origin too] induce the sweeping observation: 'Oriental people have a passion for glass'.[175] 'Orientalist' stereotypes inform the description of the 'more than modest' dwelling of the ex-librarian of the dethroned Burmese king, 'a wicker house on piles', and its occupants, 'sitting on the floor . . . chewing betel and spitting into the chinks of the floor', and 'blowing their noses at the same place . . . , without using hand-kerchiefs'.[176] In the same vein, the origins of the famous Kusolo Tou monastery in Burma are traced back to the 'very original' views of the dethroned king of Burma that building monasteries and erecting golden stupas would 'expiate his sins' and 'the cruel tricks of the oriental despot, whose distorted fantasies knew no restraints, would be blotted out of his future existence'.[177] The same 'Orientalist' stereotypes are reflected in tracing the origins of the city of Mandalay, created in 1858. It was the fantasies 'and caprices of the oriental ruler', which 'decorated this low lying swampy plain from the Irawadi up to the flat hills on the east with an entire row of quaint buildings', without 'magnificent private houses or building', unlike in Western cities. But then, 'it was always so in South-east Asia'. For, the ancient ruins of India 'testify to the fact that Indians have preserved either the traces of structures of religious importance, temples of monasteries or the remains of fortresses'. Private buildings were always lowest in priority.[178]

Minaev forgets that building houses of worship for expiation is neither original nor Oriental. Likewise, expiation for sin was the motive behind the building of many monuments in medieval England.[179]

MINAEV'S RUSSIA, 'ORIENTALISM' AND INDIA

The pride and anxiety over Russian superiority that determined Minaev's attitude toward Indian Orientalists, individual Europeans or the 'Russian factor' in India and the Afghan War would not be understandable except by reference to his inferiority complex of 'secondary modernity'.[180] Thus when a British military official advised treating a misbehaving Burmese in their ship 'like the Russians', Minaev's shocked reaction was, 'As if, in Russia people are hanged for such an act, or even such reasoning is conceivable!' He also brings up an incident where the Englishmen were worse off than Russians in dealing with racial difference. Whenever a Gujarati merchant and his son, travelling with them in a first class cabin, appeared in public, they 'were stared at and searching glances were cast on them'. He patriotically compares Russia's tolerance of such sartorial novelty with the 'intrusive looks' and aggressive comments from the British fellow passengers: 'I asked myself "Is something like this is conceivable in Russia?" With what a pompous carriage would a Tartar prince have moved about amongst Russian passengers?'[181]

The reaction reflects the nineteenth-century contentions of Russian 'Orientalism' about 'British racism versus Russian assimilationism', with the former having weakened the foundations of the Empire 'so much that their possessions were ripe for conquest'.[182] But Minaev does not understand that pride about Russia's tolerance of the incongruous airs of a princely Tartar in a public place indicates his complicity with a European modernity that regards the Tartar as an Oriental ethnic specimen. Moreover, he shows having the nagging feeling, diagnosed by Tlostanova, that 'the Orient that the Russian empire got through its colonial efforts was also second-rate, not like the one of Europe'.[183] Also noticeable are his words that the 'power and authority the Chief Commissioner [Governor-General] . . . wields . . . such liberty . . . could not be dreamt of by any of the Russian Generals who were temperamentally martial but officially civilians'. Minaev was struck by his huge salary, and lifestyle of 'a big landowner in a vast mansion', giving 'fetes and dinner in which a legion of barefooted red-liveried servants serve to the guests European delicacies spoilt by the manipulation of the black skinned native cook'. He notes that this luxury was also emulated by the delegates of 'Her Britannic Majesty' in the provinces on a lower scale.[184] He is astounded that Lyall[185] drew a salary of £ 10,000, and remarks: 'Was there ever any empire like the British empire in India? Compared to it what was the ancient Roman empire and what is the contemporary Russian empire? The empire of the great Moguls cannot stand any comparison with it. . . . This handful of harmless strangers . . . exert far more influence on Indian life than any foreigner had done at any time'.[186]

Obviously, these words stem from Minaev's complete identification with the Russian imperial logic. Bongard-Levin and Vigasin point out that in a speech at the St. Petersburg University in 1884, that is just before the third journey, Minaev affirmed that Russia's interest in India was merely caused by the affinity of the two cultures, and there was never 'any serious thoughts in Russia of a campaign against India or of conquering it', and that he 'contrasts Russia's friendly attitude towards India with British colonial policy, which he condemns'.[187] But then why is Minaev so keen to elicit the opinions of all sections of Indians on a possible invasion from Russia? And why does he compare the imperial fortunes of England with that of Russia in these terms?

> The British have been surprisingly lucky during the passage of the present century in Europe. They have not suffered any kind of defeat—either military or diplomatic, nor an inch of their dominion has been taken away from them. *Nothing like Jena, Sevastopol or Sedan figured in their history* of the nineteenth-century. Outside Europe in their historical life *there were of course critical moments: the first Afghan war, the sepoy rebellion and finally the troubles in Sudan; but they came out of these victorious* [italics added].[188]

This contraposition of these two sets of military confrontations, and the recounting of these 'favourable conditions which . . . created self-confidence' in the minds of the British is obviously set in the backdrop of psychology of the 'Great Game'.[189] Otherwise it would seem completely out of tune with the very next sentences, where Minaev differentiates between England and Russia in terms of the binary of the mercantile and the heroic.[190] The key to Britain's shopkeeper's mind is not so much fear of Russia, as the wrong basis of this fear. As Minaev puts it, 'They are afraid of a clash with Russia, but they dread, as it appears, only the cost exactly as a wealthy man would be afraid of the distribution of his funds on a huge scale, funds which were meant for some other purpose. But about the victory they are confident'.[191] Like most Russian Orientalists Minaev crosses swords with Russia's detractors who confuse Russia's land-based Central Asian foray and 'contiguous empire' with England's maritime expansion. 'They . . . have a completely inaccurate picture about Russia and her relations with the Central Asiatic countries', and so 'think that even one small reverse may shake and even totally impair the strength of a military power like Russia . . . a country which has lived through Plevna, the fight with the biggest Muslim power!'[192] According to Minaev, Russia's presence in Central Asia is motivated by higher things. While, in the West greed for money 'is considered to be the basic principle . . . the permanent motive for moving forward', any move without such apparent motives is 'either condemned or some secret motive is ascribed to it'. The myopia born of this materialism makes the English misunderstand the true propeller of Russia's foray into Central Asia, as merely 'a threat to India', and not as an '*overflow of Russian might into the sands* and barren steppes', or as an '*an evidence of sincere service to humanity*' [italics added].[193]

These words place Minaev on par with Vereshchagin regarding the liberating role of Russia Central Asia, and the ideal form of colonialism. Vereshchagin compared the Russian position in Turkestan with 'that of France in Algeria' and thought that procurement of enough land to plant a numerous Christian and civilized population among the 'uncivilized Mahomedan population' was needed for real colonization.[194] Minaev says the same thing about India when he says, 'There are no colonists here, there are no settled Englishmen here. A third generation Englishman in India is a rarity', implying that British rule in India was to that extent fragile.[195] Actually, he goes one over Vereshchagin in eulogizing Russia's beneficial influence even in British India in absentia, where 'nothing in the nature of a big job is undertaken without its having something to do with Russia'.[196]

BRITISH CIVILIZING MISSION IN BURMA AND INDIA: MINAEV'S DILEMMA

But what was Minaev's 'curatorial' Indology trying to protect, prevent or preserve in India? The question is important because he did not believe that given the nature of Orientals the colonial civilizing mission in India had any chance of success. Minaev's India was, as with 'Orientalists', unchanging and immutable. Colonial modernization of India in 1885 seemed to him to be a surface reality that misled the undiscerning traveller, 'acquainted with India from the show-end', and getting everywhere 'an identical impression . . . of the might of European influence on the East. . .'. These were manifest in the 'European caravanserai . . . shops where merchandise of the west is offered for sale to Europeans'; improved 'roads of communication', specimens of 'western architecture'; 'a horse drawn tram car'; 'an English or vernacular newspaper'; natives talking in English; and 'students with English books in their hands', surprisingly 'acquainted with all the problems of the day in Europe'. But what these 'outward manifestations of the civilized life of Europe' did not convey was that '*all this has been superimposed* and *the essence of oriental life has not in the least been*, and cannot be *affected by this*' [italics added].

One reason behind this was that Westernization left the essence of 'oriental life' in India untouched, except for the infinitesimal English-speaking intelligentsia: 'People here lead their life as of old, and those problems which agitate the western society do not exist for them. An insignificant minority amuses itself with the thought of realizing western political ideals. For the masses these ideals and the problems connected with them are not easy to understand.'[197]

Now, Minaev does not stop at branding colonial modernity as stunted, but also unwittingly introduces the binary of reason and prejudice to distinguish the Occident from the Orient. After admitting that for the masses here 'life is regulated by customs', he essentializes the East generally and not just the masses in its rural areas as hide-bound and customs-driven. Here every custom is of divine origin. Reason cannot explain it; and such understanding is not even necessary. This is because, 'for the masses the less understandable a custom is, the more enduring is its reputation of divine origin. It has struck deep roots into life—and nobody would think of delving far down for them. *Incomprehensibility and even absurdity of a custom are as if in essence the special signs of a custom's divinity and its strength*' [italics added]. Because of this unchallenged 'supremacy of the ancient custom' underneath a surface modernity,[198] even the English-educated elites, 'actually a weak minority trained in British political ideas, who have learnt to repeat aphorisms taken from English books word for word', would not 'support any legislative measures calculated to change any religious or social customs'. Minaev says derisively, 'And this minority talks of progress!' For the common masses even the question did not arise, because they 'hate; and are frightened of all kinds of changes'. This is why in India 'customs and innovations live side by side without coming into collision with each other'.[199] Besides, modernization was an imposition, since the material products of colonial civilization were not required by the common Indians, who 'only wonder and do not at all need these things'. Still this 'luxury—this demand for comfort—is inoculated like a small-pox vaccine', in the service of the colonialists' greed for money.[200]

Minaev did not, however, seem to realize that the current imperviousness to social reforms through the mediation of the colonial state was a post-1857 phenomenon, caused not only by the colonial state's wariness of social legislation, but by the demand of the new politics of nationalism for a rollback of the state from the social sector. As a result he essentialized India and the subcontinental Orient; failed to grasp the extent to which classical India had managed an enormous amount of change under the surface of continuity;[201] and did not expect colonial civilizing mission to go beyond the veneer. For, apart from blind obedience to customs and resistance to changes of any kind, another factor that incommoded change was Indians' servile obedience to superiors. In Burma this servility was primarily occasioned by the teachings of the betel-chewing Buddhist monks,[202] but was also active outside the religious domain. In India, he sees it in the son of Indologist Mahesh Chandra Nyayaratna, serving in the financial department on a handsome salary, giving his whole income to his father, causing the cryptic comment: 'There it is, the joint family system!'[203]

Because of this vision of India as 'Orient', Minaev remained very much equivocal about the whole idea of progress in the Indian subcontinent, in the senses of secularization and modernization of its socio-political processes. For him 'progress' in colonial India was 'one of those words which are most frequently used without any clarification', a word by which 'everyone understands a step which is in conformity with his political convictions, and would promote the success of those convictions'.[204] But while pillorying colonial conception of progress, his vision of modernity in India or Burma was not altogether consistent. The inconsistencies come out first in contradictory views about the educational systems in these countries, in both clerical and western influenced schools. First, his views about the curriculum at the famous U Baya Toya monastery in Burma, where six monks taught twenty pupils, are ridden with internal contradictions. He criticizes the course of study for concentrating on 'Pali texts with Burmese translations'. No 'secular subject is studied. Very little attention is given to arithmetic, orthography and Burmese poetry'. After giving a list of Pali texts and Burmese translations mastered by the students, and himself certifying 'how smartly and fluently they could quote' and explain them, and then their knowledge of the life of Buddha, he complains that boys 'are not taught religious geography' and that is 'why they do not know where Buddha Gaya is'.[205] But another school, the U-Thilawentha school in Pa-Zun-Daung, was criticized because the curriculum was both secular and modern, and Pali was neglected, being kept as an optional with 'Sanitations', which most of the boys chose. Even those who had selected Pali did not 'study with particular care even the little that is prescribed for them'. For, none of the children carrying Pali books in their hands could give 'a single satisfactory answer to any of the questions' put before him on this subject, including those on 'the most common words'.[206]

Sometimes Minaev's opposition to secular curriculum goes to absurd limits. He is aghast that even a monk like Maung Po Hmin, who was 'opposed to the appointment of Sasanabain [Buddhist Bishop] by the British Government', and 'did not even form part of the deputation which handed over a memorial to the Viceroy', did not understand the danger of exposing his students to a secular

Eurocentric map, a veritable 'poison he has brought into his monastery'. For, after 'looking at this map', students 'will learn to lose faith in the truth of the words of the Great Teacher; in vain they will search for Sumeru and Jambudwipa'. And 'no kind of resourcefulness and no matter of Jesuitism could in these circumstances save the Buddhist society from unbelief'.[207] Apart from curriculum, the schools around the Shwe-Zan-daw monastery were unsatisfactory because of their difference from Russian or European schools, in that the monk was found sitting 'in the middle, sewing a yellow robe', surrounded by 'boys seated on mats with blackboards before them, on which are written a few sentences from *Mangalasutra*'.[208] The only Buddhist school not to attract adverse comments was run by the erudite monk Muninda of U-Giang, where pupils studied sacred texts like *Abhidhammatthavibhavanī*, *Prātimokṣa*, *Khuddasikkha*, *Ka khāvitaraṇī*, etc., under twelve monks (*Upasampanna*), for five months.[209]

By contrast the course of study was better in the 'Normal School', an institution presumably patronized by the British, where 'teachers are trained for monastic schools'. Minaev speaks of it as 'that laboratory which produces the means of analyzing Buddhism and ancient Indian culture'. There pupils do not study the 'English language but read. . . . Arithmetic, Algebra, History of India, Geography, History of England and Burma'.[210]

It is not difficult to divine why none of the courses of Burmese schools could satisfy Minaev. Buddhism was in crisis in Burma. Minaev saw that 'It is struggling desperately but is losing ground under its feet . . . but western culture and unbelief are striking it death blows'. The problem was that while the traditional educational system neither assured Orientalist knowledge nor fought superstitions, the new educational system harmed the moral foundations of education. As Minaev summed it up, 'In the monastic schools they read only excerpts, and in life see crude superstition. But once superstition is destroyed by western culture, the credit of moral teachings is also undermined'.[211] Minaev feared that this tradeoff between rationalism and morals in the British system of education will give rise, in Burma, to 'an intelligentsia like that in India', not good for 'either of the two worlds'.[212] Another fear was that the colonial educational system would make knowledge completely Eurocentric. For example, at the U-Thilawentha school better 'answers were being given to the questions of geography. A little Samanera knows thoroughly all the principal cities of Europe including Petersburg'. But he does not know Pali enough.[213] But Minaev could not always take clear sides in the scholasticism/ rationalism, tradition/modernity divide in the curriculum.

Anyway, colonial modernization presented Burma with many tough choices, none of which Minaev could fully accept. He could not reconcile himself to the vision of a modern Burma without Buddhism or Pali. He did not like it when 'an enlightened Burmese' said that 'Buddhism is not on the decline, but the study of Pali is'.[214] But his consolation was: 'The Burmese read little and know only what is necessary for performing the customary rites. But this they are not giving up'.[215] However, just three weeks later he had to admit that both were endangered: 'Buddhism is on the decline, worldly people do not wish to know about Buddhism and do not wish to learn Pali but they are learning English. How to remove this deplorable state of affairs!'[216]

Minaev's opposition to the colonial transformation of Buddhist Burma was evenly matched by his nostalgia for a Buddhist Burma, where 'during the reign of the king there were about ten thousand monks'. The king spent liberally for them, and not only monks in Mandalay, but 'many others outside the capital' could count on 'maintenance by the king', and benefit from his generosity. The change was reflected in the lamentation of a monk at the big Myothit Atwinwoon Minkyoung monastery, that compared to his present few pupils, 'during the reign of the king some monks had as many as five hundred pupils'.[217]

What appears strange is that though Minaev had little respect for the monks' learning and their erudition, he clearly dislikes the idea of a Burma without these monks and their uninformed Buddhism. He imagines 'the yellow robes whisper privately', that there would be 'an end of teaching', as 'soldiers will occupy the country the destiny of which has been determined . . . annexed or declared a protectorate'. The 'capital of devout Buddhists will become the new centre of propagation of unbelief among the natives'; the monks, now suddenly valorized as 'these pillars of learning', will be there no more; and 'in [a] few years' time the new unbelieving generation will replace the generous donators of today'.[218]

So the monks criticized frequently before, for living parasitic, 'idle lives', with their limited knowledge, have suddenly become defining features of an essentialized Burma, where the 'triumph' of the West will usher in a new world of 'unbelief'.

Why does Minaev not want India or Burma to fall subject to Westernization? One important reason seems to be that the development supposed to come was not what the common people of these countries wanted; and it benefited mostly the colonial masters. He recalls that when as a tourist he was 'deprived of all the amenities of civilized life', in a 'wild country', he had momentarily thought that 'it would be excellent if this wild country could be taken in hand by the western master'. But now he argues that it would be 'excellent' only for the 'man of the west . . . who wishes to live under conditions created by western culture'. The native people neither needed them, not were going to use them, though these conditions were being installed at their cost.[219]

Besides, Minaev did not like the way in which the British colonial state was interfering in the nature and structure of Burmese Buddhism by appointing as a Bishop ('Sasanabain') for Buddhists a person who neither commanded respect of the monks or the laity,[220] and cut a sorry figure on the occasion of the return of the image of Buddha—taken away by the British—to the Buddhists by Lord Dufferin.[221] Sufferance of the colonial imposition of a bishop for Burmese Buddhism was traced back squarely to the 'revolutionary effect' of the secular schools on the slackening of the faith of the Burmese.[222]

Minaev was further concerned that the 'private individuals' whom the government praised for doing 'works of public utility' were undermining the Buddhist underpinnings of Burmese society. They had constructed bridges, excavated tanks and wells, erected guest-houses, in short everything that is prescribed by Buddhist charity. At Rangoon where schools are run by the state, Christian 'missionaries with their schools are undermining the basis of native religion', and 'twelve new Kiauns i.e. monasteries have been built'.

He asks sardonically, 'What more do you want? And is this not an act of faith?'[223]

Finally, Minaev pillories the aggressive Western modernity, typical of the British civilizing mission, which is destroying the uniqueness of the civilization of the Orient. That is why arriving at Rangoon for the first time he was afraid of the spoliation of 'a city beyond the limits of the Aryan world and on the borderline of two worlds and two ancient cultures, Chinese and Indian. From here starts the far east over which the man of the West is beginning to dominate'.[224] Again, looking around the landscape of Burma, dotted with 'the golden cupolas of the stupas, small houses on piles, and an abundance of tropical vegetation' from the steamer, he realized once again that the British civilizing mission was nothing but a smokescreen for the greed of the Western man: '. . . how wonderful is God's earth! Look around, and you will begin to see why man of the West has made his way into this place. Why, there must be gold mines around!'[225] He was horrified that this Buddhist idyll will be gone with the wind of change. That was why he even supported the Burmese monks' nativistic resistance to curricular modernization, when they declared 'geography and English language mortal sins, heresy and so on', but was doubtful of its impact, as it has not 'held anybody back from the study of the English language, Arithmetic, Geography etc'. Rather 'the number of people studying holy scriptures is decreasing?'.[226]

Minaev was very unsure about the outcome of the British civilizing mission, and of what it would leave of pristine Burma. And he makes his point very clear that the 'first inroad of civilization into a culturally underdeveloped country', would be like 'an inundating downpour or a stormy gust of a tornado', unhinging the 'the entire structure of life'. But while the new thing would take a long time to 'strike its roots into the conquered soil', it will leave a 'tabula rasa' for a long time. He quotes Emile Zola's *Germinal* to posit that the motive behind the so-called Western civilizing mission was 'domination by capital and all the evils are the necessary consequences of that domination'.[227]

It is partly because of his academic fixation with Buddhist India and partly his dislike of capitalistic modernization that Minaev did not or could not fully sympathize with the early nationalist movement in India, and the efforts of the Congress in this regard. Some students of Indo-USSR relations show Minaev as an indefatigable supporter of the nationalist movement in India, because he 'attended the founding meeting of the Indian National Congress in Bombay', [228] and praised its efforts for the 'development of feeling of nationalism in India, for the unification of India'.[229] We have not, however, found supporting words in Minaev's *Diaries*, except the non-committal entry about travelling with Surendra Nath Banerjee, the 'President of the Bombay Session' while going from Bombay to Calcutta. Minaev engaged him 'into a conversation' about 'what practical results they expected from the conference'. Banerjee reportedly said it would ensure growth of 'national feeling in India and unity of Indians'. Minaev simply adds that he 'pointed out that people from different corners of India gathered at the conference'.[230] But rather than sharing Banerjee's optimism about the potential of the Congress, he seemed to be more receptive to Mahesh Chandra Nyayaratna's 'indifference' towards the Bombay Conference and his dislike of Surendra Nath Banerjee, who not only 'speaks Bengali badly', but had 'sent his wife and son to London for their education on the English pattern', and had himself 'become a perfect Englishman'. He also seemed to share Nyayaratna's dislike of the growing influence of Anglicized Bengalis in British and princely bureaucracies in India, and in nationalist politics, and the 'decadence in the knowledge of Sanskrit'. As a result of this young people 'do not want to study Sanskrit; they prefer the English language. Study of Sanskrit is encouraged neither by Government nor by private individuals.' Minaev was thinking that 'Western education is denationalizing the Bengalees. And yet these people are the messengers of the new idea of nationalism'. People who 'have forgotten their mother tongue and their ancient motherland, are dreaming of western forms of government and representation therein . . .'. For him the Congress was just as insignificant as these people, whom Western education was 'denationalising'. Finally A. Aluktuk's claim is disproved by the words: '*Hume formed the Congress. This is his idea*' [italics added].[231]

But irrespective of this trivialization of the Congress, Minaev's tirade against colonial spoliation of the Orient is total. He does not distinguish between colonialisms, in terms of their impact upon the Burmese. The Bishop ('Sasanabain') had said 'either through naivety or foolishness . . . that the French were better than the English. He said the same thing about the Russians'. But Minaev differs. The French might have been 'more condescending and gentle to the Burmans', but 'at the same time would have led a more depraved life'. Minaev's judgement is '*All western people are the same—they are covetous and ruthless*' [italics added]. He resents that crucial decisions affecting the futures of independent countries were being made in Western metropolises. Thus, 'people knowing nothing about Burma assemble, seriously argue and try to come to an agreement . . . about whether Burma can deal with its own property according to its own discretion'.[232] He satirizes the expectations of the British that the 'natives' will remain grateful to them for the benefits of Western civilization and culture that they had brought to India. He dramatizes their arrogant demand of grateful submission in the following words:

> You want to be our equal? You think you can get along with our trusteeship and more than that, you want your old, native rulers! Oh nigger! Drop this idle fancy. You are black. On Sundays you do not read the Bible—and therefore you can never be equal to a blueblooded Briton and a good Christian. You chew betel and spit from time to time: is it conceivable that our ladies will sit side by side with you? You are not grown up, nigger! *You are as though a baby* and without our guardianship and our handsomely paid leaders you cannot do for a long, long time yet. Idle are your fancies, oh nigger! [italics added].[233]

The invocation of the binary of childhood/adulthood in the above passage distinguishes Minaev from British 'Orientalists' in spite of his 'secondary modernity' and complicity with Russia's State interests. Also his travelogue is free of many of the stereotypes of the other European or Russian travel narratives. He was not comparing and contrasting all the time; nor was he in his nostalgia judging all the things unfamiliar to him in India in a negative light. His description of the plundering in and of Burma by the British, the resistance to it by the Burmese and the petulance of the British at this resistance is objective and truthful. While the basic problem in Burma was between the Bombay Burma Trading Corporation and Thi-baw, the Burmese ruler, the British government interposed, and against all its assurances to the contrary 'entered the war and occupied the border without fight'. As a result the 'Hampshire soldier looted treasures, bought a pony for himself, has a capital in the savings Bank, goes about on his own horse and becomes indignant when a Burman shoots at him from behind a bush'. If the words above do not remind one of US soldiers in Iraq, or indeed of a Russian soldier in Turkestan, the following will: 'He may loot and fire at a Burman from his Snider, but the Burman must be submissive and must not be obstinate. He should not dare defend his freedom and plot against the Briton a series of unpleasant skirmishes in the coming hot days.'[234]

THE RETURN AND MINAEV'S DIFFERENCE

Minaev was no homesick Nikitin, lost in an alien land, no haughty Vereshchagin, not even a well-meaning but embittered Lebedev. While journeying along the river Irawaddi on board the ship *Du-Bhun*, the exquisitely beautiful landscape reminded him of his native Russia. He seemed to be on the Volga; the small hamlets seemed 'Russian settlements'; and 'Htis, the golden domes of the Orthodox churches'.[235]

This return-time nostalgia notwithstanding, he thoroughly enjoyed his stay in India, despite Britain's suspicions, as when he was not given the report of the journey of Sarat Chandra Das to Tibet by a government official,[236] or when he was not initially allowed a visit around the King's library in Burma.[237] And he could place the difference of India in its context. While journeying along the river Irawaddi in a steamer he notices that 'Burmese ladies [women] are bathing without taking off their skirts but completely uncovering the upper portions of their bodies . . . alongside, almost bare-bodied coolies . . . dragging wooden logs to the steamer.' But he does not decry it like a Nikitin or his West European successors. Rather, as his steamer moves on after weighing anchor, he shifts to a description of the riverside natural landscape, dotted with 'the never failing—stupas, now white with golden cupolas, now unplastered brick-red . . . a mass of stupas and monasteries along both the banks'[238]

Even when Minaev is describing the unhygienic conditions in the city of Mandalay, and the habit of its residents of defecating in public, the tone is objective. Good and bad aspects of city life come in quick succession. After description of the 'appalling stink and squalor' and people performing 'their morning ablutions in a seminude condition', comes the description of 'a lot of green all around'.[239] Of course the Burma that he wants to see maintained is an Oriental idyll, containing all the binaries in which the Orient is sought to be distinguished from the West. In front of a Buddhist temple he exhorts his readers to 'go to the holy place', and 'have a look at these strange pious people', who in spite of 'all the efforts of the cultured man . . . still believe and pray with devotion and *childish simplicity* and sing hymns before the holy of holies *in words not understood by them*' [italics added]. While the 'staircase leading to the upper square as much resembles a bazaar as it does the threshold of a temple', with shouts of 'Lemonade! Lemonade!' intensifying the similarity, one is 'all the same at a place of prayer and in the midst of people whose faith has not evaporated'. Any doubt on this score, after looking at 'the pillars worn by the passage of time, at the room with half ruined fretwork and at the worn out and broken steps', evaporates when one is on the upper square, where too many shrines seem 'too little for the devotees', and among 'shrines, statues, small stupas . . . the Shwe-dagon in the shape of a golden bell . . . humming with a crowd of people . . . is as if a museum of curios and an ethnological exhibition for the non-Buddhists'.

Colonial civilizing mission disturbs the idyll, for 'round this Shwe-dagon, in close proximity, West is marching by its right forcibly acquired', with 'fortifications and guns sticking out of the hills'. Minaev gets nostalgic about Rangoon as it was 'at the beginning of the present century. There are no bamboo huts nor mud houses here . . . there is not the same pack of mongrels whose barking and yelping the vanguard pioneers of British culture complain of, and here the cleanliness of the streets is not in charge of the pigs, as it used to be in the beginning of the present century.'[240] This nostalgia about the Orient comes with a strange uneasiness about the return to Russia: 'Motherland! Return to my native land does not at all cheer me . . . No, it is necessary to go home. Here idleness is growing'.[241] One might construe this passage as the fatigue of a person who was ill and would die four years hence. But still there is something more to it, a suggestion of the enticing languor of the East. Minaev was half enjoying and half distrusting it. Even his matter-of fact prose cannot fully hide this tension. After endorsing the comparison made by Anglo-Indians between Darjeeling and Kapua, Minaev complains that 'This climate, these fascinating natural surroundings incline one towards laziness'. He finds a villa 'with the inscription "Nirvana"', aptly named, as had he stayed here another month 'I would become a complete parasite. I am already beginning to feel the fascination of loafing and idling in contemplation and imagination'.[242]

This is what the West dreads as the Orient, the Continent of Circe, the place of the 'Lotos-Eaters', where the most purposive Westerners get deflected from their rational goals. The Orient is not meant for those who work. Darjeeling was saying to the Indologist, in the words of Shakespeare, the Great Bard:

> Be not afeard: the isle is full of noises,
> Sounds and sweet airs, that give delight, and hurt not,
> Sometimes a thousand twangling instruments
> Will hum about my ears; and sometimes voices,
> That, if I then had waked after long sleep,
> Will make me sleep again: and then, in dreaming,
> The cloud methought would open and show riches
> Ready to drop upon me; that when I wak'd.
> I cried to dream again.[243]

Strangely, Minaev echoes the great poet's words on board the ship in his final journey back home: 'I am sorry to leave India . . . I am waking up as if from a very pleasant dream'.[244] But Minaev's European soul was also echoing the words of Tennyson:

> Then some one said, 'We will return no more';
> And all at once they sang, 'Our island home'
> Is far beyond the wave; we will no longer roam.[245]

The most accomplished and the most successful among the Russian Orientalists in India, who 'aimed at a comprehensive study of ancient and modern India', not losing sight either of the progress of scientific philology and Sanskrit literature, or of the study of that 'India which did not find expression in ancient literature or which more or more departs from its native past', [246] could not shake off the conceptual blinkers of 'Orientalism'. What better proof of the entrapping power of its gaze?

NOTES

1. Bongard-Levin and Vigasin, *Image of India*, p. 82; also see Aleksandr Gnaīūk-Danil'chuk, *Tagore, India, and Soviet Union: A Dream Fulfilled* (Calcutta: Firma KLM, 1986), pp. 19–20.
2. Morrison, 'Russian Rule in Turkestan', p. 676.
3. Barranikoff, 'Biographical Sketch of I.P. Minayeff', in Minayeff, *Travels in and Diaries of India and Burma*, pp. 23–35 (hereinafter *Travels*); Bongard-Levin and Vigasin, *Image of India*, pp. 82–5; and Kemp, *Bharat-Rus*, pp. 214–15.
4. See I.P. Minayeff, *Pali Grammar: A Phonetic and Morphological Sketch of the Pali Language*, with an introductory essay on its form and character (1872), translated from Russian into French by M. Stanislav Guyard, rendered into English by Charles George Adams (Rangoon: Albion Press, 1882).
5. Sahni, *Crucifying the Orient*, pp. 21–6.
6. For Dayananda and his possible source see L. Polyakov, *Le mythe aryen. Essai sur les sources du racisme et des nationalisme* (Bruxelles, 1971/87), in Christophe Jaffrelot, 'The Idea of the Hindu Race in the Writings of Hindu Nationalist Ideologues in the 1920s and 1930s: A Concept between Two Cultures', in Peter Robb (ed)., *The Concept of Race in South Asia* (New Delhi: Oxford, 1995), pp. 330–1.
7. Minayeff, *Pali Grammar*, pp. i-ix.
8. Bongard-Levin and Vigasin, *Image of India*, pp. 92–7.
9. See Edwin Gerow, 'Untitled Review of *Image of India*', in *Journal of American Oriental Society* 107: 2 (April–June 1987): 360–1; and Nina Rao, 'Review: *Image of India*', *Social Scientist* 14: 7 (July 1986): 71–7.
10. See T. W. R. Davids, 'Review of I.P. Minayeff's "Recherches sur le Bouddhisme"'. *The American Journal of Theology*, 1: 1 (January 1897): pp. 166–8.
11. Ibid.
12. See Erik Naumovich Komarov, *Indo-Soviet Cooperation: Historical Background and Present Day Development* (New Delhi: Allied Publishers, 1976), p. 1.

13. See for example, Philip C. Almond, *The British Discovery of Buddhism* (Cambridge University Press, 1988/2007); and Donald S. Lopez, *Curators of the Buddha: Study of Buddha under Colonialism* (Chicago and London: Chicago University Press, 1995). Friedrich Max Müller satirizes him as 'one of our most celebrated Pâli scholars, the great Russian traveller', who has thrown 'the whole Buddhist chronology, so far as it had been accepted by . . . nearly all scholars back into chaos' in the context of the dating of Buddhaghosa. See Max Müller, *The Dhammapada and the Sutta Nipata: Buddhist Texts*, ForgottenBooks. Org, p. 6, retrieved through books.google.co.in, on 31 March 2011.
14. Serebriany, 'Marginal Notes', pp. 81–3.
15. Ibid., p. 85.
16. See Jan Willem Jong, *A Brief History of Buddhist Studies in Europe and America*, original from the University of Virginia (Delhi: Sri Satguru Publications, 1987), pp. 18, 19, 25 and 26.
17. See Judith S. Amtzis , John Deweese and Dzogchen Khenpo Chöga (eds.), *Drops of Nectar: Khenpo Kunpal's Commentary on Shantideva's Entering the Conduct of the Bodhisattvas*', vol. 1, Version: July 2004, compiled and translated by Andreas Kretschmar, Śāntidéva's Bodhisattva-caryāvatāra, according to the tradition of Paltrül Rinpoche, commentary by Khenpo Kunpal, chapter one, with oral explanations by Dzogchen Khenpo Chöga, compiled and translated by Andreas Kretschmar, http://www.tibet.dk/pktc/onlinepubs.htm, http://www.kunpal.com/, visited last on 3 June 2008, pp. 12–13, fns. 69 and 71.
18. The authority, D.N. Shastri, is quoted in James Thrower, *Marxist-Leninist 'Scientific Atheism' and the Study of Religion and Atheism in the USSR* (Berlin, New York: Walter de Gruyter, 1983), 'Appendix IV: Bibliographical Survey of Soviet Work Relating to Buddhism, Christianity and Islam', p. 419.
19. J.A. Naik, *Russia's Policy towards India: From Stalin to Yeltsin* (New Delhi: M.D. Publications, 1995), p. 2.
20. I.P. Minayeff, *Ocherki Tseilona i Indii iz putevykh zametok russkogo*, St. Petersburg, 1878, vol. I, p. iv, cited in Morrison, 'Russian Rule in Turkestan', p. 676.
21. See Alex Marshall, *Russian General Staff and Asia*, pp. 141–2.
22. N.A. Khalfin, 'Indian Missions in Russia in the Late Nineteenth Century and British Historiography of International Relations in Asia', in *Modern Asian Studies*, 21: 4 (1987): 639–46. The missions Khalfin takes up for discussion are of: (i) Rao Raja Telasingh Bahadur to the Russian Consul in Resht (Iran) on behalf of a group of maharajahs (of Marwar, Bikaner and Jaipur) in December 1860; (ii) Abdurrahman-Khan and Sarfraz-Khan,

envoys of Maharajah Ranbir Singh of Kashmir in 1865 to M.G. Chernayev, the governor of the Turkestan Region; (iii) Gaukhar Sultan, son of the chief minister of Indore, to Tashkent on 18 July 1876; (iv) mission headed by Baba Karm Parkash sent by Maharajah Ranbir Singh, which reached in June 1870; (v) Gurcharan Singh, a member of the Namdhari sect, sent by Baba Ram Singh, their leader, with a letter to Katta–Kurgan near Samarkhand to deliver it to the Governor-General; (vi) Maharajah Dulip Singh, Son of Ranjit Singh, who arrived at Moscow in 1887. Ibid, pp. 639–44.

23. See P.I. Shastitko (ed.), *Russko-Indiiskie Otnosheniya v XIXv* Docs. 73–8 (Moscow, 1997), pp. 181–201, translated in Purabi Roy (ed.), *Russo-Indian Relations in the Nineteenth Century: A Selection of Documents* (Calcutta: Asiatic Society, 1999), and Morrison, 'Russian Rule in Turkestan', p. 676.
24. Khalfin, 'Indian Missions', p. 643.
25. 'Editorial Note', in *Ivan Pavlovich Minayeff, Travels in and Diaries of India and Burma*, pp. 9 and 21–2; and Bongard-Levin, *Image of India*, p. 87.
26. Bongard-Levin, *Image of India*, p. 85.
27. Kemp, *Bharat-Rus*, p. 220.
28. See 'Editorial Note', p. 11.
29. Ibid., pp. 12–13.
30. Kemp, *Bharat-Rus*, p. 215.
31. *Travels*, 2nd *Diary*, 5 March 1880, p. 74.
32. Ibid., 17 March 1880, p. 77.
33. Ibid., 20 March 1880, pp. 77–8.
34. Ibid.,15 May 1880, p. 102
35. *Travels*, 3rd *Diary*, 23 December 1885, pp. 116–17.
36. Ibid., 19 December 1885, p. 112. For Sandeman's importance see A.L.P. Tucker, *Sir Robert G. Sandeman, K.C.S.I.: Peaceful Conqueror of Baluchistan* (London: Society for the Promotion of Christian Language, 1921), Kessinger Publishing's Legacy Reprint Series, 2010.
37. *Travels*, 2nd *Diary*, 20 February 1880, p. 65.
38. Ibid.,14 February 1880, p. 61
39. Ibid., 2 March 1880, p. 74.
40. Ibid., 11 April 1880, p. 85.
41. Ibid., 10 May 1880, p. 98; here Minaev is speaking of T.M. Rao, who became Dewan of the native states of Travancore, Indore and Baroda, where he followed the modernizing policies of the British. See *Travels*, p. 237.
42. Ibid., 27 March 1880, p. 81.
43. Ibid.,16 and 18 April 1880, pp. 90–1.
44. Ibid., 27 March 1880, p. 80.

45. Ibid., 8 April 1880, p. 85.
46. Ibid., *Diary of the Third Journey*, 14 December 1885, p.109. All references from p. 104 onwards are from it.
47. Ibid., 17 December 1885, p. 111.
48. Ibid., 23 December 1885, p. 116.
49. *Diary of the Second Journey*, 22 January 1880, pp. 45, 219.
50. Ibid., pp. 46, 221.
51. Ibid., 26 January 1880, p. 48. In the backdrop of the contours and limits of political agitation in the Bombay Presidency, under various groups and persons, the 'liberal party' could be none other than the Liberal Party in Britain. The Poona Sarvajanik Sabha had in 1880 already greeted the new regime led by Liberal Lord Ripon and the 'Liberal party' as 'the true representative members for India' in the British Parliament, who at least genuinely sympathized with the aspirations of the people of India'. See Richard P. Tucker, 'The Proper Limits of Agitation: The Crisis of 1879–80 in Bombay Presidency', in *The Journal of Asian Studies*, 28: 2 (February 1969): 339–55, especially pp. 350–5.
52. *Travels*, 3rd *Diary*, 26 December 1885, p. 118.
53. Ibid., 16 January 1886, pp. 132–3.
54. Ibid., 29 December 1885, pp. 119–20.
55. Ibid., p. 120.
56. Bengal was one of the few locales of radicalism in India in the 1880s. See Sumit Sarkar, 'Radicalism of Intellectuals in a Colonial Situation: A Case Study of Nineteenth Century Bengal', *Calcutta Historical Journal*, 2: l (July–December 1977): 71.
57. *Travels*, 3rd *Diary*, 4 and 5 March 1886, pp. 190–2.
58. Ibid., 8 March 1886, p. 193.
59. *Travels*, 2nd *Diary*, 27 January 1880, p. 48. Editors comment that actually he is speaking of English newspapers published in India, p. 222
60. Ibid., 8 February 1880, p. 57.
61. As Minaev wrote, 'judging from his conversation with me, he has no clear idea about Russia' Ibid., 8 February 1880, p. 59.
62. *Travels*, 2nd *Diary*, 22 February 1880, p. 66.
63. *Travels*, 3rd *Diary*, 2 January 1886, p. 120.
64. *Travels*, 2nd *Diary*, 20 February 1880, p. 65. The fellow Russian is mentioned as S.P.P, and the editors provide no clue about him or her.
65. Ibid., 24 February 1880, pp. 68–9.
66. *Travels*, 3rd *Diary*, 29 December 1985, p. 122.
67. *Travels*, 2nd *Diary*, 3 February 1880, p. 53.
68. Ibid., 4 April 1880, p. 83.

69. Ibid., 14 April 1880, p. 88.
70. Ibid., 27 March 1880, p. 80.
71. Ibid., 3 May 1880, p. 97.
72. Ibid., 14 May 1880, p. 101.
73. *Travels*, 2nd *Diary*, 22 February 1880, p. 66.
74. Ibid., 3 February 1880, p. 52.
75. Ibid.
76. Ibid., 3 February 1880, p. 60.
77. Ibid., 9 February 1880, pp. 56–7.
78. Ibid., 14 February 1880, p. 61.
79. Ibid., 24 April 1880, p. 92.
80. Mahadev Moreswar Kunte (1835–88), Marathi historian and Sanskrit scholar and a well-known Indian expert of Buddhism, in Minaev's rating 'was not all well read in this subject', although 'he is interested in Buddhism'. *Travels*, 2nd Diary, 29 January 1880, p. 49.
81. Kashinath Trimbak Telang (1850–93), prominent worker in the Indian nationalist movement in western India; later became the president of the Bombay branch of the Asiatic Society in 1892; editor of the *Deccan Star*; and wrote a number of historical and historico-philological works. Ibid., 31 January 1880, p. 49.
82. *Travels*, 2nd *Diary*, 7 May 1880, p. 98.
83. Nyaratna was Principal of the Sanskrit College and Companion of the Order of the Indian Empire (C.I.E.) (1836–1906). *Travels*, 3rd *Diary*, 5 January 1886, p. 122.
84. *Travels*, 2nd *Diary*, 10 May 1880, pp. 98, 237.
85. Ibid., 3 February 1880, p. 50.
86. Ibid., 24 February 1880, p. 69.
87. Ibid., 28 February 1880, p. 73.
88. The translator has written Arabs for Afghans. Ibid., 29 April 1880, pp. 94–5.
89. Travels, 2nd *Diary*, 27 March 1880, p. 80.
90. Ibid., 3 May 1880, p. 97.
91. *Travels*, 3rd *Diary*, 12 and 14 December 1885, p. 107.
92. Ibid., 5 January 1886, p. 123.
93. Ibid., 22 March 1886, p. 201. Lyall refers to Sir Alfred Comyn Lyall (1835-1911), Lieutenant-Governor of North West Provinces, and Chief Commissioner of Oudh (North-West Provinces) from 1882 to 1887, i.e., during Minaev's visits.
94. *Travels*, 2nd *Diary*, 22 January 1880, pp. 46, 221.
95. Ibid., 25 January 1880, p. 47.

96. Ibid., 31 January 1880 pp. 49–50; 5 February 1880, p. 54; 17 March 1880, p. 77; 4 April 1880, pp. 82–3; and 11 April 1880, p. 87,
97. Ibid., 18 April 1880, p. 91.
98. Ibid., 16 April 1880, pp. 91–2. For the armed revolt organized by Vasudeo Balwant Phadke in Maharashtra from March to May 1879, British calumny against him, his trial from 22 October to 7 November 1879, and his transportation for life and death in Aden Jail in 1883 see Venkatesh Shastri Joshi, *Vasudeo Balwant Phadke: First Indian Rebel Against British Rule* (Bombay: D.S. Marathe, 1859), passim, esp. pp. 118, 191; and Richard I. Cashman, *The Myth of Lokamanya: Tilak and Mass Politics in Maharashtra* (Berkeley: University of California Press, 1975), pp. 28–30.
99. Ibid., 3 May 1880, p. 97.
100. Ibid., 13 May 1880, pp. 100–1.
101. Ibid., 5 May 1880, p. 98.
102. *Travels*, 3rd *Diary*, 22 December 1885, p. 115.
103. *Travels*, 2nd *Diary*, 2 March 1880, p. 74.
104. See n. 57 of 'Introduction'.
105. *Travels*, 2nd *Diary*, 11 April 1880, pp. 87, 223.
106. As Tagore said government by the British Nation was like Western brands of tinned food, 'as little touched by the human hand as possible'. It is a regime where our rulers need not know our language, need not come into personal touch with us except as *officials*; they can lead us on a certain path of policy and then pull us back again with the manipulation of *office red tape*' (italics added). See R.N. Tagore, *Nationalism*, Macmillan Pocket Edition (Madras: Macmillan India Ltd., 1985), p. 10. Arendt says, 'Aloofness became the new attitude of all members of the British services; it was a more dangerous form of governing than despotism and arbitrariness because it did not tolerate the last link between the despot and his subjects, which is formed by bribery and gifts. The very integrity of then British administration made despotic government more inhuman and inaccessible to its subjects than Asiatic rulers or reckless conquerors had been.' See Arendt, 'Race and Bureaucracy', *The Origins of Totalitarianism* (New York: Harcourt, Brace and Company, 1951), pp. 184–221, especially 184, 207, 212.
107. *Travels*, 2nd *Diary*, p. 82, Notes, p. 233.
108. For this term see Benedict Anderson, *Imagined Communities: Reflections on the Origins and Spread of Nationalism*, fourth impression (London: Verso, 1983), pp. 44–9.
109. *Travels*, 3rd *Diary*, 22 December 1885, pp. 115–16.

110. Ibid., 11 March 1886, p. 195. By 'Black Hole' Minaev is here referring to the incident of 20 June 1756 where Nawab Siraj-ud-Daulah's troops rounded up allegedly 146 captives and placed them in an 18 sq. ft. punishment cell in the fort, where after a terrible night only 23 survived. For an objective account of this over-hyped and exaggerated incident see Kate Teltscher, '"The Fearful Name of the Black Hole": Fashioning an Imperial Myth', in Bart J Moore-Gilbert, *Writing India: 1757–1990: The Literature of British India* (Manchester: Manchester University Press, 1996), pp. 30–51. 'Kanpur brutalities' refer to the order of Nana Sahib, leader of the Sepoy Mutiny, while retreating from Cawnpore before the advancing British army, to execute his civilian hostages. Around 200 English women and children were killed in the 'Bibigarh', or 'House of the Ladies' on 15 July 1857. For how the over-exaggerated brutalities were captured by the colonialist discourse to turn it into one of the biggest bogeys of post-Mutiny British rule in India, see Jenny Sharpe, *Allegories of Empire: The Figure of Woman in the Colonial Text* (Minneapolis: University of Minnesota Press, 1993), pp. 63–7; Indrani Sen, *Woman and Empire: Representations in the Writings of British India* (1858–1900) (Hyderabad: Orient Longman, 2002), pp. 24–6; and Rudrangshu Mukherjee, *Spectre of Violence: The 1857 Kanpur Massacres* (New Delhi: Penguin Books, 1998). The words of Minaev prove that he unwittingly believed colonial accounts of both the incidents and treated them as just deserts, or at least as a barometer of the Indians' hatred for the British.

111. For partisan European versions of the annexation of Burma see D.G.E. Hall, *Europe and Burma: A Study of European Relations with Burma to the Annexation of Thibaw's Kingdom, 1886* (London: Oxford University Press, 1945). For books written for children see Margaret B. Synge, *The Story of the World: Book V: The Growth of the British Empire*, first published in 1905 (Chapel Hill, NC: Yesterday's Classics, 2006), pp. 172–9. For more objective and more recent books see Terence R. Blackburn, *The British Humiliation of Burma* (Bangkok: Orchid Press, 2001), and Anthony Webster, *Gentlemen Capitalists: British Imperialism in South East Asia*, 1770–1890 (London: Tauris Academic Studies, 1998), pp. 135–66. For a sympathetic history of the resistance in Burma, see Parimal Ghosh, *Brave Men of the Hills: Resistance and Rebellion in Burma, 1825–1932* (London: C. Hurst and Co. 2000).

112. *Travels*, 3rd *Diary*, 14 December 1885, pp. 110–11.

113. *Travels*, 2nd *Diary*, 20 and 21 January 1880, pp. 44–5.

114. *Travels*, 3rd *Diary*, 14 December 1885, p. 109.

115. Cited in Sahni, *Crucifying the Orient*, p. 14.

116. *Travels*, 3rd *Diary*, 16 December 1885, p. 110.
117. Ibid., 7 January 1986, p. 124.
118. Tagore, *Europe Prabāsīr Patra*, in *Rabindra Racanabali*, low-priced edition (Kolkata: Visvabhāratī, 1986–91), vol. I, p. 818, hereinafter *RR*.
119. *Travels*, 2nd *Diary*, 24 January 1880, p. 45.
120. *Travels*, 3rd *Diary*, 11 March, 1886, p. 195.
121. *Travels*, 2nd *Diary*, 10 March 1880, p. 75.
122. Ibid., 27 March 1880, p. 81.
123. *Travels*, 3rd *Diary*, 12 January 1886, p. 126, and 7 February 1886, p. 166.
124. Ibid., 13 January 1886, p. 129.
125. Ibid., 14 February 1886, p. 174.
126. Ibid., 17 February 1886, p. 176.
127. Ibid., 7 February 1886, p. 166.
128. Most of the Soviet books make much of his meetings with them, see Bongard-Levin and Vigasin, *Image of India*, pp. 89–92, and Kemp, *Bharat-Rus*, p. 218.
129. See Ronald Inden, *Imagining India* (Oxford: Basil Blackwell, 1990), p. 37, cited in Wilhelm Halbfass, 'Research and Reflection: Responses to My Respondents', in Franco and Preisendanz (eds.), *Beyond Orientalism*, p. 3.
130. *Travels*, 2nd *Diary*, 24 January 1880, p. 46. 'Prarthana Samaj', is literarlly 'Prayer Society'.
131. For this see Ashis Nandy, *At the Edge of Psychology* (New Delhi: Oxford University Press, 1993), p. 58
132. *Travels*, 2nd *Diary*, 24 January 1880, p. 46. The explanatory notes inform that the Arya Samaj was founded by Dayananda Saraswati in 1875, while the 'Prarthana Samaj' was founded by him before in 1849, with its main following among Marathis. Ibid., p. 220.
133. *Travels*, 2nd *Diary*, 26 January 1880, p. 48.
134. Ibid., 3 February 1880, p. 53.
135. Ibid., February 1880, undated, p. 58.
136. Ibid., 29 January, 1880, p. 49. Explanatory notes add that Kunte was Marathi historian and Sanskrit scholar teaching at the Elphinstone College; Ramakrishna Gopal Bhandarkar (1837–1925) was noted Marathi scholar, philologist and historian; and the other was Rao Bahadur Shankar Pandurang Pandit, noted Indian philologist, at the time of Minaev's second trip to India, senior translator of eastern languages, working under the Government of Bombay Presidency. See n. 32, p. 223.
137. Ibid., 28 February 1880, p. 71.

138. Ibid., 15 May 1880, pp. 101–2.
139. *Travels*, 3rd *Diary*, 3 and 4 January 1885, p. 121. The person referred to is Sir John Ware Edgar, author of *Report on a Visit to Sikhim and the Thibetan Frontier in October, November and December, 1873* (Calcutta: Bengal Secretariat Press, 1874).
140. *Travels*, 3rd *Diary*, 17 January 1886, pp. 134–5. Subhuti was one of Budhha's ten major disciples, best known as the recipient of the *Diamond Sutra*. Wariyapola Sri Sumangala was a Budhist monk who lived in early nineteenth century in Ceylon, and who was famous for taking down the Union Jack and hoisting the Sinhalese lion flag at the convention that passed on control of the country to the British in 1815. Later during the rebellion of 1818, he removed the Tooth Relic of the Buddha from the Temple of the Tooth, and gave it to the leaders of the rebellion. He was arrested and convicted for treason the same year. While giving these two unrelated names Minaev was perhaps testing the knowledge of the monk about the tradition and modernity of Buddhism.
141. Ibid., 23 January 1886, pp. 141–2.
142. This is the Pali rendering of full title of the spiritual mentor of the Burmese king, or the Rajaguru. The exact translation of the words, as given by the editors are, 'Teacher of the supreme King of Kings, of the great religion; Teacher of the General of the shining religion; Teacher incomparable in the tradition of the pure religion; adorned with garlands of flowers.' Note 271, pp. 251–2.
143. Ibid., 24 January 1886, pp. 142–3.
144. Ibid., 13 and 14 February 1886, pp. 172 and 174.
145. Ibid., 26 February 1886, p. 187.
146. The dictionary meaning of 'pabbajita' is 'one who has gone out from home, one who has given up worldly life and undertaken the life of a bhikkhu recluse or ascetic'. See T.W. Rhys Davids and William Stede, *The Pali-English Dictionary* (New Delhi: Asian Educational Services, 2004), p. 414. The editors add that by the three vows Minaev is informing that 'Accepting the three refuges (Buddha, the teaching and the community—the Buddhist trinity) and having taken an oath to fulfil the commandments a person becomes a member of the Buddhist community.' 'Pabbajito' is the Pali title of a Buddhist monk who has completely renounced the worldly life. *Travels*, 3rd *Diary*, n. 344, pp. 260–1.
147. Ibid., 6 February 1886, p. 164.
148. Ibid., 17 February 1886, p. 175. Jatila is a Pali word signifying a hermit who wears matted plaits of hair. 3rd *Diary*, n. 364, p. 262.
149. 'Hpungi' is a Burmese word meaning a Buddhist monk. 3rd *Diary*, n. 365, p. 262.

150. Ibid., 17 February 1886, p. 175.
151. Ibid., 17 March 1886, p. 198.
152. See nn. 43 to 54 of Chapter 5.
153. Ibid., 17 March 1886, pp. 200–1.
154. *Travels*, 2nd *Diary*, 4 February 1880, pp. 52–3.
155. The explanatory notes suggest that the 'reference is apparently to "Kulatatwanirupana" (actually *Kulatattvaṇirūpaṇa*), one of the works of Vedanta' and to 'obviously *Taratamya*, also one of the works of Vedanta (Madhavan School)'. Ibid., n. 112, p. 232.
156. Ibid., 25 March 1880, p. 80.
157. *Travels*, 3rd *Diary*, 17 February 1886, pp. 62–3; 2nd *Diary*, 24 February 1880, pp. 67–8; 25 February 1880, p. 69; 2 March 1880, p. 73; and 16 March 1880, pp. 75–7.
158. *Travels*, 3rd *Diary*, 16 January 1886, pp. 131–2. See n. 241.
159. Ibid., 29 January 1886, pp. 149–50; 2 February 1886, pp. 156–7; and 4 February 1886, p. 158.
160. See n. 16 of 'Introduction'.
161. *Travels*, 2nd *Diary*, 28 February 1880, p. 73.
162. Ibid., 2 May 1880, p. 97.
163. James Grant Duff (1789–1885) served India between 1805 and 1822, and authored the well-known *History of the Mahrattas*, vols. 1, 2 and 3 (London: Longman, Rees, Orme, Brown, and Green, 1826).
164. *Travels*, 2nd *Diary*, 21 February 1880, p. 65.
165. Ibid., 11 April 1880, p. 85.
166. *Travels*, 3rd *Diary*, 7 February 1886, pp. 164–5.
167. Ibid., 25 January 1886, p. 144; 1 February 1886, p. 154.
168. Ibid., 2 February 1886, p. 158.
169. Ibid., 27 January 1886, pp. 146–9.
170. Ibid., 29 January 1886, p. 150.
171. *Travels*, 2nd *Diary*, 4 February 1880, pp. 52–3.
172. Ibid., 18 January 1880, p. 46.
173. Ibid., 3 February 1880, p. 52.
174. Ibid., p. 53.
175. *Travels*, 3rd *Diary*, 30 January 1886, p. 153.
176. Ibid., 2 February 1886, p. 157.
177. Ibid., 29 January 1886, p. 149.
178. Ibid., 7 February 1886, p. 165.
179. We learn from an entry by one Mr. Urban in *The Gentleman's Magazine*, titled 'Notices of Tavistock and its Abbey' that the Tavistock Abbey was built originally as a monastery by the wife of King Edgar, for expiation of

a crime committed by him in respect of one of his deceitful courtiers. *The Gentleman's Magazine*, published and printed by F. Jeffries, 1830, pp. 114–15, books.google.com/books?id=I0p5TZ5bLmcC... , last visited on 17 August 2008.

180. Tlostanova, 'The Janus-faced Empire Distorting Orientalist Discourses', pp. 1–11.
181. *Travels*, 3rd *Diary*, 2 March 1886, Calcutta, pp. 188–9.
182. Morrison, 'Russian Rule in Turkestan', pp. 674–6.
183. Tlostanova, 'The Janus-faced Empire', pp. 1–3.
184. *Travels*, 3rd *Diary*, 25 February 1886, pp. 185–6.
185. Minaev is referring to Sir Alfred Commyn Lyall, then Lieutenant- Governor of the North-Western Provinces and Oudh. See S.C. Mittal, *India Distorted: A Study of British Historians in India*, vol. 2 (New Delhi: M.D. Publications, 1996), p. 285.
186. *Travels*, 3rd *Diary*, 26 March 1886, pp. 204–5.
187. See Bongard-Levin, *Image of India*, p. 85.
188. *Travels*, 3rd *Diary*, 21 December 1886, p. 114. 'Jena' refers to Russia's failed ambitions to establish control in Germany with a united 'Third Germany' alongside Austria and Prussia in early 1813, immediately after Napoleon's disastrous Russian campaign. See Alexander Grab, *Napoleon and the Transformation of Europe* (Basingstoke: Palgrave, 2003), pp. 108–9. 'Sevastopol' alludes to the siege of Sevastopol (8 October 1854–9 September 1855), the major operation of the Crimean War, in which British and French troops, joined by Piedmontese troops, besieged and finally captured the main naval base of the Russian Black Sea fleet. But in the eleven month siege neither the allies nor Russia succeeded in ending the stalemate. See Harold E. Raugh, *The Victorians at War: 1815–1914: An Encyclopedia of British Military History* (Santa Barbara: ABC-CLIO, 2004), pp. 295–6. Reference to 'Sedan' is in the context of the Franco-Prussian War (1870–1), in which within months the two main French armies suffered ignominious defeats at Sedan and Metz at the hands of Prussians and their South German allies. Before the Prussian victory, Russia had suggested intervention by the neutral powers to redress the European balance and preserve the integrity of France. Being rebuffed by Austria and Prussia, Russia denounced the restrictions imposed on it in the Black Sea by the 1856 treaty. But to preempt a Russo-British compromise on this issue Bismarck concluded an armistice with France in early 1871. Subsequently the London Conference of February 1871 forced from Russia the concession that international agreements should not be renounced unilaterally. In return, St. Petersburg regained her

sovereignty over the ports and littoral of the Black Sea. She also became a resurgent power after the decline of France. But the greatest power on the European continent was now the new German Empire. See John Lowe, *The Great Powers, Imperialism and the German Problem, 1865–1925* (London and New York: Routledge, 1994), pp. 38–9. The references to these three moments in Russia's imperialist ambitions and particularly to 'Sedan' prove that Minaev was ruing the lost opportunities of Russia.

189. The 'Great Game' is a term used to denote the strategic rivalry and conflict between the British and the Russian empires for mastery over Central Asia. See Peter Hopkirk, *The Great Game: The Struggle of Empire in Central Asia* (New York: Kodansha International, 1994).

190. This differentiation has deeper roots than appears at first sight. As a component of 'Occidentalism', or the critic of Enlightenment and the West, the binary between heroes and merchants that denounced the 'West European civilization', 'the ideas of 1789', the 'commercial values' and the 'Komfortismus' that were epitomized by West Europe, arose in Germany and also Russia. See Ian Buruma and Avishai Margalit, *Occidentalism: The West in the Eyes of Its Enemies* (New Delhi: Penguin Books, 2004), pp. 50–9, and 82–99.

191. *Travels*, 3rd *Diary*, 21 December 1886, p. 114.

192. Ibid. Originally known as the city of Pleven, in the state of Bulgaria, Plevna was known by this name during the Russo-Turkish War of 1877, where the occupation of the city held the key for claiming victory in the war. After five months of bloody siege, the Russians could enter the town on 10 December 1877 and claim victory. Here 'the biggest Muslim power' refers to Turkey.

193. Ibid., 18 December 1885, p. 112.

194. See n. 73 of Chapter 5.

195. Minaev, *Ocherki Tseilona i Indii*, vol. 2, p. 16, cited in Morrison, 'Russian Rule in Turkestan', pp. 681–2.

196. *Travels*, 3rd *Diary*, 14 December 1885, p. 110.

197. Ibid., 8 December 1885, p. 105.

198. Ibid., 9 December 1885, pp. 105–6.

199. Ibid., p. 106.

200. Ibid., 10 December 1885, pp. 106–7. Here Minaev's stress on artificial needs was echoed much later by Tagore. See Rabindranath Tagore, 'Swadesī Samrāj' (Native Society), *Atmaśaktī*, *RR*, vol. 2, p. 626.

201. For an original explication of how pre-colonial Indian society absorbed change through the processes contraction-expansion-contraction, see Rabindranath Tagore, 'Bhāratavarṣhe Itihāser Dhārā' (The Course of

History in India'), in *Paricai*, *RR*, vol. II, 575–92. Bernard S. Cohn has shown how Hinduism has all through its history harboured 'two opposed but contradictory processes: absorption and compartmentalization', not only for indigenously manufactured 'others', but also for outsiders. See Cohn, *India: The Social Anthropology of a Civilization* (New Delhi: Oxford University Press, 1971/2001), pp. 64–8.

202. *Travels*, 3rd *Diary*, 24 January 1886, p. 143.
203. Ibid., 11 March 1886, pp. 194–5.
204. Ibid., 9 December 1885, p. 106.
205. Ibid., 13 January 1886, p. 128.
206. Ibid., 24 February 1886, pp. 180–2.
207. Ibid., 25 February 1886, p. 185.
208. Ibid., 16 January 1886, p. 132.
209. Ibid., 17 January 1886, p. 133.
210. Ibid., 14 January 1886, p. 130.
211. Ibid., 13 January 1886, p. 129.
212. Ibid.
213. Ibid., 24 February 1886, pp. 180–1. 'Samanera' (sâmaṇera) means a novice monk.
214. Ibid., 14 January 1886, p. 130.
215. Ibid., 15 January 1886, p. 131.
216. Ibid., 13 February 1886, p. 173.
217. Ibid., 9 February 1886, pp. 168–9; 23 January 1886, p. 141.
218. Ibid., 9 February, pp. 169–9.
219. Ibid., 9 February 1886, p. 169.
220. Ibid., 14 February 1886, p. 173.
221. Ibid., 23 February 1886, p. 180.
222. Ibid., 24 February 1886, pp. 182–3.
223. Ibid.
224. Ibid., 12 February 1886, pp. 172.
225. Ibid., 20 January 1886, pp. 136–7.
226. Ibid., 2 March 1886, pp. 189–90.
227. Ibid., 5–9 April 1886, pp. 208–9.
228. See Peter J.S. Duncan, *Chatham House Papers: The Soviet Union and India*, The Royal Institute of International Affairs (London and New York: Routledge, 1989), p. 15.
229. See A. Aluktuk, 'Indology in the Soviet Union', in *Studies on the Soviet Union*, p.105, cited in Naik, *Russia's Policy towards India*, p. 2.
230. *Travels*, 3rd *Diary*, 2 January 1886, p. 120.
231. Ibid., 5 January 1886, pp. 122–3.

232. Ibid., 22 March 1886, pp. 202–4.
233. Ibid., 29 March 1886, pp. 206–7.
234. *Travels*, 3rd *Diary*, 11 February 1886, p. 170.
235. Ibid., 17 January 1886 p. 135.'Hti' refers to the umbrella or top ornament found in almost all pagodas in Burma as also in present Myanmar, made of stone or metal coated with gold. See John Falconer, Luca Invernizzi, et al., *Burmese Design and Architecture* (Hong Kong: Periplus, 2000), pp. 21 and 32.
236. *Travels*, 3rd *Diary*, 9 March 1886, p. 194.
237. Ibid., 29 January 1886, p. 150.
238. Ibid., 20 January 1886, p. 136.
239. Ibid., 24 and 25 January 1886, p. 143.
240. Ibid., 19 February 1886, pp. 177–9.
241. Ibid., 17 March 1886, pp. 199–200.
242. Ibid.
243. William Shakespeare, *The Tempest*, in *The Complete Works of William Shakespeare* (New Delhi: Oxford & IBH, 2005), III. ii. p. 17.
244. *Travels*, 3rd *Diary*, 3 April 1886, p. 208.
245. Alfred Tennyson, 'Lotos Eaters', in *The Collected Poems of Alfred Lord Tennyson* (Hertfordshire: Wordsworth, 1994), pp. 81–5, especially p. 82.
246. Kemp, *Bharat-Rus*, pp. 215–16.

Afterword

In the 'Introduction' of this book we decided to tell about Russia's encounter with India, as seen through travel literature and related cultural productions of select Russian travellers. And we started by agreeing with Serebriany's suggestion that since 'Europe' and even more 'the West' are not cultural monoliths, the narrative device of telling about the encounter between the West and India in just one single story would be rather artificial and inadequate. Besides, even if a single story is narrated, Eastern and Southern European strands ought to be grafted into the general canvas.[1] But after delving into the encounter between Russia and India through the seven travelogues we have also realized the problems of starting with sub-stories or subplots, as spelt out by Halbfass in his response to Serebriany. Serebriany suggested that the 'rather subdued and marginal' response of Russia to the 'encounter between Europe and India' underscores 'its generally marginal role in Europe'. But not agreeing with him, Halbfass asks: 'What then about Spain, which has virtually no tradition of Indian studies?'[2]

Halbfass's disagreement stems from the fact that despite everything said about 'Russia's ambivalent attitude toward Europe . . . on the one hand, and the ambivalence of its acceptance by the rest of Europe on the other', Russia never permanently became 'Europe's internal Orient'. We agree. For, at least three of our travellers, Saltykov, Vereshchagin and even Lebedev, encoded themselves mainly as Europeans. Besides, 'the Russian exploration of Indian and Buddhist thought has been part of the general European scene, and it has closely interacted with it'.[3] We have seen the incontrovertibility of this position when dealing with Minaev's academic Indology and Buddhism.[4] Again, Alexis Saltykov was more of a Frenchman than Russian. And if one remembers the development, maturation and reception of Vasily Vereshchagin's anti-war art the same argument of interaction with Europe would operate with greater force.[5]

But regardless of the amount of Russia's insulation from or interaction with Europe, Halbfass's main reason against such substories or sub-plots is that if 'it is true that Europe is not a 'cultural monolith', can we really say that France or Germany (which was not even a political entity in those days) are such monoliths?'[6] We agree with his point because Serebriany's own list of exclusions does not indicate a Russian monolith. For, the people excluded are not only those 'who professed or profess Orthodox Christianity, that is Russians, Ukrainians, Bulgarians etc.', but comprise 'those who were, or still are the followers of Islam, for example, the Muslims of Bosnia, or the Volga Tartars, or, for that matter, the Turks'; and possibly 'even those Muslims who live within the confines of geographical Europe. . . . Bulgarians, Rumanians, Serbs, Ukrainians'.[7] The current Caucasian cultural protest against Vereshchagin's Orientalist art would reveal the hollowness of any Russian monolith, equally overarching in Russia's east.[8] So attempts to construct a Russian sub-plot, with what a commentator on Halbfass calls, 'a more ample appreciation of texts',[9] to counter the hegemony of a European metanarrative of encounter with India would not really help. For, a Russian narrative would not include the Volga Tartars or the Muslim peoples of the peripheries of Russia's contiguous empire. As we have seen with Vereshchagin or even with Saltykov, while describing the people of Persia, Caucasia or Turkestan they wanted to test their culture on the anvil of Russian culture that revealed the inanity of a Russian monolith.[10]

The question may then legitimately arise why we chose a Russian sub-plot to find out the difference of Russian Orientalism. A genuine answer to this question would have two components. The first is that we have chosen not Russian Indology per se for our point of entry, but Russian travelogues. And there is no doubt that they are neglected. In a very comprehensive book on European travel literature in south India[11] neither Nikitin nor Saltykov are as much mentioned by name. Marco Polo is assigned a whole chapter,[12] in spite of wide controversies about the authenticity of his *Travels*.[13] But Nikitin, the seven manuscripts of whose travels are remarkably consistent, and whose pages contain some useful insights into the Bahmani rule and 'some useful second-hand evidence as to Vijayanagar', does not even find a single mention in the index. This merely proves that the eyes of the Russian travellers are not considered 'European'.

The second component to this answer has to remember that in the 'Introduction' we mentioned that the European metanarrative of 'Orientalism' is ruptured by three voices: the 'curatorial', the 'magisterial', and the 'exoticist', which complicate the Foucauldian formula of power/knowledge.[14] We wanted to find out what mix of these three voices we find in Russian Orientalism. Of course, Soviet Orientalism tried to pass it off wholly as 'exoticist'. Bongard-Levin and Vigasin reformulated the voices as 'the "colonial" and the "romantic"', and while ascribing the first trend to the English and French tradition of Orientalism, reserved the second for German and the Russian tradition.[15]

This is not an apt description of Russian Orientalism because all of it was not 'romantic'. Rather, comparative study of European and eastern languages, including Sanskrit, in Russia was dictated both by national interest and linguistic pride. If the former owed to the presence in Russia's periphery of different peoples and different languages, and a number of eastern nations professing Buddhism, the latter was occasioned by the perceived similarities of Russian with Sanskrit and their supposedly common origin.[16] Actually we have shown in the chapter on Minaev how foreign policy interests of the Russian state were sought to be promoted through one of Russia's foremost Indologists.

Our study has also showed that all the Russian travel literature and related cultural productions did not deviate equally from West European Orientalism. If Nikitin anticipated many of the established archetypes of 'Orientalist' observation, Efremov and Daniebegov were completely shackled by them. While Saltykov was either freer of or more tolerant towards them, Vereshchagin, in spite of his 'progressive', anti-war and anti-exploitation credentials, evinced all the manifestations of 'a secondary Orientalism' and a 'secondary Eurocentrism'[17] in his depiction of Transcaucasia and Central Asia.[18] Further, the image of the artist that comes out from both volumes of their travels in India, is that of a 'virile' Westerner exulting amidst Oriental effeminacy and appearing more or less as a big Russian bully. Minaev is seen to be more concerned about the future of Russia in India in his *Diaries* than about the Indological treasures in India, and is proving the pretensions of Orientalist discourse 'as a form of knowledge that is both different from and superior to, the knowledge that the Orientals have of themselves'.[19]

However, in Lebedev, whether as a translator of Bengali plays, creator of the Bengali proscenium or writer of grammar and composer of dialogues, 'Orientalism'—in its Russian sub-plot—buys back much of its debt of sin. And he redeems the entire corpus of 'Orientalist' knowledge, not through the excellence of his cultural production, but through his hermeneutic ability to enter the heart of Indian culture against heavy odds and thousand pains inflicted by his English detractors. That is why Kolkata loves him too. Even the plot of land where he constructed his stage is a permanent research concern of Bengali scholars, who have not tired of searching for its exact location amidst the constant changes of localities, street names, houses and their owners, and other topographical changes in Calcutta. If after devoting six pages to it Hayat Mamud could not settle the issue,[20] seven years later another researcher conclusively proved where this building was located, namely, 37 Ezra Street.[21]

Research for location of a theatre where a play could be staged for only one or two nights is of no intrinsic significance, except as testimony to love for a man who wanted to know India, even after more than 200 years. Such love was reserved for only another man, a Portuguese and a poetaster, 'Anthony Kobiāl' or 'Anthony Phiringī'. Asked by his challenger Thākur Sinha why he did not have shirts on him, he retorted sardonically,

> 'I'm living happily in this Bengal in Bengali dresses;
> Shedding all shirt and hat, Thakre Singh, my brother-in-law,
> Removing all their vestiges'. [Translation mine][22]

Finally, a naturalized Portuguese poetaster legitimized Nikitin's nightmarish *dhoti*.

NOTES

1. See n. 27 of 'Introduction'.
2. See Wilhelm Halbfass, 'Research and Reflection: Responses to my Respondents', in Franco and Preisendanz, *Beyond Orientalism*, p. 155.
3. Ibid.
4. See nn. 3–18 of Chapter 6.
5. See nn. 2–33 of Chapter 5.
6. Halbfass, 'Research and Reflection', p. 156.
7. Serebriany, 'Some Marginal Notes on India and Europe', pp. 77–8.
8. See nn. 80–1 of Chapter 5.
9. Francis X. Clooney, S.J, 'Wilhelm Halbfass and the Openness of the Comparative Project', in Franco and Preisendanz, *Beyond Orientalism*, p. 39. For Halbfass's response to this suggestion, see Halbfass, 'Research and Reflection', p. 145.
10. See n. 13 of Chapter 4 and nn. 35–88 of Chapter 5.
11. See Joan-Pau Rubiés, *Travel and Ethnology in the Renaissance: South India through European Eyes, 1250–1625* (Cambridge: Cambridge University Press, 2000).
12. See 'Marco Polo's India and the Latin Christian Tradition', in Rubiés, *Travel and Ethnology in the Renaissance*, pp. 34–84.
13. A well-known commentator on Orientalism says: what 'is known of the book is highly ambiguous, no actual original exists, every manuscript that comes down to us is different, containing interpolations, interpretations, mistakes and additions from earlier copyists', and the greatest ambiguity about the book is 'caused by a recent claim that Marco Polo may not have visited China at all . . .'. See Ziauddin Sardar, *Orientalism*, pp. 4–5, and 14–15.
14. See n. 15 of Chapter 1.
15. Bongard-Levin and Vigasin, *Image of India*, p. 61.
16. Ibid., pp. 61–3.
17. Tlostanova, 'The Janus-faced Empire', pp. 1–3.
18. See nn. 35–88 of Chapter 5.
19. Inden, *Imagining India*, cited in Franco and Preisendanz, *Beyond Orientalism*, p. 3. See nn. 136–9 of Chapter 6.
20. Mamud, Lebedeff, pp. 350–5.
21. Salil Sarkar, '25 No. Domtolla Street: Kichhu Tathyānusandhān' (No. 25 Domtollah Street: Some Researches), in *Natya Academy Patrika* 2 (January 1992): 18–26.
22. See Bandyopadhyay, *Bāṅglā Sāhityer Sampūrṇa Itibṛtta*, p. 272.

Bibliography

PRIMARY SOURCES: ORIGINAL TRAVELOGUES AND OEUVRES

Daniebegov, Rafail, *A Journey to India by Rafail Daniebegov: A Georgian Nobleman*, translated from Georgian [into Russian], Moscow 1815 tr. and ed. P.M. Kemp in *Russian Tavellers to India and Persia 1624–1798: Kotov, Yefremov, Daniebegov*. Delhi: Jiwan Prakasan, 1959.

Garrett, H.L.O., I.E.S, *The Punjab a Hundred Years Ago, As Described by V. Jacquemont (1831) & A. Soltykoff (1842)*, tr. and ed. Garrett, Punjab Government Record office, Monograph No.18 Patiala: Languages Department, Punjab, 1971.

Heber, Reginald, *Narrative of a Journey through the Upper Provinces of India from Calcutta to Bombay, 1824-1825 (With Notes upon Ceylon): An Account of a Journey to Madras and the Southern Provinces, 1826, and Letters Written in India, In Two Volumes*. New Edition, London: John Murray, Albemarle Street, 1856. Digital copy by http://books. Google.com/.

Jacquemont, V., *Letters from India: Describing a Journey in the British Dominions of India, Tibet, Lahore, and Cashmeer, during the Years 1828, 1829, 1830, 1831 Undertaken by Order of the French Government by Victor Jacquemont, Travelling Naturalist to the Museum of Natural History, Paris*, 2nd edn. vol. I, London: Edward Churton, 26, Holles Street, 1835, digital copy by http://books. Google.com/.

Lebedev, Gerasim, *A Grammar of the Pure and Mixed Indian Dialects*, 3rd enlarged edn., edited with notes, biographical sketch and bibliography on the writings of Lebedeff by Mahadev Prasad Saha, Calcutta: Firma K.L. Mukhopadhyay, 1801/1988.

——, *The Impartial Observations on the Brahmanean System in Eastern India (Bezpristrastnoe sozertsanie sistem vostochnoy Indii Bramgenov svyaschenuikh obryadov ikh I narodnuikh obichayev* (1805).

Minaeyff, I.P., *Pali Grammar: A Phonetic and Morphological Sketch of the Pali Language*, with an Introductory essay on its form and character (1872), tr. from Russian into French by M. Stanislav Guyard. Rendered into English by Charles George Adams. Rangoon: Albion Press, 1882.

—— *Minayeff Ivan Pavlovich, Travels in and Diaries of India and Burma*, tr. Hirendralal Sanyal, compared with the Russian text by Sunil Bhattacharya, language edited by Satish Chandra Sen Gupta, Calcutta: Eastern Trading Company, 1956.

Moorcroft, William and George Trebeck, *Travels in the Himalayan Provinces of Hindustan and the Panjab; in Ladakh and Kashmir; in Peshawar, Kabul, Kunduz and Bokhara, 1819–1825*, 1st pub., London: John Murray, 1841, New Delhi: Munshiram Manoharlal, 2005.

Nikitin, Afanasii, *Voyage Beyond Three Seas: Afanasy Nikitin 1466-1472. With Hindi and English Texts* [*Khozenie za tri moria Afanasiia Nikitina*] (ed.) S.N. Kumkes, Moscow: Geografgiz, 1960.

Saltykov, Alexei Dmitrievich Kniz, Voyages *Dans L'Inde*; *Lettres Sur L'Inde*, Paris, Amyot, Rue De La Paix, 1848, digital copy by http://books. Google.com.

—— *Voyages dans l'Inde : Pendant les anees 1841–2–1843, 1845–6*, H. Gache editeur, 1841–6, Rue de la Victoire.

—— *Voyages Dans L'Inde et En Perse* par le Prince Alexis Soltykoff, Paris, V. Lecou, Editeur, 10, Rue Du Bouloi, 1853, Paris : Typographie Plon Frères. Imprimeurs De l'Empereur, digital copy by http://books.google.com

Vereshchagin, V.V., *Vassili Vereshchagin: Painter–Soldier-Traveller: Autobiographical Sketches*, vols. 1 & 2, tr. from the German and the French by F.H. Peters, London: Richard Bentley and Son, 1887.

Vereshchagin, Vasily, *Oil Painting Reproduction from Tamsquare Art*, http://*www.tamsquare.com/artist/Vasily-Vereshchagin/* - retrieved on 25 May 2008.

—— 'Vereshchagin en Asia: Dias del futuro pasado'. http://www.futuropasado.com/?p=1021 - 29k, retrieved on 25 May 2008.

Yefremov, Filip, *The Travels of Filip Yefremov in the Kirghiz Steppes, Bukhara, Khiva, Persia, Tibet and India and His Return thence to Russia*, tr. and ed. P.M. Kemp, *Russian Travellers to India and Persia 1624–1798: Kotov, Yefremov, Daniebegov*, Delhi: Jiwan Prakashan, 1959.

SECONDARY LITERATURE

BOOKS

Almond, Philip C., *The British Discovery of Buddhism*, Cambridge: Cambridge University Press, 1988/2007.

Amtzis, Judith S., Deweese John and Dzogchen Khenpo Chöga, *Drops of Nectar: Khenpo Kunpal's Commentary on Shantideva's Entering the Conduct of the Bodhisattvas*; vol. 1, version: July 2004, Śantideva's Bodhisattva-caryāvatāra, according to the tradition of Paltrül Rinpoche, commentary by Khenpo Kunpal, chapter one with oral explanations by Dzogchen Khenpo Chöga, compiled and translated by Andreas Kretschmar, http://www.tibet.dk/pktc/onlinepubs.htm, http://www.kunpal.com/, retrieved on 3 June 2008.

Anderson, Benedict, *Imagined Communities: Reflections on the Origins and Spread of Nationalism*, London: Verso, 1983.

Andreeva, Elena, *Russia and Iran in the Great Game: Travelogues and Orientalism*. Abingdon, Oxon: Routledge, 2007.

Arendt, Hannah, *The Origins of Totalitarianism*, New York: Harcourt, Brace & Company, 1951.

Bandyopadhyay, Asit Kumar, *Bāṅglā Sāhityer Sampūrṇa Itibṛtta* (A Complete Account of Bengali Literature), Calcutta: Modern Book Agency, 1998–9.

Bandyopadhyay, Tarashankar. *rogya Niketan* (Home for the Healing), 8th rpt. edn, Calcutta: Prakash Bhavan, 1969.

Banerjee-Guha, Swapna, *Men, Women and Domestics: Articulating Middle Class Identity in Colonial Bengal*, New York City: Oxford University Press, 2004.

Barooshian, Vahan D, *Artist at War*, Gainesville: University Press of Florida, 1993.

Bassin, M., *Imperial Visions: Nationalist Imagination and Geographical Expansion in the Russian Far* East, *1840–1865*, Cambridge: Cambridge University Press, 1999.

Bayly, C.A., *Empire and Information: Intelligence Gathering and Social Communication in India, 1780–1870*, Cambridge: Cambridge University Press, 1999.

Benois, Alexandre, *The Russian School of Painting*, tr. from the original Russian by Abraham Yarmolinsky, London: T. Werner and Lawrie Ltd., 1916.

Bhabha, Homi K., *The Location of Culture* (1994), rpt. edn., London and New York: Routledge, 1995.

Bharucha, Rustam, *Theatre and the World: Performance and Politics of Culture*, London and New York: Routledge, 1993.

Bhatia, Nandi, *Acts of Authority/Acts of Resistance: Theatre and Politics in Colonial and Postcolonial India*, Ann Arbor: University of Michigan Press, 2004.

Bhatia, Tej K., *A History of the Hindi Grammatical Tradition: Hindi-Hindustani Grammar, Grammarians, History and Problems*, Leiden, The Netherlands: E.J. Brill, 1987.

Bhattacharyya, Benoytosh, *An Introduction to Buddhist Esoterism*, Delhi: Motilal Banarsidass, 1989.

Billig, Michael, *Banal Nationalism*, New Delhi: Sage, 1995.

Blackburn, Terence, *The British Humiliation of Burma*, Bangkok: Orchid Press, 2001.

Borovsky, Victor, 'The Organisation of the Russian Theatre 1645–1763', in Robert Leach and Victor Borovsky (eds.), *A History of the Russian Theatre*, Cambridge: Cambridge University Press, 1999.

——, 'The Emergence of the Russian Theatre', ibid.

Breyfogle, Nicholas, *Heretics and Colonizers: Forging Russia's Empire in the South*, Ithaca. N.Y.: Cornell University Press, 2005.

Briggs, A.D.P., 'Pre-Revolutionary Russian Theatre', in Neil Cornwell (ed.), *The Routledge Companion to Russian Literature*, London: Routledge, 2001.

Brower, D. and E. Lazzerini (eds.), *Russia's Orient: Imperial Borderlands and Peoples, 1700–1917*, Bloomington: Indiana University Press, 1997.

Brubaker, Rogers, *Nationalism Reframed: Nationhood and the National Question in the New Europe*, Cambridge: Cambridge University Press, 1996.

——, 'Myths and Misconceptions in the Study of Nationalism', in J. Hall (ed.), *The State of the Nation: Ernest Gellner and the Theory of Nationalism*, Cambridge: Cambridge University Press, 1998.

Burbank, Jane and David L. Ransel (eds.), *Imperial Russia: New Histories for the Empire*. Bloomington: Indiana University Press, 1998.

Burnim, Kalman A., *David Garrick, Director*, Carbondale: Southern Illinois University Press, 1973.

Cashman, Richard I., *The Myth of Lokamanya: Tilak and Mass Politics in Maharashtra*, Berkeley: University of California Press, 1975.

Chatterjee, Sudipto, 'Mise-EN-(Colonial)-Scéne: The Theatre of the Bengal Renaissance', in Ellen J. Gainor (ed.), *Imperialism and Theatre: Essays on World Theatre, Drama and Performance*, London: Routledge, 1995.

Chattopadhyay, Bankimchandra, 'Bāṅglā Sāhityer Ādar' (Appreciation of Bengali Literature) *Bankim Racanavalī* (1954), vol. 2, 15th rept., ed. Bagal Jogeshchandra, Calcutta: Sahitya Samsad, 2004.

Chaudhuri, Nirad C., *The Continent of Circe: Being an Essay on the People of India*, London: Chatto and Windus, 1966.

Chrisman, Laura, 'The Imperial Unconscious? Representations of Imperial Discourse', in P. Williams and L. Chrisman (eds.), *Colonial Discourse and Postcolonial Theory: A Reader*, New York: Columbia University Press, 1994.

Cohn, Bernard S., *India: The Social Anthropology of a Civilization*, Delhi: Oxford University Press, 1971/2001.

——, *Colonialism and its Forms of Knowledge: British in India*, Princeton, N.J.: Princeton University Press, 1996.

Courtney Locke, J. (ed.), *The First Englishmen in India*, New Delhi: Munshiram Manoharlal, 1997.

Dalrymple, William, *The Last Mughal: The Fall of A Dynasty, 1857*, London: Bloomsbury, 2007.

Davids, T.W. Rhys and William Stede, *The Pali-English Dictionary*, New Delhi: Asian Educational Services, 2004.

Duncan, Peter J.S., *Chatham House Papers: The Soviet Union and India*, The Royal Institute of International Affairs, London and New York: Routledge, 1989.

Ferguson, John, *A Dictionary of The Hindostan Language* . . . T. Cadel in The Strand, MDCCLXXIII [1773].

Furber, Holden, *John Company at Work: A Study of European Expansion in India in the Late Eighteenth Century*, Cambridge, Mass.: Cambridge University Press, 1951.

Gandhi, Leela, *Postcolonial Theory: A Critical Introduction*, New Delhi: Oxford University Press, 1999.

Ghosh, Ajit Kumar, *Dinabandhu Mitra: Makers of Indian Literature*, New Delhi: Sahitya Akademi, 1998.

Ghosh, Parimal, *Brave Men of the Hills: Resistance and Rebellion in Burma, 1825–1932*, London: C. Hurst and Co., 2000.

Gilchrist, John Borthwick, *Oriental Linguist*: *An Easy and Familiar Introduction to the Popular language of Hindoostan* . . . Calcutta: Ferris and Greenway, 1798.

——, *The Hindee-Roman Orthoepigraphical Ultimatum*. . . . London: Black, Kingsbury, Parbury and Allen, 1820.

——, *Dialogues, English and Hindoostanee: For illustrating the Grammatical Principles of the Strangers' East Indian Guide*, London: Kingsbury and Parbury, and Allen, 1826.

——, *Preface* [*to A Dictionary English and Hindoostanee, A Grammar of the Hindoostanee Language and The Oriental Linguist*], Calcutta: The Mirror Press, 1798.

Gleason, Abbot, *A Companion to Russian History*, Chichester, Malden: Wiley-Blackwell, 2009.

Grab, Alexander, *Napoleon and the Transformation of Europe*, Basingstoke: Palgrave, 2003.

Greenleaf, Monica, *Pushkin and Romantic Fashion: Fragment, Elegy, Orient, Irony*, Stanford, Stanford University Press, 1994.

Guha-Thakurta, P., *The Bengali Drama: Its Origin and Development*, Trübner's Oriental Series, first published in 1930 by Kegan Paul, Trench, Trübner & Co. Ltd., London: Routledge, 2001.

Hall, D. G. E., *Europe and Burma: A Study of European Relations with Burma to the Annexation of Thibaw's Kingdom, 1886*, London: Oxford University Press, 1945.

Hall, J., *The State of the Nation: Ernest Gellner and the Theory of Nationalism*, Cambridge: Cambridge University Press, 1998.

Halperin, Charles, *Russia and the Golden Horde: The Mongol Impact on Medieval Russian History*, Bloomington: Indiana University Press, 1985.

Hobsbawm, Eric J. and Terence Ranger (eds.), *The Invention of Tradition*, Cambridge, Cambridge University Press, 1983.

Hopkirk, Peter, *The Great Game: The Struggle of Empire in Central Asia*, New York: Kodansha International, 1994.

Inden, Ronald, *Imagining India*. Oxford: Basil Blackwell, 1990.

Jaffrelot, Christophe, 'The Idea of the Hindu Race in the Writings of Hindu Nationalist Ideologues in the 1920s and 1930s: A Concept between Two Cultures', in Peter Robb (ed.), *The Concept of Race in South Asia*, New Delhi: Oxford University Press, 1995.

Jalal al-'Azm, Sadik, 'Orientalism and Orientalism in Reverse', Reading 8, in George Ritzer and Zeynep Atalay (eds.), *Readings in Globalization: Key Concepts and Major Debates*, Chichester; Malden: Wiley-Blackwell, 2010.

Jersild, Austin, *Orientalism and Empire: North Caucasus Mountain Peoples and the Georgian Frontier, 1845–1917*, Montreal: McGill-Queen's University Press, 2002.

Jong, Jan Willem, *A Brief History of Buddhist Studies in Europe and America*, Delhi: Sri Satguru Publications, 1987.

Joshi, Venkatesh Shastri, *Vasudeo Balwant Phadke: First Indian Rebel Against British Rule*, Bombay: D.S. Marathe, 1859.

Kapany, Narinder Singh and Kerry Brown, 'Introduction', in Kerry Brown (ed.), *Sikh Art and Literature*, London and New York: Routledge, 1999.

Karatchkova, Elena, 'Ghost Towns and Bustling Cities: Constructing a Master Narrative in Nineteenth Century Jaipur', in Carol E. Henderson and Maxine K. Wesgrau (eds.), *New Directions in Tourism Analysis—Raj Rhapsodies: Tourism, Heritage and the Seduction of History*, Aldershot, Hampshire: Ashgate Publishing Limited, 2007.

Katsev, Allison Y., 'In the Forge of Criticism: M.T. Kachenovskii and Professional Autonomy in Pre-Reform Russia', in John T. Sanders (ed.), *Historiography of Imperial Russia: The Profession and Writing*, Armonk, N.Y.: M.E. Sharpe, 1999.

Kaviraj, Sudipta, 'The Culture of Representative Democracy', in P. Chatterjee (ed.), *Wages of Freedom: Fifty Years of the Indian Nation-State*, New Delhi: Oxford University Press, 1998.

Kaye, Sir John William, *The Administration of the East India Company: A History of Indian Progress*, London: R. Bentley, 1853.

Kelly, Catriona, 'The Origins of the Russian Theatre', in Robert Leach and Victor Borovsky (eds.), *A History of the Russian Theatre*, Cambridge: Cambridge University Press, 1999.

Khalid, Adeeb, 'The Making of a Colonial Society: The Russian Conquest', in Khalid, *The Politics of Muslim Cultural Reform: Jadidism in Central Asia* Berkeley: University of California Press, 1998.

Khodarkovsky, Michael,' "Ignoble Savages and Unfaithful Subjects": Constructing Non-Christian Identities in Early Modern Russia', in Brower and Lazzerini, *Russia's Orient.*

King, Blair P., *Partner in Empire: Dwarakanath Tagore and the Age of Enterprise in Eastern India*, Berkeley and Los Angeles: University of California Press, 1976.

Klein, Christina, *Cold War Orientalism: Asia in Middlebrow Imagination, 1945–61*, Berkeley: University of California Press, 2003.

Knighton, W., *Forest Life in Ceylon*, in 2 vols., London: Hurst and Balckett Publishers, 1854.

Komarov, Erik Naumovich, *Indo-Soviet Cooperation: Historical Background and Present Day Development*, New Delhi: Allied Publishers, 1976.

Lopez, Donald S., *Curators of the Buddha: Study of Buddha under Colonialism*, Chicago and London: Chicago University Press, 1995.

Lowe, John, *The Great Powers, Imperialism and the German Problem, 1865–1925*, London and New York: Routledge, 1994.

Lynn, John A., 'The Heart of the Sepoy: The Adoption and Adaptation of European Military Practice in South Asia, 1740–1805', in Emily O. Goldman and Leslie C. Eliason (eds.), *The Diffusion of Military Technologies and Ideas*, Stanford: Stanford University Press, 2003.

Mackay, Alexander, *Western India: Reports Addressed to The Chambers of Commerce of Manchester, Liverpool, Blackburn, and Glasgow, by Their Commissioner, The Late Alexander Mackay, Esq.*, ed. James Robertson, London: Nathaniel Cooke, 1853.

Majumdar, D.N. and T.N. Madan, *An Introduction to Social Anthropology*, 4th edn., New Delhi: National Publishing House, 1989.

Majumdar, Kamal Kumar, *Antarjalī Jātrā*, Kalikata: Kathashilpa, [1369]1962.

Majumdar, Ramesh Chandra, Hemchandra Raychaudhury and Kalikinkar Datta, *Advanced History of India*, London: Macmillan, 1951.

Majumdar, Ramesh Chandra, *History of Modern Bengal*, Calcutta: G. Bharadwaj, 1978.

Maksimovich Bongard-Levin, Grigori and Aleksei Alekseevich Vigasin, *The Image of India: The Study of Ancient Indian Civilization in the USSR*, Moscow: Progress Publishers, 1984.

Mamud, Hayat, *Gerasim Stepanovich Lebedeff*, Dhaka: Bangla Academy, 1985.

——, *Gerasim Lebedeff*, Calcutta: Paścimbanga Nāṭya Academy, 1995.

Marx, Karl, 'The Future Results of British Rule in India' (1953), excerpted in

Marx on India, ed. Iqbal Husain, with 'Introduction' by Irfan Habib, and Appreciation by Prabhat Patnaik, sponsored by Aligarh Historians Society, New Delhi: Tulika Books, 2006.

McClintock, John and James Strong, *Cyclopaedia of Biblical, Theological, and Ecclesiastical Literature*, New York: Harper, 1883.

McDermott, Rachel Fell, *Revelry, Rivalry and Longing for the Goddess of Bengal: The Fortunes of Hindu Festivals*, New York: Columbia University Press, 2011.

McReynolds, Louise, *Russia at Play: Leisure Activities at the End of the Tsarist Era*, Ithaca, New York: Cornell University Press, 2003.

Mehta, Binita, *Widows, Pariahs, Bayadères: India as Spectacle*, London: Associated University Press, 2002.

Metcalf, Thomas R., *Ideologies of the Raj*, New Delhi: Cambridge University Press, 1998/2005.

Minayev, Ivan, *Old India—Notes on Afanasy Nikitin's "Voyage Beyond the Three Seas"*, tr. Arun Mohanty, ed. Eugenia Vanina & Irina Chelysheva, New Delhi: Har-Anand, 2010.

Mittal, S.C., *India Distorted: A Study of British Historians in India*, vol. 2, New Delhi: M.D. Publications, 1996.

Mitter, Partha, *Much Maligned Monsters: History of European Reactions to Indian Art*, 2nd edn., Chicago: Chicago University Press, 1992.

Mukherjee, Rudrangshu, *Spectre of Violence: The 1857 Kanpur Massacres*, New Delhi: Penguin Books, 1998.

Müller, Max, *The Dhammapada and the Sutta Nipata: Buddhist Texts*, ForgottenBooks. Org., retrieved through books. google. co. in, on 31 March 2011.

Nandy, Ashis, *The Intimate Enemy: Loss and Recovery of Self under Colonialism*, first paperback edn., New Delhi: Oxford University Press, 1988.

——, *At the Edge of Psychology*, New Delhi: Oxford University Press, 1993.

Naik, J.A., *Russia's Policy towards India: From Stalin to Yeltsin*, New Delhi: M.D. Publications, 1995.

Negrov, Alexander I., 'Dmitrii Bogdashevskii (1861-1933): His Hermeneutical Approach', in Negrov, *Biblical Interpretation in the Russian Orthodox Church: A Historical and Hermeneutical Perspective*. Tübingen: Mohr Siebeck, 2008.

Neumann, Iver B., *Russia and the Idea of Europe: A Study in Identity and International Relations*, London and New York: Routledge, 1996.

Niranjana, Tejaswini, *Siting Translation: History, Post-Structuralism and the Colonial Context*, Hyderabad: Orient Longman, 1995.

Oaten, Edward Farley, *European Travellers in India: During The Fifteenth, Sixteenth and Seventeenth Centuries; The Evidence Afforded by them With Respect*

To Indian Social Institutions & the Nature and Influence of Indian Governments, London: Kegan Paul Trench Trübner and Company Ltd., 1909.

O'Hanlon, Rosalind, *Caste, Conflict and Ideology: Mahatma Jotirao Phule and Low Caste Protest in Nineteenth-century Western India*, Cambridge: Cambridge University Press, 1895.

Orlich, Captain Leopold Von, *Travels in India, Including Sinde and Punjab* tr. from the German by H. Evans Lloyd, vol. II, London: Longman, Brown, Green and Longmans, 1845.

Owen, Wilfred, 'A Terre (Being the Philosophy of Many Soldiers)', in Jon Silkin (ed.), *The Penguin Book of First World War Poetry*, London and New York: Penguin Books, 1996.

Pavlov, Vladimir Ivanovic, *The Indian Capitalist Class: A Historical Study*, New Delhi: People's Publishing House, 1964.

Ram, Harsha, *The Imperial Sublime: A Russian Poetics of Empire*, Madison, University of Wisconsin Press, 2003.

Raugh, Harold E., *The Victorians at War: 1815-1914: An Encyclopedia of British Military History*, Santa Barbara: ABC-CLIO, 2004.

Ray, A.K., *A Short History of Calcutta: Towns and Suburbs*, Census of India, 1901, Calcutta: Riddhi-India, 1982.

Roy Purabi (ed.), *Russo-Indian Relations in the Nineteenth Century: A Selection of Documents*, Calcutta: Asiatic Society, 1999.

Royle, Nicholas, *After Derrida*, Manchester: Manchester University Press, 1995.

Said, Edward, *Orientalism: Western Conceptions of the Orient*, Harmondsworth: Penguin, 1978/1995.

Sardar, Ziauddin, *Orientalism*, published by arrangement with Open University Press, New Delhi: Viva Books Limited, 2002.

Raazani, Jahan, 'Wilfred Owen', *Poetry of Mourning: The Modern Elegy from Hardy to Heaney*, Chicago: The University of Chicago Press, 1994.

Riasanovsky, Nicholas, 'Asia through Russian Eyes', in W.S. Vucinich (ed.), *Russia and Asia: Essays on the Influence of Russia on the Asian Peoples*, Stanford, CA.: Hoover Institution Press, 1972.

Rodinov, Mikhail, '"Profiles under Pressure": Orientalists in Petrograd/Leningrad, 1918–1956', in Michael Kemper and Stephan Connermann (eds.), *The Heritage of Soviet Oriental Studies*, Abingdon, Oxon and New York: Routledge, 2011.

Sahni, Kalpana, *Crucifying the Orient: Russian Orientalism and the Colonization of Caucasus and Central Asia*, Bangkok, Thailand: White Orchid Press, 1997.

Schimmelpenninck van der Oye, David, *Russian Orientalism: Asia in the Russian Mind from Peter the Great to the Emigration*, New Haven: Yale University Press, 2010.

——, 'Imperial Roots of Russian Orientalism' in Kemper and Conermann (eds.), *The Heritage of Soviet Oriental Studies*, 2011.

Sen, Indrani, *Woman and Empire: Representations in the Writings of British India (1858–1900)*, Hyderabad: Orient Longman, 2002.

Serebriany, Sergei D., 'Some Marginal Notes on India and Europe', in Eli Franco and Karin Preisendanz (eds.), *Beyond Orientalism: The Work of Wilhelm Halbfass and its Impact on Indian and Cross Cultural Studies* (1997), 1st Indian edn., Delhi: Motilal Banarsidass, 2007.

Shakespeare, William, *The Tempest*, in *The Complete Works of William Shakespeare*, New Delhi: Oxford & IBH, 2005.

——, *King Lear*, New Delhi: Oxford & IBH, 2005.

Sharpe, Jenny, *Allegories of Empire: The Figure of Woman in the Colonial Text*, Minneapolis: University of Minnesota Press, 1993.

Sleeman, Colonel William Henry, *Ramaseeana or a Vocabulary of the Peculiar Language Used by the Thugs, With an Introduction and Appendix, Descriptive of the System Pursued by that Fraternity and of the Measures which Have Been Adopted by the Supreme Government of India for its Suppression*, Calcutta: G.H. Huttman, Military Orphan Press, 1836.

Spivak, Gayatri Chakravorty, 'Subaltern Studies: Deconstructing Historiography' (1985), in Donna Landry and Gerald Maclean (eds.), *The Spivak Reader: Selected Works of Gayatri Chakravorty Spivak*, New York and London: Routledge, 1996.

Stacy, R.H., *India in Russian Literature*, Delhi: Motilal Banarsidass, 1985.

Steadman-Jones. Richard. 'Etymology and Language Learning at the Start of the Nineteenth-Century', in Piet Desmet (ed.), *The History of Linguistic Grammatical Praxis: Proceedings of the XIth International Colloquium of the Studienkreis 'Geschichte der Sprachwissenschaft'* (Leuven, 2–4 July), Leuven: Peeters, 2000, http://books.google.com, retrieved on 11 April 2009.

——, *Colonialism and Grammatical Representation: John Gilchrist and the Analysis of the 'Hindustani' Language in the Late Eighteenth and Early Nineteenth Centuries*, Oxford: Blackwell Publishing, 2007.

——, 'Richardson's Barometer: Colonial Representation in Grammatical Texts', in Natasha Glaisyer and Sara Pennel (eds.), *Didactic Literature in England 1500–180: Expertise Constructed*, Aldershot: Ashgate Publishing Limited, 2003.

Suny, Ronald Grigor and Terry Martin (eds.), *A State of Nations: Empire and Nation-Making in the Age of Lenin and Stalin*, New York: Oxford University Press, 2001.

Synge, Margaret B., *The Story of the World: Book V: The Growth of the British Empire*, Chapel Hill, NC: Yesterday's Classics, 2006.

Tagore, R.N., *Chhelebelā* (*My Boyhood Days*), *Rabīndra Racanābalī* (*Collected Works of Tagore*), low-priced edition on the occasion of Tagore's 125th birth anniversary, Kolkata: Visvabhāratī, 1986–91, vol. 9.

——, 'Jīvita o Mṛta', *Galpaguchchha. Rabīndra Racanābalī*, vol. 9.

——, *Europe Prābasīr Patra, Rabīndra Racanabalī*, vol. I.

——, *Nationalism*, Macmillan Pocket Edition, Madras: Macmillan India Ltd., 1985.

——, 'Swadesī Samāj' (Native Society), *tmaśakti, Rabīndra Racanabalī*, vol. 2.

Teltscher, Kate, *India Inscribed: European and British Writing on India 1600–1800*, Oxford India paperbacks, New Delhi: Oxford University Press, 1997,

——, ' "The Fearful Name of the Black Hole": Fashioning an Imperial Myth', in Bart J. Moore-Gilbert (ed.), *Writing India: 1757–1990: The Literature of British India*. Manchester: Manchester University Press, 1996.

Tennyson, Alfred, 'Lotos Eaters', in *The Collected Poems of Alfred Lord Tennyson*, Ware (Hertfordshire): Wordsworth, 1994.

Thornton, Edward, *Illustrations of the History and Practices of the Thugs, and Notices of Some of the Proceedings of the Government of India, for the Suppression of the Crime of Thuggee*, London: W.H. Allen and Co., 1837.

Thrower, James, *Marxist-Leninist 'Scientific Atheism' and the Study of Religion and Atheism in the USSR*, Berlin, New York: Walter de Gruyter, 1983.

Tucker, A.L.P., *Sir Robert G. Sandeman, K.C.S.I.: Peaceful Conqueror of Baluchistan*, London: Society for the Promotion of Christian Language, 1921, Kessinger Publishing's Legacy Reprint Series, 2010.

Vasudevan, Hari, 'The Solitude of Afanasii Nikitin in his "Voyage over the Three Seas"', in Geeti Sen and Molly Kaushal (eds.), *Journeys: Heroes, Pilgrims, Explorers*, India International Centre, New Delhi: Penguin Viking, 2005.

Vereshchagin, V.V. et al., *Artists Look at India* (a collection of Russian paintings on India starting with Vereshchagin), Moscow: State Fine Arts Publishing House, 1955.

Vereshchagin, V.V., 'Realism' (1895), *Khudozhnik* 1891, no. 1, tr. Robert Russell, with notes by Alexey Makhrov, and Robert Russell, *Russian Visual Art Criticism*, 1800–1913, primary text in translation. www.hrionline.ac.uk/rva/texts/ver/verbib.html-. retrieved on 24 May 2008.

——, 'On Progress in Art' ('O progresse v iskusstve') F.I. Bulgakov, *V.V. Vereshchagin i ego proizvedeniia*, St Petersburg: Tipografiia A.S. Suvorina, 1905, www.hrionline.ac.uk/rva/texts/ver/verbib.html, retrieved on 24 May 2008.

Vivekananda, Swami, *Prācya o Pāscātya* (The East and the West), 25th edn., Kolkata: Udbodhan Karyalaya, 1902/2009.

Weber, Max. 'Prefatory Remarks', in *Collected Essays in the Sociology of Religion* (1920), ed. Stephen Calberg with New Translation and Introduction, Chicago: Fitzroy Dearborn Publishers, 2001.

Webster, Anthony, *Gentlemen Capitalists: British Imperialism in South East Asia, 1770–1890*, London: Tauris Academic Studies, 1998.

Werth, Paul W., *At the Margins of Orthodoxy: Mission, Governance, and Confessional Politics in Russia's Volga-Kama Region, 1827–1905*, Ithaca: Cornell University Press, 2002.

Wileman, David, 'Review', of *The Travels of Rafail Daniebegashvili in India, Burma and Other Asian Countries, 1795–1827*, ed. L.I. Maruashvili, Academy of Sciences of the Georgian SSR, Vakusthi Institute of Geography, Moscow: Progress Publishers, 1969.

Wœrkens, Martine van, *The Strangled Traveler: Colonial Imaginings and the Thugs of India*, tr. Catherine Tihanyi, Chicago: University of Chicago Press, 2002.

Wright, Caleb, *Lectures on India*, Boston: Caleb Wright, 1851.

——, *Historic Incidents and Life in India*, Chicago: J. A. Brainerd, 1867.

Journals

'An Account of the Books for the year 2002', in *Asiatic Annual Register, or A View of the History of Hindustan and of the History, Commerce and Literature in India, for the Year 1802*, London, printed for J. Debett, Picadilly and T. Caell Jun. and W. Davis, Strand, 2005, http://google.com./retrieved on 11 October 2010.

Bassin, Mark, 'Russia between Europe and Asia: The Ideological Construction of Geographical Space', *Slavic Review*, 50: 1 (Spring, 1991): 1–17.

Banerjee, Anindita, 'By Caravan and Campfire: Chorasani Narratives about Hindustan and Afanasij Nikitin's "The Journey Beyond Three Seas"', *Die Welt Slaven* XLVIII (2003): 69–79.

Bayly, C.A., 'Knowing the Country: Empire and Information in India', *Modern Asian Studies* 27: 1(1993): 3–43.

'Contemporary Literature', *The Westminster Review*, LXI (January and April 1854), American Edition, New York: Leonard Scott and Co., 1854: 158.

Davids, T.W.R, 'Review of Minayeff's Recherches sur le Bouddhisme', in *The American Journal of Theology* 1:1 (January 1897): 166–8.

'From Simla to Chinese Tartary', *Calcutta Review* XLVI (1867): Article VII: 158–87.

Ezzaher, Lahcen E., *Writing and Cultural Influence: Studies in Rhetorical History, Orientalist Discourse, and Post-Colonial Criticism*, Comparative Cultures and Literatures Series, vol. 18, New York: Peter Lang, 2003, cited in Kermit E. Campbell, *Rhetorical Review* 2: 1, p. 12 (February 2004), http://www.nnrh.dk/RR/index.html, retrieved on 13 November 2008.

From the Athenaeum: 'Life in Persia in the Middle of the Nineteenth Century', *The International Monthly Magazine of Literature, Science and Art*: Making of America Project, III (April–July 1851): 105–8.

Gerasimov, I., S. Glebov, A. Kaplunovsky, M. Mogilner and A. Semyonov, 'In Search of a New Imperial History', Novaia imperskaia istoriia postsovetskogo prostranstva, Kazan, 2004, pp. 7–29, PDF article obtained from http://www.zeitgeschichte-online.de/zol/portals/_zf/documents/pdf/abimperio.pdf-, retrieved on 20 May 2008.

Gerow, Edwin, 'Untitled Review of *Image of India*', *Journal of American Oriental Society* 107: 2 (April–June 1987): 360–1.

Hardgrave Jr., Robert L., 'The Representation of Sati: Four Eighteenth Century Etchings by Balthazar Solvyns', *Bengal Past and Present* 117 (1998): 57–80, retrieved from asnic.utexas.edu/hardgrave/Satiart.rft.html on 25 January 2008.

Khalid, Adeeb, 'Russian History and the Debate over Orientalism', *Kritika: Explorations in Russian and Eurasian History* 1: 4 (Fall 2000): 691–9.

Khalfin, N.A., 'Indian Missions in Russia in the Late Nineteenth Century and British Historiography of International Relations in Asia', *Modern Asian Studies*, 21: 4 (1987): 639–46.

Kirchner, Walther, 'The Voyage of Athanassius Nikitin to India, 1466–72', *The American Slavic and East European Studies* V (1946): 46–54.

Knight, Nathaniel, 'Grigor'ev in Orenburg, 1851–62, Russian Orientalism in Service of Empire?', *Slavic Review* 59: 1 (Spring 2000): 74–100.

Lelyveld, David, 'Colonial Knowledge and the Fate of Hindustani', *Comparative Studies in Society and History* 35: 4 (October 1993): 665–82.

Lenhoff, Gail, 'Beyond Three Seas: Afanasij Nikitin's Journey from Orthodoxy to Apostasy', *East European Quarterly* 13: 4 (1979): 431–47.

Makdisi, Ussama, 'Ottoman Orientalism', *The American Historical Review* 107: 3 (June 2002): 768–96.

Martynuk, Igor S., 'Toward Understanding the Art of Modern Diasporic Ideology Making: The Eurasianist Mind-Mapping of the Imperial Homeland (1921–34)', *Journal of the Interdisciplinary Crossroads, Thematic Issue: The Limits of Exile*', ed. D. Kettler and Z. Ben-Dor, 3: 1 (April 2006): 93–116, retrieved from www.jic.in/contents31.htm - 15k -, on 27 April 2008.

Maxwell, Mary Jane, 'An Orthodox Russian's Spiritual Voyage in the Dar al-Islam, 1468–75'. *Journal of World History* 17: 3 (September 2006): 243–66, obtained from Proquest Research Library, Document View, pp.1–19, http://proquest.umi.com/pqdweb?index=3&did=1126906851&SrchMode=3&sid+1&F, retrieved on 23 January 2008.

Morris, A.S., 'The Journey Beyond Three Seas', *The Geographical Journal* 133: 4 (December 1967): 502–5.

Morrison, Alexander, 'Russian Rule in Turkestan and the Example of British India, c. 1860-1917'. *The Slavonic and East European Review* 84: 4 (October 2006): 666–707.

——, '"Applied Orientalism" in British India and Tsarist Turkestan', *Comparative Studies in Society and History* 51: 3(2009): 619–47.

Rao, Nina, 'Review: *Image of India*'. *Social Scientist* 14: 7 (July 1986): 71–7.

Riasanovsky, Alexander V., 'A Fifteenth Century Russian Traveller in India: Comments in Connection With a New Edition of Afanasiî Nikitin's Journal', *Journal of the American Oriental Society* 81: 2 (April–June 1961): 126–30.

Palat, Madhavan K., 'Tsarist Russian Imperialism', *Studies in History* 4: 1 and 2 (1988): 157–285.

Rahman, Tariq, 'The British Learning of Hindustani', *Pakistan Vision* 8: 2: 19–20. www.pu.edu.pk/psc/journal/PDF-FILES/Tariq-2%20new.pdf -, retrieved on 13 November 2008.

Sahadeo, Jeff, '*Conquest, Colonialism, and Nomadism on the Eurasian Steppe*', *Kritika* 4: 4 (Fall 2003): 942–54.

Sahai–Achuthan, Nisha, 'Soviet Indologists and the Institute of Oriental Studies: Works on Contemporary India in the Soviet Union', *Journal of Asian Studies* 42: 2 (February 1983): 323–43.

Sarkar, Sumit, 'Radicalism of Intellectuals in a Colonial Situation: A Case Study of Nineteenth Century Bengal', *Calcutta Historical Journal* 2: 1 (July–December 1977): 65–71.

Sen, Amartya, 'Indian Traditions and Western Imagination', *Daedalus* 126: 2 (Spring 1997): 1–26.

Schimmelpenninck van der Oye, David, 'Vasilij V. Vereshchagin's Canvases of Central Asian Conquest', *Cahiersd'Asie centrale* (En ligne), 17/18/2009, mis en ligne le 26 mai 2010: 179–209, retrieved on 6 August 2011.

Solomon, Rakesh H., 'Culture, Imperialism, and Nationalist Resistance: Performance in Colonial India', *Theatre Journal: Colonial/Postcolonial Theatre*, 46: 3 (1994) 337–40, courtesy http://www.jstor.org/stable/3208610.

——, 'From Orientalist to Postcolonial Representations: A Critique of Indian Theatre Historiography from 1827 to the Present', *Theatre Research International* 29 (2004): 111–27.

Tillettt, Lionel R., 'Afanasy Nikitin as a Cultural Ambassador to India: A Bowlderized Soviet Translation of His Journal', *Russian Review* 25: 2 (April 1966): 160–9.

Tlostanova, Madina, 'The Janus-faced Empire Distorting Orientalist Discourses: Gender, Race and Region in the Russian/(post)Soviet Constructions of the Orient', obtained from *Worlds and Knowledge Otherwise*, www.jhfc.duke.edu/wko/dossiers 1.3/contents.php-10k: 1–11, retrieved on 9 May 2008.

——, 'Life in Samarkand: Caucasus and Central Asia vis-à-vis Russia, the West and Islam', *Human Architecture: Journal of the Sociology of Self-Knowledge* 1(Fall 2006): 105–16, www.highbeam.com/doc/1P3-1559750411. html - retrieved on 10 May 2008.

Tolz, Vera, 'European, National and (Anti-) Imperial: The Formation of Academic Oriental Studies in Late Tsarist and Early Soviet Russia', *Kritika: Explorations in Russian and Eurasian History* 9: 1 (Winter 2008) (New Series): 53–81.

——, 'Orientalism, Nationalism and Ethnic Diversity in Late Imperial Russia', *The Historical Journal* 48: 1 (2005): 127–50.

Tucker, Richard P. 'The Proper Limits of Agitation: The Crisis of 1879-80 in Bombay Presidency', *The Journal of Asian Studies*, 28: 2 (February 1969): 339–55.

Urban, Mr., 'Notices of Tavistock and its Abbey', *The Gentleman's Magazine* 47 (February 1830), 114–15: books.google.com/books?id=I0p5TZ5b LmcC... , retrieved on 17 August 2008.

Yekelchyk, Serhy, 'Interpreting Russia's Imperial Dimension', *Canadian Slavonic Papers*. (September–December) 2004: 1–9. findarticles.com/p/articles/mi_qa 3763/is.../ai_n11849950/ -, retrieved on 23 May 2008.

Internet Sources

'Afanasy Nikitin'. Wikipedia, en.wikipedia.org/wiki/Afanasy_Nikitin; Minwala Shabnam, *Times News Network*. 28 January 2002. www.russian-centre-mumbai.com/en/admin/.../shabnam_minwalla.doc., retrieved on 24 May 2008.

Caucasus and Central Asia Newsletter, The Caucasia and Central Asia Program at the University of Berkeley, California, Issue 9, Spring 2006, http://socrates.berkeley.edu/~bsp/caucasus/, retrieved on 19 May 2008.

Chakrabarty, Dipesh, 'Postcoloniality and the Artifice of History: Who Speaks for 'Indian' Pasts?, *Representations* 37 (Winter, 1992): 1–26.

Friedlander, Peter, 'Travel Talk: Phrases for Travellers in India', coombs.anu.edu.au/SpecialProj/ASAA/biennial-conference/2004/Friedlander-P-ASAA2004.pdf, retrieved on 24 June 2008.

'The Greeks', *Banglapedia, National Encyclopedia of Bangladesh*, www.banglapedia.org/httpdocs/HT/G_0203.HTM, retrieved on 10 Noember 2011.

'In the Footsteps of Afanasy Nikitin', by a Staff Reporter, *The Hindu*, online edition, 27 March 2007, www.hindu.com/2007/03/27/stories/2007032701190500.htm—visited on 1 April 2008.

Mahalingam, Sudha, 'The Challenges of Travelling through Russia', *The Hindu*, online edition, 28 November 2006.

Rahman, Tariq, 'The British Learning of Hindustani', *Pakistan Vision* 2: 19–20, www.pu.edu.pk/psc/journal/PDF-FILES/Tariq-2%20new. pdf, retrieved on 26 June 2008.

Sahni, Kalpana, 'Light Within: Foreign Exchange: Fiddler on the Loose', *Daily Times*, Saturday, 9 April 2007, http/ sajshirazi.blogspot.com/2007/04/foreign-exchange-fiddler-on-loose_08.html - 31k, visited on 23 October 2008.

South Asia at Chicago: Fifty Years of Scholarship, IV, 'Recurrent Themes in the Representation of South Asia', http://www.lib.uchicago.edu/e/su/southasia/50yrs4.html - 13k, last visited on 1 May 2008.

Vereshchagin, Vassili V., '1865 Caucasus Molokane and Leapers: Eye-witness Report, by Vassili V. Vereshchagin', www. molokane.org/books/Veresehchagin/1887.html; and en.wikipedia.org/wiki/Karabakh–, retrieved on 11 December 2009.

Index

Adelung Johan Christophe 39, 109, 112, 121, 154, 159, 162, 273
Alayev, L.B. 83
Almond, Philip C. 322, 332n13
Aluktuk, A. 316, 333
Amtzis, Judith S. 322
Anderson, Benedict 33, 51, 326
Andreeva, Elena 48
Anglophiles 106–7, 165, 283–4, 297
'Anthony Kobiāl' or 'Anthony Phiringī' 327, 338
Arendt, Hannah 295, 326
Asiatic Annual Register 109–10,121, 154
Assumpcam, Frey Manoel da 111, 157

Bandyopadhyay, Asit Kumar 153n75
Bandyopadhyay, Bireswar 158
Bandyopadhyay, Tarashankar 151
Banerjee, Anindita 78, 84
Banerjee, Surendra Nath 316
Barooshian, Vahan D. 214–15, 218–20, 224, 243, 246, 261–3, 265–7, 269
Bassin, Mark 25, 30, 49–50
Battle, Joseph 135–6
Bayly, C.A. 48n14, 156n109
Beissinger, M. 32, 51
Bengalee style 135
Bengalee Theatre 137–8
Benois, Alexandre 215–16, 262
Bezpristrastnoe 106, 139–40, 142, 161–2
Bhabha, Homi K. 17, 48
Bharucha, Rustam 136, 160
Bhatia, Nandi 160n184
Bhatia, Tej K. 111, 155
Bhattacharyya, Benoytosh 267n112, 290
Blackburn, Terence R. 33, 327n111
Blair, P. 207
Bongard-Levin, Grigori Maksimovich 38–9, 41, 53, 59, 65, 83, 85–6, 94, 111, 149–50, 155, 271–2, 275, 277, 321, 323
Borovsky, Victor 159
Bowlt, John E. 269n164
Breyfogle, Nicholas 230, 264
Briggs, A.D.P. 133, 159
Brower, Daniel 30, 50n38, 228
Brown, K. 178
Brubaker, Rogers 33
Buddhism 39–40, 247–50, 253–4, 271–2, 275–9, 281, 298–301, 312–14, 322, 325, 329, 335, 337
Burnim, Kalman A. 160n176
Buruma, Ian 332n190

Calcutta Gazette 44, 103–4, 135, 159–60
Calcutta Play-House 129
Calcutta Theatre 134, 136–7
Carol, Lewis 267n128
Cashman, Richard I. 326n98
Catherine the Great 132, 137
Central Asia 48, 53, 239, 266, 332
Chakrabarty, Dipesh 51n45
Chatterjee, Indrani 91, 149
Chatterjee, Sudipto 138, 153
Chatterjee, Suniti Kumar 99, 125, 152, 154
Chattopadhyay, Bankimchandra 107
Chaudhuri, Nirad C. 149n1
Chrisman, Laura 20, 49
Cohn, Bernard S. 41, 114

Communist Party of India (CPI) 100
Concerts of Lebedev 38, 103–4, 153, 297
Conermann, Stephan 52–3n66
Conti, Niccolo 43–4, 63, 74–5, 78, 88–9, 98
Cooper, Frederick 51n45

Dalrymple, William 195
Daniebegov, Rafail [Daniebegashvili] 89, 93–9, 124, 149–51, 337; 'antarjalī' 96; details of his journey 91; foolish Kashmiris and 99; Georgian or Russian travelogue 93; and idol worship 95–9; and expansionist efforts of England 98–9; polyandry 99–9; skewed demography 95–9; on suttee 95–9
Das, Golok Nath 110–11, 121, 125, 127, 129, 158
Das, Sisir Kumar 125, 158
Dickens, Charles 267n128
Dirks, Nicholas 114, 118

Edgar, John Ware 329n139
Efremov, Fillipp S. 89–92, 95, 337; archetypes of observation 337; asceticism and physical penance 91; barbarism 47, 91–3; cow-worshippers 91; depiction of riverside life in Bengal 91; Ezzaher, Lahcen E. 114, 155n103; journey details of 149n6; slavery, idolatry and forced 'Antarjalī' 91–3; superficiality of observation and attendant miscomprehension 92; *Travels of Civil Councilor Yefremov in Bukhara* 90; *Yefremov in Bukhara, Khiva* 90
Europe 17–18, 22–6, 28–9, 33–4, 36, 38–40, 49, 51, 53, 63, 99–102, 145, 162–4, 187, 306–7, 335–6
Ezzaher, Lahcen, 114

Ferguson, John 109–12, 115–17, 122, 154, 156
Franco, Eli 49
Friedlander, Peter 113–15
Furber, Holden, 150n29

Gandhi, Leela 48, 55
Gargi, Balwant 135
Garrett, H.L.O. 190, 205, 209–11
Garrick, David 134, 160
Gellner, Ernest 33, 51
Geraci, Robert P. 30
Gerasimov, I. 35
Gerow, Edwin 321n9
Ghosh, Ajit Kumar 161n194
Ghosh, Parimal 327n111
Gilchrist, John 109–10, 112–18, 120, 122–3, 154–6
Goswami, Madan Mohan 127
GPMEID (Grammar of the Pure and Mixed Indian Dialects) 103, 108–12, 114, 122, 124, 129, 152, 154–9
Grab, Alexander 331n188
Greenleaf, Monica 30, 50
Grierson, George 102, 109
Guha-Thakurta P. 153, 160

Hadley, George 109–11, 115, 122, 154
Halbfass, Wilhelm 23, 38, 49, 53, 164, 278, 335–6
Halhed, N.B. 139, 157n133
Hall, D.G.E. 327n111
Hall, J. 51
Halperin, Charles 50n33
Hardgrave Jr, Robert L. 54n93; dominance of 'Orientalist' archetypes in travelogue 169; pre-determined notions and gossip in travelogue 170
Heber, Reginald 167–71, 180, 184, 199
Henderson, Carol E. 204n2
Hindu divinity 41, 46, 65, 70, 182

Hobsbawm, Eric J. 33, 51n44
Hopkirk, Peter 331–2n189, 332
Hroch, Miroslav 33
Hyde, Justice John 130

Ignatieff, M. 51n46
Inden, Ronald 298
India Gazette 103
India, archetypes of orientalist observations of 41
Indian People's Theatre Association in Calcutta 100

Jacquemont, Victor V. 167–8, 170–1, 205–6; disapproval of Oriental studies 168; disparagement of Sanskrit 170; empathetic approach toward contemporary India 171; ethnocentric biases 170; magisterialism 170
Jaffrelot, Christophe 158, 321
Jalal al-'Azm, Sadik 161
Jaroslavl 100
Jersild, Austin 33–4, 52n52
Jones, William 20, 99, 122, 138, 146, 148, 206
Jong, Jan Willem 278
Joshi, Venkatesh Shastri 326n98

Kalpanik Saṃbadal 158n147, 159n164
Kapany, Narinder Singh 207n54
Karatchkova, Elena 168, 170, 204, 206
Katsev, Allison Y. 84n15
Kaufman, General Konstantin P. 218–19, 226–8, 233, 239, 279–80
Kaviraj, Sudipta 84
Kaye, Sir John William 113n115, 211
Kelly, Catriona 130, 159
Kemp, P.M. 41, 59, 74, 89, 165, 272
Kemper, Michael 52n66, 41, 52–3, 59, 62, 73–4, 76, 89–91, 94, 97–8, 105–7, 121–6, 141–2, 145–6, 165, 272, 281
Khalfin, N.A., 280, 322–3
Khalid, Adeeb, 20, 22, 30, 49–50, 239, 266
Khodarkovsky, Michael 83, 88
Khorasani travelogues 56
King, Blair P. 207n36
Klein, Christina 53n77
Knight, Nathaniel 20, 30–1, 49–50
Knighton, W. 205n10
Knyaz, Alexei Dmitrievich Saltykov 205n9
Komarov, W. 321

Layton, Susan 30
Lazzerini, E. 30, 50n38
Lebedeff, Gerasim Stepanovich 101, 114, 124, 136, 138
Lebedev, Andrej K. 47, 89–90, 99–114, 117–30, 133–48, 152–3, 156–63, 262, 270, 318, 335, 338
Lebedev, Herasim Stepanovich 47, 89, 99; authorial controversy about *Kālpanik Saṃbadal* 126; biography 100–3; career as violinist 100, 105; comedies he translated 105; compared with Jones 109; comparison with other Hindi grammarians 109; concerts in Calcutta 103; CPI-inspired remembrance of 100; dialogues in his Grammar 108; doubts of espionage 137; GPMEID as grammar 103, 109; GPMEID from the perspective of dialogues 112; GPMEID in the context of Russian Indology 109, 112; hermeneutic ability 99; humility 99; *Impartial Observations*, and its chapters 121; initiator of first Bengali proscenium 338; Orientalism 138–49; proscenium and its 'Bengalee Style' 129, 135; lexicographical turn 108–10; linguistic endeavours 108, 110–

11; movement to Calcutta 121; myth of an adventurer 100, 102; pioneer of modern Bengali prose, 121; and Pundits 141–2; simple conspiracy theory behind his harassment and ouster 136–7; source of *The Disguise* 124; special value of endeavours of 105–6; translator of two plays 124; unfortunate exit from Calcutta and its effect on theatre in Bengal 137–8
Lelyveld, David 154
Lenhoff, Gail 78, 81
Little Theatre Group 100
Locke, J. Courtney 149
Love is the Best Doctor 124–6
Lur'e, Ja. S. 87
Lynn, John A. 150n31

Mackay, Alexander 205
Madan, T.N. 151
Mahalingam, Sudha 84n13
Majumdar, Ramesh Chandra 135
Majumdar, D.N., 151n47
Majumdar, Kamal Kumar 149n13
Makdisi, Ussama 51–2n50
Mamud, Hayat 100–4, 124–5, 127–8, 135–7, 144, 148
Margalit, Avishai 332n190
Marr, Nikolai 16, 30, 48
Marshall, Alex 239
Marshall, P.J. 157n135
Martynuk, Igor S. 52n61
Maruashvili, L.I. 93–4, 150
master-servant discourse in Hindi grammarians' dialogues 114
Max Müller, Friedrich 322n13
Maxwell, Mary Jane 78
McClintock, John 54n84
McDermott, Rachel Fell 207n40
McReynolds, Louis 133
Metcalf, Thomas R. 161n199
Mill, James 20, 206
Minayev, I.P. 85n17, 321n3; difference from other Russian Orientalists, 299; doubts of espionage 285; oeuvre, 271–3; philological and linguistics-based solution of debate about Aryans 273–5; as scholar of Pali and Buddhism 275–8
Minayev's *Diaries:* about Burmese monks 300–1; about Burmese War and its aftermath 295–6; about discontents against British rule and its significance 292–5; about disposition of native royalty about Russia 282–5; about Indian Indologists 298–9; about level and sources of awareness of Russia among common people 287; about non-Russian Westerners and Englishmen 296–8; about 'radical India' 286; about Russia's image of 'secondary modernity' 287; about 'unofficial India' 286; anxieties about superiority/inferiority of Englishmen and Europeans to Russians 297–8; 'curatorial' voice 337; dilemma about colonial civilizing mission in Burma and India 309–18; in Soviet eyes 208–1; interest of Russian State in 279–80; noble motivation behind Russia's presence in Central Asia 308; 'Orientalism' and India 306–8; pangs of separation from India, 280; revealing contents 282, 295; as source of Indology 278, 298–9; supporters and detractors of the Afghan War and Russia 285–92
Minwala, Shabnam 84n8
Mitter, Partha 46, 54
Mohanty, Arun 84–5n17

Moorcroft, William 94
Morris, A.S. 61, 63, 67–8, 74
Morrison, Alexander 20, 37, 41, 270, 279–80
Muhammad, Kājī Dīn 125
Muhammad, Khoja 79
Mukherjee, Rudrangshu 327n110
Mukherjee, Sujit 158n153

Naik, J.A. 182, 322, 333
Nandy, Ashis 17, 48, 328
Negrov, Alexander I. 267n124
Neumann, Iver B. 24, 49
Nikitin, Afanasy 15, 43, 47, 53, 56–92, 217, 272, 318, 336–8; archetypes of India and their sources of 64–73; on Bidar as political centre of India 65; bowdlerization of *Khozenie* 64; on cultural life of the Hindus and of the Muslims 71; on dhoti 65; on easy sexuality of Eastern women 66; essential identities of 78–83; ethnocentrism of 73; familiar 'Orientalist' mode of compare and contrast 71; on fear of being 'surrounded by other faiths' 76; grouse against the Muslims in India 75; on Hindu divinity/pantheon 65, 70; imputed secularism of 75–7; India's interest in 57–8; influence of *Chorasani* narratives on impressions of 68; *The Journey Beyond the Three Seas* 56; *Khozenieza tri morya* 56; on loose morals of Indian men 66; on nakedness of Indian women 66; on obstacles to indo–Russian trade 75; Orientalization of the *Journal* 72; on Parvat as religious hub of India 70; quasi conversion of 81; on religious customs of the Hindus 65; Russia's glorification of 63–4; spiritual transformation of 78, 80; voyage of 56–7; wails of 75–7
Niranjana, Tejaswini 115, 156
Novitskii, V.F. 96, 151

O'Hanlon, Rosalind 156–7n124
Oaten, Edward Farley 43, 54, 68, 74–5, 87–9, 149, 151
Oldenburg, S.F. 16, 30, 37, 48, 142, 272, 278
Orient 15–19, 22–3, 29–31, 48–50, 86, 88, 98, 152, 156, 161, 228, 239–42, 264–6, 309–11, 319–21, 327
Oriental Renaissances 29, 38, 41, 163, 270
'Orientalism' 15–24, 27–8, 30, 34, 36, 41–2, 47, 64, 83, 89, 138, 163–4, 213–14, 298–9, 306, 337–8; as discourse 23, 64; encounter between India and the West 24; as imperial project 23, 83; as one single story 24; as pathology in the Western psyche 17–18; as sum of several different stories 24; travelogues as sources of 15; Tsarist 'Orientalism' 27
'Orientalist' 17–21, 23, 30, 47, 66–7, 71, 89, 91–2, 108–9, 166, 228–9, 238–42, 250–2, 297–9, 304–5, 336–8; the 'curatorial', the 'magisterial', and the 'exoticist' 47, 337; discourse 56; stereotypes 56, 89, 99; voices in 'Orientalist' representations 19, 23
Orlich, Captain Leopold Von 211
Owen, Wilfred 220, 263

Palat, Madhavan K. 27–8, 32, 49–52, 265
Paria of Bernadin Saint-Pierre 182
Pavlov, Vladimir Ivanovic 207

Peter the Great 24–5, 28, 102, 131
Petrovna, Tsarina Elizaveta 132
Postcolonial analysis/theory 16, 48–9, 55, 251
Preisendanz, Karin 49
Proscenium 129–30, 135–6, 138, 338
Purchas, Samuel 46, 211, 267

Rahman, Tariq 155
Ram, Harsha 89, 149
Ramazani, Jahan 263n16
Rangacarya, Adya 125
Raugh, Harold E. 331
Ray, A.K. 150, 160
Ray, Bharat Chandra 105, 153–4
Razumovsky, Count Andrey Kyrillovich 100–1
Rhys Davids, T.W. 276, 329
Riasanovsky, Nicholas 27, 50, 60, 65, 74, 83, 85–7
Rodinov, Mikhail 53
Romanov, Aleksei Mikhalovich 131, 133; Alexander II 29, 31, 223, 225; Peter the Great 24–5
Roy, Parama 210
Royle, Nicholas 86
Rozario, Dom Antonio da 157
Rozen, Baron Viktor 30
Rubiés, Joan-Pau 339
Russia: colonization by 34; conquest of Central Asia and Turkestan 27; as contiguous empire 33–4, 308, 336; cultural Russification 30–1, 113; and debate about Europe 24; discrete territorial massif between Europe and Asia 24; distinctive position between East and West 20, 34–5; its identity as state or empire? 29, 32–6; as important Oriental player 22; Nizhnyi Tagil in central Urals, physically embodying dual identity of Russia 26; its relationship with its Asian borderlands 20–1; Russia's 'applied Orientalism' 22, 24–32; ways of encoding Russia's Orient 22
Russian empire 22, 27, 29–30, 34–6, 131, 288, 306–7, 332; post-colonialist take on 35
Russian Indology 37, 112, 336
Russian Orientalism 112, 163–4, 204, 213; and inferiority complex regarding Europe 28; Peter the Great 24–5, 28, 102, 131; and secondary Eurocentrism 21, 24, 235, 238, 337; and sense of inadequacy 27; and tsarist imperialism in East 27–8; tsarist imperialism masquerading as 'Orientalism' 27; and Westernizer–Slavophile debate 28, 163
Russian Orientology 37, 162, 270; Silver Age of 37
Russian state 25, 29, 33, 35, 39, 50, 93, 163, 214, 218, 225, 231, 270–1, 278–9, 281, 337
Russo-Tartar relations 27

Saha, Mahadev Prasad 104
Sahadeo, Jeff 32, 51
Sahni, Kalpana 15, 28, 32, 48–9, 101, 152, 264–6, 273, 321, 327
Said, Edward W. 16
Saint-Pierre, Jacques-Henri Bernardin de 182, 208
Saltykov Knyaz, Alexei Dmitrievich 205
Saltykov, A.D. 40, 47, 53, 70, 127, 163–8, 171–204, 189, 207–12, 335–7 (*also see* Saltykov Knyaz, Alexei Dmitrievich); admitting of alternative possibilities 196; aesthetic detachment 165; alleged acceptance of European stereotype of the strangler 167

attempt to fit him into an 'Orientalist'-Eurocentric framework 166; on Bombay 172, 182; on Calcutta 169, 173; catholicity of 180; charge of Eurocentrism against 166; cityscape of Amritsar 178; compared with other contemporary travellers 167–71; contemporary stereotyping of the travelogue 164–7; court of Sher Singh, son of Ranjit Singh, in Lahore 190; on courts of big and small native kings 172; courts of Tanjore, Pudukkottai, Thiruvantapuram, Travancore, Gwalior, Amritsar 185; on decadence of the historical places 172; on Delhi 176; about Englishmen in India 166; 'exoticist' and 'curatorial' tone of Saltykov's oeuvres 165; faithful description of image and iconic grammar of Hindu divinities 183; goddess Kālī 169, 182–3; grotesque temples in Bombay 182; on Hindu idols and festivals 172; on Indian cities and their inhabitants 172; about Indian women 202; about Indians 175, 183, 188; on Jaipur 177; king of Lahore 190–1, 202; on Lahore, Orientalist's paradise 177–8; lighthearted depiction of the deadly goddess Kālī 184; on looks of the Bengalis 175; on Madurai and its Hindu temple 181; mixture of 'voices' in travelogue 171; monstrous idols in Bombay 182; on nascent civil society of the new cities 171; negative depiction of Bahadur Shah II 194; on nobility of Calcutta 175; on Puri in Orissa, 182; on Simla 179; on social practices 172; stereotypes of observation, *antarjalî*, burning of corpses, suttee, and *thugs* 196–200; on temple city of Benares 176; on temple complex at Kancheepuram 179; on temples, shrines and religious places 172; a travelogue ignored 164–7; on vices of the traditional society and culture 172; on virtues of traditional society and culture 172

Samra, Chattar Singh 160

Sardar, Ziauddin 18, 48, 252, 339

Sarkar, Salil 339n21

Sarkar, Sumit 324

Satī (or suttee) 41–6, 54, 92, 95, 98–9, 169, 196–201

Savitskii, P.N. 36, 52

Secondary Orientalism 21, 228, 233, 235, 258, 296, 301, 337

Semenov, L.S. 86–7

Sen, Amartya 19, 48

Sen, Indrani 327

Serebriany, Sergei 23–4, 38, 49, 53, 56, 200, 205, 278, 322, 335–6, 339

Shakespeare, William 210, 320, 334

Sharpe, Jenny 84, 327

Shastitco, Petr Mikhailovich 53

Shastitko, P.I. 280, 323

Shastri, Venkatesh 326

Slavophile thought 21

Slavophilism 40

Sleeman, Colonel William Henry 211

Smirnova-Rakitina, Vera Alekseevna 153

Solomon, Rakesh H. 134, 136, 159–60

Soltykoff, A. 164, 167–8, 204–5

Spivak, Gayatri Chakravorty 41, 54

St. Petersburg 28, 34–5, 37, 40, 58, 84, 131–2, 153, 173, 214–15, 219, 235, 265, 271, 280, 294

Stacy, R.H. 38–9, 53, 84, 112, 155, 204

Steadman-Jones, Richard 115–16, 156
Stede, William 329
Stoler, Ann Laura 51
Strakhovsky, Leonid 33, 52
Strong, James 54
Suleri, Sara 265
Sumarokov, Alexander 132
Suny, Ronald Grigor 33–4, 51
Swift, Jonathan 267

Tagore, Rabindranath 97, 151n38, 140, 297, 321, 326, 328, 332
Tambov 271
Tarkapanchanana, Jagannatha 139
Teltscher, Kate 15, 18–19, 45, 48, 54, 87, 138–9, 146–7, 152, 161–2, 202, 211, 251, 267–8, 299, 327
Tennyson, Alfred Lord 320, 334
Thankappan Nair, P. 101, 152
Theatre Halls in Calcutta 95, 100, 102, 129
Theatre in Russia 133
Thompson, Ewa M. 30, 50
Thornton, Edward 211
Thrower, James 322
Tillettt, Lionel 61, 67–8, 78, 86, 88, 322
Tlostanova, Madina 21, 49, 228, 240–1, 264, 266, 268, 306, 331, 339
Tolz, Vera 15–16, 22, 28–32, 37–8, 48–51, 270
Transcaucasia 21, 229
Travel narratives 15, 32, 41, 47, 68, 317
Trebeck, George 150
Tucker, A.L.P. 323
Tucker, Richard P., 324

van der Oye, David Schimmelpenninck 23, 49–50, 52, 214, 269
Valkenier, Elizabeth Kridl 261, 269
Vapha, V.K. 83
Vasudevan, Hari S. 57, 65, 77, 82, 84, 86, 88
Vereshchagin (Mrs): about conceited upper caste 'tchaprassi' and a spirited Indian dog 251, 260–2; debunking of Koupgenlama 253; depraved natives 256–7; doctrine of transmigration of souls passed off as superstition 251; inevitable subordination of the 'Orient' 260–2; mundane and non-spiritual lamas 254; non-rational Buddhism in the Himalayas 247; polyandry in the hills and travails of hill women 254–6; self-image of a white goddess 258–60; Sikkim's king, presumptuous and miserly 257; superstitious and competing religions in the Himalayas 246–8; about Vereshchagin's 'energetic measures' 261; virile Vereshchagin and effeminate Indians 243; Western quackery vs. Eastern charms 258
Vereshchagin V.V. 34, 47, 49, 213–29, 231–70, 301, 308, 318, 335–7 (*also see* Vereshchagin, Vasily); admission of the liberating potential of war 220; appraisal of Vereshchagin's 'Orientalist' gazes by post-Soviet postcolonialists 239; archetypes of observation in Central Asia: slavery, pauperism, vagrancy, mendicancy, and Russian deliverance 233–8; archetypes of observation in Transcaucasia: fanaticism, wildness, deviance and degeneration 229; as artist 216; artistic and textual production in Caucasia, Turkestan and Central Asia 217–18; as battle painter 217–23; biography 214–17; contents of battle painting analysed 217, 221–3; as

European encoding himself in the context of Asian backwardness 241; in Himalayas and their 'secondary Orientalism' 242; identity of; 'Orientalism' as power/knowledge even in Russia 214; 'Orientalist' art depicting inferiority of Russia's 'Orient' 238–42; paintings that soured relations with tsar and court 241; plea for stronger form of Russian colonization of Central Asia 218; reasons of getting into the Kaufman team 226–7; Russian Orthodox lens about Dukhobors, Molokans, and Leapers 232; sectarian deviations of Dukhobors, Molokans, and Leapers 229; self-tormentation in Shiite festival of Muharram 229; supporter of Russia's expansion in the east 226; suspect pacifism 217; Tashkent as 'Orient' 262; urge to remain in the thick of battle 219
Vereshchagin, Vasily 47, 213, 270, 335
Vernadsky, G. 36, 52
Victor Borovsky 159
Vidyasundar 110, 138, 154
Vigasin, Aleksei Alekseevich 47, 53, 131, 163, 165, 167, 169, 171, 173, 175, 177, 179, 181, 183, 185, 203–5
Vivekananda, Swami 73, 87
Volkov of Yaroslav 129–30
Volkov, Fyodor 129–33
Vyatka 90

Weber, Max 191, 209, 271
Webster, Anthony 327
Werth, Paul W. 33–5, 52
West's discourses about 'the Orient' 16
Westminster Review 165, 205
Wielhorsky, Count M. 85–6
Wileman, David 93–4, 150
Willem, Jan 278
Wilson, Horace Hayman 150, 206
Wœrkens, Martine van 166, 196, 205, 210
Wright, Caleb 199, 211

Yaroslavl 131–2
Yefremov, Filip 47, 90, 149–50